SOUTHLAND WRITERS

i

SOUTHLAND WRITERS.

BIOGRAPHICAL AND CRITICAL SKETCHES

OF THE

LIVING FEMALE WRITERS OF THE SOUTH.

With Extracts from their Writings.

BY

IDA RAYMOND.

IN TWO VOLUMES.

VOL. II.

PHILADELPHIA:
CLAXTON, REMSEN & HAFFELFINGER,
819 & 821 MARKET STREET.
1870.

STEREOTYPED BY J. FAGAN & SON.

PRINTED BY MOORE BROTHERS.

CONTENTS

VOLUME II

ALABAMA.

MISSISSIPPI.

FLORIDA.

TENNESSEE.

VIRGINIA.

NORTH CAROLINA.

SOUTH CAROLINA.

MARYLAND.

TEXAS.

ALABAMA.

MADAME ADELAIDE DE V. CHAUDRON.

THIS lady, who stands unsurpassed as translator of the now famous Mühlbach novels, is a resident (we believe, a native) of Mobile. Her father was Emile De Vendel, a teacher of some distinction in a country where teaching is regarded as one of the professions, and where intellect, education, and birth are principally valued as the "open sesames" of good society. Adelaide de Vendel was married early to Mr. West of St. Louis: he was a lawyer by profession. After his death, she resided in Mobile, where she contracted a second marriage with Mr. Paul Chaudron. Left again a widow, she was compelled by misfortune to adopt her father's honorable occupation, and being well qualified by her talents and accomplishments, she assumed the charge of a seminary for young ladies, a position she still fills.

She is known as an author principally from her translation of the "Joseph II." of the Mühlbach novels, and also for her compilation of a series of readers and a spelling-book, during the late war. These were published in Mobile, and adopted in the public schools of that city; they are regarded as really excellent text-books.

The "Round Table," a journal not usually too favorable in its judgment of Southern authors, speaks thus of the translation of the "Joseph II. and his Court":

"The translation of this volume is unusually praiseworthy. Some small things might be said by way of criticism, but we pass them in deference to its general superiority. A translator is to be tested by the success with which the spirit of the original is preserved in the translation. To translate words is a simple task, but to re-embody the original work in its spirit in the translation is the work of genius. Madame Chaudron, to achieve this result, has dared to assume the responsibility of a free translation, and has succeeded."

"Joseph II." was published during the war by the late S. H. Gœtzel, of Mobile, and was the introduction of the now well-known Mühlbach romances into the United States.

Mrs. De Chaudron is much appreciated in the society of Mobile; she has fine conversational powers, an excellent memory, and a happy facility in imparting ideas and knowledge gathered from general reading; her fine musical powers make her an acquisition to any circle; her *spécialité* is decidedly the acquisition of foreign languages.

MISS KATE CUMMING.

MISS CUMMING hardly can be classed as a "writer" in the professional interpretation of that term, "Hospital Life in the Army of the Tennessee" being her only contribution to the literature of the country.

Miss Cumming is of Scotch descent, and has resided in Mobile since childhood.

"Hospital Life in the Army of the Tennessee" was published by John P. Morton & Co., Louisville, Kentucky, in 1866. Says a reviewer:

"At the first glance over the title-page of this book, the reader will, very likely, form an opinion of it from the work written by Miss Florence Nightingale after the Crimean War. But Miss Cumming's book is of a very different character. Miss Nightingale confined herself almost entirely to her life in the hospitals at Scutari and its vicinity, and gave minute directions upon the subject of nursing the sick and wounded, the management of hospitals, and general clinical treatment. Miss Cumming aims to do more than this. She was constantly with the army in the field, received the wounded in nearly every action, and assisted in organizing the field hospitals in the memorable campaigns in Tennessee, Kentucky, and finally in Georgia, when the army was retreating. She has told the story in a plain, straightforward manner, made up from the diary kept through the war; and has presented a very fair history of the operations of the Western army under Bragg, Johnston, and Hood. To the soldiers of the Army of the Tennessee, and to their relatives and friends, this book contains much that is interesting. An heroic woman leaves her comfortable home in the Gulf City, and offers her services as a matron in the corps of field-nurses. She devotes her whole time to the care of the sick and wounded soldiers, sees to the cleansing of their hospital wards, attends to their food, and often with her own hand prepares delicacies for those prostrate with wounds or burning with fever. But she is not located in some interior village, where everything is quiet, and food plenty; her place is in the field. She follows the army in all its wanderings, prepares lint and provides stimulants when a battle is expected, and establishes temporary sick-wards in the first building to be had, when the battle has been fought and the wounded are being brought in. For four years Miss Cumming followed this army-life, and every evening, after the fatigues of the day, spent a few moments over her diary, recording the incidents that transpired around her, 'all of which she saw,' to paraphrase the expression of Cæsar, 'and a part of which she was.'

"The book is almost a transcript of that field-diary. It has been but little altered, and still bears evidences of haste in some parts, as if the words were written just before starting for Dalton or Atlanta, when the army was retreating; and of fatigue in others, as if jotted down after being all day ministering to the sick. But while some may complain of this crudity, if we may so call it, there can be no doubt that this adds very much to the spirit or piquancy of the book. Its main beauty is, that the words convey all the force and testimony of an eye-witness, or even of an actor in the events recorded."

LAURA S. WEBB.

MRS. WEBB is "one of the many" Southern women who have suffered much and lost their all by the war. For several years she contributed poems and sketches to various papers, under the signature of "Stannie Lee." Dr. W. T. Webb, the husband of Mrs. Webb, fought gallantly as a private, as lieutenant, and as captain, and was then surgeon in the Seventh Mississippi Regiment. He contracted consumption in the army, and died after the close of the war, leaving his widow with three little children.

Mrs. Webb became a teacher in the St. Joseph's Institute, Mobile, and in the spring of 1868 published a little volume entitled, "Heart Leaves," to which the following is the introduction:

"Read not through prismatic light
These sorrow-shaded leaves,
For they are from a heart where oft
The spell of sorrow weaves!
No genius rare dwells in the soul
From whence these leaflets came,
And the writer does not seek for them
The laurel-wreath of fame.
Yet sometimes from these humble leaves
There comes an inward moan,
That wells from the depths of a bleeding heart,
By saddened memories torn.
Like some deserted fountain,
Choked by advancing years,
The waters of that heart ooze out
In silence and in tears."

THE HOME OF MISS EVANS.

"'T is the home of the beautiful, the home of the true,
Where the jewels of thought that hallow the view,
Are linked with flowers that bloom in the soul,
Down deep where the waves of genius roll!"

Not long since, we paid a visit to Miss Evans in her home, near the city of Mobile. It is a sweet, secluded spot, where thought can revel in the sunshine of joy, and weave into deathless garlands the jewels that glow in the brain and the soul. All whisper of peace and breathe of beauty around the home where Augusta J. Evans holds communion with her pen and soul. The enchantment that clusters around all that belongs to fame, clings thickly about the homestead which her pen has rendered classic forever.

Previous to our visit, we had never met Miss Evans, and, as we had often read and admired her works, it was with pleasure we wended our way through the gravelled walks that led to her dwelling. Our summons at the door was answered by a servant, who ushered us into an elegantly furnished parlor, where we awaited the appearance of Miss Evans. While sitting there alone, we noted the rare beauty of the paintings that *breathed* upon the walls. They were master-works of master-minds, that had drunk deeply of inspiration, and had left the impress of their souls on the canvas that now glowed with life. But not long did we feast our gaze upon these glorious works of art, for soon Miss Evans entered, and *then* we saw nothing but her. She advanced to greet us with extended hand and pleasant smile, and soon we found ourselves conversing with her who has won the brightest wreath of Southern fame. She was robed in an evening dress of pale blue silk, that suited well with her complexion of pearly whiteness. It would be difficult to determine which pleased the most, her loveliness, the beautiful simplicity of her toilet, or her conversation. All harmonized, all suited, all *charmed*.

There is no pedantry or affectation about her; she converses fluently, and the words ripple musically from her lips, as if they were the glad murmur of a happy heart. May she be forever blest and happy; for though the "Sunny South" is blighted and darkened, and many of her truest hearts are sorrowful and sad, yet may our gifted writer never feel her soul wrapped in the pall that *deep* sorrow weaves!

We spent a delightful hour in her company, and then, as we had other pressing engagements, we rose to take our leave. Miss Evans accompanied us to the outer door, and as we bade her adieu, as she stood there in the doorway, with the golden light of sunset bathing her fair brow, we felt that though, perchance, we were destined never to linger near her again in life, yet our soul would forever keep her memory green.

Miss Evans is tall and queenly in her bearing, graceful and swanlike in her movements, and there is a charm about her manner that wins the heart at once. Her "eyes are thrones of expression," and seem to burn with their glorious beauty down into the caverns of the soul. But the crowning beauty of that classic face is written on the brow, where the seal of intellect is impressed. 'T is a fit resting-place for the wreath that she has won with the genius of her soul. May no poison ever lurk beneath those laurel-leaves that twine with dewy freshness around that beauteous brow! Alas! how oft is the chaplet of fame given those who drink deepest of the cup of woe! But never may the chalice of bitterness be pressed to the joy-wreathed lips of Augusta J. Evans; may the night-time of sorrow never cling around her heart where the spell of genius lingers.

"Oh! why is it forever willed
  That hearts where brightest shine
The gifts of feeling, deep and rare,
  Must deepest steep in sorrow's brine?
'T is but to teach the gifted one
There is no rest till heaven is won!"

Genius is a glorious, but yet a *fearful* gift — a gift that wreathes the soul with the sweetest and most treasured flowers of the heart, bathes them with the dew that welled from the deep urn of the soul, and causes that heart and soul, with all their buds of beauty and of hope, to twine with deathless grasp around an *earthly idol.* Then for a brief, glad while, flashes of wild joy quiver through the deep chambers of the soul where the fire of genius burns, and then — ask of the ashes of desolation that lie on the hearthstone of the heart.

We have woven Miss Evans, her home and genius together, as they are one and the same, except the *blight* that so often withers the greenest wreath. We will not link the bands of sorrow with the destiny that we predict for her. The hand of fate *may* leave her brow unscathed.

'T is appropriate to link her name with that of genius, as she is the child, and her home the abode of genius. And the place that her footprints have marked, the birds that have sung at her windows, the breezes that have kissed her brow and cheek, and the flowers that bloom round her home, are blessed forever by the spell that her presence has cast.

And though she may wander beneath the blue skies of Italy, and gaze with rapture on its glorious sunsets; though she may tread the sunny shores of France, and inhale the fragrance of its delightful clime; and though Switzerland, the land of beauty, may thrill her soul with joy "in her wanderings from home," yet we know that "backward, still backward," will her heart ever turn to her sunny-bright home near the "Mexican sea."

MRS. ANNIE CREIGHT LLOYD.*

ANNIE P. CREIGHT, in 1863, published several short articles in prose and verse in the "Gulf City Home Journal," of Mobile, her first appearance in print. The editor of that journal, in alluding to Miss Creight's contributions, remarked:

> "Miss Creight has put in our hands, with evident trepidation and timidity, several short papers. We saw some faults, but we thought that they could be remedied by a little encouragement, and we gave them to the public. We thought if we would assist the bird to learn to fly, that it would fly very well after a while."

And the editor truly prophesied, for since that time Miss Creight has made for herself quite a to-be-envied place among "Southland writers." Her first novelette appeared in the "Army Argus and Crisis," Mobile, and was entitled "Garnet; or, Through the Shadows into Light;" which was followed by "Hagar; or, The Lost Jewel," which we consider superior to any of her published novelettes. These novelettes have had the honor of republication in the columns of a Mississippi paper, since the close of the war.

In the summer of 1867, Mrs. Lloyd was the successful competitor for a prize offered by the "Mobile Sunday Times" for the best romance; "Pearl; or, The Gem of the Vale," being the title of the successful novelette.

Miss Creight was born in Abbeville, South Carolina: she is yet young in years, and with careful study and judicious pruning of her narratives will accomplish something worthy of herself and her country. At an early age, Miss Creight removed to Mississippi; was educated in Aberdeen, where she graduated in 1859; deprived of parents, she came to Mobile, Alabama, and shared the home of an uncle; in 1866, she was married to William E. Lloyd, and resides in Mobile, occasionally writing as a recreation.

* Extracts from her writings were accidentally destroyed.

MRS. E. W. BELLAMY.

MRS. E. W. BELLAMY ("Kampa Thorpe") has not, as yet, accomplished a great deal in the literature of her country, but what she has published she has cause to be proud of. Her novel "Four Oaks" was published by Carleton, New York, 1867. The "Round Table," New York, under the impression that "Kampa Thorpe" was of the masculine gender, thus alludes to "Four Oaks":

"This is a story of every-day life, in which all the incidents are probable, and, what is yet more rare, the characters are all perfectly natural. A number of men and women, differing in age though not in station, are brought together on terms of pleasant acquaintanceship, and there is a more liberal allowance than usual of intelligent men and brainless nonentities, of sensible women and those torments of modern society, women of an uncertain age on the lookout for husbands; and although there are no diabolical villains, there are mischief-makers enough to occasion unpleasant complications, which, together with mysterious miniatures and family secrets, combine to sustain an interest which the events of the story would not otherwise suffice to keep alive.

"The scene opens in the pleasant town of Netherford, where, after a severe round of introductions to the forefathers and relatives of the heroine, we are presented to a charming, good-hearted, and beautiful girl, a little spoiled, rather self-willed, and somewhat too self-reliant, but so true and honest, so free from all the vices which attach to the fashionable and fast young lady of the present day, that we are grateful to the author who awakens our interest for a woman equally endowed with vitality, modesty, and common sense. There is an absence of all romance about a life passed among such restless and ill-assorted people as form the society of Netherford, but the author has refrained from giving us any exaggerated or extravagant scenes; he is thoroughly consistent and natural, and his imagination has evidently been greatly assisted by personal observation."

And a Southern editor and critic of experience (Major W. T. Walthall) thus reviews the book:

"We have subjected this volume to careful reading — a reading much more careful than we are in the habit of giving to any new novel.

"We confess having commenced 'Four Oaks' with some nervous apprehensions — fear lest it might prove like too many books by Southern authors, which task the ingenuity of an indulgent reviewer to effect an awkward compromise between candor and charity in the expression of his opinion. They have to be 'damned with faint praise,' or eased off with unmeaning platitudes. 'Four Oaks,' we are happy to say, is not one of such books. We have read it through with continually increasing interest, and have laid it down with that paradoxically pleasant regret which busy people rarely have the luxury of feeling in finishing a book — regret that it is ended.

"Considering the temptations held out by the examples of some of the most successful novels of the day, 'Four Oaks' is to be commended almost as much for what it is *not*, as for what it is. It is not a 'sensational' story. There is not a battle, nor a duel, nor a ghost, nor a murder, and but one pistol-shot in it. [We do not object to a reasonable use of these elements of interest in a novel, but it is very refreshing to meet with one that can be just as interesting without them.] It has no violations of the letter or the spirit of the seventh commandment — no sentimental apologies for vice — no poetic idealization of acts and passions which in the honest language of the Scriptures are called by homely names that would be inadmissible in elegant fiction. Without a particle of prudery or pretension, it is imbued with the very atmosphere of purity — purity not *inculcated*, but taken for granted. To say that the author is a lady, *ought* to be sufficient to make all this follow as a matter of course; but, unfortunately, some of the lady novelists of this generation have taught us a different lesson.

"Nor does the author of 'Four Oaks' delight in twisting and torturing human passions and feelings into agonies of strange attitudes and fantastic developments. Her characters are men and women, with loves, hates, hopes, fears, joys, sorrows, faults, and follies, like those of other people.

"Neither is 'Four Oaks' a device for showing off the learning of the author. She shows the effects of culture, but not its processes. There is, perhaps, rather too much botany in one of her chapters, but this is an exception to the general rule.

"Again, 'Four Oaks' is neither political, polemical, nor philosophical. Thoroughly Southern as it is, the word 'Southern' scarcely occurs in it, nor is there anything said of patriotism, or chivalry, or the sunny South, or the peculiar institution. Its locality is defined only by its general tone, spirit, and the language, manners, and usages of the people who figure in it. It has no theory to maintain, nor any 'mission' to fulfil.

"It is needless, however, to specify the negative merits of 'Four Oaks,' when it has so many that are positive. It is a story of every-day life. Its materials and its style are of the most unpretending sort. We are introduced in the early chapters into the society of a pleasant little circle of people in 'the town of Netherford,' on the 'banks of the Ominihaw,' and these people constitute nearly all the personages of the story. The heroine is far from being a model of propriety. She is full of faults and foibles, which sometimes provoke the friendly reader and make his interest and sympathy tremble in the balance for a moment, but she is sure to carry away his heart in the end. Her education is lamentably imperfect when she is first introduced. She likes picnics and dancing better than books, has never read even 'The Lady of the Lake,' and 'The Burial of Sir John Moore' is new to her; but she has a heart, and an honest one, and she is witty and beautiful. Herein, as we think, the author again shows good sense. We have a great respect for plain women. They often make admirable nurses, friends, mothers, sisters, and even sweethearts and wives for those who are indifferent about beauty, but they do not answer for heroines of romance. Even Jane Eyre has to marry a blind man. But Harry Vane is not only beautiful — she is bewitching in every sense. We may vow that she is unworthy of being loved, but she wins us back in the course of the next minute, and binds us faster than ever. The progress of her character, and the quiet but steady growth of its improvement, are among the most interesting features in the book; and yet there is no parade made of it. The art of the artist is admirably concealed.

"We have never read anything more thoroughly and unaffectedly natural than the characters, the conversation, and incidents of this book. It exhales the very odor of the groves, the fields, the forests, and the ancestral homes of Virginia or the Carolinas; and yet, as we have already said, neither Virginia nor Carolina is mentioned. There are no tedious and elaborate descriptions of scenery or analyses of character: the touches that set them before us so vividly are imperceptible. The humor of some passages is delightful. It must be a dull soul — totally insensible to mirth — that can read unmoved such scenes as the account of the first meeting of the Quodlibet, or that of Mr. Dunbar's courtship, or his prescription of 'earthworms and turpentine,' or some others that might be specified.

"But it is in the love-scenes of 'Four Oaks' that its chief charm consists. Trite as is the theme, it is still that which stirs most deeply the human heart, and has the most universal attraction for human sympathy. We have often seen its influences depicted with more power, but never with so much of exquisite grace, delicacy, and fidelity, as in this book. Without a particle of sentimentality to repel the most fastidious taste, it unites all the truth and tenderness of the sentimental school with the sparkle of the gayer and lighter sort, and touches of exquisite delicacy, which could proceed only from a woman's pen, and which may be appreciated, but scarcely described or analyzed.

"We forbear to say anything more in praise of 'Four Oaks.' What we have said is not said from any undue partiality, for we know the writer only by reputation — scarcely even by name. We are sensible, too, of some faults in her book. It has, to a certain degree, that fault from which scarcely any lady writer — perhaps none — is entirely free: the fault of diffuseness. But then, there is this difference: the works of most women (and perhaps of most men too) would be improved by reducing them to one-fifth of their dimensions; in the case of 'Four Oaks,' we could not possibly *spare* more than one-fifth. There is an artistic fault in the too rapid introduction of characters in the beginning. The mind of the reader is confused, and one has to look back for explanation oftener than we like in the hurry of novel-reading.

"The sum of the whole matter is, that 'Four Oaks' is the most delightful book that we have read for a long time. It is the very book to be read aloud either by the winter fireside or the summer seaside, with one congenial listener, or a circle of such listeners, and to leave all parties more genial, more happy, more thankful to the Creator for his good gifts, more charitable toward his creatures. It is very rarely that we could conscientiously recommend the author of a new novel to repeat the effort, but in this case we very much hope that 'Four Oaks' is only the beginning of a series. 'Kampa Thorpe' has not mistaken her vocation."

Mrs. Bellamy is a widow, and is a teacher in a seminary at Eutaw, Greene County, Alabama. Her essays contributed to the "Mobile Sunday Times" are beautiful and elegant articles, and we imagine she is an ardent lover of "nature and nature's God."

From her first book, one can judge that in the future something which the "world will not willingly let die" will be forthcoming.

A SUMMER IDYL.

When woodlands spread their denser screen,
  And wheat is reap'd on sunburnt plains;
When apples blush for looking green,
  And berries ripen in the lanes;

When bees go robbing clover-fields,
  And barefoot truants wade the brook,
Or 'neath the shade the forest yields
  They seek them out some breezy nook;

When summer weaves her slumb'rous spell
  Of dreamy murmurs, lulling care,
Till Thought lies dormant in his cell
  To watch the castles rise in air;

What vocal rover haunts the land,
  Roaming adown the dusty walks,

Or in the stubble takes his stand,
  And loudly of the harvest talks?

From sylvan coverts far and near
  A name is called from morn till night,
And questions asked in accents clear
  About the crop of Farmer White;

That vague, mysterious crop of peas
  The gleaners of the feather'd gown
Are waiting eagerly to seize
  When "Bob" shall lay his sickle down.

O Bob, Bob White! where doth he dwell?
  And wherefore do they call his name?
And who is he?—can any tell?
  Can any whisper whence he came?

Have any seen him on the hills,
  Industrious at the dawn of day?
Have any spied him by the rills,
  Dozing the noontide hours away?

Perchance he is akin to Kate
  Who did the deed without a name,
Or that poor Will whose luckless fate
  The twilight babblers oft proclaim.

"A man of words, and not of deeds,"
  He dwells in an unreal clime,
And takes his ease in sunny meads,
  Unjostled by the march of time.

In those fair realms beyond the stream,
  That parts the infant from the man,
I see this farmer in a dream,
  With kindly eye and cheek of tan;

A jolly wight, who loves his pipe,
  And knows the cunning speech of birds,
But parleys o'er his peas unripe
  To teach his reapers human words.

An echo from old Babyland,
  His name, across the vanish'd years
By summer breezes lightly fann'd,
  Brings happy thoughts bedew'd with tears.

What tireless rambles through the wood,
  What revels round the bubbling spring,
By slopes whereon the stout oaks stood,
  And held the grape-vine for a swing!

O summer days! O summer joys!
  That come not as they came of old;
Their charm still lingers in the voice
  Now piping from the sunlit wold.

Wherefore be blessings on the bird
  That warbles with such magic art;
What time his "airy tongue" is heard,
  The past illuminates the heart!

JULY, 1868.

TRANSITION.

"BRILL ON THE HILL," ALA.

How soon will end the Summer days!
  Though thick and green the forest-leaves,
Already Autumn's golden haze
About the woods and hilly ways
  A veil of tender radiance weaves.

Oh! what is in the Autumn sun,
  And what is in the Autumn air,
Makes all they shine and breathe upon,
Ere yet the Summer days are gone,
  Look so exceeding sweet and fair?

E'en weeds, that through the Summer rain
  Grew wanton, and o'ertopped the flowers,—
Rude children of the sunburnt plain,—
Bud out and blossom, not in vain,
  Around the Summer's faded bowers.

For long ago the violets fled,
  The pansy closed its purple eye,
The poppy hung its uncrowned head,
And on the garden's grass-grown bed
  The lily laid her down to die.

No more the roses bud and blow;
  The few late beauties that remain

Are tossed by rough winds to and fro,
And all their fragrant leaves laid low
  And scattered by the latter rain.

Like some old limner's quaint design
  The sunlight's checkered play doth seem,
And through the clusters on the vine,
As through a goblet filled with wine,
  Soft, shimmering sparkles gleam.

The red-cheeked apples thickly grow
  About the orchard's leafy mass,
But when they hear the tempest blow,
Through twisted boughs they sliding go
  And hide within the tangled grass.

No more the partridge's whistle rings;
  The dove her plaintive cry has ceased,—
From tree to tree, on restless wings,
The mock-bird flits, but never sings:
  The west wind rocks an empty nest.

All harmonies of Summer fail!
  The vaulting insects cease to sport;
The songs of bees alone prevail,
The wingèd traffickers that sail
  From flowery port to port.

Upon the hills and in the fields
  A few pale flowers begin to blow;
A few pale buds the garden yields,
A few pale blooms the hedge-row shields;
  Summer consents not yet to go.

O yellow leaf amid the green!
  Sad presage of the coming fall,
Soon where your withered tent is seen
Shall Autumn's gorgeous banners screen
  The incipient ruin over all!

Though sadly to ourselves we say,
  "The summer days will soon be o'er,"
Yet who may tell the very day
Whereon the Summer went away,
  Though closely watching evermore?

With sailing clouds the heavens teem,
  That beckon like impatient guides,
And like the gliding of a stream,
Like thoughts that mingle in a dream,
  The Summer into Autumn glides.

She goes! and leaves the woods forlorn;
  For grief the birds refuse to sing;
Bare lie the fields that laughed with corn;
But of each garnered grain is born
  The certain promise of the Spring.

SHADOW-FAME.

"Where be those old divinities forlorn
That dwelt in trees?"
Plea of the Midsummer Fairies.

The imagination of the poet, says Madame de Staël, forms a link between the physical and moral world—by building upon that secret alliance of our being with the marvels of nature. From this "secret alliance" sprang the exquisite creations of the elder bards, divinities that dwelt within the enveloping bark, and lived, suffered, and died with the tree, ofttimes walking abroad and communing with man.

Those days are passed away: the imprisoned hamadryads walk no more abroad, yet not altogether silent do they dwell within their homes of bark. The forests still whisper unto man sweet idyls of the spring, or sigh forth sad elegies of autumn, and still orchards yield their gracious fruits, and hide within leafy bowers "all throats that gurgle sweet." Green boughs still throw soft shadows on the summer grass when the noon burns hot, and wave a breezy welcome.

The story of that memorable tree in Eden, so closely interwoven with man's destiny, is but the beginning of the intimacy that has so long existed between mankind and the children of the forest and the garden; as though the trees had followed the "exiles of Eden" out into the forlorn and dreary world to shelter and sustain them—how often, in after-ages, to prove a most sure refuge in the day of adversity! Nor was this all; faithful monitors from a ruined paradise, with arms forever stretching upward, they point man to the skies! Judea's stately palm sheltered the wife of Lapidoth in peace while "the children of Israel came up to her for judgment;" but an avenging oak in the wood of Ephraim seized the rebellious son of David, and held him aloft while Joab's three darts clove their way into his heart. When Zaccheus, in the press and crowd of Jericho, would see the Saviour of mankind, a sycamore lent its strong back to this man "of little stature." The fig-tree that withered at a word bore testimony to Christ's divinity; and it was under the shade of trees that he went out to pray when there were none to watch with him.

In attestation of the universal sympathy between mankind and the heaven-aspiring trees, the religious myths of all lands have consecrated some tree to eternal homage. The ancient Hindoos, who believed in hamadryads, were accustomed every year to celebrate at great expense the marriage of the shrub Toolsea with the pebble-god Saligram. The *Enada Mina* of Lamaism has its heaven-born *Zampa* tree, bearing fruit for the sustenance of the *Lahen*, spirits whose radiant bodies sufficed them for light until they partook of the forbidden fruits of *Shima*, the earth. Ormuzd, the great principle of light and good in the Persian mythology, after creating the sky, sun, moon, and stars, fire, wind, and clouds, and bidding the mountains rise, called forth the tree *Hom*, the first in the vegetable world, the perfect type of all trees.

The coffin of Osiris, stranded among the rushes of Byblos on the Phœnician coast, found a safe asylum when the pliant reeds knit themselves together, and grew into a mighty tree, enclosing the murdered god.

The Greeks had their sacred olive, and their sacred fig-tree, and that renowned Dodonian oak where the wood-pigeon whispered of hidden things, nay, the tree itself had uttered speech, and even its dismembered limb that ploughed the deep prophesied unto those early navigators seeking the Golden Fleece. And the Romans in their *Ficus Ruminalis* long preserved the memory of that wild fig by the yellow Tiber, where the wolf nourished Rome's twin founders.

The rugged imagination of the Scandinavians pictured the huge ash, Yggdrasill, supposing the universe sending forth roots that reached to the dwelling of the gods, the land of the giants, and the dreary regions of perpetual cold and darkness. At one of these roots was the deep well where wit and wisdom lie hidden.

The Druids held the oak sacred, and never suffered one to be cut. It is said the cathedral of Strasbourg stands upon the spot where a tree grew, worshipped by the rude tribes that dwelt along the Rhine. Haply it was the very oak to which the zealous Boniface courageously laid the axe, thick with interlacing boughs, that furnished the great model of the intricate Gothic arches.

Islam never doubts the miracle of the acacia-tree, that suddenly sprang up in the dim dawn to veil the entrance of that cave of Mount Thor, wherein the Prophet and Abu Beker had taken refuge the first morning of their desperate hegira. Nor less credible, according to the Arabian chroniclers, is the miracle of the groaning date-tree of the mosque of Medina, disconsolate at the Prophet's withdrawal from its supporting trunk. Perhaps it was in grateful memory of this timely service and this delightful flattery that Mohammed assigned to trees so conspicuous a *rôle* in his fantastic paradise.

The date-tree he buried beneath his pulpit, there to await the final resurrection, when it shall be transferred to Al Jannet to bear fruit for true believers.

The beautiful faith of Babyland consecrates a mystic growth, which springs up in a midwinter night, ablaze with blossoms of taper-flame, laden with the fruits of Santa Claus, and musical with the "bells of Yule."

Rabbinical fable and monkish legend have contributed to the fame of trees; the rabbis aver that the true cross was made from a tree which grew from a slip of the tree of life brought by Adam from Eden; and the monks of Glastonbury affirm that the thorn of which our Lord's crown was made was perpetuated in England by Joseph of Arimathea when he founded the abbey in the Vale of Avalon.

But the light of accepted history casts a blaze of glory around many honored trees that need not the aid of fable to enhance their merits. What memories of valor and heroic adventure do they record among the nations, as though the hamadryads had stepped forth and stamped a page of history.

Switzerland has her lime at Môrat and the long-vanished tree of Altorf, under which Tell's little son stood with the apple on his head; France has her two pear-trees of Ivry; Sweden her pine of the Lungsjo Forest, where Gustavus Vasa found shelter; England her Royal Oak of Boscobel; America her Charter Oak and her Liberty Elm, and the sad South her "Seven Pines," breathing their odorous sighs over heroes who died in vain.

The great lime of Môrat was not standing there when the bold Duke of Burgundy led his forty thousand men one summer day before the gates of the little town, escaping when the battle was done by "dint of hoof."

> "Here Burgundy bequeath'd his tombless host,
> A bony heap through ages to remain;
> Themselves their monument."

When, after three hundred years, the Burgundians of the French army destroyed the ghastly "ossuary," what more fitting monument to the memory of the victory patriotism gained over oppression could the Swiss have raised than this broad-spreading tree?

The tree of Altorf, where Gemmi Tell stood when his father's unerring arrow clove the apple on his head, is veiled in the mists and shadows of a vague tradition, at which the critic frowns; but it is sometimes well to cultivate "a wise credulity." Who would forego the delight of believing that the tower of Altorf's public square, with its rude pictures of Tell's brave exploits, marks the very spot where the shadows played upon the trembling peasants, awaiting the verdict of the Alpine bow.

No monument rises where the two pear-trees of Ivry died upon the field of glory; but on that memorable day when Ivry, the obscure, burst into immortal glory, Henry IV. bequeathed these trees to fame, linked with "the white plume of Navarre;" for here was the rallying point he gave his troops.

Doubtless the pine-tree of the Lungsjo Forest has long since vanished away; it was already decaying when Gustavus Vasa made his bed beneath its boughs; but so long as Sweden reveres the memory of that young prince, who in the obscurity of the Dalecarlian mines formed the bold scheme of liberating his country, so long will she cherish the recollection of the decaying pine. Here did the wounded and hunted prince find shelter three days and nights, while the Danish emissaries sought him in vain amid the dwellings of man.

Conspicuous among all the trees of fame stands the Royal Oak of Boscobel,

> "Wherein the younger Charles abode
> Till all the paths were dim,
> And far below the Roundhead rode
> And hummed a surly hymn."

Of this memorable and unique adventure Charles himself has left an account in that paper attributed to him among the Pepysian MSS. in Magdalen College, Cambridge. This pollard oak, whereof the branches grew so propitiously bushy and thick, stood not within the wood of Boscobel, where the fugitive king had previously passed a most miserable day, sore with fatigue, and wet with the September rain. Major Careless pointed it out from the windows of Pendrell's house, standing among several others in an open field. Thither came Charles and the faithful cavalier at dawn, and here they passed the weary day, Charles sleeping with his head in the Major's lap: while "going up and down in the thicket of the wood, searching for persons who had escaped," wandered the vengeful Roundheads. Nor is Charles the only monarch who, in the hour of need, found safety by climbing a tree. It is related of Louis VII., of France, that when the army he was conducting to Palestine was attacked at dead of night by the Turks, he climbed a tree while the battle raged amid darkness and disorder, escaping only at dawn to find his camp almost deserted.

Charter Oak stands first upon America's list of renowned trees. It grew upon Wylly's Hill, now within the city limits of Hartford, where it was found flourishing in the perfection of its glory when the first inhabitant of the name settled on the hill. Perhaps, as Cowper supposes in the case of Yardley Oak, a deer's nimble foot scooped a hollow for an acorn, and the forest winds nursed it into vigorous growth, while mysterious nature, working by unseen forces, formed the cavity at its root, where Andros never dreamed of seeking the missing parchment.

The original Liberty Tree was one of a grove of elms in Boston, which has long since given place to bricks and mortar. The inscription on its trunk brought it under the displeasure of the British, who cut it down in 1774. It has been characteristically recorded by a Yankee that it furnished fourteen cords of wood. But the flame it kindled the British could not quench. Every town in "the original thirteen" consecrated a tree to liberty. A live-oak in Charleston was the rallying point of the South Carolina patriots in the days of stamp-act excitement. Here did Christopher Gadsden raise his voice against oppression, and for this very reason the live-oak shared the fate of the elm at Boston. Sir Henry Clinton ordered its demolition in 1780. It is not said how many cords it yielded, but enough remained of the stump to furnish cane-heads, as heirlooms, and a ballot-box, presented to the "'76 Association," but which was unfortunately consumed in the conflagration of 1838.

How long shall Richmond's Seven Sighing Pines whisper the story of that "glorious day in June"? Yea, though their branches wither and their trunks decay, their voice still will echo amid the ruins of a nation's shattered hopes, like that faint murmur of the multitude heard at nightfall in the Alhambra's haunted courts.

"Old trees," says an English writer, "without the aid of an oracle to consecrate them, seem to have been some of the most natural objects of that contemplative and melancholy regard which easily passes into superstitious veneration." Erasmus could not be convinced that trees felt not the first stroke of the axe; and Evelyn, who so revered the British oaks, says he could never hear the groans of a falling tree without a feeling of pity. How pathetically does he record his vexation of spirit at the demolition of that "most glorious and impenetrable holly-hedge," at Sayes Court, through which it was the Czar Peter's pleasure to ride in a wheel-barrow! The "tongues in trees" sometimes babbled unto deaf ears: the Vandal from the Baltic, to whom, in an evil hour, Evelyn lent his mansion, had little regard for any forest-growth, save that he found well-seasoned under a carpenter's lumber-shed.

The legends of classic antiquity are rich in that beautiful sympathy which man finds in nature. We read of the Babylonian mulberry, of which the fruit turned red with the blood of Pyramus and Thisbe; the bare almond-tree of Phyllis the forlorn, bursting into leaf at the touch of her late returning lover; and of that spiry group upon the tomb of Protesilaus by the Hellespont, that ever, as they grew tall enough to catch a view of Troy's fatal shore, shrank and withered at the sight. Therefore would it seem that poets have a prescriptive right to make them friends among the trees, and doubtless the poets of every age and of every clime have been enamored of a hamadryad. We know that a laurel grew spontaneously upon the tomb of Virgil, or perchance some "light-winged dryad of the trees" planted it there, to die a martyr at the hands of the admirers of the Mantuan bard. And the Persians tell us the nightingales sing sweetest in the boughs that shadow Rocknabad, where Hafiz sat.

In the grounds of Donnington Castle, whence the "morning-star of song" sent forth his sweet music to the world, an oak as late as the days of Queen Elizabeth was known by the name of Chaucer's Oak. In its shadow, it is said, he wrote many of his later poems, and to the memory of Edward and Philippa he left two green monuments in the "King's Oak" and the "Queen's Oak," which he named for them.

The three-peaked hill of Eildon, above the town of Melrose, once nourished in its soil the tree under which stood Thomas of Ercildoun, poet and seer, while he delivered his prophecies to a credulous people. This tree exists no longer; but the spot is marked by a stone that takes its name from the Eildon Tree.

Shakspeare conferred an immortality upon the mulberry he planted in his garden at Stratford that Francis Gastrell could not take away. The infamy of this man shall endure as long as the fame of the tree he so ruthlessly destroyed. Well did he deserve the execrations that followed him through the streets of Shakspeare's native town. The mulberry shares the honor of Shakspeare's favor with a crab-tree on the roadside from Stratford to Bedford. The reputation of this town may be divined from its sobriquet of "drunken Bedford;" the ale brewed here tripped up the poet's home-returning feet, and laid him low in the shadow of this tree to pass the night. Herne's Oak, too, in Windsor Forest, owes far more of its fame to the airy creatures of the poet's brain than to the frightful spectre of the horned hunter that haunted there on winter nights. It was cut down in 1795 by the king's order, being totally decayed.

Penshurst, in Kent, boasts of "Sir Philip Sidney's Oak," where the hero of Zutphen loitered in the shade, nurturing those noble sentiments that beautified his life and were the ornament of his death.

Pope, who did so much to improve the English taste in gardening, has not left his fame destitute of sylvan monuments. Seven miles from Windsor, in the village of Binfield, was a neat brick building, which England's great satirist describes as his "paternal cell":

"A little house with trees a-row,
And, like its master, very low."

A short distance from this house, amid a grove of beeches, stood one favored tree, where this forest-warbler, *recumbens sub tegmine fagi*, won his early fame. It is represented as a huge bare trunk, stretching forth one attenuated branch; it bears the inscription, "Here Pope sung," cut in large letters in the bark, and for many years annually renewed by the care of Lady Gower, of Workingham. But the willow, the far-famed weeping-willow of the Twickenham Villa, died of old age in 1801. It was a cherished foundling, a hardy twig bound round some precious curiosity from a foreign land. Pope reared it in that renowned garden where he amused himself "planting for posterity," and this little twig from the banks of the Bosphorus sent forth its shoots all over England, and even into the gardens of the Empress of Russia.

There is an ancient forest on the banks of Ouse, whither the bard of Olney often strayed, soothing his melancholy in sweet converse with nature. Within the hollow of Yarkley Oak he would sit for hours

"With hearers none,
Or prompter, save the scene,"

pondering the beauties of Kilwick and Dinglebury, that he knew so well how to make "live in description and look green in song." Yardley Oak was known for ages by the name of "Judith;" it is supposed that it was planted by Judith, niece of William the Conqueror, who received the counties of Northampton and Huntingdon for her dower. The fame that attaches to this oak threatens to prove its destruction, and the Marquis of Northampton, upon whose estate it stands, has been obliged to threaten with the penalties of the law all those who shall injure or deface it.

An elm in the church-yard of Harrow-on-the-Hill grows by a tomb which is still known there as "Byron's tomb." Here sat the incipient poet in the happy school-days, "and frequent mused the twilight hours away." Thus he wrote of it years afterward, when his heart yearned for the days that would never come again. At Newstead he planted an oak, with which he connected his own fate, and which he celebrated in verse when he found it pining from neglect.

Romance, too, has cast her spell upon the gardens and the groves, and tells strange, delightful tales of the hamadryads' power over men, of groans from hollow oaks, and trees that wither at the memory of horrid deeds.

Abderaman the Just, in the loneliness of his grandeur, turned from the pomp and magnificence with which he had surrounded himself at Cordova, to indulge, in the shade of his date-tree, sweet memories of Araby the Blest, the land for which his soul was sick.

Xerxes once stopped his vast army to pay court to a plane-tree, decking it with gold and gems and the gay fabrics of the Eastern looms; and a Roman consul cherished a beech-tree under which he slept, and often refreshed its roots with wine. This was a common practice among the Romans, and Caligula may have done the same to that huge palm they called his "nest," where he was wont to assemble his parasites, who could enjoy the luxury of the shadow and the breeze, but into whose callous hearts the sweet lessons of benevolence taught by trees never found an entrance.

Louis le Débonnaire whiled away one pleasant hour, we may safely affirm, planting the rose-tree by the church-walls of Heidelberg, forgetting the cares of state and his rebellious sons. Many long years after his broken heart had gone to its refuge in the island-tomb of the Rhine, his rose-tree continued to flourish and to bloom,—only a few years since it was reported as still vigorously climbing the church-walls. A rose-tree of the ninth century well may challenge credulity, but this rose would hardly smell as sweet by any other name.

Neither the historian nor the traveller would seek for the holly-bush of Bosworth Field, yet is there not the good old English proverb, "Cleave to the crown though it hang on a bush," to testify to the fact that Lord Stanley did not find the crown in the mire, but saw it glittering in a holly-bush, where a peasant hung it when it fell from Richard's head? This proverb was first spoken in 1485, and who would not rather believe it than all the histories ever written?

On the borders of the elf-haunted forests of the Vosges, a voice prophetic, that could not speak unto the dull ear of Charles, stirred the aspiring heart of the innkeeper's daughter. Far away the tumult of battle raged over desolated France; near by her young companions pursued their rustic sports; but Joan sat silent by the fountain, while, among the leaves of the lime bending over her, she heard the Archangels, Michael and Gabriel, promising victory.

Tradition tells a fearful story of a hollow oak among the mountains of Merionethshire: the ferocious Glyndwr here hid away the body of the murdered Sele, until the oak groaned and drooped under the curse of its awful secret,

"And to this day the peasant still
With cautious fear avoids the ground,
In each wild branch a spectre sees,
And trembles at each rising sound."

However the story of Jane McCrea be told, the pine-tree is still standing near Fort Edward, though blighted by the memory of the piteous tragedy enacted in its shade.

After these wild stories, how pleasant it is to fancy the doughty Peter Stuyvesant issuing from his yellow brick house on genial afternoons, to sun his silver-embossed leg of wood under the veteran pear-tree, while the smoke of the distant city curled over the trees in the "Bowerie Lane"! Haply the tree made a compact with Peter to stay and watch the city's growth. The companions of the orchard fled, dismayed and stifled by the march of improvement that, gorgon-like, turned all to stone, but dauntlessly the pear-tree stood its ground, defying the stones that usurped the carpet of clover and grass at its feet, heralding the spring, as was its old-time custom, with fair white blossoms, and ripening every autumn fewer and fewer of the old Dutch governor's favorite fruit, while the mighty city strode behind it.

Who has not seen Cupid's foot-prints on a tree, the mystic hearts and darts — signs by which the ubiquitous little god may be traced even along the walls of doomed Pompeii. These sylvan *graffiti* mark that curious crisis in a man's life when he is prompted to study the language of flowers, and to make a confidant of a hamadryad.

In the garden of the Generalife, "the house of love," as the name signifies, the cypresses of the Moors yet stand; among them is the famous *Cipres della Regina Sultana,* where the fair prisoner of the harem held her stolen interviews with her lover, Abencerrages. It may have been by this very tree that he took the fatal step into the Sultana's balcony which brought a bloody death upon so many of his tribe.

The ill-starred Duke of Monmouth carved upon a tree in Nettlestede Park the simple name "Henrietta," a touching monument to the lady of his love. Little he thought, while he shaped the letters, what a charm their fate would bequeath unto this tree.

The melancholy Vanessa, at Marley Abbey, was accustomed to plant a laurel in her garden, with her own hands, to commemorate the visits of Swift. The garden is crowded with these witnesses of the double-dealing dean's perfidy.

"All under the greenwood tree," memories of robber-life cluster thickly. In the lawless days of these *mira gens, socii arborum,* when the judges went on their circuit, they were accompanied by a strong guard of armed men. A great oak between Carlisle and Newcastle was long remembered as the spot where this cavalcade were accustomed to halt for dinner.

Epping Forest was so dreaded a robber-haunt that no person dared pass through it alone. It lay to the north of London, and near the city bounds was the famous Fairlop Oak, of which the boughs stretched out so wide. Here the Sunday fairs were held, and mountebanks and dancing-girls amused the idle crowd, while the denizens of the greenwood mingled unknown among them. Fairlop Oak is not now to be found in Epping Forest, but in the church of St. Pancras, where it forms the pulpit.

The oaks of Clipstone and of Welbeck Parks are linked with the memory of Robin Hood. Clipstone Park, the property of the Duke of Portland, existed before the Conquest, and Robin Hood's Trysting-tree, the gnarled Parliament Oak, is 1,500 years old. The Duke's Walking-stick, in Welbeck Park, is perhaps the tallest of trees, being higher than Westminster Abbey. In the same park is the famous Greendale Oak, with an archway through its trunk, once wide enough to admit a carriage, but slowly and steadily closing up. Trees take strange freaks sometimes, and we will no more doubt the pictures of the willow by Napoleon's tomb, that, leaning on a stump, cast his shadow on the sky, than we doubt the existence of those enchanted and aërial Moors guarding the treasures of the Sierras of Spain. We know the cypress that was blown down on the estate of Vespasian got upon its *roots* again, only because Vespasian was to be blessed with grandeur and prosperity.

Among those trees which kept open house, as it were, the Talbot Yew, of Tankersley Park, would permit a man on horseback to turn about very comfortably within its hollow boll, but the *Caztagno de' cento Cavalli* surpasses this by ninety-nine horsemen; whether Queen Joanna and her one hundred attendants could comfortably turn about within the bark of that hospitable giant of Mount Ætna, where they were sheltered from the rain, it is hazardous to declare. It is certain that not quite one hundred years ago a little hut was built within its enormous hollow for the accommodation of those engaged in gathering and preserving the chestnuts. The Sicilians call this "the oldest of trees," and as there is no possibility of estimating its age, they run little risk of contradiction. Nevertheless, the vague and wavering belief excited by this assertion fades utterly away in the shadow of the *six thousand years* M. Decandolle assigns to the cypress of Santa Maria de Tecla, near Oaxaca. The Pre-Adamites might have dwelt beneath its boughs in the days when Jan-ben-Jan ruled the Genii. Had the sloe-thorn, which took root and bore fruit in the shepherd's breast, belonged to this era of marvels, the Archbishop of Tarragon had not testified in vain to the truth of the only story of the trees at which credulity grows restive.

The reverence for aged trees is not confined to the Philippines, though all do not believe them to be the chosen abodes of ancestors. It has been the amusement of the learned to count the rings in transverse sections of trunks, and all the world listens and applauds. To be really venerable, a tree must reckon its age, not by years, but centuries. After M. Decandolle's statement, one will readily believe that the cypress exceeds all trees in longevity. A cypress in the garden of Chapultepec is considered by Humboldt to be upward of 5,000 years old. The cypress of Somma, in Lombardy, sinks into insignificance before these veterans of Mexico; it is only 1,900 years old, but it lived in the time of Julius Cæsar, and Napoleon himself turned out of his way, when he made the road of the Simplon, to avoid interfering with it. A yew at Braburn, Kent, is computed to have seen 3,000 years, and one at Fortingal, in Scotland, very nearly as many. But as long as a stump stands upon Lebanon or Olivet, it can never be true that our reverence for aged trees is in proportion to the years they number. The "glory of Lebanon" is reduced to twelve gigantic cedars; "their great age," says an American traveller, "is strikingly apparent in their gnarled and time-worn trunks." The best authorities are agreed that this grove, which is found at Bisharri, nearly opposite Tripoli, contains the original growth of Libanus, of which Isaiah spake so eloquently. The praise of the prophet is all-sufficient for their fame, but the Arabs of the Mount tell many strange stories of miracles enacted in their shade, and the petty vanity of man has cut away the bark in many places, and scarred the white and fragrant wood with names. Isaiah's Mulberry-tree, which is supposed to mark the spot where he was sawn asunder, stands, or did once stand, at the end of the causeway built across the mouth of the Tyropœon, that deep ravine which intersects Jerusalem from north to south.

The olives of Gethsemane are eight in number, enclosed within a wall and strictly guarded. In the shadows of this sacred grove, where Christ uttered his sublime and touching prayer, there comes a vision of that Tree of Life the beloved disciple beheld on the Isle of Patmos: "and the leaves of the tree were for the healing of the nations." In the New Jerusalem there shall not lack man's pleasant companion of the garden and the grove.

MISS MARY A. CRUSE.

MISS CRUSE is a native of Huntsville, Alabama, one of the most beautiful and hospitable little cities of the "Southland." Charles Lanman, in one of his volumes, thus alludes to this little city:

"It occupies an elevated position, and is hemmed in with high hills, from the summit of which it presents an uncommonly picturesque appearance. . . . . It is supplied with the best of water from a mammoth spring, which gushes from a rock in the centre of the town; and this, with the array of from one to two hundred saddle-horses which are daily collected around the county court-house square, ought to be mentioned as among the features of the place. But on becoming acquainted with the people of Huntsville, the stranger will find that they are the leading character."

This was an *ante-bellum* view, yet in this latter particular the people are not changed. The Cruse family are from Maryland, and one that would take position anywhere for their refinement and peculiar sprightliness of intellect. Sam Cruse, as he was universally termed, Miss Mary Anne's father, was a man of great probity and manliness of character, one of the first citizens of Huntsville. In the person of Mr. William Cruse, an odd old-bachelor uncle, the town of Huntsville will long remember an unfailing fund of witticisms and quaint peculiarities which will render his memory delightful. "Billy Cruse" was a curiosity, an oddity, a genius, but leaving his fame, however, entirely to tradition.

Miss Cruse, even at school, began to distinguish herself, by the studiousness of her deportment and the rapidity with which she acquired her tasks. Even then the germ of the future authoress might be discovered. She frequently indulged in poetic flights when very young, in which the partial eye of friendship found buds of future promise, though I believe she has not in maturer years given any of her poetry publicity. She is highly cultivated and a fine classical scholar. She is a woman of warm friendships, rather secluded, however, in her tastes; lavishing her sentiments upon a choice few, of great uprightness and enthusiasm of character. It was in part through her exertion and earnest work in the cause that the Sunday-school and Church of the Nativity, at Huntsville, have increased in numbers and usefulness. Her books, entitled "The Little Episcopalian," and "Bessie Melville," a sequel to the former, show the beauties of religion, are pleasingly written, and were and are very popular among Sabbath-school scholars and children of a larger growth. The writer acknowledges to have read those volumes with pleasure and profit not many years ago. These tales were written more especially for the Sabbath-school of the Church of the Nativity.

During the "war," when Huntsville was occupied by Federal troops, Mr. Sam Cruse was one of the old citizens who was sent to "Dixie" on very short notice, because he loved his Southern country too well to declare himself against it. We believe Miss Cruse accompanied him, and they were "refugees" for many months.

Since the close of the war, (1866,) Miss Cruse has published her most ambitious work, "Cameron Hall: A Story of the Civil War."

"A story," the author modestly tells the reader, "which was completed before the termination of the war, the result of which, so different from our anticipations, seemed at first to necessitate a change, or at least a modification of many of the opinions and hopes confidently expressed by some of the characters. Upon reflection, however, it was decided to leave it as it is; a truthful picture, as it is believed to be, not only of the scenes and events which occurred immediately around the author's home, but also of the inner thoughts and feelings, the hopes and expectations, in a word, the *animus* of the Southern heart."

And "Cameron Hall," which we are pleased to say was a success, is, as the author says, "a work belonging rather to truth than to fiction,—a claim which will be acknowledged by thousands of hearts in our 'Southland.'"

The "Round Table," a New York journal that is not at all partial to anything from the South, and not near as consistent and reliable a "Review" as the "Nation," the latter being very Radical in politics, but just in literature, attacks "Cameron Hall" in a very savage manner. It says:

"To any one who is at once a rebel and an Episcopalian, we unhesitatingly recommend 'Cameron Hall.' It is hard to decide where to commence enumerating its undesirable characteristics. Perhaps the most apparent is a preternatural long-windedness." (And the "Round Table" continues at some length.)

"Cameron Hall" would be improved by judicious pruning: there is too much of it — yet it is so pure and fresh. To read it after reading a sensation novel, is like getting up early in the morning: it was very hard to start, and awful dull and sleepy to dress in the shuttered, dark room; but once up and out, how fresh and pure and sweet! There is something so earnest and unsullied in it.

Miss Cruse, like all Southern women, was a loser by the war; but she wasted no time in idly repining, and is teaching the "young idea how to shoot" in her pleasant home at the foot of "Monte Saño." And she is appreciated and loved, quietly going on the even tenor of her way.

THE WAKING OF THE BLIND GIRL BY THE TONES OF THE GRAND ORGAN.

"Have you ever been to Switzerland, Charles?" asked Uncle John.

"No, sir."

"Then it will be worth while for you to go with us. I will tell you, Charles, and would have told you before; but I don't want Agnes to know what she is going for, since surprise will add to her pleasure. In the quiet old town of Fribourg there is a cathedral containing an organ which has but one superior in Europe, and an organist whose marvellous execution is quite as wonderful. It is the only pleasure that I know on the Continent that can be enjoyed by the blind as much as by those who can see; and I am especially anxious that the child, who has been disappointed in being able to recover her sight, should at least enjoy that. Were it not for this, I would go home in the next steamer."

. . . .

They reached Fribourg early in the afternoon, and Uncle John was rejoiced that they had at last arrived at their destination, and he determined to remain there until Agnes should be thoroughly rested.

As they drove rapidly through the streets, Charles saw enough to excite his curiosity, and make him anxious to study in detail the features of this singular-looking place. Its situation is most romantic, the town being divided by immense ravines, spanned by bridges, two of which are suspension bridges, the only link to bind this quaint old town to the present. Everything else seems to belong to the far-distant past, and is black with the smoke, and dust, and mould of age. Upon one of these bridges Charles stood, and looked with wonder into the ravine below, where men looked almost as small as children. The bridge is said to be as high above the street underneath it as the precipice of Niagara, and it certainly seemed to our traveller to be a dizzy height. He was so absorbed that the gathering clouds failed to attract his attention, when all at once he was aroused by the large, heavy drops of rain. The storm came as suddenly and violently as only it can come in mountain countries, and by the time he reached the hotel it was pouring in torrents, with severe thunder and lightning.

He found Agnes asleep upon the sofa, and Uncle John watching her anxiously.

"I am uneasy about her, Charles," he said. "She was so bright and well at Chamouni, I thought that the Swiss air was going to work wonders for her; but to-day she has been more languid than I have seen her since she left home."

"That is nothing. The child is tired, and a few days' rest will make her as strong as ever."

"Everything is adverse to my plans to-night, Charles," said Uncle John, going to the window, and looking out at the pouring rain and the flooded streets. "The rain and her indisposition combine to upset a favorite project of mine."

"What is that, sir?"

"It is an old man's whim, which I know will excite a smile, even if it does not awaken a doubt with regard to my sanity. For days I have been indulging a pleasant sort of dream about taking her asleep to the cathedral, and having her awakened by that wonderful organ-music. It would be such a delightful surprise to the child! You don't know how much I dislike to give up the idea."

"The plan is rather impracticable, sir," answered Charles, smiling, "especially on such a night as this."

"Her condition, Charles, alone renders it impracticable. If I were certain that she was only tired, and not sick, I would not hesitate to try it, for I know that I could protect her from the rain."

"Why not wait until to-morrow night, as we are to stay here some days?"

"Because the organist will not play again, either to-morrow or the next night. He is a professor of music in Berne, and only comes here on certain nights in the week to play for the benefit of travellers, for many lovers of music come to Fribourg especially to hear its wonderful performance. Besides, I want Agnes to hear the music before she knows what I brought her here for."

"How is she to get to the cathedral?"

"In my arms."

. . . .

The rain had temporarily ceased, and Charles said if they would go at once they could perhaps reach the cathedral before it rained again.

It was very dark when they went into the street, and the feeble light of the lantern was almost quenched in the surrounding gloom. Uncle John carried Agnes with gentleness and dexterity, that showed he knew how to take care of her. When they reached the cathedral, they found the doors not yet opened, and they were compelled to stand and wait. As one and another were added to the waiting group, they looked with wonder and curiosity upon the foreigner with his singular burden; but, unconscious that he was the object of interest or remark, he leaned against the heavily carved portal, and in his anxiety to keep Agnes from being awakened, he forgot all else. Presently the crowd gave way to a man who approached with a lantern, and motioning Uncle John aside, he swung open the heavy doors. All was black darkness within, except that in the dim distance Uncle John and Charles saw one feeble ray, which they followed, until they found it was the sexton's lantern, by the light of which he was seating persons in the other end of the church. By degrees, their eyes became accustomed to the darkness, and looking around and above them, where two or three glimmering lights betrayed the position of the organ, they selected a seat at a proper distance.

It was a strange audience that was assembled in the Fribourg Cathedral on that stormy night — men and women, and one blind child; some from a distant continent beyond the sea; from Britannia's Isle; and others who were born and reared in the same old town which had singularly enough produced the sweetest of organs and the most gifted of musicians. There they all sat in the stillness and darkness of midnight. Scarcely a whisper was heard, and a reverent silence pervaded the assembly.

Presently the deep, trembling notes of the organ broke the stillness, and deeper, and louder, and more tremulous they grew, until it was difficult to believe that the rushing wind, of which it was so wonderful an imitation, was not sweeping wildly through the cathedral aisles. Uncle John felt a thrill pass through Agnes's frame as she sprang up and called aloud:

"Uncle John!"

He clasped her hand tightly, and whispered:

"Here I am, Agnes."

She was satisfied. She knew not, cared not where she was, or how she had come there; she knew that Uncle John was with her, and that she was listening to her own dear organ, and she was happy.

The strange performance went on. Thunder, lightning, wind, and storm exhausted themselves in wild unearthly music, and then died away in a strain so sweet and low that it might almost have been mistaken for an angel's whisper. Quicker and quicker grew the throb of the childish heart, and tighter was the grasp with which she clung to Uncle John, but she did not speak. It was a double spell that bound him, for he heard the music through Agnes's ears and felt it through her soul. Sometimes its crushing power made the stone walls tremble, and then gradually the strain wandered farther and farther away, until all that was left was a soft, sweet echo, so pure and so distant that it might have been awakened in the snowy bosom of the far-away Mont Blanc.

At length there was a long pause: artist and instrument seemed alike to have exhausted their wealth of harmony. Uncle John's hand had grasped Agnes's shawl, when there stole through the gloom such a strain of heavenly sweetness that his outstretched arm was arrested, and though he was not unfamiliar with this strange music, still he listened in breathless wonder, as he had done the first time that he ever heard it.

Sweeter than the softest flute it floated through the air, and presently another strain was interwoven with it — a low, subdued, liquid tone of the human voice, that blended with each organ-note the most exquisite harmony. It did not strike the ear; the listener knew not that it reached the heart through the medium of a bodily organ; it seemed to melt and flow at once into the very soul.

Agnes was very still; she clung closely to Uncle John, and scarcely dared to breathe.

At length it was all over; the last note died away, and they waited, but in vain, for another awakening. Presently a soft whisper said:

"Uncle John, come close."

He leaned down, and she asked, softly:

"Uncle John, is it heaven?"

He did not reply, but the tears sprang to his eyes — tears of pleasure at the thought that he should have given her so much happiness.

The audience quietly dispersed. The storm was over; the elements had ceased their strife, as if to listen, and the spirit of sweet peace had been wafted upon the wings of that music until it seemed to rest upon earth, and air, and sky.

LILIAN ROZELL MESSENGER.

LILIAN T. ROZELL was born in Kentucky; her parents were Virginians, and were both fond of Poetry and Music. Hence it is not difficult to conjecture whence the daughter's genius, for at the parent fount her young soul quaffed. Her love of nature, of the beautiful, the grand and weird, was manifested at an age when most children think of toys and sweets. When a little child, she delighted in oratory, in climbing some elevation and imitating speakers she had heard, in either prose or verse; and when not roaming the shades of moss-haunted woody places, she loved to fly a kite and to shoot a bow and arrow. From these early years she was a poet, for of all features of nature's glory, the clouds always furnished her more exquisite enjoyment; and the study of astronomy and natural philosophy dispelled so many fond illusions concerning the mystery of the clouds, that she almost regretted knowledge, and looked back on ignorance *then* as bliss.

All of Miss Rozell's family are of a melancholy, sensitive, musical temperament; and she is not sanguine, and is often and suddenly the victim of most depressing melancholy: in this particular she is said to be completely Byronic, if not his counterpart in genius.

Considering that Miss Rozell has never had the aid of a large library, or the advantages to be derived from literary groups, but worked in silent gloom and isolation without help or practical aid, her verse cannot be expected to be of a very hopeful strain.

The death of her father caused a change in her prospects, inasmuch as it was the reason for the shortening of her school-days; but she expects to study all her lifetime — not always to sing her lays like the mountain streams, but aim to mount higher and higher.

It was after her father's death, when everything seemed dark indeed around the young girl, that she wrote her first verses, and the subject was "Night." She was in her sixteenth year when the first publicity was made of her poems. Colonel M. C. Gallaway was her "Fidus Achates." That true-hearted gentleman was the first to offer the young poetess and orphan a sympathetic hand. Her maiden effusions appeared in the "Memphis Avalanche," under the *nom de plume* of "Zena Clifton."

Miss Rozell was married in her seventeenth year to Mr. Messenger, editor of a newspaper at Tuscumbia, North Alabama — a man of strong, clear understanding, blameless as a man and as a politician. He died in 1865, four years after their marriage, leaving his young widow and one son.

During the war, when the Federal troops plundered Tuscumbia, they took a journal of manuscripts, principally lyrics, belonging to Mrs. Messenger. General Dodge tried to recover it, but did not succeed.

Mrs. Messenger has contributed many beautiful poems to the "Louisville Journal," Memphis papers, and "New York Home Journal." Her most ambitious poems are lengthy, narrative poems, yet unpublished. One of these poems purports to be an epic, and has for its subject "Columbus the Discoverer." The theme of a second is "Charlotte Corday;" and "Penelope, the Wife of Ulysses," is the subject of a third.

Mrs. Messenger is a very sweet and earnest poet; and I verily believe, had she been in a Northern literary clique, with all the advantages to be derived therefrom, she would now be a particular star in the firmament of poesy.

She is yet in her youth; and, with a desire to become a worthy contributor to her country's literature, to be recognized as a devout worshipper in the sacred temple of the Muses, she must succeed. Says she: "If I can aid in soothing any hearts, or help to inspire noble ambitious souls, it will be a sweet reward."

Mrs. Messenger possesses good musical talents, and has fine talent for landscape painting. "Next to being a great poet, I should love to be a glorious painter," says she.

Mrs. Messenger's home is in Tuscumbia, a small town in the northern part of Alabama.

THE OLD WHARF.

AT PINE BLUFF, ARK.

Sad, broken, and scarred, with a careworn look,
It is never a place that a fay might haunt,
This brown old wharf, where the murky waves
Forever in idle monotone chaunt

A story which seems but nothing sometimes,
Save a babble of foolish and quaint old rhymes;
Like the broken fragments of winds that fell
With sweet spring, swept to her flowery dell,
Or yet to their deep-toned caves,
Whose soft blue gloom hath defied the sun,
But the love-warm rays of the moonlight won.

Sad, broken, and scarred, with its careworn look —
And no one thinks it can ever be more
Than the brown old wharf by the idle waves,
With hurrying cloudlets passing o'er;
But I often think if these could speak,
How its mummied secrets would crumbling break,
And tell of the thousand steps that passed,
(In a day near by, in a far-off day,
Which may never return, or which may be the last,)
And whisper of farewells again,
That divided true hearts, and severed true hands,
When over the South and its sweet summer-lands
Hung the fiery Cross of Pain.

On the grim, gory mount of war it gleamed,
And woman, the weeper, was mourning there,
One farewell cleaving brave hearts and brave hands,
And fate seemed bound in the bands of prayer —
But only seemed; and the same waves tell,
By the old wharf brown, whatever befell,
When their barks drew near, and others sailed out,
Far off in the far-away!
Eyes there are, yet gazing through time's dim gray,
That is flecked with the gold of that dawning day.

Four times and three, at the old wharf brown,
With a cloven heart have I said good-bye,
And my secret left, and dreamed it the last,
While the slow sad waves passed on with a sigh.
But once they bore off a form enshrined
In death's dim dusk; and once they chimed
To a marriage-bell, on a blue June-day;
That, too, passed out in the far-away.
And I sometimes fear that a welcome more
Will never come back from the brown old shore,
Though an army with banners of joy stood there,
Where the phantoms of hundred farewells are.

ICONOCLAST.

With the morn of hope, the star of love,
  And strength of faith, man meets his life,
  And hears the gentle music-strife
Of rainbow wings, and clouds that move
With fleecy feet through light above,

And songful winds that deftly leave
  Hints of a hundred sweets, which steal
  From star-kissed flowers while they kneel
In sun-worship and softly breathe
Halos of prayer their brows to wreathe;

Giving the days new melody,
  So that he calls life very good;
  And carves in beauty's solitude
Fair forms of that divinity
Which haunts his soul on land and sea.

These idols of his fondest care,
  Close bound with golden bands of love,
  That all his nobler nature move,
He places on the altars fair
Within his soul, and worships there,

Saying, "They 're safe in beauty's dawn,
  Within this fane, — nor life nor death,
  Nor any mist that sorrow hath
Across this radiance shall be drawn
To blot one star from out my morn:

"Here 'mong my idols I will dwell,
  Nor aught of fear shall e'er intrude;
  Earth shall not touch my solitude,
While sighs of love that softly swell
Just sway my temple's silver bell."

But then a something men call fate —
  Perhaps creation's negative —
  Shadows the temples where they live,
Breaking them with its hand of hate,
And death and woe within create.

And while this dark Iconoclast
  Doth every idol break or mar,
  "Too many images there are
For perfect light," says Faith at last;
"Go leave thine idols with the past."

DENIAL.

The myrtles flushed like a crimson snow
From an evening crimson cloud,
And a dew-lipped rose half breathed aloud,
"I will kiss thee, kiss thee, sweet;
Then in thy veins will a magic flow,
And thou shalt forever, ever know
Of beautiful mysteries here that meet
In the silken folds of my heart,
The same which fill the earth with mist
  As they softly come and go."

But I answered, "Nay, I have mysteries more
Than the human tongue can tell;
They have built me a sorrow-home full well,
And I'll none of thee, lest there may be
One thought less for my loved one gone,
  Gone forever from me."

The sweet stars came to the dusky gate
Of night, and they whispered low,
"Come out unto us! Come, bathe in the glow
  Of a soothing, subtle fire!
With our golden wine we wait, we wait,
That thy soul may drink and evermore hate
The old earth there which hath bred thee woes,
  And thou be lifted higher.
We've tow'rs of gold, and kingdoms of light,
Where all things pleasantest be,
To loosen the fetters that fetter thee:
And never has blown the breath of a blight
O'er our seas of magical flame;
And hallowed mysteries, just the same
As those which link the rose's heart
To sea and sky and our burnished hills,
May heal thee yet, and thy soul, perplext,
  Be freed from human ills."

But I said, "Not so; for I will not drink
Of your wisdom's golden wine,
Lest I lose one thought of a love divine
  That's gone forever from me;
For I scorn all heights and depths that win
One thought from the thoughts I nurse for him
  Now gone forever from me."

A memory pale came unto my soul,
And folded its wings, and said,
"O pilgrim, if now with me thou 'lt wed,
I'll feed thee on fragments sweet
Of beautiful hopes, and the bits of wings
Of thy broken dreams,
And echoes dim of the murmurings
Of a lost love's silent lips:
I'll fan thee to rest with sleep's soft sigh,
And thou shalt glide o'er a mystic deep
At last to a day gone by,
Whose light was the light of his love-lit eye—
And his smile shall encircle thee."

And I said, "Ah, yes, with thee I'll wed;
But not with an angel e'en
Would I stay one hour, if it came between
  My love, and my loved one dead;
And in my grief, like an autumn-leaf,
I could crush and scorn all things that win
One sweet thought which I nurse for him
  Now gone forever from me!"

SARAH E. PECK.

MRS. PECK has, since the close of the war, contributed many interesting sketches to the literary journals of the South; and principally excelled in sketches for children — writing like a good, true mother.

Sarah Elizabeth Peck is a native of Morgan County, Alabama.

> "She is industrious, knits and reads by day, and reads and knits by night. Her husband and children are as often entertained by the music of her sewing-machine as by the reading or recital of some new story."

Mrs. Peck was educated principally at Columbia, Tennessee. She was eminently successful in drawing and painting, as well as in tastefully modelling figures in wax. Several years previous to the war, while in wretched health, confined to her room most of the time, she amused the tedium of her confinement by making extracts from her readings. These she arranged alphabetically under different heads. The title was, "A Dictionary of Similes, Figures, Images, Metaphors, etc." She has been engaged for some time in preparing this work for the press. Says a friend of this lady, alluding to this work:

> "This is truly an eclectic work. It is too large for a bouquet; shall I say that it is a garden into whose rich soil she has transplanted the choicest cuttings of the most celebrated rosaries?"

Mrs. Peck's home is near Trinity Station, on the Memphis and Charleston Railroad.

JULIA L. KEYES

IS the eldest daughter of Prof. N. M. Hentz and Mrs. Caroline Lee Hentz, and was born at Chapel Hill, N. C., in the year 1829. At the time of her birth, her father filled the chair of modern languages in the University of North Carolina, but, while Julia was yet an infant, he resigned his professorship and removed to Cincinnati. He did not, however, remain here long, but finally located in Florence, Ala., and in connection with Mrs. Hentz, opened a school for young ladies. It was called Locust Dell Academy, and soon became one of the most popular institutions in the South. Locust Dell! ah! it is music to the ear of many matrons throughout the South.

It was at Locust Dell that the larger portion of Julia's childhood was spent. She was an artless, happy little girl, beloved by her associates, and admired by all who knew her for the simplicity of her nature. With such associations, and with such a mother, it is not singular that she should, even at an early age, have imbibed a literary taste; and yet whatever distinction she may have attained has been done without the slightest expectation that her name would be mentioned among the female writers of the South. No such ambition has ever moved her heart and pen. From Florence, her parents removed to Tuscaloosa, Ala., in the year 1842, and took charge of the Female Institute at that place. Tuscaloosa was then the capital of the State, besides being the seat of the University. The period during which her parents resided there were days of pleasantness to Julia. They were perhaps the very happiest of her girlhood. Beloved and admired by all, with scarcely a care to disturb her peace, her young imagination painted the future with hues even brighter and more beautiful than those that then adorned her sky, for a vision of the Land of Flowers was ever in her heart. She knew that an abode would be prepared for her in that sunnier clime, for there was one, the object of her own and her parents' choice, who would there make himself a home.

From Tuscaloosa, Professor Hentz, in 1846, removed to Tuskegee, Ala., where, in the same year, Julia was united to Dr. J. W. Keyes, to whom for several years her hand and heart had been plighted.

Soon after, she bade adieu to parents and home, and went with her husband to Florida, at that time the place of his residence. It was here, in the early years of her marriage, amid the mournful music of the pines and the bright flowers of the far South, she wrote some of her sweetest poems. She wrote, as we have already intimated, not for gain or glory, but from that poetic impulse of which all true poetry is born. It was, we believe, in the third or fourth year of her marriage she composed those beautiful lines, "To My Absent Husband." We append a few stanzas:

"Why does my spirit now so oft
In fancy backward rove?
As beautiful in mist appears
That golden year of love.
Why do I love to live again
My first year's wedded life?
Oh! I was then so young and glad—
A childlike, happy wife.

"Swiftly these few short years have fled,
And I am happy yet;
But oh! those bright and sunny days
My heart will not forget.
No care had I to make me look
Beyond those hours of bliss,
No griefs that only mothers have,
No moments such as this.

"And these dear little ones, that bind
My heart so near to earth,
So twine around me that I bless
The hour that gave them birth.
And then, my husband, thou hast been
Kind, gentle, true to me,
And these bright living links have drawn
Me nearer unto thee.

"This happiness is sweet and pure;
But then so much of pain
Is mingled with our love and joy
In this domestic chain,
That I am wont to wander
To those bright sunny hours
When life was joyous, and my path
Was ever strewn with flowers.

"But think not that I would again
My girlhood's hours recall;
I'd rather bear life's ills with thee
Than to be freed from all,
And be without thy loving care,
Thy fond, protecting arm,
Thine ever constant, anxious wish
To shelter me from harm."

A few years passed quietly away, and she who had been the happy, hopeful girl was now a matron, immersed in the cares of a household, and that tender solicitude which never sleeps in a mother's breast was hers; and yet in that land where the birds sing and the flowers bloom always, and where the stars from the deep azure sky seem to look so dimly and sadly over the stillness of earth, and where, too, the sound of the sighing pines and surf-beaten shores is heard, her feelings would oft constrain her to give expression to them in verse. Few, however, of the many poems written at that period of her life have ever been given to the public.

The year of 1856 was an eventful one, and one, too, of great sorrow to Mrs. Keyes; for in that year she lost her gifted mother. She, too, had wandered to this beautiful land; for the remaining members of the family followed soon after Julia's marriage. In one of those rare and fatal spells of cold which cut down the orange and lime trees, Mrs. Hentz was attacked with pneumonia — her last illness. Nor was this Mrs. Keyes's only bereavement. In the latter part of the same year her father, who for several years had been in feeble health, died, and on the same day a beautiful and interesting little boy of five years, to whom her heart most tenderly clung. And yet she bore all these heavy afflictions in the spirit of meekness and humble reliance upon the goodness of Him who "doeth all things well."

In the year 1857, Dr. Keyes removed to Montgomery, Ala., where he had his home until the close of the war. During her residence in this city of the South, so "lovely for its situation," her time was greatly occupied in household affairs; yet some of her best poems were written in the midst of these domestic cares. The writer of this sketch, who was an inmate of her home, has often wondered at her economy of time. After doing a large amount of sewing in the day, she would sometimes give us a poem, composed while plying the needle, and written down at odd moments.

We may here remark that her poetical talent would probably never have been known beyond the home circle, had not her husband drawn from her portfolio her fugitive pieces and given them to the public, he being, perhaps, her greatest admirer. This, as we may suppose, has given her a stimulus, without which her pen would remain idle.

In 1859, she obtained the prize for the best poem under sixty lines of the "Southern Field and Fireside." The poem is called "A Dream of Locust Dell," and is considered the most touchingly beautiful of all her published productions. Certainly, few can read it without being touched by its beauty and pathos.

During the "war," Doctor Keyes was absent from home — an officer in the army — and Mrs. Keyes was left with all the cares of a large family upon her; and she patiently and cheerfully bore up under all her burdens, for her soul was strengthened and nerved by that holy and active patriotism which clothed with such undying glory our "women of the South."

The fate of war was adverse to the cause he advocated, and Dr. Keyes felt that the South, under the rule of its conquerors, was no home for his family, and he went to Brazil, where they now reside.

Above all and beyond all, Mrs. Keyes trustingly, steadily, and hopefully looks to a union of all that are dear to her in that "rest which remaineth to the people of God."

A DREAM OF LOCUST DELL.

What spell of enchantment is that which enthralls me
  When winding the mystical mazes of dreams?
What spirit is that which alluringly calls me,
  And leads me away over mountain and streams?

I see from afar a rich landscape unfolding —
  A beautiful grove — a lake sleeping below —
'T is my own Locust Dell once more I 'm beholding,
  As on wings of the zephyr there floating I go.

I have reached it again, and the misty reflection
  Of childhood o'erpowers me with pleasure and pain;
These musings — they seem but a dim recollection
  Of something I 've lost that I cannot regain.

I wander along in this lethean existence;
  I weep, and my tears fall like dew on the grass;

I see a white mansion, not now in the distance;
 I touch my own gate-latch, and entering I pass.

So lightly and cautiously treading, I enter
 The hall where my voice in its infancy rung;
I pause for a moment when reaching the centre,
 And list for the sound of some welcoming tongue.

The quivering moonbeams and shadows are falling
 Like ghostly illusions along the dark floor:
Why suddenly thus is that vision appalling?
 Why throbs my wild heart as it ne'er throbbed before?

To open the chambers I now am unwilling;
 No farther the mansion I wish to explore;
I feel a strange dampness the atmosphere filling —
 The cold wind is rushing within the hall-door.

Oh! where are the loved ones? Oh! where have they wandered?
 Why stands the dear homestead thus bared to the blast?
'T was thus, while weak, fainting with anguish, I pondered,
 That memory appeared with a scroll of the past.

The spirit of slumber still did not forsake me —
 Again, as on wings of the zephyr, I flew;
The cool, vap'rous breath of the morn did not wake me;
 I threaded the labyrinth of dreaming anew.

I saw by a clear gushing fountain a flower —
 On its bosom a drop of the crystalline spray;
I stooped, but the spell of some magical power
 Prevented my taking the blossom away.

I watched the bright pearl-drop; it slowly distended —
 The blush of the rose seemed the hue of the sky;
I saw a new world in the ether suspended —
 Its groves and its lakes I could faintly espy.

Amid clustering trees a white mansion was gleaming —
 Two wandered together beneath the soft shade;
The pearl-drop has fallen — I wake from my dreaming
 To see the long shadows the sunbeams have made.

Oh! I know 't is the absent I 've seen in my sleeping!
 Unto mansions our Saviour prepared they are gone;
Love's vigilance still o'er their child they are keeping;
 When I pass the dark valley I 'll not be alone.

AUGUSTA J. EVANS.

SOME critics of the sterner sex profess to believe that female writers skim over the surface of thought; jump at conclusions without pausing to note the various steps or arguments by which those conclusions were attained; exercise imagination more than reason; and address themselves to the emotions rather than the intellect. That this is true in some instances cannot be denied, but it is far from being universal. Examples to the contrary cluster around us "thick as leaves at Vallambrosa," among whom the subject of this sketch stands foremost. But even admitting the truth of the above proposition for the sake of argument, are we not creatures of feeling as well as of thought, and are the affections *less* important in the economy of nature than the intellect? Do not our spirits crave the beautiful as well as the useful? What would the world gain by turning its flowers into forest-oaks, or its sweet green hills into impregnable mountains?

I would refer all who imagine that women are incapable of deep metaphysical research and close logical reasoning, to the writings of Miss Evans, who, in grappling with infidelity — the hydra-monster of the present age — has placed herself among the first in point of polemic ability and literary acumen, and justly merits the title of the De Staël of the South. Like the author of "Corinne," she approaches a subject with a fearless, independent spirit, and gives it the whole energies of her mind.

Augusta J. Evans is the eldest child of the late M. R. Evans, formerly a merchant of Mobile; and connected on her mother's side with the Howards, a prominent family of Georgia. She was born near Columbus, Georgia, but while she was yet a child, her parents moved to Texas. The subsequent year they divided between Galveston and Houston, and early in 1847 removed to the then frontier town of San Antonio. The Mexican war was just then at its height, and this was a place of "rendezvous" for the soldiers sent out to reinforce General Taylor. Here, between the lawlessness of the soldiery and the mixed character of the inhabitants, society was completely disorganized. There were no schools worthy of the name, and the education of the little Augusta was conducted entirely by her mother, a lady of great moral and intellectual worth. Like Madame Le Vert and Mrs. Mary E. Bryan, Miss Evans owes everything to her mother, and is withal a bright example of the efficiency of home culture.

Amid the wild, uncultivated scenes around San Antonio, with scarcely a companion but her mother, (for her brothers were some years younger than herself,) she imbibed that strong, free spirit which breathes through all her works. Here she delighted to ramble about the crumbling walls of the Alamo, with her hand clasped in her mother's; while nature's grand and gloomy solitude, and the dark and bloody tragedy which had so recently been enacted in and around those walls, stirred up the latent enthusiasm of her precocious young soul. There she first dreamed of authorship. She longed to describe the wide-spread Alameda, and tell of the treachery and cruelty that marked the fall of the Alamo and the brave men who perished in that fall.

After a residence of two years in San Antonio, Mr. Evans and family removed to Alabama, and settled in Mobile, where they have resided ever since. There Miss Augusta entered school, but her health failing from the confinement, she returned to her first *alma mater*, her much revered and excellent mother.

At the age of seventeen she wrote "Inez: A Tale of the Alamo," designed to show the errors and abuses of Papacy as revealed to her in San Antonio, and to embody the principal features of the Texan war of independence. "Inez" was published anonymously in 1855, by Harpers, New York: while hardly a "success," it was not a failure. Since Miss Evans has become famous, a New York firm has published "Inez" without her consent—at least, the "copyright" had, we believe, passed from her control. For several years after the publication of "Inez," she wrote nothing, except a few book-notices for the papers. And consequently great was the surprise when "Beulah" appeared, creating a sensation throughout the country. It was published in 1859, by Derby & Jackson, New York. This book immortalized Miss Evans's name, a book much abused by certain critics, and much admired and read by everybody else. Its merit is abundantly shown in the fact that, coming from an unknown girl of twenty-three, it ran through editions of twenty-one thousand copies in little over a year.* Its great popularity is to be attributed, in some degree, to the original-

* Since the publication of "Macaria" and "St. Elmo," there has been a great demand for "Beulah," and even "Inez."

ity of its principal characters. Beulah Benton is not exactly like any girl who ever lived; and yet when we remember the bitter sufferings of her early life, her subsequent opportunities for mental culture, her genius, and the seclusion in which she lived, her character is perfectly natural. She is not as gentle, amiable, and *loving* as we could wish her to be; and the possession of some of those "amiable weaknesses" so charming in pretty women would make her much more lovable; but if this were the case, the book would be without those strong peculiarities which are its most attractive features. Had Beulah's mind been less imbittered by early wrongs, she might not have struggled with those doubts which constitute the groundwork of the book; she most probably would never have groped through the labyrinth of infidelity, and learned by experience that the weary soul can find no rest but in the religion of the Bible.

Miss Evans's home is in Summerville, about three miles from the city of Mobile, on one of the city railways. "There is nothing dreamy or eccentric about her. She is a healthy, practical, straightforward, Christian woman." She is a member of the Methodist Church, and we believe is the leader of the choir in the St. Francis Street church of Mobile. Dr. Jerome Cochran, of Mobile, says:

"Her most remarkable characteristics seem to me to be an enthusiasm, at the same time simple and childlike, and large and generous to a degree not very common among women; and a resolute, energetic will, that will not allow her to swerve from any enterprise she has once deliberately undertaken. She has an immense capacity for work. Her genius is the same triumphant faculty that has made so many people famous in this world's history — the genius of labor. Her fluency of speech is sometimes a matter of legitimate astonishment; and yet, I believe, she does not compose very rapidly. She copies her manuscript with a great deal of care, in very clear, regular, legible chirography, with hardly a blot or an interlineation on hundreds of pages. She is a very womanly woman, and is an unwavering opponent of all the new-fangled doctrines that would lead the sex to invade the time-honored prerogatives of masculine humanity. She has her faults and her weaknesses, no doubt; else she would not be human. But she is a genuine woman, and no counterfeit imitation of one — a woman full of generous feeling and high aspirations, and who is most highly esteemed by those who know her best."

During the days of the Confederacy, Miss Evans was devoted to the cause of the South and to the soldiers. An encampment a short distance from her residence was entitled, in her honor, "Camp Beulah."

Here she was a constant visitor. "While the soldiers lived, one bright spirit never forsook them; when they died, her eloquent tongue gave them counsel and comfort." It was a rare treat to pass the evening at Miss Evans's home; and her parlors and piazza never lacked for guests highly entertained by her conversation and that of her sisters.

It became a "military necessity" to destroy the beautiful trees about Summerville, as it was expected that there might be fighting in that direction, and it was thought advisable for Mr. Evans's family to remove to the city. Mobile was crowded with people, and house-room was in demand, and they fixed up the second and third floors of their father's store, fronting the river, and for several months occupied the same in a kind of "camping-out style." In the popular acceptation of the term, Miss Evans is not a *bas bleu;* for, as some one humorously remarked, "like the girls in the history of 'Sergeant Dale,' she sings psalms and darns stockings equally well."

In 1864, West & Johnston, Richmond, published "Macaria; or, Altars of Sacrifice." The motto of which was, "We have all to be laid upon an altar; we have all, as it were, to be subjected to the action of fire." By many persons this is considered Miss Evans's best book. No man or woman ever had such a subject as that, or ever will have again.

Says one critic in a Confederate journal:

"In examining a work of this kind, the first question is, What, taken as a whole, are the characteristics of the plot and the principal characters? In this respect 'Macaria' is unexceptionable. The plot is *vraisemblable,* and well sustained throughout; the characters are deeply interesting and never inconsistent. From the moment that Irene, the heroine, is introduced to us, she is lofty in her aspirations, independent in spirit, and almost eccentrically just in judgment, and so she remains to the last. When she appears in the second chapter, these qualities are justly represented as influenced by the inexperience of youth, and by the *brusquerie* inseparable from motherless training, masculinity of association, and unrestricted indulgence. She answers her Aunt Margaret with almost offensive pertness, but in the same breath evinces a sturdy spirit of self-reliance, and an utter disregard of conventional pretentiousness. With Electra she presently betrays a charming though unexpressed degree of sympathy for the afflicted Mrs. Aubrey; immediately afterward she more boldly and distinctly shows it to Russell; she does not fully express it, however, till she asks her father for the means of carrying it into practical effect; and she fully unmasks its force only when, after receiving her father's terrible rebuff and refusal, she finally obtains the aid she requires from Dr. Arnold. And, as thus portrayed, she continues in character to the latest period of her life to which the author has conveyed us, with such modifications alone as are justly attributable to such increased experience and advantages of association as she enjoyed. These were not very extensive. Their effect is properly represented as correspondingly limited, and she leaves our company still open to improvement in most of the salient points of her character — still needing the chastening effects of an acquaintance with the hard actualities and the softening joys and beauties of real life; still lacking the gentleness begotten of constant association with feminine youth, and amiability, and joyousness.

"Her father, Leonard Huntingdon, is portrayed as well as is Irene herself. The intensity of his uncontrolled passion startles us as we read of his outburst on learning that it is Mrs. Aubrey — the Amy who had refused his proffered hand — to serve whom Irene had asked two hundred dollars of him. But it is far from being without the pale of probability. His conduct is nothing compared with that of Mr. Bronte, the father of Currer and Acton Bell, toward poor Charlotte, as well as the rest of his family. And we may remark here that there are in 'Macaria' not a few features which would suggest to the readers of the Bronte biography, by Mrs. Gaskill, a curious though distant similarity with many of those which this lady has portrayed of that strangely unhappy though distinguished family. There are, for instance, the same traits of cramped and undirected genius on the one hand; on the other, the same mixture of severe yet well-meant desire for justice, and of anxious yet harsh paternal feeling; there is the same prohibition of the marriage of the daughter; there is even the savage bull-dog, 'Keeper,' and Emily's control over him, to contrast with Irene's gentle and affectionate Paragon; there is the unhappy denouement in both cases. And other similarities and contrasts may be found. They go no further, however, than to illustrate the assertion that there is nothing improbable in either the plot or the characters of 'Macaria' which we have noticed. There is not the slightest ground for supposing that they suggested any of Miss Evans's portraitures.

"In Russell and Electra we have two characters equally as well drawn as those of Mr. Huntingdon and his daughter; and it is not a little worthy of observation that each pair of the characters should be so naturally represented as to afford a very striking illustration of the doctrine of physical and mental heritage, as well as of the effects of surrounding circumstances. That the salient qualities of Irene's attributes are derivable from her father is too obvious to need enforcement. And that Russell and Electra, as cousins, inherited like qualities is not less clear, when it is considered how they had struggled to achieve a glorious fame, and throughout maintained their individuality and force of character. This illustration is carried farther, indeed, in the case of Russell and his father. Controlled as they may have been by the former, the same passions that led his father to his unhappy end were undoubtedly present and strong in him.

"Mrs. Aubrey and, Jacob Watson, Hugh and Harvey Young, Uncle Eric and Clifton, Dr. Arnold and Lawyer Campbell, are all as life-like as it is possible to make them. The piety of the blind widow is as pure as human nature seems capable of cultivating — too God-like in charity for bigots, too holy in faith for infidels, too confident in hope for the thoughtless. The sordid villany of Watson is constantly met with, and, thank heaven! as constantly, sooner or later, meets its reward. And what a beautiful contrast is that presented between the recklessness of Hugh and his untimely end, and the goodness and firm resolution of Harvey Young! How much alike in goodness of heart, though differing in sentiment and manner, are Clifton and Eric, the generous lawyer and the warm-hearted old-bachelor physician!

"And nowhere, as we have said, does one of these characters fail. From beginning to end they contribute to the development of the plot, and nowhere do they flag — nowhere do they violate the attributes we ascribe to them as soon as we know them."

Mr. Salem Dutcher, at the time editing a journal in Augusta, Georgia, thus reviews "Macaria":

"In 'Macaria,' the authoress of 'Beulah' has ventured on a dangerous experiment. She has endeavored to write a story of American life — our hard, bare, prosaic, unnovelistic American life — in an ultra classic and super-erudite style, and has failed. It was necessary from the very nature of things that she must have failed — but has at least done as well as any, where none could fully succeed. The narration of life in the New World is not to be written in Græcisms, or told by all the recondite philosophizing of science. We are neither a classic nor a profound people, and any attempt to portray us by a style appropriate to such, must strike us with as painful incongruity as those French melodramas where Hannibal wears red-heeled shoes and Cato harangues in a *roquelaire* and a tie-wig. The characters in 'Macaria,' or the main characters at least, are three in number — for, disdaining even the traditional duality, perhaps because it is traditional, the authoress has given us a trinity of chief personages. There is Russell Aubrey — the very type of the American self-made man. There is Irene Huntingdon, the self-poised, 'faultily faultless' daughter of a stern millionaire; and there is Electra Gray, a large-eyed, fervid devotee of Art. Russell Aubrey is, when the scene opens, a dry-goods clerk, and Irene and Electra, school-girls. Prompted by pride and ambition, the hero devotes his spare hours to study, is received into a lawyer's office, goes to Europe, returns, is admitted to the bar and prospers, dabbles in politics, and 'in the course of the political cataclysm' (*Macaria*) is elected to the legislature. He loves Irene, and Electra loves him. Feelings conflict, strange love-experiences occur. Aubrey has ambition to distract him; Electra also serves two masters — Love and Art; and Irene, who finally discovers her heart is Aubrey's, mingles with her contemplations on that subject the astronomical contemplation of the heavens. The plot thickens. The triple, or rather sextuple thread of the tale becomes inextricably involved. Then the war breaks out, and the Gordian knot is — as is classically proper — cut by the sword. Aubrey becomes a soldier, and proves himself a good one. He serves faithfully, is wounded unto death, and expires in Irene's clasping arms, a noble victim offered up on a pure 'altar of sacrifice.' At his death the proper duality is restored — though that duality is of one sex, for 'Macaria' is strange to the last. Irene and Electra become heart-sisters, one ministering to the soldier and the poor, and the other pouring out her artist soul over a high-art painting, *The Modern Macaria* — a battle-scene, where the Federal flag trails in the dust, and the white-robed Angel of Peace stops the touch-hole of a cannon.

"Such is a rapid enumeration of 'Macaria's' salient points. The design of the work we have already characterized as impossible of accomplishment, and the conduct of the story is marred by a flashy show of erudition. These are grave defects — exceedingly grave, as affecting equally design and execution; and yet, in spite of all, 'Macaria' is a fine book. It is thoroughly readable, it will be productive of good, and has not a few most tender and graceful passages — so tender and so graceful that we could wish to have heard less of *æons* and *chiliasms*, and more of love and duty. Here the authoress excels. The heart — the great, loving, clinging, lovable heart — is peculiarly the province of woman, and few there be who can touch its softest chords like the authoress of 'Beulah.' Striking those chords as she did in 'Beulah,' many will hang upon her words and bless her for the comfort and happiness they bring. Forsaking the substance for the shadow, and striving to reach the head rather than touch the heart, there are few who will not feel that she is giving but husks to the hungry. Classic allusion and metaphysic theory are 'caviare to the general,' and it is for the general the novelist should write. Those who love the classics will not look for their beauties in a modern romance; and the devotees of science are still less likely to forsake the tomes of fact for the *brochures* of fancy.

"But *cuique in sua arte credendum est* — let credit be given every one in his own craft. It may be thought that we speak too harshly of 'Macaria;' and 'Macaria' shall speak for itself.

"Here is the passage which describes the star-gazing of Irene. It is night, and she watches the heavens:

"'In panoramic vision she crossed the dusty desert of centuries, and watched with Chaldean shepherds the pale, sickly light of waning moons on Shinar's plains; welcomed the gnomon (first-born of the great family of astronomic apparatus); toiled over and gloried in the Zaros; stood at the armillary sphere of Ju, in the days of Confucius; studied with Thales, Anaximander, and Pythagoras; entered the sacred precincts of the school of Crotona, hand-in-hand with Damo, the earliest woman who bowed a devotee at the starry shrine, and, with her, was initiated into its esoteric doctrines; puzzled with Meton over his lunar cycle; exulted in Hipparchus's gigantic labor, the first collection of tables, the earliest reliable catalogues; walked through the Alexandrine school of *savans*, misled by Ptolemy; and bent with Uliegh Beigh over the charts of Samarcand. In imagination she accompanied Copernicus and Tycho-Brahe, and wrestled with Kepler in the Titanic struggle that ended in the discovery of the magnificent trinity of astronomic laws framed by the Divine Architect when the first star threw its faint shimmer through the silent waste of space. Kepler's three laws were an unceasing wonder and joy to her, and with a fond, womanly pride she was wont to recur to a lonely observatory in Silesia, where, before Newton rose upon the world, one of her own sex, Maria Cunitz, launched upon the stormy sea of scientific literature the '*Urania Propitia.*' The Congress of Lilienthal possessed far more of interest for her than any which ever sat in august council over the fate of nations, and the names of Herschel, Bessel, Argelander, Struve, Arago, Leverrier, and Maedler were sacred as Persian *telefin.* From the 'Almagest' of Ptolemy, and the 'Cométographie' of Pingré, to the 'Mécanique Celeste,' she had searched and toiled; and now the sublime and almost bewildering speculations of Maedler held her spell-bound.'

"This is the style we dislike — the false, strained, would-be Frenchy, ready-made scientific style, distressing to the reader, and unworthy the writer. It glitters, yet it is not gold. But here is the pure gold itself — pray that the successors of 'Macaria' have more of it. Russell Aubrey is dying. They have brought him to the rear, and as his life is fleeting fast away in Irene's arms, he speaks:

"'" I should like to have seen the end of the struggle — but Thy will, O my God! not mine."

"'He lifted his eyes toward heaven, and for some moments his lips moved inaudibly in prayer. Gradually a tranquil expression settled on his features, and as his eyes closed again he murmured faintly:

"'" Irene — darling — raise me a little."

"'They lifted him and rested his head against her shoulder.

"'" Irene!"

"'" I am here, Russell; my arms are around you."

"'She laid her cheek on his, and listened to catch the words; but none came. The lips parted once, and a soft fluttering breath swept across them. Dr. Arnold put his hand over the heart — no pulsation greeted him; and, turning away, the old man covered his face with his handkerchief.

"'" Russell, speak to me once more."

"'There was no sound — no motion. She knew then that the soldier's spirit had soared to the shores of Everlasting Peace, and that not until she joined him there would the loved tones again make music in her heart. She tightened her arms around the still form and nestled her cheek closer to his, now growing cold. No burst of grief escaped her, to tell of agony and despair:

"But, like a statue solid set,
And moulded in colossal calm,"

she sat mute and resigned, at the foot of the Red Dripping Altar of Patriotism, where lay in hallowed sacrifice her noble, darling dead.'

"Bating the poetry and the many capitals at the close — for human extremity never quotes poetry or employs capitals — this is nobly written. It is true, and therefore touching. It is feeling, and therefore felt. It is worthy of the authoress of 'Beulah,' and as far superior to the stringing together of *microcosm* and *macrocosm, almagest* and *telefin, chiliasm* and *adyta* as the eloquence of Pericles surpassed the mouthings of Cleon."

Miss Evans is of medium size, small-waisted, a neck fair, and a perfect model for a sculptor. Her hands and feet are those of a Southern lady, very small and tidy. She looks as if she would weigh about one hundred and fifteen pounds, and to the eye of an artist resembles Power's Greek Slave more than the Venus de Medici or the Venus of Canova.

After the close of the war, Miss Evans proposed to erect a monument to the Confederate dead; but it was objected to by those in authority.

"St. Elmo" was published in 1867, by Carleton & Co., New York, and soon acquired the reputation of being the "most praised and best-abused novel" ever published in this country by a woman.

Says the "Round Table," in a lengthy notice of this book:

"'St. Elmo' is a curious mixture of power and weakness — of insight and superficiality — of creative vigor, and of tame imitation; and while it evinces of real merit sufficient to stock half a dozen of the domestic fictions from female hands to which we are so well accustomed, it at once falls short of the ideal the writer herself unquestionably had in view, and persuades us that with time, perseverance, and a rigid chastening of style, she can produce something far better. . . . .

"'St. Elmo' is an interesting story, if it is in some respects a stilted and pretentious one. It is a promising story, if not a particularly robust or original one."

From the many reviews and notices that have appeared of "St. Elmo," we have selected one, written by Dr. Jerome Cochran, of Mobile, and printed in the "Home Monthly," Nashville, to make our extracts:

"It is not necessary to read the title-page to know that 'St. Elmo' is the work of the same warm, true heart, and of the same resolute, aspiring mind to which the world is indebted for 'Beulah' and 'Macaria.' We have here, in still higher development, the excellences for which those two books were remarkable; the same love of inanimate nature; the same confident assertion of the dignity and blessedness of labor; the same impatience of all servility, meanness, and duplicity; the same immaculate purity of conception, thought, feeling, expression; the same beautiful sympathy with all the forms and phases of self-abnegation and self-sacrifice; the same reverent appreciation of the metaphysical and ethical doctrines of the Christian religion; the same unswerving devotion to Duty — stern daughter of the voice of God; and, in a word, the same abounding enthusiasm, the same abiding faith in all things beautiful, and true, and good. . . . .

"In spite of all its faults, 'St. Elmo' is a genuine, earnest book; a strong, honest, rich book; a book brimful of fine thought, graceful feeling, and brilliant imagination; a book which no other woman could have written, and of which it may be safely said that in its day and generation it will do some good in the world. In the ordinary sense of the word, it is not a sensational book. It derives no part of its interest from perverse ingenuity of plot, nor from the skilful management of some tantalizing and perplexing mystery, with its customary train of evanescent and shadowy fascinations. And yet it throws over the reader a spell which he cannot shake off, which enchains his attention from the first chapter to the last, and will not allow him to stop until the end is reached.

"It is easy to say that the style is inflated and ambitious; but more than this is necessary to describe it fitly. It is always clear and strong, and rich with every variety of rhetorical embellishment. Sometimes it is imbued with the truest and tenderest pathos, and affluent of music as the song of the nightingale. Sometimes it is all aglow with the fire of eloquence, and gleams and flashes like a sky all stars. And this is its fault. It is too rich, too brilliant, too liberally garnished with those ambitious polysyllables, words sesquipedalian of learned strength and thundering sound, which were such favorites with Dr. Johnson and Dr. Parr. It seems at times to walk on stilts; and very often, in passages which are in other respects beautiful exceedingly, we come across some verbal monstrosity, or some incongruous comparison dragged in by the heels, which provokes us beyond measure. There is too much glitter. We grow weary of the unchanging splendor — of the prodigal opulence of similes, metaphors, and recondite allusions.

"The plot is extremely simple. Edna Earl — this name, by the way, is not musically correct — Edna Earl, the heroine, is a simple country-girl, the daughter of a carpenter. Bereft in early childhood of both father and mother, she grew up, until her twelfth year, near Chattanooga, Tennessee, ignorant of worldly knowledge, and of the guile which so often keeps it company, under the shadow of Mount Lookout, and the care of her grandfather, Aaron Hunt, the blacksmith, when, he also dying, she is left alone in the world, without kith or kin, and takes the cars for Columbus, Georgia, with the intention of working in the factory for a living, and of educating herself as she best can. Providence, which watches over the sparrows when they fall, does not favor the factory scheme, having quite other fortune in store for the stricken wanderer; and the train which carries Edna collides with another, with the usual quota of broken heads and limbs. Edna, badly hurt, but with some life left in her, is taken to Le Bocage, the palatial residence of the Murrays, to be watched and tended until she recovers from her injuries. Her sweet, patient temper, together with her gifts of mind and body, wins so much of Mrs. Murray's good opinion, that it is arranged that she shall remain at Le Bocage until she is qualified to teach; and her education is intrusted to Mr. Hammond, the venerable pastor of the village church, under whose care her hungry intellect devours an immense amount of miscellaneous mental food, including Greek and Latin, and even a little of Hebrew and Chaldee, her unfeminine curiosity perversely leading her to seek acquaintance with Eddas, Sagas, Talmuds, Targums, and Egyptian, Greek, Roman, and Scandinavian mythologies, instead of resting satisfied with the usual feminine varieties. At Le Bocage she makes the acquaintance of St. Elmo Murray, the hero of the book, the master of the house, and the only son of her benefactress. St. Elmo, like Phillips' Napoleon, is grand, gloomy, and peculiar. He is also handsome and rich—his beauty, to borrow a simile from Edgar Poe, dark and splendid, like that ebony to which has been likened the eloquence of Tertullian—his wealth of such fabulous abundance as to enable him to gratify the most extravagant whims of his extravagant imagination. He had grown up with his heart full of generous sympathy for humanity's toiling and suffering millions, and with his head full of philanthropic schemes for the amelioration of humanity's abounding miseries. The darling friend of his youth, Mr. Hammond's son, whom he had overwhelmed with benefactions, betrayed his confidence with treachery most foul. The beautiful woman whom he loved with all the fervor of his passionate nature was cruelly unfaithful to her vows. He tore the false woman from his heart with scorn and loathing; the false friend he killed in a duel. Soured into misanthropy and skepticism, fierce, moody, implacable, taking no delight in man, nor woman either, he heaped bitterest maledictions and anathemas upon the whole hated race of human beings, and devoted himself, soul and body, heart, mind, and estate, to the service of the infernal gods. This man, trampling all the charities and nobilities of human nature under his irreverent feet, Edna regards, first with fear and aversion, then with pitying wonder, and then—inexorable, inevitable fatality—with blind, passionate love; illustrating the truth of Pope's familiar lines:

"'Vice is a monster of such frightful mien,
As to be hated needs but to be seen;
But seen too oft, familiar with its face,
We first endure, then pity, then embrace.'

"And how does St. Elmo feel, think, act toward the poor orphan girl whom accident had thrown under his roof? She was human, and therefore, in his opinion, vile. She was woman, and therefore, according to his philosophy, false. But when he found her always clinging resolutely to the right; when years of temptation and trial left her always faithful and true—always 'pure, womanly'—his stoical misanthropy gave way. The love that had been cast out of his fierce heart, and buried out of sight for so many years, revisited the glimpses of the moon. He struggled against it; but it would not down at his bidding. At last, clasping her in his arms, covering her lips with passionate kisses, he poured into her ear the dark history of his life, into her heart the perilous burden of his passionate love. Here is the crisis of the book. For a weak woman, under the circumstances, there would have been no hope. But Edna is not weak. In spite of the mesmeric fascinations which invested her lover as he stood before her like an archangel fallen—in spite of the love that pleaded for him out of the depths of her woman's heart—she will be none of his; she will not degrade her womanhood by marrying a man whom she knows is not worthy of her.

"They parted; she to pursue a brilliant literary career in New York—to win money, reputation, hosts of friends, everything necessary to gratify her ambition. She is admired and praised, and her hand is sought by men most brilliantly endowed in mind and person and in this world's perishable goods. But her heart still clings, with unreasoning affection, to St. Elmo; and so, poor, proud, honest woman that she is, the flattering offers are all declined. In the mean time, Edna's love of St. Elmo—for well the wicked man knows she cannot help but love him—is the one star, radiant of hope, which shines in the dark sky that overshadows him. He will make himself worthy of Edna; with that prize before him, his lexicon has in it no such word as fail. He mends his ways. The lips that have so often uttered God's name in curses, now tremble in pious supplications. All that he can do to atone for the folly and wickedness of his misspent life he does. And the peace that passeth all understanding descends from the heaven of heavens into his heart once more. He is ordained to the ministry. Mr. Hammond's venerable hands are laid upon him in benediction, and his mother's heart blossoms like the rose. Rehabilitated in the sight of men and of angels, he seeks Edna Earl. She cannot be more just than God—cannot condemn the man whom God has pardoned; and so she takes him the usual way, for better or for worse, to love, honor, and obey. . . . .

"The character of Edna has at least one of the merits which criticism demands—it is true to nature. Miss Evans puts herself, more or less, into every book she writes. Beulah is like her in many things; Irene is like her in many things; but Edna is her finished and authentic portrait of herself. The biographical details of Edna's life are not applicable to Miss Evans, and in personal appearance they are widely different; but in moral and intellectual character they are precisely the same. As Edna feels and thinks, so feels and thinks Miss Evans; and just as Edna talks, Miss Evans talks. The most dazzling conversational bravura of Edna in the book is not one whit more keen, polished, and brilliant than Miss Evans's impromptu conversations

5

in real life; and Edna's self is not more worthy to be loved and honored than the gifted lady whose fancy painted her.

"Miss Evans has done well in 'St. Elmo;' but she can do better. She has the native power of thought, the energy of will, the shaping-power of imagination, and the triumphant faculty of labor, which sweeps all difficulties from its path, all the qualifications that are necessary to produce a truly great book — a book that will deserve to live, and that will live."

Miss Evans was married, on the 1st of December, 1868, to Mr. L. M. Wilson, of Mobile. Her residence is at Summerville, very near the home of her girlhood. She has in the press of Carleton a novel written before her marriage, which will be eagerly welcomed by the many admirers of her former works.

INDEPENDENCE.

"Clara, I have been commissioned to invite you to spend several days with us, until you can select a boarding-house. Dr. Hartwell will be glad to have you come."

"Did he say so?" asked the mourner, shading her face with her hand.

"He told me I must bring you home with me," answered Beulah.

"Oh, how good, how noble he is! Beulah, you are lucky, lucky indeed." She dropped her head on her arms.

"Clara, I believe there is less difference in our positions than you seem to imagine. We are both orphans, and in about a year I too shall be a teacher. Dr. Hartwell is my guardian and protector, but he will be a kind friend to you also."

"Beulah, you are mad, to dream of leaving him, and turning teacher! I am older than you, and have travelled over the very track that you are so eager to set out upon. Oh, take my advice; stay where you are! Would you leave summer sunshine for the icebergs of Arctic night? Silly girl, appreciate your good fortune."

"Can it be possible, Clara, that you are fainting so soon? Where are all your firm resolves? If it is your duty, what matter the difficulties?" She looked down, pityingly, on her companion, as in olden time one of the athletæ might have done upon a drooping comrade.

"Necessity knows no conditions, Beulah. I have no alternative but to labor in that horrible treadmill-round, day after day. You are more fortunate; can have a home of elegance, luxury and —"

"And dependence! Would you be willing to change places with me, and indolently wait for others to maintain you?" interrupted Beulah, looking keenly at the wan, yet lovely face before her.

"Ah, gladly, if I had been selected as you were. Once, I too felt hopeful and joyous; but now life is dreary, almost a burden. Be warned, Beulah; don't suffer your haughty spirit to make you reject the offered home that may be yours."

There was a strong approach to contempt in the expression with which Beulah regarded her as the last words were uttered, and she answered coldly:

"You are less a woman than I thought you, if you would be willing to live on the bounty of others when a little activity would enable you to support yourself."

"Ah, Beulah! it is not only the bread you eat, or the clothes that you wear; it is sympathy and kindness, love and watchfulness. It is this that a woman wants. Oh! was her heart made, think you, to be filled with grammars and geographies and copy-books? Can the feeling that you are independent and doing your duty, satisfy the longing for other idols? Oh! Duty is an icy shadow. It will freeze you. It cannot fill the heart's sanctuary. Woman was intended as a pet plant, to be guarded and cherished; isolated and uncared for, she droops, languishes, and dies." Ah! the dew-sparkle had exhaled, and the morning glory had vanished; the noontide heat of the conflict was creeping on, and she was sinking down, impotent to continue the struggle.

"Clara Sanders, I don't believe one word of all this languishing nonsense. As to my being nothing more nor less than a sickly geranium, I know better. If you have concluded that you belong to that dependent family of plants, I pity you sincerely, and beg that you will not put me in any such category. Duty may be a cold shadow to you, but it is a vast volcanic agency, constantly impelling me to action. What was my will given to me for, if to remain passive and suffer others to minister to its needs. Don't talk to me about woman's clinging, dependent nature. You are opening your lips to repeat that senseless simile of oaks and vines: I don't want to hear it; there are no creeping tendencies about me. You can wind, and lean, and hang on somebody else, if you like; but I feel more like one of those old pine-trees yonder. I can stand up. Very slim, if you will, but straight and high. Stand by myself; battle with wind and rain, and tempest-roar; be swayed and bent, perhaps, in the storm, but stand unaided, nevertheless. I feel humbled when I hear a woman bemoaning the weakness of her sex, instead of showing that she has a soul and mind of her own, inferior to none."

"All that sounds very heroic in the pages of a novel, but the reality is quite another matter. A tame, joyless, hopeless time you will have if you scorn good-fortune, as you threaten, and go into the world to support yourself," answered Clara impatiently.

"I would rather struggle with her for a crust than hang on her garments asking a palace. I don't know what has come over you. You are strangely changed," cried Beulah, pressing her hands on her friend's shoulders.

"The same change will come over you when you endure what I have.

With all your boasted strength, you are but a woman, have a woman's heart, and one day will be unable to hush its hungry cries."

"Then I will crush it; so help me heaven!" answered Beulah.

"No! sorrow will do that time enough; no suicidal effort will be necessary."

AFTER THE FUNERAL.

Back to a desert home, whence the crown of joy had been borne. What a hideous rack stands at the hearth-stone, whereon merciless memory stretches the bereaved ones! In hours such as this, we cry out fiercely: "The sun of our life has gone down in starless, everlasting night; earth has no more glory, no more bloom or fragrance for us; the voices of gleeful children, the carol of summer birds, take the mournful measure of a dirge. We hug this great grief to our hearts; we hold our darling dead continually before us, and refuse to be glad again." We forget that Prometheus has passed from the world. Time bears precious healing on its broad pinions; folds its arms compassionately about us as a pitying father; softly binds up the jagged wounds, drugs memory, and though the poisonous sting is occasionally thrust forth, she soon relapses into stupor. So, in the infinite mercy of our God, close at the heels of Azrael follow the winged hours, laden, like Sisters of Charity, with balm for the people.

RUNNING THE BLOCKADE.

"Well, Miss Grey, I shall place you on Confederate soil to-morrow, God willing."

"Then you are going to Mobile?"

"Yes; I shall try hard to get in there early in the morning. You will know your fate before many hours."

"Do you regard this trial as particularly hazardous?"

"Of course; the blockading squadrons grow more efficient and expert every day, and some danger necessarily attends every trial. Mobile ought to be pretty well guarded by this time."

The wind was favorable, and the schooner ploughed its way swiftly through the autumn night. The captain did not close his eyes; and just about daylight, Electra and Eric, aroused by a sudden running to and fro, rose, and simultaneously made their appearance on deck.

"What is the matter, Wright?"

"Matter! why, look ahead, my dear fellow, and see where we are. Yonder is Sand Island light-house, and a little to the right is Fort Morgan. But the fleet to the left is hardly six miles off, and it will be a tight race if I get in."

There was but a glimmering light rimming the east, where two or three stars burned with indescribable brilliance and beauty, and in the gray haze and wreaths of mist which curled over the white-capped waves, Electra could distinguish nothing. The air was chill, and she said, with a slight shiver:

"I can't see any light-house."

"There is, of course, no light there, these war times; but you see that tall, white tower, don't you? There, look through my glass. That low, dark object yonder is the outline of the fort; you will see it more distinctly after a little. Now, look right where my finger points; that is the flag-staff. Look up overhead — I have hoisted our flag, and pretty soon it will be a target for those dogs. Ha! Mitchell! Hutchinson! they see us! There is some movement among them. They are getting ready to cut us off this side of the Swash channel! We shall see."

He had crowded on all sail, and the little vessel dashed through the light fog as if conscious of her danger, and resolved to sustain herself gallantly. Day broke fully, sea and sky took the rich orange tint which only autumn mornings give, and in this glow a Federal frigate and sloop slipped from their moorings, and bore down threateningly on the graceful, bounding schooner.

"But for the fog which puzzled me about three o'clock, I should have run by unseen, and they never would have known it till I was safe in Navy Cove. We will beat them, though, as it is, by about twenty minutes. An hour ago I was afraid I should have to beach her. Are you getting frightened, Miss Grey?"

"Oh, no! I would not have missed this for any consideration. How rapidly the Federal vessels move! They are gaining on us."

Her curling hair, damp with mist, clustered around her forehead; she had wrapped a scarlet crape shawl about her shoulders, and stood, with her red lips apart and trembling, watching the exciting race.

"Look at the frigate!"

There was a flash at her bow, a curl of white smoke rolled up, then a heavy roar, and a thirty-two pounder round shot fell about a hundred yards to the right of the vessel.

A yell of defiance rent the air from the crew of the "Dixie" — hats were waved — and, snatching off her shawl, Electra shook its bright folds to the stiffening breeze, while her hot cheeks matched them in depth of color.

Another and another shot was fired in quick succession, and so accurate had they become, that the last whizzed through the rigging, cutting one of the small ropes.

"Humph! they are getting saucy," said the captain, looking up coolly, when the yells of his crew ceased for a moment—and with a humorous twinkle in his fine eyes, he added:

"Better go below, Miss Grey; they might clip one of your curls next time. The Vandals see you, I dare say, and your red flag stings their Yankee pride a little."

"Do you suppose they can distinguish me?"

"Certainly. Through my glass I can see the gunners at work; and, of course, they see you. Should not be surprised if they aimed specially at you. That is the style of New England chivalry."

Whiz — whiz; — both sloop and frigate were firing now in good earnest, and one shell exploded a few yards from the side of the little vessel, tossing the foam and water over the group on deck.

"They think you have hardly washed your face yet, Miss Grey; and are courteously anxious to perform the operation for you. But the game is up. Look yonder. Hurrah for Dixie and Fort Morgan!"

From the dim flag-staff battery bellowed a gun.

The boom of a columbiad from the fort shook the air like thunder, and gave to the blockaders the unmistakable assurance, "Thus far, and no farther."

The schooner strained on its way; a few shot fell behind, and soon, under the frowning bastions of the fort, whence the Confederate banner floated so proudly on the balmy Gulf breeze, spreading its free folds like an ægis, the gallant little vessel passed up the channel, and came to anchor in Mobile Bay, amid the shouts of crew and garrison, and welcomed by a salute of five guns.

THE MODERN MACARIA.

The canvas, which she leaned forward to inspect more closely, contained an allegorical design representing, in the foreground, two female figures: one stern, yet noble-featured, crowned with stars, triumph and exultation flashing in the luminous eyes — Independence, crimson-mantled, grasping the Confederate banner of the Cross, whose victorious folds streamed above a captured battery, where a Federal flag trailed in the dust. At her side stood white-robed, angelic Peace, with one hand over the touch-hole of the cannon against which she leaned, and the other extended in benediction. Vividly the faces contrasted — one all athrob with national pride, beaming with brilliant destiny; the other wonderfully serene and holy. In the distance, gleaming in the evening light which streamed from the west, tents dotted a hillside; and, intermediate between Peace and the glittering tents, stretched a torn, stained battle-field, over which the roar and rush of conflict had just swept, leaving mangled heaps of dead in attestation of its fury. Among the trampled, bloody sheaves of wheat, an aged, infirm Niobe mother bent in tearless anguish, pressing her hand upon the pulseless heart of a handsome boy of sixteen summers, whose yellow locks were dabbled from his death-wound. A few steps farther, a lovely, young wife, kneeling beside the stalwart, rigid form of her husband, whose icy fingers still clutched his broken sword, lifted her woful, ashen face to heaven in mute despair; while the fair-browed infant on the ground beside her, dipped its little, snowy, dimpled feet in a pool of its father's blood, and, with tears of terror still glistening on its cheeks, laughed at the scarlet coloring. Just beyond these mourners, a girl of surpassing beauty, whose black hair floated like a sable banner on the breeze, clasped her rounded arms about her dead patriot lover, and kept her sad vigil in voiceless agony — with all of Sparta's stern stoicism in her blanched, stony countenance. And, last of the stricken groups, a faithful dog, crouching close to the corpse of an old silver-haired man, threw back his head and howled in desolation. Neither blue shadows, nor wreathing, rosy mists, nor golden haze of sunset glory softened the sacrificial scene, which showed its grim features strangely solemn in the weird, fading, crepuscular light.

I. M. PORTER HENRY.

MRS. HENRY is perhaps best known as a contributor to General Hill's magazine, "The Land we Love," and other Southern papers and magazines, under her maiden name of Ina M. Porter, also publishing under the *nom de plume* of "Ethel Hope." She is a native of Tuscaloosa, Ala., a daughter of Judge B. F. Porter, a South Carolinian by birth, and the writer of occasional verses of considerable poetic merit. Mrs. Henry from a very early age indulged in literature, always happy when she was able to sit near her father and write.

For several years, her "youthful" muse sang Indian legends, vague fancies, the beauties of her mountain home, and revelled in the mists which shrouded the rolling hills, or grew ecstatic on the bosom of the lovely Tennessee River; yet she wandered, sighing for some deeper song to sing. She felt that power within her which must be perfected through deeper emotions than those called forth by the calm beauty of nature, some key-note more sublime than caves, chasms, and mighty waters. It came — when the war-cry sounded through our land, she knew that the "South" was her theme.

Through the sufferings of her countrymen and women, she learned that poets could find no higher strain than love of right and hate of wrong — no holier subject than truth.

Judge Porter made his home in Greenville; now a thriving little town, on the line of the Mobile and Montgomery Railroad.

Miss Porter wrote a play during the second year of the war, entitled "None but the Brave Deserve the Fair," which was performed at the Mobile Theatre, and subsequently at Greenville, for the benefit of the "Confederate Soldiers." In Simms's "War Poetry of the South," "Lament for Mumford" and several other poems commemorative of the struggle of the South appear from this drama. Miss Porter's prose articles during the war were mostly on topics of local interest, or upon some practical question applicable to the wants and means of aiding our soldiers.

The "Roadside Stories," appearing in "The Land we Love," were truly excellent pictures of "life in Dixie." Few, to read them, would think they were written under adverse circumstances — written during that period of desolation which followed the surrender of the "Confederate cause."

Judge Porter's family shared the common heritage of Southrons, and were left with little to wear and little to eat; and to add to these "evils," sickness surrounded them.

A friend tells me that Miss Ina Porter and her mother were the only available workers on the place — all the others sick, and the servants all left, except one, a girl, who had the small-pox, and was of no assistance. Mrs. Porter was physician and nurse, and Miss Ina cook and maid of all work. Under these circumstances, not favorable to literary labors, the "Roadside Stories" were written. We mention these facts to show the heroic spirit that animated one of *our* bright stars among "Southland Writers," and can truly say she is but a representative of the many in her "will to do."

In October, 1867, Miss Porter was married to Mr. George L. Henry, and continues to reside near Greenville, Butler County, Ala. She continues to "wield her pen" when other duties and health permit — for, we regret to say, her health has not been good, and the death of her father was a severe blow. Mr. and Mrs. Henry have begun the battle of life with "Confederate weapons," warm hearts and strong wills; and success and happiness must crown their hearth-stone.

RIMMER.

I stand before thee, Rimmer,
  And as thy chosen wife
Am exultant in the glory —
  Crowning glory of my life.

Wind no rosy veil about me,
  My actual self to hide;
As a real — not ideal —
  Look upon your future bride.

You smile at my odd fancies;
  Smile — but know me as I am,
Or our voices ne'er can mingle
  In the holy marriage-psalm.

You flatter me, gay Rimmer;
  You call my eyes sky-bright!
Have you seen the blue skies darken
  At the falling of the night?

You vow my cheeks are petals
  From living roses rent;
Ah, the roses wither, Rimmer,
  When the summer shine is spent!

There! my unbound hair you 're calling
  Golden eddies of the morn!
Do you know the dawn-waves whiten
  When the yellow sun is gone?

If you love me, if you trust me,
  Erring, human, as you see,
Give your honor to my keeping,
  As I give my own to thee.

My life I cast before thee;
  Its pages lie unclaspt;
Read from alpha to omega,
  Judge the future by the past.

Canst thou mete as I have measured
  Truth as boundless as the sea?
Speak! my heart will not be broken —
  Ha! 't is glorious to be free!

Oh, forgive me, noble Rimmer!
  No love nor faith I lack;
But the wedding robes are holy
  As the coffin's solemn black!

Our souls are God's, not ours —
  My heart is all I bring;
Lift me higher, royal lover;
  I crown thee — O my king!

CCEAN SIGHS.

A sigh-laden, whispering shell of the sea
Whispers a tale of the deep to me;

It echoes the moans,
The sobs and the groans,
That were heard one night on the roaring wave,
When a ship went down no hand could save.

I shuddering list to the sighs and moans,
The piteous shrieks and maddening groans,
And wish they could sleep
In the moaning deep,
And nought but murmurs sweet and low
Could rise as the waves reel to and fro.

Shell of the sea, listen to me,
Cease that wild, shuddering song of the sea!
Some spirit bright
Went down that night,
Chanting a pæan of joy and peace;
Thy sighing and groaning, thy shuddering cease!

Ah, faintly it floateth. Hush! Mark the soft tone
Dreamily, dreamily sighing alone!
A lullaby motion
Stirs the green ocean,
And heaves from its bosom a boat of bright shells,
Her topmast aglow with silver-tongued bells.

Dark spirits, be still! Whence cometh that light?
Are moonbeams or starbeams so dazzling to sight?
A voice in the air
Sighs — 'tis the bright hair
Of an earth-cradled maiden lost in the sea,
Lulling the storm with her sweet lullaby.

Her wistful blue eyes are watching a sail
That soareth on proudly, through calm or fierce gale;
I hear the shell say,
As the moans die away,
That her prayers flutter upward on silvery beams,
Like white-breasted doves cleave the sky of our dreams.

Two white arms encircle her lover alway,
Her floating hair spangled with glittering spray;
Awaking or sleeping,
The love-watch she 's keeping;
And bright is the path o'er the ocean's soft breast,
With her hand on the helm and the sailor at rest.

Come, dreamer, and list, ere the vision has flown;
The ocean-bell's chime is dying — is gone!
But I wonder no more,
Bright shell of the shore,
That a voice wild and thrilling, yet sweet as can be,
Floats weird-like and solemn across the deep sea!

MISERERE.

Holy Mary!
Thou hast known the woe of life,
Thou art past the bitter strife:
Look upon us from thy rest,
Bear our sorrow on thy breast,
Holy Mary!
By thy gentle name I bear,
By this womanhood I wear
Broken-hearted! let me lean
On thy bosom, Heaven-Queen!
Miserere!

Holy Mary!
Does the blood, heroic shed,
Cry in vain? Alas, our dead!
May I see the patriot's name
High in heaven, through sword and flame,
Holy Mary!
May the purple path they trod
Lead my weary feet to God;
Slumberers on historic plain,
Teach my hand to wear its chain.
Miserere!

Holy Mary!
Crown the victors; they have won
Freedom through thy martyred Son:
Lo! the silvered Cross is high,
Borne aloft to Southern sky!
Holy Mary!
Gloria! for those who fell
On their spotless shields; 'tis well!
Sigh thou with us — stricken band,
Miserere, motherland!
Miserere!

Holy Mary!
Giant sorrows drag their length,
Noiseless in their deadly strength;
I have wept — ah, let me weep!
Rock my tearless heart to sleep,
Holy Mary!
Guide me to thy sweet relief;
By our sisterhood of grief,
Bear the Father every cry,
Woman-angel! sigh for sigh!
Miserere!

OUR DEAD.

Written for the Anniversary of the Floral Decoration, April 26, 1868.

The evening shadows lift themselves and turn
Toward the west, whene'er the pure-faced moon
Comes out with silver wand to watch the world.
Thus, when an angel-sentry walks the earth,
Or stands in breathless beauty o'er Our Dead,
The greatness of my sacred theme revealed,
I shrink away in silent awe. My hands
Are filled to finger-tips with silent love;
My head bows down with holy reverence,
And I can only cry, Alas, Our Slain!
Traitors — assassins — they are called, because
They dared to stand as bulwarks round our homes.
They stood — they fought — they fell — as did the Greeks
Around Etolia's walls; and we who live
Are only left to toil in blackened woe,
To shameless grief and utter misery!
To mark the bloody path across our land
O'er heaps of bones, and barren, ashen plains;
To hear the cry of Rachel while she sits
Like some lone bird beside her ruined nest,
Who calls, and calls her missing ones in vain!
They fell. Thank God, the Dead, at least, are free!

There are shafts of spotless crystalline that rear
Themselves, at God's behest, beyond the stars;
The noblest shaft is reared to Martyrdom.
It bears upon its beauteous shining scroll

Coeval dates with birth of worlds — and lo!
The loftiest name was called from Bethlehem.
Ah! those whose garments trail in their own blood
Have placed their names anear the aureole
That clothes His name — the God-man, Jesus Christ.
Oh! countless thousands sheathed their dripping swords,
And laid themselves, in tattered gray, to wait
And rise in ranks, at muster-roll of God!
Can *we* forget? Say, can a father's curse
Rest on the son who died for Honor's cause?
And can a mother slay her first-born child?
Can comrades cease to think of those who bore
The brunt of conflict, marching side by side —
Forget how youth forgot his beardless face,
Made battle beauteous with his val'rous arm,
And reared his living walls across the plain,
Or closed the dear, dead eyes, when all was o'er?
Can sisters coldly touch the honored blade
That lies across a fallen brother's bier?
Ah! can the grave with all its cold, cold bands
Confine the soul? or life with heartless sounds
Drown the sad wail of love in widowed hearts?
Man has the electric current in his grasp,
But can he turn one flash upon its way?
The Atlantic holds a cord within her breast
That thrills two hemispheres, and bears a word
In wondrous motion through the pathless deep;
But who, save God, can bid one wave, "*Be still!*"
Ay, point thy swords to yonder cloud, and guard
The lurid light within its awful folds,
And bind one wavelet of the restless sea,
Ere Southern hearts forget our Southern dead!

No drums are heard, save those whose muffled beat
Are heard in homes where black-robed women sit
By vacant chairs, to lean the pallid cheek
Against the folded suit of faded gray,
And kiss its stains; or turn at every sound
To watch for those who never, never come!
Or in the breasts of little ones, who hear,
With wondering eye and flushing cheek, of him
Who went away, and never came again!
Our flag is folded o'er our darling dead;
And, like Merope's gentle face, that turns

Upon her sister Pleiades with tears,
Its cross is blurred with mists of human woe!
Its folds are bloody as the bannered west,
When slowly through the castled clouds there float
The kingly colors of the setting sun:
But search its field — thou canst not find one blot
Of shame, to make us curse the day they died!
We hand them thus, in stainless winding-sheet,
Back to the God who gave, and called them home!

As long as April hangs his light green shield
Upon the dark-clad forests of the South,
And in his dewy mantle comes to kiss
The blush upon the cheek of queenly May,
Or plume with feathery ash her spotless brow,
Let vet'rans (battle-scarred) repeat the tale;
And while we women list, (with kindling cheek,)
We'll twine the new-born flowers of spring, and gem
Their fragile cups with homage true of tears.
We'll bid the laughing birds, that learned to sing
In happier days, to hush their songs, and fly
Across the Gulf to where, in Torrid heat,
The Arawanda hides among the palms,
With lifted head and drooping wing, to toll
The weird, sad music of her mystic bell.
Ay, while we wander through the land of graves,
To lay our gifts of love on every mound,
Fair bell-bird, Arawanda, come and rest
In snowy flocks upon our sighing pines;
Here in the sweet magnolia dip thy spotless beak,
And toll a chorus, while we maidens chant
A nation's requiem for her sleeping sons!

DIRGE.

(Air — *"I would not live alway."*)

Bend low, weeping willows, our harps must be strung,
Our princes have fallen, their dirge must be sung!
A pæan of glory for heights they have gained,
A low wail of sadness for captives unchained!

Let it rise from the valleys in heart-thrilling song,
Till hundred-voiced mountains its echoes prolong;

On through the Gulf waters, by Southern breeze whirled,
The requiem sounds o'er the sea to the world!

Nay, hush thy loud pealing, thou merry-lipped bell,
The spires standing silent our story can tell;
Peal softly and sweetly, and blend in the sky
The call to a bridal with notes of a sigh!

Blow gently, wind-trumpets, among the fresh flowers,
That rise from the bosoms of loved ones of ours;
They have drawn their rich hues and their sweet-scented breath
From the hearts of dead heroes, from gardens of Death!

Bring myrtle, magnolia, bay, orange, and lime,
With boughs of green palm in its stateliest prime;
Bring straight, slender cedars, as types of their youth,
And white-hearted lilies, to witness their truth.

Red roses, that bear in the depths of your breast
The stain of lost battles, that bloom where They rest,
Above the long file of the soldiers asleep,
Ye lift happy faces, while we mourners weep!

Ye speak, through the tints of each beautiful cheek,
A wisdom more lofty than mortals can speak;
Of a Hand that has touched you, and lo, from the tomb
Ye are risen, from ashes to loveliest bloom!

Faith tells us they live on the shores of the blest,
The Great Shepherd watches His flock while they rest;
But orphans an-hungered cry out for the slain
And pale women shudder with heart-breaking pain.

O roses, with faces like widows, dead-white,
Mute watchers by grave-stones, say, what of the night?
Ah, sweets, ye are voiceless as they, and your bloom
Is spotless as angels'; watch on by the tomb.

But, by the long watch o'er our graves ye have kept,
By every heart broken, by every tear wept,
I charge ye, fair flowers, these tokens to bear
To the dead, love eternal — to the living, a prayer!

Winds, forests, and flowers the same message tell
Of rest for the weary who fought the fight well —
Of homes for the homeless — of tears wiped away —
Of crowned, faithful servants — of night lost in day!

The same which was spoken where Lazarus slept,
When the head of our Saviour bowed down while he wept:
To sorrowing women He speaks now as then,
(And weeps with us, Southrons,) Our Dead rise again!

Eternal Justice speed the day when Truth
Stamps Falsehood in the dust, and cries, "Oh, shame!"
Till then we mourn for those who fell asleep.
Recording angel! thine's the hand to pen
The glorious history of each nameless grave!
Thine to record our unrecorded dead!
Oh, they have died as mighty men of old;
As crownèd princes lead them up to God!

As Danish sailors stay the graceful oar
To watch Vineta's spires, and hear her bells
Chiming beneath the waves of Rügen's lake,
They tell in whispers of a time to come,
When solid earth shall heave each placid wave,
Till from her hold they shrink away appalled —
Then men shall marvel when they see arise
A peopled city from her deep-sea grave,
Awakened from her wondrous sleep of years —
Thus I await, with patient trust, God's time.

This wreath of loving words and sparkling tears
I gather from the garden of my heart,
And offer, kneeling, to my country's sons.
I pray each faithful heart to come with me
To every sacred spot where Southrons lie:
With folded arms, they dream sweet dreams of home,
Regardless of the foe — GOD IS ON GUARD!

Sleep on, brave men, nor heed the rush of worlds;
Nor taunt, nor tears can move your lips to speak,
Nor hearts to beat; but if your spirits turn
With tenderness to those who mourn your loss,
Accept this tribute from a woman's hand,
Of truth to God, her native land, and you!

6

CATHERINE W. TOWLES.

AMONG the writers of the "Southland" who have labored in the "heat of the day," never ceasing in the good work of providing interesting, instructive, and moral literature for her countrywomen, may be named Miss C. W. Barber; for by her familiar maiden name is she best known to the readers of Southern periodical literature.

Miss Barber was born in Charlemont, a romantic little town in Northern Massachusetts, on the 25th day of October, 1823. She was the daughter of a farmer, and her earliest recollections are of green pastures, where fed herds and flocks; rich meadows, where waved the tall grass ready for the mower's scythe, and fields of golden grain ripening in the sunshine. She early began her literary career, sending verses to the country newspapers while yet a mere child. These verses were favorably received by the reading public, and were frequently copied into other journals. Hon. Whiting Griswold, now of Greenfield, Mass., was her principal teacher; he was at the time a student in Amherst College. He brought her books to read from the college library, and encouraged her to study and literary effort.

In 1846, soon after the death of her father, she came South to reside in the family of her brother. Her literary reputation followed her, and contributions were solicited of her by Southern journals.

In 1849, she received two prizes, one for the best tale, and one for the best poem, written for the "Madison Family Visitor," a literary and family journal started in Morgan County, Geo., and was solicited to take charge of its literary department; and did so, and continued editress of this paper for three years. It was during this period that she wrote a series of tales for the "Masonic Signet and Journal," which were so well received by the fraternity that they were collected into a volume, and published in New York under the title of "Tales for the Freemason's Fireside." Shortly afterward she wrote a series of "Odd-Fellow Tales," which were published in a volume, entitled "The Three Golden Links."

In 1861, Miss Barber became connected with the "Southern Literary Companion," a paper published by I. N. Davis, a blind man, in the town of Newnan, Georgia. To this journal she contributed some elegantly written novelettes, and articles on subjects "humorous, grave, and severe." Her connection with this paper continued until the close of the war. In the spring of 1866, she became editress and proprietress of a literary paper published in Newnan, called "Miss Barber's Weekly," which was continued until August 29th, 1867, when Miss C. W. Barber became the wife of Hon. John C. Towles, of Lafayette, Ala. She now resides on her husband's plantation near that place.

Although of Northern birth, Mrs. Towles is Southern by acclimation and long residence, and she considers Alabama her home; for to her it is now "a land of rest."

MRS. JULIA SHELTON.

("*Laura Lorrimer.*")

"GENIUS — native talent."

LAURA LORRIMER possesses "genius of a rare order," and several years ago was noted as one of the most promising of the young writers of the South. In December, 1855, she married Mr. J. A. Shelton, of Bellefonte, Alabama, at which place she resides at the present time, having two children, a son and daughter.

Julia Finley was born on the Cumberland River, Tennessee, and at an early age commenced "poetizing." She was one of George D. Prentice's galaxy of poets — of which Amelia Welby was probably the best known. The South, and indeed the whole country, owe much to this gifted and noble Kentuckian, for his helping hand and encouraging words to young aspirants for literary fame.

"Laura Lorrimer" was a contributor to the various journals and magazines, North and South — Godey's "Lady's Book," "Louisville Journal," and "Field and Fireside," among others.

THE FEVER-SLEEP.

A PRIZE POEM.

There was a Hecla raging in my soul,
Of wild emotions which might not be stilled.
Through its dim arcades flashed the murky light,
In fitful corruscations, and each niche
Grew all irradiate. On the year's broad breast
Four months had wreathed their coronals and died,
For it was May, but in my fevered soul
The sweet May flowers had withered, and upon
Its myrtle garland slept a mildew blight.

One year ago that very May, I bent,
In love and faith, beneath the deep-blue heaven,

And as the stars went floating up its arch,
My soul was floating on the passionate breath
Of new, strange music to a fairy land.
Life then was golden-tinted: I had not
One unbelieving thought; I could not link
The purple glory of my dreams in one;
They wavered, flashed, and paled like sunset gleams,
Through the proud arches and pilastered domes
Of Southern climes. Oh! I had never known
Aught half so blissful, and I lived an age
In every breath which chronicled that hour
Of my existence. Immortality
Seemed charactered upon it, and I heard
The low, sweet chiming of a thousand streams,
Which swept their crystal through the amaranth bowers
Of Aiden, and the mystic language grew
Articulate. I seemed to hear them say
That love like this could never die; that through
The march of centuries to Eternity,
Its hymn of adoration still would rise
And tremble on the air. I have had dreams
Which crowned my spirit as I walked amid
The shadowy vale of visions, with a band
Of all unearthly radiance, but, oh! none
So bright as those which clustered round me on
That sweet May midnight, when my eyelids drooped,
Dank with the dews of slumber on my cheek,
And the soft echo of love's thrilling words
Still lingering around me. How my soul
Grew gently luminous with gleaming wings,
As the night-sky with stars!

May came again;

But my hot brow seemed banded with a chain
Of living fire. My senses all were bound
In the dread fetters of a fever-sleep.
I struggled with my thraldom, and my thoughts
Wandered within a narrow, darkened cell—
Pale, wingless phantoms, striving to unlock
The gates of destiny. Then strange, wild birds,
With eyes of fire and wings of lurid flame,
Perched close beside me, and, from time to time,
Sank deep their vulture beaks into my heart.
I knew they were my incarnated passions, which
The fever-demon mockingly had called

Into a fierce existence. Closer still
They flocked around me, and I was upborne
Upon their rushing pinions through the stars,
On, on to "outer darkness." There are orbs,
Which ages since flashed down a golden ray,
Whose earthward journey yet is scarce begun,
And we had passed the farthest; now we stood
At the closed gates of dread, eternal Night.
"*Room*," shrieked, half humanly, each vulture throat,
"*Room for our burden.*" Fetterless, the winds
Roamed the abyss, and answered, "*There is none!*"

Time had not winged another moment ere
Light flashed upon my eyelids. On the earth
How one short moment oft has crowned my soul
With years of rapture, and I have grown old,
Even in the folding of one warm caress!
Another moment, and a star-throned isle
Gleamed in the blue beneath us. "We must rest,"
Moaned my fierce carriers; "*room is for us here,*
In this fair planet; *here* our weary wings
Shall leave their burden." Wooingly the waves,
From their blue, throbbing bosoms, whispered "*Come.*"
It was a lovely world: its temples lay
Like heavy snow-rifts, in the gentle light
Of seven bright moons. It was a paradise,
Which I had never imaged, even amid
My wildest visions. Opiate incense rose
From nameless flower-buds, like the heavy mists
From the damp earth, and every nerve grew faint
With dreamy languor. I was all alone,
That star-world's sovereign. It had never yet
Felt the soft stirring of an angel-plume
In its calm air. The chiming of the wave,
The wind's low footstep, and the wild bird's song,
Were all its music. But my heart-strings still
Were linked to earth, and to earth's passion-dreams.

One cloud may veil the "day-god's" fiery steeds,
Even in the zenith of their blue-arched path;
And now earth-shadows severed from my soul
The soft, gold arms of the caressing light.
Wiser than I have tangled up their prayers
In the dark tresses of a haughty head,

And sung a hymn to clay instead of God;
And I — am but a mortal; so I had
An *idol* with me, e'en among the stars,
A name to which my soul forever sang
As to a deity, and whispered words
Of half-unearthly worship.
Hours or months,
It might have been, grew gray and died, but yet
There came no day. My spirit could not count
Time's heavy throbbings, but the very air
Seemed faint and tremulous with an unseen
And mighty presence. Four bright pinions came
Floating above me, and then wavered down,
Like the gold leaves of autumn, by my side.
Beautiful angels were they, Love and Faith,
But Love stood nearest, bending o'er my heart,
As if to count its throbbings. God had sent
Visible angels, thus to symbol forth
The thoughts invisible which filled my soul.
Oh, in the heavens, Israfel's sweet lute
Ne'er to his fingers thrilled as did my heart
To the soft music of their murmured words —
That angel lullaby! My lids drooped down,
Charmed with its opiate. To the land of dreams,
I bore the vague, sweet echoes of the song:

Slumbers be thine,
Gentle and deep;
Queen of the star-isle,
Rest in our keep!

Chased by our pinions,
Trouble shall fly,
Ever around thee
Rise Love's lullaby.

Faith ever near thee
Guardian shall stand,
Love round thy forehead
Twine her bright band.

The music died in wailings. O'er the sky
Swept a dark tempest, and my star-isle shook
To its foundations; fiery lavas rolled
In desolating fury down the slopes

So grand with beauty, and the temples fell
In shapeless masses on the trembling earth.
My angel guards had fled; beside me stood
A demon presence, giant-like and stern.
Fearfully beautiful twined the iris crown
In the black billowy locks which swept away
From the lost angelhood of his broad brow—
Fit rival for the passions glowing fierce
And tiger-like in the wild orbs beneath.
Silent in demon majesty he stood,
But ever and anon the heavy wings
Shook almost to unfolding, and the mists
Dropped from them, leadenly, upon my brow.
All, all was silence, save the wild heart-throbs
Which strove to burst their prison; for I shrank
In voiceless terror from the bitter smile
Which curved the haughty lips, and from the stern
And blasting gaze of those dark, fiery eyes.

I rose and strove to fly; but demon wings
Flapped heavily around me, and a voice
Which filled the universe hissed in my ear
The awful words: "Down! down! to meet thy doom.
Thou hast lost heaven for earth, and staked thy soul
Against a mortal's love. For one whose brow
Is crowned with amaranth, thou hast flung down
The gauntlet to Omnipotence. Depart!"
I was a wanderer. A mark was set,
Like Cain's, upon my forehead; and alone,
Amidst the mighty forests of the West,
I writhed my way. Like sleeping Titans lay
The mountain ranges in the dim gray light
Which heralded the dawn. Before me rolled
The ocean, with its hungry waves astir,
Leaping in eager bounds upon the strand,
Like wild beasts on their prey.
"Alas," I cried,
"Alas for thee! my own sweet spirit-love!
Thou art not now beside me; but thy deep
And passionate words are floating round my heart
Like angels in the darkness, and again
I drink a haunting music from their swell;
Their memory comes like echoes from the past,

The blessed past. Will no one ope the gates,
And lead me backward to that glorious state,
And to the idol of my girlhood dreams
And their wild fervor?"
Then a genius came,
And he unlocked the caverns of the deep;
Then bore me downward to the blue-sea halls,
And midst those coral grottos cooled my hands
In crystal vases. There the opal shone
With mystic radiance, and the emerald wreathed
The pale, dead brows, which gleamed up white and strange
Amid the sea-weed. Oh! they slept with pearls
And all things beautiful, and the great waves
Forever pealed a requiem o'er them, and
Thus shall they sleep until time's dying throbs
Shall shake the universe.
"Go seek thy love,"
Whispered the spirit, and a mocking smile
Bent his red lip; "perchance he sleepeth here
In Neptune's regal palace."
One by one
I numbered o'er the dead, and wandered on
For weary miles. I lifted raven curls
From many a brow, and bent o'er many a lip;
But yet saw none which bore the spell of his
For whom I sought with hopeless, patient love.
Soft through the waters, gleaming like a star,
Flashed a clear ray. "Sweet love!" I murmured then,
"Be this the guide to lead my steps to him."
Fresh glories gleamed around me. Rainbow-hued
And crimson sea-flowers climbed a coral arch,
And draped a regal couch; and there he lay,
Not pale and dead, but warm and rich with life.
Age yet had pressed but lightly on the brow
So glorious in its beauty, and those curls
Of raven darkness swept its marble breadth
In shadowy magnificence. The eyes
Had learned not coldness from the frozen years
Which rolled their heights between us; the full lips
Were curving their rich crimson in a smile,
And angel pinions drooped with silvery sheen
From the broad shoulders. Like a peal of bells,
He syllabled my name. I never thought
If he had wings on earth, or was so fair,

But still I nestled in his warm embrace;
And then he said, one cabalistic word
From him would ope those portals as the sun
Unbars the gates of day. With trumpet-voice
He breathed the mystic spell. A thousand flowers
Seemed blending all their blossoms into one;
A thousand music-echoes seemed to sweep
Into infinitude, and dazzling rings
Of golden light, in widening circles, flashed
Athwart my vision, and my fever-dreams
Were torn apart, as by a wizard spell.
Yet one remained—the sweetest one—to be
A sweet *reality*. A proud face bent
O'er my pale brow, and wooing, loving words
Charmed my weak senses. All athirst, I drank
The God-sent nectar, and my pulses beat
With healthful throbbings. Life to me once more
Was beautiful, and the great boundary-line
Which spanned my Eden was Eternity.

THE LEPER'S CHILD.

Daughter of Judah's race, thine eye is bright,
  Thy red lip's beautiful and scornful curl
Regnant with pride; thy heart is free and light
  In its first blooming. Oh, most radiant girl!
Alas! that bitterness and gloom must now
Shadow the whiteness of thy pure young brow!

No more amid those purple-gleaming bowers,
  Draped with the Orient's many-tinted dyes,
Rich with the perfume of a thousand flowers,
  Will, in calm slumber, droop thy dreamy eyes.
Listen, O Zara! ere my brain grows wild:
A curse is on thee—*thou'rt the leper's child!*

My own sweet one, Gehazi's awful sin
  Is clinging to thee; ere one fleeting year,
Its loathsome crust will whiten o'er thy skin;
  Save to me only, thou wilt be a fear,
A form of dread to every passer by:
There now is nothing for thee but to die.

Zara, sweet June was in her depths of bloom
  On thy first birthday, ere I knew that he,

Round whom my love was circling like perfume,
Bore the dread curse which soon will rest on thee,
While I, calm, careless, like a dew-bent flower,
Slept, all unconscious of this horrid hour.

A whirlwind swept my dreams. *His* crimson lips
Were wooing mine with love's sweet honey-dew,
And his proud eyes lay half in sad eclipse,
Beneath the lids which veiled their midnight hue.
The air was heavy with his grief; he said,
"Young, bright, and sinless, better were she dead:

Dead ere —" Oh! let me veil the words which came,
To coil like fiery adders in my breast,
And from his parched lips burst like gusts of flame.
Zara, forgive him — he is now at rest;
But while life's pulses in thy bosom glow,
Oh! *never curse another with thy woe* —

As *I* have *thee.* Cast love's sweet poison by:
It was distilled for other lips than thine;
And, had I known how soon its bliss would fly,
Its venom never would have moistened mine.
Then, my soul's idol, veil thy pure young face,
And *die* — the *last of an accursed race.*

"AS ARTLESS AS A CHILD."

"As artless as a child?" The downward bending
Of her pale lips returns a bitter "no;"
It is no girlish impulse which is sending
From heart to cheek that deep and fitful glow.
It is that she has learned a truer linking
For words and thoughts than that she studied o'er,
So long ago, when utterance and thinking
Both the same meaning to her spirit bore.
Around her brow there rests a golden glory,
Like the faint shadow of an angel's crown,
Where ringlets bright as Hope's bewildering story,
Float, like the mists of sunset, softly down.
Love *seems* with folded pinions sweetly dreaming,
Nursed in the shadows of her violet eyes;

And yet, alas! alas! it *is* but *seeming*,
'T is Falsehood wears the boy-god's radiant guise.

"As artless as a *child?*" That low, rich laughter
Rings out above her heart's wild wail of pain,
And nothing earthly now can ever waft her
The peaceful dreams of childish hours again.
Like the rose-scented, seaward-roving breezes
Which hover round the coast of Malabar,
Her tone's soft witchery every spirit seizes,
And leads it captive, in love's chains, afar.
Yet (cold Iconoclast) one picture only
Of those in childhood crowned with rainbow light
Hangs in her bosom, desolate and lonely,
A star of beauty 'mid the gloom of night.
And when youth's rose-tint from her cheek has faded;
When age's silver glory crowns her brow;
When sorrow's darkest mists her soul have shaded,
That one dear picture will be bright as now.

"As artless as a child?" Alas! there lingers
Within her bosom now but *one fresh flower;*
'T was planted by the blind god's fairy fingers,
One gentle autumn at the twilight hour.
The chill December watched its glorious blooming,
And May's white-clouded, blue, caressing skies
Still kept the vigil, and at spring's entombing
Gave for a guardian June's voluptuous eyes.
She whispers love-words to it when the fringes
Which shade her eyes have curtained them to dreams,
And kisses it when bright-haired morning tinges
With golden shadows crystal-footed streams.
Ah! there are flowers whose laggard petals never
Unfold, save o'er a century's dying hour;
But none like this, whose radiance lasts forever:
Eternity keeps watch above this flower.

JEWELS FOR LETHE.

Jewels for Lethe! Genii, bring the key —
The heart's the casket where those jewels be.
The bright-winged angel, which, in purple state,
Sat, with furled pinions, singing at the gate,

Has drawn the bolts, and sought a prouder throne,
Leaving the rich insignia there alone —
The heart's crown-jewels. Fling them side by side
In the calm crystal of the Lethean tide.

Jewels for Lethe! Bring the brightest first,
(Love's ruby coronet;) in times of erst
It was the fitting crown for beauty's brow,
An emblem meet for knighthood's holiest vow
And fearless worship. Now, oh! who may dare
Unscathed its wreath of flashing light to wear?
Where can it find a softer, calmer grave?
Oh! cast it unpolluted in the wave!

Jewels for Lethe! Ha! a laurel-wreath
Carved out from emeralds; but close beneath
Lie jagged thorns; the heavy golden clasp
Is a coiled serpent, holding in its grasp
A wounded dove. Poor bird! how like to thine
Their fate who round their fair young temples twine
That wizard! Be it buried deep,
Where, charmed to silence, Lethe's waters sleep.

Jewels for Lethe! Jewels from the heart,
Why, when its regal visions all depart,
Should the regalia linger? Well it were
They ne'er had burned in princely splendor there.
Give the dark waters yet another gem,
Brightest but one in life's star-diadem:
When *Love* and *Glory* sleep beneath the tide,
Faith too should veil its radiance by their side!

Jewels for Lethe! Ah! no more there be;
Upon the empty casket turn the key;
And if its guardian angels e'er come down,
They must bring jewels for another crown,
And in Elysium forge another key;
This, Lethe, is an offering unto thee.
Shroud *Love*, and *Faith*, and *Fame* beneath thy flow:
What are they all but synonyms for *Woe?*

MISSISSIPPI.

SALLIE ADA VANCE.

SALLIE ADA REEDY was born in Northern Alabama. Captain James Reedy, her father, removed to Lexington, Mississippi, during her infancy.

Miss Reedy was early inclined to study; was passionately fond of reading, and had the advantage of careful and judicious culture.

While a child in years, she began to write in verse, and her early poems exhibit the same thoughtful tone, the same impassioned tenderness which can be seen, ripened and refined, in her later writings.

In 1860, her poems, which had appeared from time to time in the various periodicals of the South, were collected for publication in book-form. The "war" caused the idea to be abandoned for more auspicious times.

In 1865, about the close of the war, Miss Reedy entered upon a new phase of womanhood: she was married to Mr. Vance, and resides in Lexington, the home of her childhood.

The character of Mrs. Vance's poetry is subjective — her thoughts most frequently introverted — finding their field of research in the infinitely varied human heart. Yet she feels the charm of nature with all a poet's sensitive organization; and she describes the beauty of earth, sky, and ocean with the vivid truthfulness of an appreciative as well as imaginative mind. Her melody of versification is remarkable. Her thoughts ripple away into rhyme so easily that we perceive it to be their natural vehicle. Her words are always musical and well chosen.

But there are depths in her nature which have not been stirred: there are chords which have not been sounded. When these have been awakened by the hand of a larger experience, we shall see the poetry of Mrs. Vance take a wider range — a deeper and more earnest tone.

She has recently finished a poem, longer than any she ever published, which is considered by judges to be the best she has ever written.

Mrs. Vance lost her husband in December, 1868.

"Beautiful as a poet's dream" is an old saying — but here is a poet's dream that is more than beautiful:

THE TWO ANGELS.

A boy at midnight sat alone,
  And quick throbs o'er his being stole,
Like those to graver manhood known
  When high resolves are in the soul.
Two wingèd angels softly leave
  The brightest star in all the sky,
And one is fair as sinless Eve —
  The other has the serpent's eye.

Now to the boy they softly glide,
  And fold their starry wings unseen,
Then rest them, one on either side,
  And watch him as he sits between.
Each angel holds within her hand
  A spotless scroll of purest white,
For God has sent them with command
  To write the boy's resolves that night.

"I will be great!" his hot cheek burned —
  "That men shall shout in ecstasy,
When first their wondering souls have learned
  How like the gods a man may be."
The angel on the left hand smiled,
  And wrote it with suspended breath;
She knew ambition oft beguiled
  To sin and sacrifice and death.

"I shall have foes, as greatness hath,
  Whate'er may be its brilliant sphere;
But I will sweep them from my path,
  Or maim their puny souls with fear."
The angel on the left hand caught
  And wrote the proud boast with a sneer;
The angel on the right had nought
  Upon her page but one bright tear.

"Love, still the poet's chosen theme,
  Shall be a thing abjured by me;

And yet — my childhood's happiest dream
  Came to me on my mother's knee.
My mother's knee! Why what is this
  That on my lips is trembling now?
A prayer? I almost feel the kiss
  Her dying lips left on my brow.

"She'd rather hear her name and mine
  In some poor creature's night-prayer told,
Than have the proud world rear a shrine
  And write it there in burning gold."
The angel on the left awhile
  Seemed half in doubt and half in rage;
The other smiled a warm, bright smile
  That dried the tear upon her page.

"I will be brave, and ask each heart
  That faints in life to lean on mine,
And strive to do that better part
  That makes a mortal feel divine;
And, if my faults should win a foe
  Relentless through all coming time,
I'll pity you who may not know
  Compassion makes this life sublime."

The boy looked upward to the sky;
  But ere his vow was halfway done,
And ere the light passed from his eye,
  The angel on the left had flown:
The angel on the right was there,
  And for one joyful moment stood,
Then waved her bright wings on the air,
  And bore her message back to God.

Very seldom, in all the range of poetry, do we find anything so perfect in all respects as the following gem. It is unexceptionable in every respect — a lesson for life, to be conned every day by those who would worship the good, the beautiful, and the true:

GUARD THINE ACTION.

When you meet with one suspected
  Of some secret deed of shame,
And for this by all rejected
  As a thing of evil fame —

Guard thine every look and action:
  Speak no heartless word of blame;
For the slanderer's vile detraction
  Yet may spoil thy goodly name.

When you meet a brow that 's awing
  With its wrinkled lines of gloom,
And a haughty step that 's drawing
  To a solitary tomb —
Guard thine action: some great sorrow
  Made that man a spectre grim;
And the sunset of to-morrow
  May have left thee like to him.

When you meet with one pursuing
  Paths the lost have entered in,
Working out his own undoing
  With his recklessness and sin —
Think, if placed in his condition,
  Would a kind word be in vain?
Or a look of cold suspicion
  Win thee back to truth again?

There are spots that bear no flowers —
  Not because the soil is bad;
But that summer's gentle showers
  Never made their bosoms glad:
Better have an act that 's kindly
  Treated sometimes with disdain,
Than, by judging others blindly,
  Doom the innocent to pain.

STRAUSS' FIRST LOVE.

At eve they summoned the bridal crowd
  To a lofty-pillared dome,
Where the daughter fair of a lineage proud
  Went forth from her childhood's home;
And white plumes waved in the diamond light
  That shone over princely brows,
While the eye of beauty grew softly bright
  As it read love's hidden vows.

Rich tapestry trembled upon the breeze,
  And the tall wax tapers shone,
And fragrance, swept from the Southern seas,
  Stole in with the lute's low tone.
It seemed not pleasure that wildly thrilled
  The cadence of gushing song,
But bliss so deep that its depth had stilled
  The pulse of that mighty throng.

And yet there was one dark, mournful eye,
  Whose searching and soul-lit glance
Saw but one fair form as it floated by
  In the whirl of the breathless dance.
By a column tall he leaned apart,
  With a brow so deadly pale
That one might read of his broken heart
  As though 't were a written tale.

He loved with the love of a noble soul—
  'T was scorned by that haughty bride;
And the fountain, checked, all coldly stole
  O'er his heart with a frozen tide.
She had spurned the truth of the minstrel's vow,
  And given her hand to one
Who placed a crown on her fair young brow—
  For thus are the soulless won.

But hark! there burst on the deep'ning night
  A murmur of grief profound,
And the dancers paused in their giddy flight
  To catch the unearthly sound.
The minstrel poured all his breaking heart
  In melody's wailing strain,
And the bride grew pale at the sudden start
  And the swollen tensioned vein.

Still higher and deeper the music swells,
  Till the marble pillars ring;
As the song of the dying swan excels
  The lay of all birds that sing.
Then a pallor over the bride's cheek crept,
  And her brow grew coldly white
As the bridal veil that around her swept
  Like a gossamer cloud of light.

Her ducal robe wore a crimson stain,
  ('Twas the heart's red blood, I wot;)
Then pealed still higher the music-strain;
  Yet the dead bride heard it not!
The hall is deserted — the revellers fled —
  Save he of the mournful eye:
Oh! who dare tell, when the loved lay dead,
  Of his soul's deep agony?

THE SISTERS.

Those were not mortals standing there
  With eyes bent on a sleeping child,
Who, all unmindful of their care,
  Saw dreams at which his red lips smiled.
And one was blue-eyed, with a face
  Round which the brown hair closely curled
With such a soft, bewitching grace,
  It might have maddened half the world.

The other's meek eyes, raised above,
  Seemed reading trouble for to-morrow:
The brown-haired, blue-eyed one was Love;
  The other was her sister, Sorrow.
And Love's bright wings flashed here and there —
  You looked to see her float away;
But Sorrow's drooped with silent care,
  As though prepared for longer stay.

"Now, sister, give me this fair boy,"
  The blue-eyed angel gently said;
"A bosom soft and warm with joy
  Should only pillow such a head.
You've followed me where'er I roam,
  You've clung to me through many years,
And when I touch a heart, you come
  And blot the record with your tears."

The meek-eyed angel floated near,
  And took the soft hand of her sister,
And on her cheek there was a tear,
  That trembled as she gently kissed her.

"Oh, Love! thou dost remember well,
  When Eve and Adam were too wise,
And, weeping forth a sad farewell,
  We went with them from Paradise.

"They wondered at the storm above,
  And what the flowers would do without them;
I think they would have died, sweet Love,
  But that your arms were twined about them.
I loved the stars and soft, blue skies,
  And winds that sung to us at even,
And made our lovely Paradise
  Almost as beautiful as heaven.

"And so I wept, and prayed that they
  Might go from my dark presence free,
While I, the meek-eyed one, would stray,
  And weary Heaven with prayers for thee.
The guarding angel shook his head,
  And sadly pointed up above,
And said: 'Alas! it is decreed
  You part not with your sister, Love.

"'She was the fairest from her birth;
  But, pale-faced Sorrow! thou art wise;
While Love would make their heaven on earth,
  Thou 'lt mind them of lost Paradise.'
I could not leave thee then, and now —"
  But Love's bright arms were round her thrown,
And that one kiss on Sorrow's brow
  Had left a brightness like her own.

"Dear sister, this fair boy shall be
  A pilgrim at thy radiant shrine;
But every time he bends his knee,
  Half of the offering shall be thine."
The boy awoke almost in tears,
  So strange and sad the vision seemed:
Perchance he knew, in after-years,
  He had not only slept and dreamed.

MRS. MARY STANFORD.

"Ah, the most loved are they of whom Fame speaks not with her clarion voice."

ALTHOUGH few of Mrs. Stanford's productions have reached the public eye, her genius has long been acknowledged and admired by a large circle of friends. Her poetic faculty was a gift of nature, which received culture in her early education in the nunnery, near Bardstown, Kentucky. Under the oaks and magnolias of Claiborne County, Mississippi, she was born, and her maiden name of Mary Patterson will thrill the hearts and memories of many old associates and contemporaries. Her girlhood was passed amid scenes of gayety and pleasure; her ready wit, vivacity, and poetic taste, together with a graceful, petite physique, making her a charming companion and ornament to society. Her parents died when she was very young, leaving her two brothers and herself, and their estate, to the care of a relative.

Mrs. Stanford was twice married and widowed. An only son was the fruit of her first marriage; and in that son she "lived, moved, and had her being." "The ocean to the river of her thoughts," he grew to be an idol, worshipped with a devotion few mothers have given their offspring. He was her inspiration, the polar star of her life.

Freely were her private interests sacrificed in raising and equipping a battery, of which her son was first lieutenant, and subsequently captain; and no more manly, noble, and splendid talent was given the cause of the South, than when FERDINAND CLAIBORNE enlisted, and bravely fought and fell, a martyr to that cause, leaving in the memory of his mother and countrymen a monument of honor and chivalry more bright and enduring than the marble erected by his comrades on the spot where he fell. And this little tablet, pure and white and glistening, embowered in roses, and embalmed by a mother's daily kisses and tears, tells to the lingerer in the quiet little cemetery of Port Gibson the same history it told at the fortifications of Vicksburg, where, like a sentinel at his post, it guarded the lonely mound where a martyred hero slept.

Mrs. Stanford was for many years a resident of New Orleans. While the guns at Fort Sumter were still reverberating in our hearts, she pressed the farewell kisses on the lips of her son, from whom she had never been separated.

About this period, Mrs. Stanford contributed several lively tales of life in the Crescent City, and poems to the "Southern Monthly," published in Memphis.

Says she: "My writings are only to be considered for the idolatrous love that inspires them." And few mothers in our land can read her "lines" without deep feeling.

When New Orleans fell, feeling that by remaining there she could no longer guard and protect her son's pecuniary interests, she felt that the one thing left for her to do was to find her child, to be where she might at an instant's notice seek him. She had a motherless niece to care for; and not wishing to proceed on a wild, blind search for her boy, she went to the old home of her girlhood, (Port Gibson,) and found rest and sympathy with those who had loved her in the long-ago. For weeks she had not heard from her son, until she reached this place, and some returning soldiers told her of his whereabouts. When he wrote to her, he forbade her attempting to join him, urging her to remain with her old friends, "and perhaps they might meet again — perhaps he might be ordered farther South — *but he could not ask for a furlough.*"

At last, the mother's patient waiting was rewarded. Her son, who had been for over a year in East Tennessee, and in Kentucky with General Bragg, was ordered to Vicksburg with General Stevenson's Division — ordered where his mother waited for him. Need we say that the mother was soon with her son? Some months before this, finding her resources fail, being able to get nothing from New Orleans, she had opened a school for the support of her niece and self, that *she might not take from her son*, and this was in successful operation when she visited him. She found him all that a mother's loving heart could hope or pray for, but so wedded to his duties, so proud of the noble battery he commanded, that again, as he had done before, he kissed her and blessed her, and *gave her to another's charge*, and left her, to go where she could not follow. The long siege of Vicksburg succeeded.

What the year is to a mother, what it is to the country, is well told to the heart, in these few artless, plain verses:

MY NEW-YEAR'S PRAYER.

New-Year's Day! Alas! the New-Year's days
 That stalk like troubled ghosts before my sight,
From happy youth, through weary years, till now,
 When my life's sun must soon be lost in night,
And I, in death's untroubled, tranquil sleep,
Shall learn how sweet it is to cease to weep!

New-Year's Day! Yes, I remember one —
 The day I watched a little rosy face
Of six months old, with dimpling smiles
 Peep out from under folds of silk and lace:
That face, the sweetest to a mother's eyes
That ever made of earth a paradise.

And then another New-Year I recall,
 Bringing sweet prattlings I so loved to hear;
The only music I could understand,
 The only notes that ever charmed my ear,
Save th' accompaniment to this sweet song —
The steps that bore my tottering boy along.

Then, New-Year's days in numbers pass me by,
 Bearing new beauties both to heart and mind,
And adding graces to the manly form —
 I did not wonder in the three to find
All I once hoped to see united there —
My son's young promise was so passing fair.

But where, in this dark, cheerless New-Year's day,
 In thy full manhood, must I look for thee?
I shall not find in that worn face such smiles
 As dimpled through the folds of lace for me;
And stern, harsh lines are on the once smooth brow,
Babe so beloved! — a man and soldier now!

Ah! since thy mother's arms were round thee last,
 Since thou wert folded to thy mother's breast,
Since her appealing voice hath met thine ear,
 Since her last kisses on thy lips were prest,
My son, my darling, what has chanced to thee?
Loving as then wilt thou return to me?

Ghosts of the New Years! with them come the hopes
  That made the promise of thy youth more fair,
Whispering how thy manhood's love would guard
  A mother's age from every grief and care.
How canst thou be to me this guard and shield,
Thou — in constant change from tent to battle-field?

Ghosts of the New Years, visit him to-day,
  My baby once! — my country's soldier now!
Paint to his memory the unselfish love
  That, since a mother's lips first touched his brow,
Till now, when such despairing words are said,
A mother's heart has showered on his head.

Spirit of to-day! breathe in his ear the prayers
  That day and night ascend on high for him;
Unceasing, hopeful, trustful, brave and strong!
  Earth's dreams delude — its brightest hopes grow dim —
But from the ruins soars, fresh, undefiled,
The mother's prayer — "GOD BLESS AND SAVE MY CHILD."

When the siege of Vicksburg was over, and for weeks after, there was no one hardy enough to tell her "she was childless!" Weeks of darkness came, after this; but there was one thing to live for — to find the grave of her son. Once more, for one night the same roof sheltered mother and son — he in his coffin, into which she dared not look! And through the Federal army, and down the river, and amid perils and sufferings, and hardships that it is a wonder, now, she could ever endure, she brought her darling to Port Gibson — there, to live and die beside him — to be buried in his grave — in his arms, if it could be.

"DIED AT HIS GUNS."*

Extract from a letter found in the trunk of a young soldier who "died at his guns," in the siege of Vicksburg.

"DEMOPOLIS, Ala., June, 1863.

. . . . "Will you not name one of your guns in honor of my little daughter, the ——? I have not forgotten your wish to make her your patron saint; and if, in the anticipated battle at Vicksburg, your battery comes out, as I know it will, triumphant, I will present you a stand of colors, the white stripe of which shall be made of my bridal robe of *moire-antique*. . . . .

"You are placed where only brave and gallant men are called; for well the enemy

* From "Banner of the South."

know how important the acquisition of that stronghold. You may receive this on the eve of one of the grandest of the many grand battles fought for your country's freedom. For God's sake, do not falter! Let them wade through a sea of blood before they take a gun from your command."

In answer to the above, was written the following:

"BAPTIZED IN BLOOD."

Lady, when you counselled this young soldier—
This spirit bold and daring—did no voice
Whisper within you that for him, perchance,
There might be fearful prescience in your words?
And did your heart not bleed, recalling then
The soft, dark eyes that looked such love in yours,
Or danced in mirth, or proudly answered back
Your own proud patriot look of dire resolve?
Did you bethink you, then, of that sweet smile,
So full of tenderness, your startled heart,
Albeit guarded, to its depths was stirred,
As if a dream of girlhood had come back?
And did then mingle with these later dreams
Remembrance of the fresh, glad voice that made
Such music, soft or tender, sad or gay;
While came the thought, "How dear all these must be
To some fond heart that finds in them its world;
For 't is no common love proud natures win;"
And knowing this, did you not, lady, know,
To "wade through sea of blood," alas! might be
To close the eyes, take from those lips their smile,
And still the music of that voice fore'er?

"*Baptized in blood the noble gun shall be!*"
Pledge lightly made, but royally redeemed:
Whose *heart's blood* flowed to make that promise good?
Oh, noblest blood that ever dyed our soil!
Oh, truest heart that ever ceased to beat!
Oh, purest patriot of the martyr dead!
Brave blood so vainly spilt, so quickly dried—
True heart, with all its wealth of love, forgot—
Pure patriot, 'mid a country's woes passed by,
Save in a mother's proud idolatry!

Fair friend—brave comrades—weeping lady-love—
Where were ye then? Amid the tumult wild,
And through the city's wrecks, the *mother* 't was

Who sought and found the lonely grass-grown mound
Where slept her darling. 'T was the *mother's* love,
Through victor foes, and from beneath their flag,
That bore her coffined idol to a grave
Lone, still, and quiet, where the step of those
Who made her childless might not thence to stray.
The *mother* 't is who watches, morn and noon
And night, that sacred spot, o'ergrown with flowers,
And keeps upon his tomb the fadeless wreath,
Pure as his valor, fresh and green as lives
His noble memory down in her heart.
Fair friend — brave comrades — mourning lady-love —
And dear companions all — where are ye now?

In Sacred Writ we read of one whom Christ,
The blessed Saviour, at the gates of Nain,
Brought back from death to life; and gave, unasked,
Again unto the weeping mother's arms —
This one — *a widowed mother's only child!*

MRS. S. B. COX.

MRS. COX, whose maiden name was Hughes, was born in Warren County, Mississippi, five miles from Vicksburg. Her parents were Virginians, but adopted Alabama as their home, where her father, Judge Beverley Hughes, presided at the bar with distinction. They removed to Mississippi six months before the birth of the subject of this sketch, and eighteen months before the death of her father. A lady friend says: "Unfortunately for Miss Hughes, in the death of her father she lost the hand which would have been the fashioning and guiding power of her life."

Her mother married a second time—a man chilling in his manner—and her childhood passed without one genial ray of warmth to expand and open the hidden nature within her, save rare interviews with her mother, full of love and tenderness, and usually embracing one theme that was exhaustless—the virtues and graces of her father. Says Mrs. Cox, alluding to this:

"These conversations about my father were so colored by the admiration of a devoted wife, that he alone seemed to fill my idea of God's nobleman, and early became the inspiration of my life. To be worthy of being his daughter, enlisted all my faculties in every effort I made for good; no temptation beset me that I was not fortified against it by the thought, that, to yield to it would be unworthy the daughter of my father. My successes at school were alike due to this single inspiration of my life."

Miss Hughes was married very young—fourteen years and three months old on her wedding-day. Her life became very checkered: at the age of twenty-eight, when life is bright and full of joyousness to many, she became hopelessly bedridden. The trials of her life were numerous; but, to use her own language—breathings of the mother: "I was a mother, and this bore me up to live and labor for the immortal ones God had intrusted to my care."

For eight years she could not take a step, or even stand alone; and she says:

"Yet, amid all, God was very good in preserving my mind clear, and strengthening my will to conquer every repining for myself, and devote my remaining energies to the training and cultivation of my four little daughters. Up to the opening of the war, my world was found in these, my life centred in them; but a mightier appeal thrilled my being; my country called, and my whole heart responded. I felt that even the claim of my children was secondary to it, and devoted my time, my purse, and my strength, without reserve, to the sick of the Confederate army."

A friend, who is indebted to an eye-witness for his information, says:

"At one time the enemy shelled the hospital, which was near her residence. Her house, though within reach, was out of range of their guns, and she opened her doors to the inmates of the hospital, and for several weeks there were three hundred soldiers with her."

At the raising of the siege, her means were exhausted; and at the commencement of the second siege, General M. L. Smith informed her that her house had fallen within the line of fortifications, and would have to be destroyed. The Father seems strangely to provide for his creatures in the very darkest moments of their lives. Just at this crisis with Mrs. Cox, homeless and without money, her husband was discharged from active duty on account of failing health, and returned from Virginia in time to prevent her despairing, if such a hopeful mind as that of Mrs. Cox can be looked upon as "giving up." Her husband applied for and obtained government employment in the Trans-Mississippi Department, and they removed to Shreveport. The reaction from active excitement to comparative quiet prostrated Mrs. Cox again entirely to bed, and thus it was with her until the news of the fall of Vicksburg fell like a leaden weight upon her. Says she:

"For the first time, woe took the place of full confidence, and never again was the bow of hope unclouded in my heart; yet when the fall of the Confederacy was told to me, I reeled and staggered under the blow, not aware for weeks if my vitality would survive it."

The superior facilities to be found in the public schools of New Orleans for educating their daughters, decided Mr. and Mrs. Cox to make that city their home. They were scantily supplied with the "world's goods." Mr. Cox, over fifty years of age, without a son to assist him, had to begin anew the world, and for nearly two years they struggled for the necessaries of life — "a struggle such as cannot be conceived of unless felt."

Mrs. Cox had contributed to the papers of Vicksburg and Shreveport, among other articles, several appeals to the Southern people upon subjects pertaining to the war. These were published over the *nom de plume* of "Beverley." Now, in the terrible strait of poverty, the idea of writing for money came to her. Says she: "I caught at it as a drowning man clutches at a straw, and almost as hopelessly and desperately. Without an introduction to the press of New Orleans, I made my way into the journals." A writer in the "Crescent" thus refers to her:

"We think a woman, even an invalid, who can neither sit in anything but a *robe de chambre*, nor stand long enough to have her hair frizzed, like our own 'Beverley;' whose pathos moves to tears; whose philosophy makes us proud of our own sex; whose wit and sarcasms few would wish to encounter; whose faith has for years irradiated her sick-chamber with a hallowed light, is infinitely superior to a lady whose highest acquisitions are moire-antiques, thule, coiffures, tinsel, or even diamonds; whose resources for happiness are theatres, masquerades, and dancing; whose faith exhibits itself in a few Lenten visits to church; whose self-abnegation and humiliation are the changing from one luxurious diet to another perhaps a little more delicate."

In the Spring of 1869, Mrs. Cox lost the use of her right hand and arm from paralysis,—her physician ascribing it to the incessant writing for weeks to meet her engagements, for she supported her family with her brain-work.

Mrs. Cox continues to contribute to the various papers of New Orleans, and to several Northern journals, particularly to the Sunday edition of the "Times" newspaper.

SPIRIT-WHISPERINGS.

Philosophy stands up in the severe, grave dignity of truth, and demands demonstrable facts in all things. But is there nothing within us, to the intellect vague, shadowy, and undefined, which may not be reasoned upon, yet is a feeling, a consciousness from which we may reason and deduce facts as clearly as from anything material? Surely this is evident to all.

We may draw from every created thing or being an undeniable evidence of a Great First Cause or Creator. From the delicate violet, which opens its beautiful petals out upon the bosom of the brown earth, up to the dewy kisses of the night-winds; to the stone-girt mountain, which, from its burning caldron of boiling lava, hurls forth destruction and death for miles around; from the tiny insect to his own image in man,—all proclaim most unmistakably the existence of a God, the Creator of all things, and the Ruler of his creation. But perhaps the most satisfying evidence to man is the demand in his own being for a God—that universal reaching out of the soul which is found in the breast of the most benighted heathen.

Of the inspiration of the Bible, but slight evidence is given by historians since the advent of the Saviour; but it is when we compare its high and holy truths with the self-evident facts of man's life, that we find the first positive proof which is apt to be taken hold of by man. Let the unprejudiced thinker turn his mind in upon his own soul, and compare its aspirations and its longings with the truths of the Bible, and therefrom will he draw evidence beyond refutation; and therein is the mystical chain of spirit with spirit; that half-hidden, half-defined something which baffles the lore of philosophy, yet enchants and delights man.

Trouble upon trouble enters in upon the heart of man; care upon care silvers the dark threads, and bends the head low upon the stooped shoulders; the weary, aching thought of the brain, which brings no fruition; the half-requited labor, the heart-sickening disappointment in friendship and love; and man grows weary and faint, and cries out for the waters of oblivion to sweep over his soul in this dark hour of woe and despair. Then comes the small, still voice of the Spirit, and whispers: "All of earth is passing away, and heaven is eternal!"

Death lays its icy touch upon our idol, and our heart is torn until every fibre is bleeding out its own vitality, and reason staggers upon its throne. Then whispers the Spirit: "Be still, and rest in the hands of thy God." It is only a little while sooner than you that the spirit has bid adieu to the troubles of life.

A little white bird wafted its downward way from paradise, and, finding its tiny, delicate form growing cold and numb in this bleak world's grasp, sought refuge in my quiet home — for a few brief hours folded its snowy wings gently and lovingly upon my breast; but though I nestled it warmly within my bosom, and wooed it to linger with me, it gave a few farewell moans, and, softly gliding from its earthly casket, took its returning flight to paradise. Thus came and went our little babe. But a cell had been opened up in our hearts for love of her; and though we consigned to the dark earth that beautiful waxen form of purest whiteness, and other children have been born to us, love for her is still warm within my heart. That heart beats still for the angel one. Her little baby form, her eyes of heavenly blue, her mouth of sweetest mould, are yet fresh within my memory. Ah! who can doubt that we two will meet again? My spirit whispers that my heart-throbs are not for nought, but will beat on throughout eternal ages.

Ah! yes, let us listen to these sweet whisperings of the Spirit, and they will breathe into our souls strength to conquer, strength to bear. Listen to them, confide in them, and they will rob death of its sting, and open out to us a great, broad vista of ages of eternal bliss. Wife, by the death-bed of thy husband; mother, by thy dead child, take comfort from it to hush thy grief.

There is a Spirit whispering of warning and hope to the young man in a career of sin and profligacy, bidding him pause, reflect, and follow its promptings.

To the old man tottering upon the verge of a dishonored grave, it says: "Even now listen to me."

Frail woman, in thy fall and degradation, listen to it; hush it not in thy poor, sin-stained soul. When all the world turn from thee, and only sin and shame clasp hands with thee, it will prove thy best friend. It is sent to such as thee by God.

A SKETCH FROM REAL LIFE DURING THE WAR.

In a war of invasion, who can say that woman's part is not the severest? Quietly she must watch the march of the foe over the land dearer than all else to her, the land in which all the love and pride of her soul are garnered: mile by mile she must behold their devastations, and yet be denied the excitement of resistance, which almost swallows up the terror of conflict. She may ply her needle for the soldier, labor to raise provision for the army, and attend the sick and wounded. These are glorious deeds of a beautiful mission upon earth; but all these may be well performed even while a constant heart aches and a terrible dread is slowly tearing the heart-strings and wearing away life itself. Ay, she may ply the needle and force back the scalding tears "which hinder needle and thread," while they fall back upon her heart hot and burning. She may watch the writhing agony of the wounded, and the death-throes of the dying. The far-distant wail of anguish from wife, mother, daughter, and sister may ring within her ears as she folds the cold hands over the pulseless breast, and her heart echoes back the cry, while it is almost bursting with indignation against the foe who has brought such desolation to her very door. She must turn shelterless and foodless from the smouldering ashes of her home, with her children clinging to her knees, yet no hand of resistance can she raise to the barbarous deed. In silence she must accept the terrible cruelty, and, for the sake of her little ones looking to her for life, she must crave food from the hands which applied the burning torch to her home. Yes, we say that in a war of invasion woman's part is far more terrible than man's, although she may rarely face shot or shell. Look upon her powers of cheerful endurance amid these terrific trials, and we exclaim, Surely there is a heroism in it equal to any in life!

During the late war, our land abounded with instances of cheerful heroism in woman under all the dreadful terrors of an invading army; but we think that it was in country homes, often cut off from every white neighbor by the distance of several miles, that the most striking heroism was to be found.

Woman saw that the land must continue to be cultivated, that famine might be kept off, and, naturally timid and shrinking as she is, she cast all fear aside, and arose equal to the demand of the times. But it is not merely to eulogize woman that we have taken up our pen, to present our readers with a short sketch of a country maiden during the late war—a sketch true to the lives of many more than the one we present.

Mr. Kline lived in Mississippi, between Jackson and Vicksburg, near the railroad. Laura, his eldest daughter, was just sixteen when the war opened. She had been reared in all the luxury of a wealthy Southern planter's life. Just as soon as the Federal army was within reach, every able young hand, save a boy of fourteen, left and went to the enemy, leaving the old and infirm to add to the care of providing the necessaries of life.

"Wife, I suppose we may as well turn the cows and calves out together; old Charity is too rheumatic to attend to them, and I have tried in vain for two hours to milk them."

"No, indeed, papa; we cannot do without butter and milk. I can milk the cows."

"You milk! Where upon earth did you learn?"

"I learned when I was quite a little girl. Do you not remember how you and mother used to call me in from the pen and seat me in the house, lest I should grow rude and hoidenish? Well, I stole out often enough to learn to milk quite well; but, papa, you look as red as if all your blood were in your face, and you are panting as though you had been running a foot-race. It cannot be the effort of milking so much, since you did not get a drop; pray tell us what it is all about?" A mischievous twinkle stole out of the brown eyes, and rippled over the dimpled cheeks and around the cherry lips, as she looked banteringly upon her father.

"Well, Miss Saucy-box, I have had a chase after nearly every cow in the pen, and, after closing in the corner first one and then the other, have not been able to draw one drop of milk. Nor do I believe that those little white hands, which have only toyed with flowers all your life, will ever get a pint; but if you wish, you can try."

"Try! yes indeed, and milk them too. After all, I do not believe you lords of creation are half as useful as we bits of womanhood."

And the blithe creature shook her curls saucily, and rang out a merry laugh.

"Why are you taking that immense bucket, Laura. If you succeed in milking, three or four will yield milk and butter sufficient for us."

"I know that, mother; but I am not going to lose so much for our sick soldiers; you have been sending them twenty pounds of butter every week, and I intend to continue doing so."

"Things are very different now from what they have been; neither your father nor Henry can spare time to take it. How will you get it there, after it is made?"

"Never do you mind, mother; 'where there is a will there is a way.' I have it all planned very nicely."

Blithely she tripped away, with her bucket on her arm, looking back and laughing at her parents.

Twice was Mr. Kline called to bear the immense bucket in, full of the delightful beverage, and each time Laura bantered him with every step; but as he quaffed the refreshing milk after a day of toil, he gave her full permission to laugh at him so long as she succeeded.

Bright as a bird, the young girl flitted through the house and over the place, and, though you would scarcely believe her working, all was done in order and in time, and her half invalid mother was spared every extra labor. Mr. Kline had learned how much more and better work can be done by one's own hands than by servants, and they were all just becoming contented with the change in their mode of living, when the Federal army reached their neighborhood; and then began the work of devastation and ruin in real earnest. Their house soon fell into the hands of the foe, and they looked helplessly on while the flaming torch was applied to the magnificent edifice, which, in a few hours, was a heap of burning coals. They supposed that Mr. Kline had gold about him, and resorted to various tortures to extract it from him. These terrors and exposure soon snapped the attenuated threads which held together the frail life of Mrs. Kline, and in three days after she was burned out of house and home, they laid her to rest in a quiet spot in the garden.

"Laura, I feel completely crushed; there is no life nor strength left for labor and struggle. I feel that I too must die; nor can I wish to live after she is gone. What will you do, child?"

"Father, do not talk thus, do not feel thus: there are three younger than I. For these we must arouse from our grief; for these we must work on. We owe it to the helpless ones; we owe it to the dead; we owe it to your sons in the field, to our struggling country, to show that as long as we live we can be self-sustaining."

"What do you propose now, Laura? all is gone, even the roof over our heads."

"The land yet remains; the gardener's house is untouched. This contains two rooms, and is shrouded in trees, and lies in such a deep valley that it will not be likely to attract the enemy's notice. Indeed, I suppose the terrible wrong they have done us will satisfy them, and they will be willing to leave us to our poverty without further molestation. You have cows in the big black swamp; three or four of these must be gotten up, and with the provision we buried we can live until we can raise more. The negroes, except Aunt Charity and Henry, must be sent within the enemy's lines to be fed. I will give them a letter to the Yankee general, who will feed them, which is more than we can do. With this arrangement we can live, if we husband well what we have. Will you not arouse to this duty, dear father? And will you not take comfort in your children?"

"I will try, my child."

Mr. Kline followed this advice; and the heroic, noble girl hushed the sorrow for her great loss deep within her motherless heart, and arose to cheerfulness and labor for the sake of the dear ones left to her care, and the land of her birth, her love, and her pride. Industrious hands and a cheerful spirit accomplish wonders, and there was soon an air of neatness and comfort about the two rooms embowered in trees and wild vines, which refreshed and comforted the weary spirit of her almost broken-hearted father, and the little ones declared that it was nicer than the great fine house. The piano was gone, but little Eddie had run away with her guitar and hid it, and each evening, after her father had retired to bed, she played and sang, until, soothed and comforted, he dropped to sleep, as gently as a babe listening to its mother's lullaby.

The catastrophe has come. The war is ended. Fathers, sons, brothers, and lovers flock home, as the chased deer, famishing for the cooling draught, rushes to the clear, bubbling water. Two brothers out of four are welcomed back to the desolate home-spot of the Klines. They resolved to restore to the family something of their former prosperity, and with active energy they entered upon a life of labor; God blessed almost their every effort; but, strange enough to her father, Laura for the first time drooped; a shade of sadness often flitted across the lovely face, and, as days and nights passed by, deepened until it became habitual; the birdlike motion departed from the hour her mother was laid beneath the dark earth; now the regular, bright movement of the cheerful girl was gone, and every step flagged wearily, and every effort seemed a burden: yet she ceased not in her daily labor. Mr. Kline looks on in heaviness of heart, and feels that if she too goes, he will not long survive her, — nor does he wish to. He knows the glorious powers of self-reliance which have so peculiarly marked the last four years of her life, and forbears to question her, only growing tenderer and more caressing each day in his efforts to woo back light and life to her soul, knowing well what a blast and blight the fall of her loved country has cast upon a nature like hers.

It has been a cool, rosy-tinted Fall day; all animal existence seems instinct with renewed strength and life. The dogs run, frisk, and leap; the poultry crow, sing, and cackle; the horses toss their heads, bound, and frolic like country children turned out of school; the birds flit from bough to bough, and once more renew their glad spring songs; yet Laura changes not, except to look more spiritual, and wear a sweet, sad smile as she casts her eyes oftener to heaven; but the spirit of beauty, if not of life, seems to have entered her sad, quiet soul, and she has arranged her toilet for the evening with unusual care and taste: a purely white apron contrasts beautifully with the little brown figured muslin, which sits so nicely to the dainty little form, while soft, white ruffles relieve the neck and hands, and the pretty feet, laced closely in a pair of well-fitting boots, peep from beneath the short dress with every step; an exquisite blush-rose trembles in her auburn curls, while a bud and a geranium-leaf are clasped at her throat with a bright coral pin.

She has just finished milking. The cows are looking lazily contented, crunching their cuds, with their calves beside them. The little white cedar pail, filled with the snowy froth of the smoking milk, which smoke curls gracefully in thin wreaths above the frosted pile, is poised in her hands, as she pauses beneath an umbrageous oak to observe a man slowly advancing toward her on a worn-looking horse. He was thin and pale, and looked like a war-broken veteran, with the empty sleeve dangling by his side: as her eye rests upon him, she never dreams that he is a young man of only twenty-eight. A shade of pink flushes into the wan, pale face, and the dim eyes brighten as he pauses before her; the next instant a dark shade of sadness deepens in its bloodless lines, and he tries in vain to speak.

"Sir, you look weak and faint; take a cup of this warm fresh milk; it will revive your strength. Now let me hold your horse while you alight; you must tarry with us until you are strong enough to continue your journey."

The soldier was very feeble, but he was soon by her side.

"Surely my senses do not deceive me: you must be the Laura Kline I left on yonder burned hill four years ago."

"I am she, sir; but it cannot be that you are Robert Dillingham?"

Now the blood rushes in a full torrent over face and neck, while the sweet voice trembles and quivers, and the fragile form shakes like a wind-tossed leaf.

"Oh, Laura, can it be that your heart yet warms to the maimed, broken soldier?"

Now the weary, worn man flushed scarlet, and the eyes eagerly sparkled with joyous expectancy, as he clasped the little hand and looked questioningly down into the girlish face.

"Robert, can you doubt it? Did I not love you a thousand times better for these very honors, I would be unworthy the land of our birth, unworthy a noble soldier's love. I will be an arm unto you through life, as well as your devoted wife. For the first moment since our country fell, I now feel that I have something to live for, something to give me happiness even amid our great loss."

The soldier clasped her to his war-scarred breast, and tears of bliss too full for smiles fell upon her flushed face, as he pressed a fervent kiss upon the upturned brow. Disengaging herself from his embrace, the old light of life and fun broke over her smiling face, as she said:

"Come, Robert, let us go in; father will be so pleased to know that you are alive, and to see you home once more. He and the boys are doubtless wondering what has become of me — and if they are to have any milk for supper to-night. I will carry in the pail now; but in a few days I shall call you into service. But, for the world, you are not to come among my cows until the milking is over, for they have a belligerent antipathy to you lords of creation." . . . .

Mr. Kline soon divined the cause of Laura's drooping, when he saw the old light coming back to her eye and the old life to her soul, as the soldier-guest improved in health and strength day by day; and silently thanked God that she would be spared to his old age.

ELIZA POITEVENT.

PEARL RIVERS, as by her pseudonym is the "sweet singer" best known, takes her name from that beautiful stream, Pearl River, near the banks of which she was born.

Miss Poitevent is a maiden, hardly of adult years; the daughter of Captain W. J. Poitevent, a builder and owner of steamboats, and a manufacturer of lumber at Gainesville, on that river, about twenty-five miles across the plain from the Bay of St. Louis, which is now, as Gainesville formerly was, the seat of justice of Hancock County, Mississippi.

On her father's side, Miss Poitevent is of French descent; on the mother's, she is connected with the Russ family — of the Florida parishes of Louisiana and Southeastern Mississippi. Shortly after the birth of Eliza, her mother's health was so delicate that she was advised by her physician to travel, and it was decided that the "babe" should be left with her aunt, Mrs. Leonard Kimball. When Mrs. Poitevent returned, she found her babe, a healthy, rosy little girl, taking her first steps — who did not want to leave her aunt for her mother. Mrs. Kimball was childless, and had become so much attached to "little Pearl," that she earnestly entreated that she might be left with her. It was finally decided that "Pearl" should remain with her aunt.

And on the banks of the Hobolochitto, with her aunt and uncle, "Pearl Rivers" spent her pure and happy childhood. She had no playmates, and roamed the meadows and fields in search of companions. There was not a narrow path that trailed its way through the dense forest of pines that she did not know; and flowers, birds, and insects were *more* than flowers, birds, and insects to her. They were her friends and companions, and she talked to them and sang with them through many a happy day.

This poem is a true picture of her childhood, more beautifully expressed in her own "sweet language" than could possibly be told in my sober prose:

M-Y-S-E-L-F.

"Tell me something of yourself."
Letter from a Stranger — E. E. C., of Ohio.

Well, once I was a little girl,
  A-dwelling in the wood,
Beside a laughter-loving stream,
  With aunt and uncle good:

Within a rambling old log-house,
  That thought it was no sin
Through other places than the door
  To let the sunshine in:

With quaint old chimneys at each end,
  Where swallows used to come
And twitter low, "How glad are we
  To find a summer home!"

With windows low and narrow too,
  Where birds came peeping in
To wake me up at early morn;
  And oft I used to win

The Cherokees to climb the sill;
  The gossip-loving bee
To come so near that he would pause
  And buzz a word with me.

No other child grew on the place;
  A merry, roguish elf,
I played "keep house" in shady nooks,
  All by my little self.

I leaped the brook, I climbed the bars;
  I rode upon the hay;
To swing upon the old barn-gate
  To me was merry play.

I waded in the shallow stream
  To break the lilies sweet,
And laughed to see the minnows swim
  So near my rosy feet.

I rode the pony down to drink,
  He played some pranks with me;
But I had learned to hold on tight,
  And was as wild as he.

I could not keep my bonnet on;
  The briers tore the frill;
The winds untied the knotted strings,
  And tossed it at their will.

The sun grew friendly with me then,
  And still the signs I trace
Of many a merry trick he played
  Upon my neck and face.

My dress and apron bore the sign
  Of frolic wild and free;
The brambles caught my yellow hair,
  And braided it for me.

My teacher was a dear old man,
  Who took me on his knee;
And better far than vexing books
  He held a kiss from me.

I could not learn geography;
  The "States" I could not "bound;"
But many a city built by ants
  And daisy towers I found.

Arithmetic and grammar
  Were never in my line;
No measured rule was made to chain
  A spirit free as mine.

But I was quick to learn some things,
  As all the rills could tell;
I knew just where the waters bright
  With softest music fell.

I knew the names of all the birds,
  And which could sing the best;
I knew just where the speckled hen
  Had made her latest nest.

I knew how many drops of rain
  The pitcher-plant could hold,
And on the butterfly's bright wing
  How many spots of gold.

And how the spider's curious web
  Was jewelled by the dew,
And where the largest chincapins
  And whortleberries grew.

For I, though but a simple child,
  In Nature's ways was wise;
I followed her day after day
  With wonder-loving eyes.

I knew the track the ground-mole made,
  And followed it to see
Where all the windings strange would end.
  I knew the hollow tree

Where hid the sly fox-squirrel,
  And the hole where slept the hare;
But at their open, humble door
  I never set a snare.

I was a wild, but loving child;
  My little feet ne'er trod
Upon the weakest, meanest thing
  That crawls upon the sod.

They were my playmates and my friends:
  And, more than all, I knew
That if I loved his creatures well
  The Lord would love me too.

And sometimes I would lonely be,
  And so I learned to talk
To all the insects and the birds;
  And once I took a walk

To ask the sweet white violets,
  That grew down by the creek,
To learn me how to speak the tongues
  That all the flowers speak.

I thought it best to go to them;
  They are so meek, you know,
And teachers like these humble ones
  Can best God's wisdom show.

They seemed to think I was too young
  To learn their language well:
I thought I heard them ask the stream,
  Quite low, if it could tell

How many years the little maid
  Had laughed with it; for when
I guessed what all their whispers meant,
  And softly answered, "Ten,"

They smiled as though they thought it time
  The little maid should turn
From all her harum-scarum ways,
  And sit by them, and learn

The gentle words and modest grace
  That maidens all should wear;
That guards the heart and makes the face,
  Though homely, sweet and fair.

And so I softly laid my head
  Down close beside their own
Upon the fragrant mossy bed:
  And in the softest tone,

So that the zephyr could not hear
  And spread it to the breeze,
Or rustle it with laughter light
  To all the listening trees,

They taught me my first lesson through,
  And said some other day,
When they were strengthened by the dew,
  That I might leave my play,

And they would talk to me again.
  I kissed them o'er and o'er,
And deep within my heart I hid
  My wealth of flower-lore.

For something seemed to tell me then
  That I, perhaps, some day
Could tell to others what I learned
  From violets that May,—

That God would give my heart a voice,
  And send me forth to sing
Of all the honor and the love
  That nature bears her King.

So I was never lonely more;
  For flower, bird, and bee,
Though each spake different languages,
  Were understood by me.

Well, now I am a woman grown,
  And I have learned to braid
My yellow hair quite prettily
  Without the brambles' aid.

I do not climb the plum-trees now,
  Nor swing upon the gate,
For fear among the "proper" ones
  "A talk" it might create.

But though I have more quiet grown,
  I still am Nature's child,
And oft she leads me to the haunts
  And sports of childhood wild.

A new house sits upon the hill,
  Close by the river's side,
With chimneys straight and windows bold,
  And galleries long and wide,

Close-shingled roof and plastered wall;
  But dearer far would be
That old log-cabin, where the sun
  Peeped through the cracks at me.

I do not shine in Fashion's court;
  My name is scarcely known
Among the throng of worshippers
  That kneel around her throne.

But deep within the woods, amid
  A wilderness of pines,
I dwell with aunt and uncle still,
  And on my brow there shines

The happy light contentment gives;
  And in my heart I wear
This blessed truth, that God is love,
  And beauty everywhere.

When thirteen years of age, Pearl was sent to the Amite Female Seminary, in Amite County, Miss., where her many merry pranks soon won for her the name of "the wildest girl in school." She graduated at the age of "sweet sixteen," excelling in composition.

A stanch "little rebel," her first attempt at verse was to write patriotic words to several patriotic airs, which she sang to a circle of not critical, but admiring friends.

It was not until the "first year of the war" that any of her productions appeared in print.

Seeing a copy of "The South," a weekly paper published in New Orleans by John W. Overall, Esq., she was much pleased with the bold, dashing editorials, and sent several of her poems to him, trembling at the boldness of the step. Her poems were not only published, but were favorably noticed, and a friendly, encouraging letter from Mr. Overall followed. She received little or no encouragement from the members of her own family, and she considers that she owes much to her first literary friend and patient critic, John W. Overall, who introduced her to the public.

Since that time, her gift of song has won her many appreciative friends among the literati of our country, but she looks back with grateful remembrance to the one who caught the first, faint, trembling notes of her lyre.

After the discontinuance of "The South," "Pearl Rivers" contributed to the "New Orleans Sunday Times," and now contributes to the "Picayune," "New York Home Journal," and other journals.

A lady who knows her, says, "She always carries her scrap-book and pencil with her, and writes at all times."

She is one of Nature's sweetest poets, and as pure-hearted as the blue river from which she takes her name — a wild-wood warbler, knowing how to sing of birds and flowers and flowing brooks, and all things beautiful.

If "Pearl Rivers" lives, her poetical talent must increase in lustre and value as the years roll by.

A CHIRP FROM MOTHER ROBIN.

See yon little Mother Robin,
Sitting on her humble nest:
Learn from her my poem-lesson;
Nature's teachers are the best.

Other nests are lined more softly—
Larger nests than hers she sees;
Other nests are swinging higher
In the summer's gentle breeze;—

But the Robin is contented;
Mine is warm enough, she says—
Large enough to hold my birdies
Through their tender nesting-days.

Smaller cradle, warmer cover!
For my little ones, she sings;
Four there are, but see how snugly
They are tucked beneath my wings.

And I envy not my neighbors,
Redbird, Bluebird, Lark, or Thrush;
For the breeze that rocks the tree-tops
Rocks my cradle in the bush.

And the same bright sunshine warms me—
By the same kind hand I'm fed;
With the same green earth around me,
And the same sky overhead.

Though my dress is something plainer
Than my cousin's, Madame Red;
Though I have no vest of crimson,
And no gay hood on my head;—

Still, my robe of graver colors
Suits my station and my nest;
And the Master knows what costume
Would become a Robin best.

THE ROYAL CAVALCADE.

Spring is coming, Spring is coming,
  Through the arch of Pleasant Days,
With the harps of all her minstrels
  Tuned to warble forth her praise.

In her rosy car of Pleasure,
  Drawn by nimble-footed Hours,
With a royal guard of Sunbeams,
  And a host of white-plumed Flowers,

From the busy Court of Nature
  Rides the fair young Queen in state,
O'er the road of Perfect Weather,
  Leading down to Summer Gate.

Brave old March rides proudly forward,
  With her heralds, Wind and Rain;
He will plant her standard firmly
  On King Winter's bleak domain.

Young Lord Zephyr fans her gently,
  And Sir Dewdrop's diamonds shine;
Lady May and Lady April
  By her Majesty recline.

Lady April's face is tearful,
  And she pouts and frets the while;
But her lips will part with laughter
  Ere she rides another mile.

Lady May is blushing deeply,
  As she fits her rosy gloves;
She is dreaming of the meeting
  With her waiting Poet-loves.

Over meadow, hill and valley
  Winds the Royal Cavalcade,
And, behind, green leaves are springing
  In the tracks the car-wheels made.

And her Majesty rides slowly
  Through the humble State of Grass,

Speaking kindly to the Peasants
  As they crowd to see her pass.

In the corners of the fences
  Hide the little Daisy-spies,
Peeping shyly through the bushes,
  Full of childish, glad surprise;

And her gentle Maids of Honor,
  Modest Violets, are seen
In their gala-dresses waiting,
  By the road-side, for their Queen.

By her own bright light of Beauty
  Does she travel through the day;
And at night her Glowworm Footmen
  With their lanterns guide the way.

She is coming, nearer! nearer!
  Hark the sound of chariot-wheels!
Fly to welcome her, young minstrel,
  Sing the joy your spirit feels.

The "Royal Funeral," which has never been printed, is a fitting companion to the "Royal Cavalcade."

THE ROYAL FUNERAL.

THE BODY OF THE QUEEN LYING IN STATE.

There is mourning through the valleys,
  There is mourning on the hills,
And I hear a broken music
  In the voice of all the rills.

Spring, the fairest of the seasons —
  Spring, the Virgin Queen, is dead,
And a younger, browner sister
  Reigns upon her throne instead.

Royal June, with rosy fingers,
  Softly closed her violet eyes,
And within the Court of Nature
  Now in costly state she lies.

And the young Lord Zephyr, sighing,
  Yields his life upon her bier,
And the diamonds of Sir Dewdrop
  Melt away into a tear.

Brave old March, her veteran soldier,
  Covered with a tattered fold
Of the banner borne so proudly,
  Lies beside her, dead and cold.

And October, bold usurper!
  (Now his arm has feeble grown;)
On Her Majesty's dominion
  Reaps the harvest he has sown.

Fair, capricious Lady April
  Sleepeth deep and calmly nigh;
Round her lip a smile still lingers,
  Still a tear within her eye.

On a bier of withered roses
  Lies the tender Lady May,
While her constant loves, the Poets,
  Royal honors to her pay.

Low and reverently kneeling,
  Round her lovely form they throng,
And embalm her precious beauty
  With the costly myrrh of song.

Unto each she left a token,
  As a dying pledge of love:
One she gave her azure girdle;
  One she gave her rosy glove;

One she gave her silver sandals,
  Rich with shining gems of dew;
O'er the shoulders of another
  She her precious mantle threw.

But to me, the humble singer,
  Leaning on my harp, apart
From the crowd of Royal Poets,
  She has left a broken heart.

THE PROCESSION.

Hark! I hear a Voice proclaiming,
  Mournfully, Bring forth your dead!
And through Nature's holy Temple
  Has the solemn summons sped.

With the incense of her Glory
  Burning low and sweet and dim,
And the harps of all her minstrels
  Tuned to chant a funeral hymn:

In a robe of fragrance shrouded
  By the spirits of the Flowers;
In a sable hearse of sorrow,
  Drawn by weary-footed Hours:

From the silent Court of Nature
  Comes the fair, dead Queen in state,
O'er the road of Gloomy Weather,
  Leading down to Winter Gate.

Through the Summer Land they bear her,
  By a quiet, sunny way —
Through the golden Autumn Country
  To the Regions of Decay.

Over meadow, hill, and valley
  Winds the Royal Funeral,
And my spirit hears the pealing
  Of a solemn funeral knell.

She is coming nearer, nearer;
  Hark! that mournful, mournful strain;
Fly to honor her, young minstrel,
  Joining in the funeral train.

FLORIDA.

MARY E. BRYAN.

THERE is not a name among the literary stars of the "Southland" that fills a warmer place in every heart than that of Mary E. Bryan. Tastes differ about literature as about everything else; but there are somethings which challenge the universal admiration of mankind: some faces — some forms — as the "Venus de Medicis" and the "Apollo Belvidere" — and some books, although the latter are most rare. Mrs. Bryan comes as near filling this exclusive niche in the gallery of letters as any *woman of her age* who ever wrote. She does not dazzle, like the fitful light of the "Borealis race," nor sparkle like sunset on a summer sea — neither does she charm us by the smoothness and polish of her style; but she manages to creep into the hearts of her readers, as few young writers have ever done. This comes of her own earnestness — that deep, thrilling earnestness which marks all her writings, and especially her poetry. There her thoughts well up fresh and warm from the depths of a passionate heart, and never fail to meet a responsive throb in the hearts of her readers.

"Bryan — hers the words that glisten,
  Opal gems of sunlit rain!
So much the woman, you may listen
  Heart-beats pulsing in her brain!
She upon her songs has won
  Hybla's honey undistilled;
And 'from wine-vats of the sun,'
With bright nectar overrun,
  Her urns of eloquence are filled!" *

She is a poetess by nature. Largely endowed with that sense of the beautiful, which Poe called "an immortal instinct deep within the

* Mrs. L. Virginia French.

spirit of man," she gives us glimpses of the loveliness which lies beyond the common sight, and "whose very elements, perhaps, appertain to eternity alone."

Mrs. Bryan has taken no care of her literary fame; she has been at no pains whatever to extend it. She has scattered the brilliant productions of her intellect hither and thither among the periodicals of the South, as a tree flings its superabundant blossoms to the breeze; and she has taken no thought of them afterward. Whatever she writes, she finishes with care, being led to do so out of respect and love for her profession; but when written and sent to the press, it is forgotten — scarcely even being read over by her after its publication. To one who has studied her closely, the reason of this is obvious. Mrs. Bryan possesses true genius — hers is the real artist-feeling, which judges of the attained by the attempted; and nobly as she writes, she has written nothing to satisfy her own high-placed ideal — nothing that seems "worthy of her hope and aim more highly mated."

Mrs. Bryan is a native of Florida — daughter of Major John D. Edwards, an early settler of that State, and among the first and most honored members of its Legislature. Both on the paternal and maternal sides, she belongs to excellent and honorable families. Her mother, whose maiden name was Houghton, was herself an accomplished and talented lady. She lived in retirement, devoting her time principally to the education of her daughter. Mrs. Edwards was a charming woman and model mother. She made herself the companion of her daughters, (three in number,) won their confidence by her forbearing gentleness, and sympathy with their little cares, thoughts, and aspirations. She was never too much engaged to answer their inquiries, or give them any information they desired. Mary's mind opened early — too early, perhaps, for a cheerful and healthy youth. While other children played with their dolls, she roamed through the beautiful solitudes around her home, or wandered alone on the shores of the beautiful Gulf, where her parents were accustomed to spend their summers — her mind filled with dreams and yearnings that bewildered her by their vagueness. She discovered in part what these yearnings meant, when, at the age of ten years, she was sent on a visit to her aunt, Mrs. Julia McBride, so well known in Florida for her piety and philanthropy. The family of this aunt (her husband and a noble group of grown-up sons and daughters) lay at rest in the church-yard on a neighboring hill; and but for the occasional companionship of her brother, the lady lived alone. Mary could wander at will in her poetic reveries through the groves of orange and crape myrtle that embowered "Salubrity," and through the wide old gardens, scattered over with half ruined summer-houses, and enclosed by palings hung with the Multiflora and Cherokee Rose. She was never lonely; for, as she has written since:

"The poet never is alone;
The stars, the breeze, the flowers,
All lovely things, his kindred are
And charm his loneliest hours."

But this insensate companionship did not satisfy. She longed for more intelligent teachers, with a vague yearning, which she did not comprehend, until one day she chanced to gain access to the library of her uncle — Col. R. B. Houghton — who was absent on professional duties. It was the opening of a fairy world to the imaginative mind of the child. In that shadowy, green-curtained library-room, with the orange-branches brushing against the window-panes, she entered upon a new life. Her reading had been hitherto confined to her text-books, and now she revelled in the poetry of the masters, and in romances of another age. Much of what she read she understood through her mind's early development, no less than through the intuition of genius; and what her young reason could not fathom was absorbed by feeling and imagination, as one catches the tune of a song, though it is sung too far off for the words to be understood.

She read as a gifted child would do — losing her own personality in that of the characters delineated, feeling every emotion as though it were a personal experience, thrilling over deeds of heroism, shuddering over those of crime, burning with indignation as she read of cruelty and injustice, and weeping passionately over the pictures of wrong and suffering and undeserved doom. She mused and dreamed continually over the revelations thus suddenly opened to her. None guessed what influences were moulding the mind of the precocious child.

Could they not read the secret in her dreamy eyes and abstracted manner?

Her uncle did so when he returned home, and he closed his library-doors resolutely against the little, pale, wistful face.

Years after, in the prime of her womanhood, she declared to him* that those hours of stolen communion with the "spirits of the library" were more a blessing than a bane. Perhaps they were — perhaps it was to these she owed the early maturity of her mind and the variety of her style.

At eleven years old, she was sent to a boarding-school in Thomasville, Georgia. Here the shy little recluse, who had been at home among the "stately-stepping fancies" conjured up from the pages of romance and history, experienced a shrinking timidity when brought into intimate contact with girls of her own age. To her surprise she found herself far in advance of these in her studies — so efficient had been her mother's teaching, so ready her own receptive powers. She was placed in a class of young ladies, and, says Col. Houghton:

> "I remember to have seen her during an examination of the school — a slender little figure at the head of the class of grown-up girls, her pale face lit up resplendently by dark, earnest eyes, as she repeated page after page of intellectual philosophy, or musically rendered the Eclogues of Virgil. She was a special object of interest and curiosity to most of the audience there assembled, for she was known to be a religious enthusiast. A 'revival' had not long before 'converted' a majority of the girls of the boarding-school: many of them had 'backslided,' some still held to the faith in a quiet, commonplace way; only this one, prone to extremes through her ardent, impulsive nature, became a fanatic, refraining from joining in the sports and pastimes of her playmates, refusing to answer a question positively lest there might be room for a doubt, giving all her pocket-money to the poor children of the school, and (greatest sacrifice of all, to one whose love for the beautiful made her delight in bright colors and lovely apparel) rejecting the pretty garments sent her from home, and appearing, in the midst of her gayly-dressed class, in a plain, faded frock.
>
> "Her composition upon this occasion had for its theme, 'The Shadows and Sunshine of Life.' I have before me, now, a mental picture of that rapt, young face — so child-like in its contour, so old in the expression of the large thoughtful eyes, that were lighted with enthusiasm as she concluded with a brief but glowing vision of the 'land beyond the vale of shadows and fleeting sunshine.'"

This fanatical tendency, peculiarly strange in so young a child,

* We are indebted for many facts in this sketch to Col. R. B. Houghton, of Florida, formerly well known as an accomplished writer and eloquent public speaker. He has known Mrs. Bryan from her earliest youth, and by his example first gave a literary turn to her mind, that, in fertility of imagination and ease of expression, bears a considerable resemblance to his own.

greatly troubled Mary's parents, who were proud of her brilliant talents. It must have been a deep impression, for, gentle and yielding as her nature was, easily influenced by those she loved, and most sensitive to ridicule, it yet resisted entreaties, expostulation, and ridicule. In time it wore away.

"Only once," says Col. Houghton, "did she speak to me of this period of her life. 'It contained,' she said, 'agonies, that I could not again bear and live. For the least venial sin — real or imagined — I was visited by pangs of remorse. Often have I passed whole nights on my knees in prayer, unconscious of cold or fatigue in the more acute mental anguish I endured. Yet, after the long wrestle, the agonizing doubt and despair, there would come a wonderful reaction, and I would experience moments of ecstasy indescribable. I cannot understand it. It is a mystery to my maturer years.'"

Mary was then only twelve years old. A short time afterward her parents removed to Thomasville, for the purpose of educating their daughters, and made for themselves a suburban home, beautiful with vineyards, gardens, and orchards. In the years that followed, Mary wrote, and published in a Thomasville paper, poems, and a story that ran through several numbers of the paper. She was still a school-girl, hardly sixteen, when her friends were surprised to hear that she was married — married to the son of a Louisiana planter. Her marriage was as unexpected to her as it was to her friends and relatives. An hour before she took upon herself the irrevocable vows, she was sitting, school-girl fashion, on the rug before the fire in her own room, quietly studying her Latin lesson. Two hours afterward, she had bidden adieu to her girlish pursuits, to her parents, sisters, and friends, and was on her way to her husband's home on the banks of Red River. During the first year of her marriage she passed through some bitter experiences — experiences which one so young, so sensitive, and so ignorant of life, was illy prepared to meet. At the end of a year, she was visited by her father, who thought best that she should accompany him back to her old home. Of the partial separation that ensued, (partial, because she was constantly visited by her husband, who was devoted to her, and no estrangement ever existed between them,) it is not necessary to say any more than that it was deemed advisable by her father, a just man as well as an affectionate parent. There were peculiar circumstances which, in his opinion and that of her friends, made it judicious for her to postpone a return to her husband's home in Louisiana.

To divert her mind from painful thought, her father advised a renewal of her studies, with a view to completing her education; and she turned to her old text-books — sadly and listlessly at first, afterward with new energy and zeal for knowledge. She now resumed her writing for the press, and became a regular contributor to several periodicals. Among these was the "Literary Crusader," published by Mr. John Seals, at Penfield, Georgia. After writing for this paper for two years, it was removed to Atlanta, greatly enlarged and improved, and she was solicited to take part in its editorial management. She accepted the offer, went to Atlanta, and entered upon her new duties with the ardor and energy which are her distinguishing traits. She succeeded in giving to the "Crusader" an individuality it *had* not before possessed, and in making it widely and popularly known, not only throughout the South, but in the Middle and Northern States.

During the year in which she edited the "Crusader" in Atlanta, I believe that Mrs. Bryan performed more literary work and of a more varied character than any female of her age (twenty years) ever accomplished in the same length of time. The expenses of removing the "Crusader" to Atlanta, of purchasing new type and press, etc., were *so great* that the proprietor did not *consider that his finances justified his paying for contributions;* still he wished to make his paper interesting and to have it contain a variety of original reading-matter. Mrs. Bryan was equal to this emergency. She determined to the best of her ability to supply the place of contributors. She called in play for the first time her remarkable versatility, her power of changing her style "from grave to gay, from lively to severe," and she filled a page of the "Crusader" every week with the required variety of original reading-matter from her own pen. Every number contained one or more columns of "editorial" upon subjects of present interest. Then a group of sparkling paragraphs, local or critical — essays, thoughtful or humorous, and sometimes scintillating with wit — a poem — a sketch or story, and often one or more chapters of a serial tale.

In addition to the weekly task of filling so many columns of a large literary paper, and also to the trouble of proof-reading, selecting, and other duties connected with her office, Mrs. Bryan found time to pursue, at intervals, the course of reading and study she had marked out for herself. But she did so by encroaching largely upon the hours allotted to rest. Even the Sabbath was no day of relaxation, since it brought its own duties, in the care of her Bible class, of her younger band of Sunday-school scholars, and in an unfailing attendance upon divine service in the Methodist church, of which she was a faithful member.

In November of this year, she was invited to read a poem at the Commencement of College Temple, Newnan, Georgia. Her poem was an eloquent delineation of true womanhood — its sphere, its mission, and its aspirations; and it was read in her own rich, magnetic voice. After she had taken her seat, she was recalled and complimented with a diploma from the president of the college.

Before the close of the year, Mrs. Bryan felt that the unremitting toil was telling upon her health. She needed rest, and returned home, determined to write less than she had been doing. Several propositions were made for her services the next year. She accepted the offer of Col. James Gardner, proprietor of the "Field and Fireside," as being not only most liberal in salary, but most generous in its privileges. He expressly insisted that she should rest, should write at her leisure, and write with care and correction. How well she followed the latter suggestion, was shown in her first contributions to the "Field and Fireside," the noble essay, "How should Women Write," the pathetic sketch, "Cutting Robbie's Hair," and the fine poem, "The Hour when we shall Meet." (The sketch and poem are to be found in Mary Forrest's "Distinguished Women of the South.") She contributed novelettes, stories, essays, and poems. About this time she decided to return with her husband to Louisiana, and we next find her in her own quiet home, isolated from literary society, from the stimulus of applause and encouragement, and from those influences which quicken the energies and sharpen the mental faculties. Notwithstanding this, she completed her engagement with the "Field and Fireside," and entered upon a new year, beginning it with the initial chapters of "Haywood Lodge." This is a beau-ideal of a novel — "a striking fiction." The characters are as distinctly and as graphically drawn as any in "Adam Bede," or "Mill on the Floss." The scenes are sprightly and lifelike, and the plot one of intense interest. Mrs. Bryan promised a sequel to this novel — a second volume, so to speak — which has been from time to time demanded by the public, but is not yet forthcoming.

When she commenced her second engagement with the "Field and Fireside," it was at the commencement of the late war. Her husband enlisted in the service of his country, and to Mrs. Bryan was left the superintendence of the household and plantation. With these domestic duties she had little leisure for writing, yet she wrote a series of articles, vigorous in style and caustic in their satire, denouncing and exposing the system of extortion, speculation, and fraud which was undermining the Southern interest. These articles appeared in the parish paper, having a local circulation only.

When the war ended, Mr. Bryan had only honorable scars and comparative poverty. In order to contribute her mite toward rebuilding their fallen fortunes, Mrs. Bryan accepted the editorship of the "Semi-weekly Times," published in Natchitoches. She removed temporarily to Natchitoches for the purpose of superintending the paper in person, and entered upon the work with her accustomed energy and earnestness. She was now required to try her versatile powers in a direction in which they had never essayed. The "Times" was a political paper, and Mrs. Bryan's leading articles were required by its proprietor to be discussions of the grave political questions agitating the public mind. This was by no means a congenial task, but none would have guessed it from reading the bold and vigorous "leaders" which appeared twice a week in the columns of the "Times," or the pungent paragraphs, the witty and satirical comments upon contemporary opinions, or upon the ludicrous aspect of "African sovereignty."

Her work was attended by the most disheartening drawbacks. She wrote under the disadvantages of ill health, of sickness in her family, and of the necessity of devoting much of her time to the care of three young children — the eldest only five years old. In spite of these adverse circumstances, she furnished to the "Times," twice a week, not only the required columns of "editorial" and editorial paragraphs, but one or more essays, and usually a sketch, a story, or a poem.

Mrs. Bryan's stay in Natchitoches was one of misfortune, and it was terminated by an affliction — the most bitter she had ever been called upon to endure — the long, painful illness and death of her youngest child — her baby, her darling. The little sufferer (who had been a bright and beautiful boy) was suddenly and mysteriously afflicted, and lay for many weeks in the "death in life" of paralysis. It was during one of her anguished watches by that bed of silent suffering that Mrs. Bryan wrote the poem which she has called "Miserere." During the illness of her child, Mrs. Bryan exerted herself to continue her editorial duties — writing while the little one slept in her lap, or upon the bed, beside which she kept her unremitting watch; but when the little coffin was carried out from the room, and she sat down with aching heart to supply the remorseless demand for "copy," she found it impossible to collect her thoughts. The reaction had come; the long strain upon her feelings and energies showed its effects, and all she wrote was a brief adieu to the patrons of the paper.

She returned to her plantation home, but continued to contribute to the "Times." In 1868, she went on a visit to her relatives in Florida, and while there formed an engagement with "Scott's Magazine," (Atlanta.) In this magazine she published a novel, entitled "The Mystery of Cedar Bay," which will appear probably in book-form. This serial is original and thrillingly interesting.

It is difficult to convey an adequate idea of Mrs. Bryan's powers by means of extracts, owing to the variety of style. Ease and grace characterize her lighter compositions, force and vigor distinguish her graver productions.

Mrs. Bryan has frequently been called "the most gifted female writer which the South has produced." She is certainly the most versatile. It is in her power to make herself the most widely known. To do this, she must show more appreciation of her own powers — she must concentrate her energies upon some *one* work.

ANACREON.

Yon sea-like slope of darkening pines
  Is surging with the tempest's power,
And not one star of promise shines
  Upon the twilight hour;
With wailing sounds the blast is rife,
  And wilder yet the echoes roll
Up from the scenes where want and strife
  Convulse the human soul.
'T is madness rules the fateful hour;
Let me forget its fearful power;
Drop low the curtains of my room,
And in the green and purple gloom
Lose sight of angry men and stormy skies,
Gazing, Anacreon, on thy splendid eyes.

My grand old Greek! far back in time
  Thy glorious birth-hour lies;
Thy shade has heard the tread sublime
  Of passing centuries.
And yet the soul that thrilled thy lyre
  Has power to charm us still,
And with its vivid light and fire
  Our duller spirits fill.
Breathe on me, spirit rare and fine,
Buoyant with energy divine:
The light and joy of other days
Live in those blue eyes' dazzling rays;
They lift my soul from its confining cage,
The barriers of this dull and sordid age.

I dream I am a girl of Greece,
  With pliant shape and foam-white arms,
And locks that fall in bright release
  To veil my bosom's charms.
The skies of Greece above me bend—
  The Ægean winds are in my hair;
I hear gay songs, and shoutings send
  Their music on the air.
I see a bright procession pass—
The girls throw garlands on the grass—
And, crowned with myrtle and with bay,
I see thee pass that flowery way,
While swim before me smiling fields and skies,
Dimmed by a glance of thy resplendent eyes.

Prince of the Lyre! thy locks are white
  As Blanc's untrodden snow;
But, quenchless in their fire and light,
  Thy blue eye beams below,
And well the myrtle gleams among
  Thy bays, like stars of truth;
The poet's soul is ever young—
  His is immortal youth.
He dwells within that border-land
Where innocence and passion stand—
Ardent, yet pure, clasped hand in hand—
And years but add a richer grace,
A higher charm to mind and face,
While youth and beauty that his dreams eclipse,
Bend to the magic of his eyes and lips.

Oh! heart of love and soul of fire!
  My spirit bows to thee;
Type of the ideals that inspire
  My dreams eternally,
I'd be a slave to such as thou,
  And deem myself a queen,
If sometimes to my kneeling brow
  Those perfect lips might lean.
High hopes and aims within my breast
Would spring from their despairing rest,
And the wild energies that sleep
Like prisoned genii might out leap,
And bid my name among th' immortal shine,
If *fame*, to me, could mean such love as thine.

MISERERE.

Alone with night and silence, and those strange,
Those bright, unseeing, sleepless eyes, whose depth
I have searched vainly, weary days and nights,
For some sweet gleam of consciousness, some ray
Of tender recognition to break forth —
Sudden and starlike — from the vacant cloud.
It does not come; the sweet soul that looked forth
From those deep eyes wanders mysteriously
In some dim land that borders upon death,
And I sit watching, after many days,
With the tears dried upon my pallid cheeks,
Their fountains dried within my hopeless heart,
Waiting for death to make me desolate.

The roses of a lovely May breathe out
Their souls of fragrance underneath the moon;
The wind comes down from the wild grove of pines,
Vocal with wordless mysteries; I see
Its fingers toying with yon delicate leaves,
Touched with faint silver by the midnight moon;
I see the dew-gleam on the tender grass,
The thousand starry sentinels that watch
Upon the battlements of heaven; I see
All these, as if I saw not; for those eyes
Haunt me forever, turn upon me still,
Through the blank darkness made by clasping hands,

By blinding tears, and clouds of falling hair,
As with bowed head I strive to shut the sight
From the o'ertortured sense.

Oh! what to me
Is it how many flowers the May shall blow
Into young bloom with her sweet breath, since I
Must lay mine low beneath the chilly sod,
And watch the grass grow green between my heart
And the sweet face I cradled on my breast?
What is it to me how many singing larks
The morn may send to gild their soaring wings
With the unrisen sun? the voice that was
The sweetest under heaven to me is still!
I would not turn from the pale lips, whereon
Cruel paralysis — that death in life —
Has laid his numbing seal, to list the strains
The sirens sang across the classic seas.

My child, my child! my beautiful, bright boy!
In whose large eyes I dreamed that genius slept;
For whose broad brow my fancy twined the bays
That I had ceased to strive for; my fair flower,
That came when life seemed the most desolate,
And shed a brightness round its lonely waste,
And weaned the heart from the wild love of death,
And rest, and deep forgetfulness; thy lip,
Ere it could speak, quivered in sympathy
With my hot tears that fell upon thy face;
Thy baby hand lay softly on my heart
Like a charmed flower, and soothed its wild unrest.
What hopes have I not built for thee? what dreams
Of future greatness has my fancy reared,
Kneeling beside thy cradle, stroking back
The locks from thy broad temples?

Well I knew
That *my* own life had failed; that the bright hopes
And untamed aspirations of my youth,
Met by the storm of fate, had drooped their wing,
And fallen back, cold and dying, to the heart
That was their nest. Alas! I felt the cord
Of iron circumstance upon my life,
And knew that woman's sorrowful fate was mine;
That the wild energies that thrilled my being

Must throb themselves to silence; that with me
Ambition must mean only grief; but thou,
No robes of womanhood could trip thy steps
Upon the mountain-paths of fame, my child;
Thou couldst be free and fearless; thou mightst win
The goal I could not touch; mightst boldly speak
The truths I dared not utter.

Ay, I dreamed
Thy voice might thrill the great soul of the world;
And strong for truth, and brave for truth, might lead,
With clarion peal, the march of Right, and bid
Hoary Oppression tremble on his throne —
And Wrong, and Bigotry, and Hatred quail
Before its fearless utterance; that should drown
The hiss of malice, and the carping cry
Of Envy and weak Fear.

So I have dreamed,
When hope and love beat time within my breast,
And ideal visions passed with prophecies
In their deep eyes. Yet more; when I beheld
The fair land of my love laid low, and made
A land of graves and woful memories —
A slaved and conquered land, that scarcely dares
To quiver underneath th' oppressor's heel —
I did not weep; for what avail were tears,
E'en from the depths of a "divine despair,"
Before such wrong, such woe, such wretchedness,
Such desolation? So I did not weep.
A woman's tears fit only to keep warm
And moist the sod of graves; I only knelt,
With beating heart and burning cheek, above
The fair child of my hopes, and thought to breathe
And mould into his unformed being my own
Deep love, and pity, and devotedness,
And passionate sense of wrong. In time, they might
Produce the fruits I should not see: the soul
That looked forth radiantly from the clear eyes,
The hand that lay so flower-like within mine,
Might aid to win his land's deliverance,
And break the thraldom his free soul would scorn.

Alas! to-night how vain and wild they seem —
Those earthly visions — those proud hopes and dreams —;

For thee, my darling, lying like a flower,
The flames have scathed in passing, and have left
Blighted and dying, — vain and wild they seem,
As kneeling thus, I hold in mine that hand
My fancy clothed with manhood's strength and grace,
Now pale and paralyzed, while the bright mind
That was my joy and pride, alas! they say,
It will not shine again in the sweet face,
And give its radiance to the eyes I loved;
That e'en if life creeps back, and the fell fiend
Of fever quits his victim, that the mind
Will never more leap from the eyes in light,
But stay within its cell, the brain, a dim
And dreaming prisoner.
Oh! I dare not dwell
Upon the thought; better for thee and me
Were death, my darling; better this dear head
Were lain beneath the shadows of the pines
That oversweep yon City of the Dead.
And thus I give thee up, my child, my life,
To the great God who lent thee. Go, and be
Tended by angels in the land where pain
Comes not to rack the brain; from angel lips
Of loveliest music, angel eyes and brows,
Divinely calm with *love*, and bright with thought,
Learn the deep lore of heaven, and forget
The brief and pain-fraught life that only saw
The roses of one summer fade away.

BY THE SEA.

Once more, once more
Beneath the golden skies I loved so well,
Listening once more to the blue billows' swell
Upon the sandy shore —
The blue, bright waves, that in the sunlight shine
Through vistas of the feathery palm and pine.

Land of my love, once more
Thy beauty is around me: on my brow
Thy pine-trees fling their shifting shadows now,
And when the day-beams pour

Across the cloud, my steed's swift gallop shakes
The scarlet berries in thy lonely brakes.

And when the noon is high,
I see the yellowing lime and orange swinging
On branches where the wild bird's notes are ringing,
While all neglected lie
The purple figs dropped in the plumy grass,
The wild grapes hanging where cool waters pass.

And when the planets burn,
The fairest of the long-haired Naiad daughters
Holds upward, through her lake's pellucid waters,
The water-lily's urn,
And floats its broad, green leaf upon the tide,
To form an isle, where fairies might abide.

Yet strange to me they seem —
These glories of my native tropic clime;
No more its silver-flowing waters rhyme
With my own spirit's dream.
The charm has vanished, broken is the spell;
And in the woods and in the hollow dell
Strange echoes seem to shape the word farewell.

I would rebind the spell
About my brow; fling off the chain of years.
Say, what should check me? Why should time and tears
The *spirit* sear or quell?
Snatch me a wreath from yonder blooming vine!
Here let me lie, where morning-glories twine,
And round me call my olden dreams divine.

Vain! vain! the broken spell
Can never be renewed; the vanished charm
I 've vainly sought — in jessamines breathing warm;
In the magnolia's bell;
In deep ravines, where mystic waters pour
Through the cleft earth, and reappear no more.

But yesternight I stole
Down to the sea — down to the lonely sea,
Where but the starlight shone mysteriously;
And *there*, my listening soul
Heard, through the silence, every solemn wave
Speak, in deep, mournful whispers of *a grave*.

And now I know that here,
Even here — across the glory and the bloom —
There falls the shadow of that little tomb —
The grave they made last year,
Hiding beneath the sodden earth forlorn
The flower of love, my desolate life had borne.

Oh! not for me, for me,
Does the pale Naiad hold her lily-urn,
And not for me the starry jessamines burn;
Only the dreary sea
Brings *me* a message — on each solemn wave
Bearing the mournful story of a grave.

THE FATAL BRACELET.

It wanted a half-hour to midnight. The marriage ceremony had long been over, and the bride had been gayest among her guests. There was a pause in the dance just now. Vane had gone below — called down upon some business that would not wait even for bridal festivities. Flushed and sparkling, Coralyn stood at a retired window beside her partner, resting from the exercise of the dance. The night was warm, and her companion proffered to go for a glass of iced water. When he had quitted her side, she leaned from the window, drinking in the fresh air, whose balm cooled the hot glow upon her cheeks, and quieted the feverish unrest of her heart. She did not hear a stealthy step approach her; she had no warning of the proximity of danger, until a voice said in her ear: "I am late with my congratulations for such an old friend."

She turned instantly, and confronted him face to face. It was he! He was not dead. It was the dark, handsome face of the picture — darker and more sinister than ever. Had the earth opened at her feet, she could not have been more stunned, more stupefied — could not have grown whiter, or felt her brain reel with more deadly sickness.

"Do not faint!" he whispered, with a scornful smile half defined on his full lips. "What would be thought?"

The necessity for self-control brought back consciousness and strength. She glanced around — she was not observed.

"I thought — " she faltered.

"That I was dead. Very distressing thought, no doubt, to you. Happy to relieve your mind by affording you ocular proof of my existence. Probably, you thought that death alone should have kept me away from your arms. Really, you must blame the importunities of friends, which it was out of my power to resist. They kindly obliged me to accept the privilege of their residence and the society of their select guests, and insisted so strenuously upon my partaking of their hospitality for the term of my natural life, that it was only by stratagem and the devil's help that I at last got rid of the burden of their excessive kindness. See; I have brought away a token of their affection." And the escaped convict unfastened his jewelled sleeve-button, and rolling back his sleeve a little way, showed the deep scars of handcuffs on his wrist. He smiled as he saw her shudder. Then, as he quietly buttoned his cuff again, the partner of Coralyn returned with the glass of water. She would have sprung forward eagerly to his side, but a glance from the eyes she feared, restrained her. The dark stranger stepped gracefully forward.

"Permit me," he said, taking the glass from the gentleman with bland politeness, and placing it in her hand.

It would have fallen from her cold fingers, but he held it, while she drained the last crystal drop. The glass was returned to the gentleman. He was her husband's dearest friend. He would have remained by her side, had he seen or interpreted the mute, imploring look she cast upon him. He did not see it. He turned away, and left her with the man, whose easy familiarity seemed to betoken him an old friend.

She cast her eyes over the crowd — fearing and yet blindly wishing to see her husband's tall figure, and meet his eyes in search of her. Yet how could he help her? What would she dare to say to him? If he knew all, would he not fling her from him in horror? Oh! what should she do? what would become of her? Why had she ever deceived him and yielded to the temptation of securing herself within the safe, sweet shelter of home and love? What right had she to home or love? — she — she — she dared not whisper it to herself. It was horrible — horrible! True, she had been so young, so utterly ignorant; and then that cruel, terrible Margery — and her son — the fiendish being who stood now gloating upon her beauty and her terror. Could it be she had ever loved him — had trembled and blushed when he spoke to her — had watched him (the first young man she had ever seen) with a fearful, fascinated gaze, and a feeling of mingled abhorrence and admiration?

Why had he come here to-night? What would he dare to tell of her past life, when it must involve an exposure of himself — he, the escaped felon, doubtless with a price upon his head? Did he read the rapid thoughts that rushed through her brain? He stood there, watching her with folded arms, and a smile on his lips. His eyes drank in her beauty, and burned upon her with the blended fire of love and hate. The band began playing a waltz — the dancers gathered upon the floor. "Let us waltz," he said suddenly, proffering his hand. She made an involuntary gesture of loathing, and her lips syllabled a refusal. His dark brow grew blacker as he saw the abhorrence she could not conceal. His eyes flashed luridly; he bent down and whispered a word in her ear. She grew livid to the lips; her eyes fell, her hands dropped at her side. He watched her with his shining, serpent eyes and half-formed smile.

"Shall we waltz now?" he asked gayly; and passing his arm around her waist, they floated into the centre of the room among the dancers.

The music was at first slow and soft. As they swam through its languid mazes, he kept his basilisk eyes fixed upon her.

"You wear my gift," he said, tightening his grasp upon her wrist that was circled by the coiled serpent.

"Yours?" she uttered. "Nurse Margery's —"

"No; mine. The note was only a ruse to make sure of your wearing the bracelet. Margery is dead."

"Dead?"

"Dead — starved to death in a gutter, thanks to the gratitude of her foster-child." He hissed out the words between his teeth. His lips parted, and the white, carnivorous teeth shone beneath the black moustache like the teeth of a wild beast.

"Her foster-child," he continued, "that she fed when a pauper, and who, when her heirship was discovered, drove her off to starve."

"Not I, not I — it was my aunt. God forgive me, I had not courage —"

"Hush speaking of God. What is God to us? My mother will not forgive. She will torture you for it in the regions of the damned."

She cowered under the dark words and the threatening brow and eyes. What a mockery it was to be whirling round to the quickening music, flower-crowned and festally arrayed, while her spirit shrank within her through terrible shame, and her brain reeled with dizzy torture.

"And you?" she found voice to say; "why are you here to-night?"

"To crush a worm that has dared to sting me. Ha! did you think I could be deceived and trifled with, without my revenge?"

As he spoke, bending his lips so close to hers that the fiery breath was on her cheek, he grasped the serpent-bound arm so tightly, that she uttered a faint exclamation. It was drowned by the music, that now rose wilder and faster, while the dancers whirled in rapid circles over the floor, that shook with the beating of their feet.

"Scream," he whispered; "draw the crowd around you. I will then have a fine opportunity of explaining old matters."

"Have mercy," she moaned, as he whirled her relentlessly around. "Loose your grasp upon my arm. The bracelet is piercing my flesh. I am suffering intensely."

"It is the cobra's tooth," he answered, with the malignant smile of a fiend. "The bracelet is bewitched. My touch endues it with life and venom. Its head is lifted no longer; the blow is struck; the fangs are in your flesh."

"O God! I am ill. I am in terrible pain! in mercy let me stop!"

But round and round he whirled her — supporting her slender figure almost wholly by his muscular arm.

"Spare me! spare me!" she groaned. "In mercy, in mercy!"

"Did you think of mercy when you broke your faith with me?—taught yourself to scorn and hate me; drove my old mother, who had nursed you, from your presence, and deceived an honorable man into taking you as his wife—*you*, a wife! ha! ha! impostor! I would have found my sweetest revenge by exposing all—holding you up to his scorn and the contempt of the world you love so well; but I look to my own safety. I am not ready to swing just yet, or to go back to that devil's hole of punishment. I have taken a safer mode to secure my revenge."

"O God! I suffer, I suffer!"

Her head fell back heavily against him.

"Water!" he cried, "a lady has fainted."

"She has fainted! the bride has fainted!" repeated a score of voices, and the throng pressed around her in helpless bewilderment.

Vane heard the words, as he came bounding up the steps.

He strode into the room. The crowd made way as he came. He took her into his arms. He flung back the rich hair until it swept rippling to the floor. He called her by all the sweet, endearing names of love, as he applied one restorative after another. But there came no sign of life. The lips were closely crushed together, and lurid circles were darkening under the eyes.

"A physician!" he cried huskily. One stood beside him now—holding the slender wrist, which the serpent bracelet no longer clasped. He knelt down and examined her attentively. He was a man of science and experience—long a sojourner in Eastern lands.

"It is death," he said solemnly.

Vane was speechless. They took her from him to another room, and he followed like a child. As the body was borne past the physician, he pointed to the livid spots gathering upon the marble of the breast, arms, and forehead, and said: "If this were in the East, I should swear that she died from the bite of the cobra da Capelli."

And where was the murderer?—where was he with that fatal bracelet, with its concealed spring and its slender, poisoned blade—dipped in the poison of the cobra—the speediest and deadliest?

No one knew. He had disappeared in the confusion of the crowd. Only one suspected him of being a murderer.

The next day the civil authorities searched the neighborhood for an escaped convict—a desperate felon, committed for life. They went away without finding him; but some days afterward, a party of hunters in the mountains saw the vultures gathered around something at the foot of the precipice. They reached the place by a circuitous path, and found the body of a human being: the wrists and ankles were scarred as if by heavy irons, the clothing was rich, and in the pocket of the coat was found a curious bracelet of gold—in semblance a cobra serpent, in the attitude of striking, with eyes of emeralds and hood studded with rubies; on touching a secret spring, it was found that the cobra's head sprang suddenly forward, and a tiny blade leaped out from its jaws!

"Do not touch it," said the physician. "It has been dipped in the poison of the cobra."

HOW SHOULD WOMEN WRITE?

The idea of women writing books! There were no prophets in the days of King John to predict an event so far removed from probability. The women of the household sat by their distaffs, or toiled in the fields, or busied themselves in roasting and brewing for their guzzling lords. If ever a poetic vision or a half-defined thought floated through their minds, they sang it out to their busy wheels, or murmured it in rude sentences to lull the babies upon their bosoms, or silently wove it into their lives to manifest itself in patient love and gentleness. And it was all as it should have been; there was need for nothing more. Physical labor was then all that was required of woman; and to "act well her part," meant but to perform the domestic duties which were given her. Life was less complex then than now—the intellectual part of man's twofold nature being but unequally developed, while the absence of labor-saving implements demanded a greater amount of manual toil from men as well as from women.

It is different now. Modern ingenuity and Protean appliances of machinery have lessened the necessity of actual physical labor; and, in the constant progress of the human race, new fields have been opened, and new social needs and requirements are calling for workers in other and higher departments.

There is a cry now for intellectual food through the length and breadth of the land. The old oracles of the past, the mummied literary remains of a dead age, will not satisfy a generation that is pressing so vigorously forward. They want books imbued with the strong vitality and energy of the present. And as it is a moving, hurrying, changing time, with new influences and opinions constantly rising like stars above the horizon, men want books to keep pace with their progress—nay, to go before and guide them, as the pillar of fire and cloud did the Israelites in the desert. So they want books for every year, for every month—mirrors to "catch the manners living as they rise," lenses to concentrate the rays of the new stars that dawn upon them.

There is a call for workers; and woman, true to her mission as the helpmeet for man, steps forward to take her part in the intellectual labor, as she did when only manual toil was required at her hands. The pen has become the mighty instrument of reform and rebuke; the press is the teacher and the preacher of the world; and it is not only the privilege, but the duty of woman to aid in extending this influence of letters, and in supplying the intellectual demands of society, when she has been endowed with the power. Let her assure herself that she has been called to the task, and then grasp her pen firmly, with the stimulating consciousness that she is performing the work assigned to her.

Thus is apparent what has been gradually admitted, that it is woman's duty to write — but how and what? This is yet a mooted question. Men, after much demur and hesitation, have given women liberty to write; but they cannot yet consent to allow them full freedom. They may flutter out of the cage, but it must be with clipped wings; they may hop about the smooth-shaven lawn, but must, on no account, fly. With metaphysics they have nothing to do; it is too deep a sea for their lead to sound; nor must they grapple with those great social and moral problems with which every strong soul is now wrestling. They must not go beyond the surface of life, lest they should stir the impure sediment that lurks beneath. They may whiten the outside of the sepulchre, but must not soil their kidded hands by essaying to cleanse the inside of its rottenness and dead men's bones.

Nature, indeed, is given them to fustianize over, and religion allowed them as their chief capital — the orthodox religion, that says its prayers out of a prayer-book, and goes to church on Sabbaths; but on no account the higher, truer religion, that, despising cant and hypocrisy, and scorning forms and conventionalisms, seeks to cure, not to cloak the plague-spots of society — the self-forgetting, self-abnegating religion that shrinks not from following in the steps of Christ, that curls not its lip at the touch of poverty and shame, nor fears to call crime by its right name, though it wear a gilded mask, nor to cry out earnestly and bravely, "Away with it! away with it!" No! not such religion as this. It is *unfeminine;* women have no business with it whatever, though they may ring changes as often as they please upon the "crowns of gold," the "jasper walls," and "seraph harps."

Having prescribed these bounds to the female pen, men are the first to condemn her efforts as tame and commonplace, because they lack earnestness and strength.

If she writes of birds, of flowers, sunshine, and *id omne genus*, as did Amelia Welby, noses are elevated superbly, and the effusions are said to smack of bread and butter.

If love, religion, and domestic obligations are her theme, as with Mrs. Hentz, "namby-pamby" is the word contemptuously applied to her productions. If, like Mrs. Southworth, she reproduces Mrs. Radcliffe in her possibility — scorning romances, her nonsensical clap-trap is said to be "beneath criticism;" and if, with Patty Pepper, she gossips harmlessly of fashions and fashionables, of the opera and Laura Keene's, of watering-places, lectures, and a railroad trip, she is "*pish*"-ed aside as silly and childish; while those who seek to go beyond the boundary-line are put down with the stigma of "*strong-minded.*" Fanny Fern, who, though actuated by no fixed purpose, was yet more earnest than the majority of her sisterhood, heard the word hissed in her ears whenever she essayed to strike a blow at the root of social sin and inconsistency, and had whatever there was of noble and philanthropic impulse in her nature annihilated by the epithets of "bold" and "indelicate," which were hurled at her like poisoned arrows.

It will not do. Such dallying with surface-bubbles, as we find in much of our periodical literature, might have sufficed for another age, but not for this. We want a deeper troubling of the waters, that we may go down into the pool and be healed. It is an earnest age we live in. Life means more than it did in other days; it is an intense reality, crowded thick with eager, questioning thoughts and passionate resolves; with burning aspirations and agonized doubts. There are active influences at work, all tending to one grand object—moral, social, and physical advancement. The pen is the compass-needle that points to this pole. Shall woman dream on violet banks, while this great work of reformation is needing her talents and her energies? Shall she prate prettily of moonlight, music, love, and flowers, while the world of stern, staring, pressing realities of wrong and woe, of shame and toil, surrounds her? Shall she stifle the voice in her soul for fear of being sneered at as *strong-minded*, and shall her great heart throb and heave as did the mountain of Æsop, only to bring forth such insignificant mice—such productions—more paltry in purpose than in style and conception—which she gives to the world as the offspring of her brain?

It will not long be so. Women are already forming higher standards for themselves, learning that genius has no sex, and that, so the truth be told, it matters not whether the pen is wielded by a masculine or a female hand. The active, earnest, fearless spirit of the age, which sends the blood thrilling through the veins of women, will flow out through their pens, and give color to the pictures they delineate, to the principles they affirm. Literature must embody the prominent feeling of the age on which it is engrafted. It is only an isolated, excepted spirit, like Keats's, which can close its eyes to outward influences, and, amid the roar of gathering political storms, and the distant thunderings of the French Revolution, lie down among the sweet, wild English flowers, and dream out its dream of the old Greek beauty.

How should a woman write? I answer, as men, as all should write to whom the power of expression has been given—*honestly and without fear.* Let them write what they feel and think, even if there be errors in the thought and the feeling—better that than the lifeless inanities of which literature, and especially periodical literature, furnishes so many deplorable samples.

Our opinions on ethical and social questions change continually as the mind develops, and the light of knowledge shines more broadly through the far-off opening in the labyrinth of inquiry through which we wander, seeking for truth. Thus, even when writers are most honest, their opinions, written at different times, often appear contradictory. This the discerning reader will readily understand. He will know that in ascending the ladder, upon whose top the angels stand, the prospect widens and changes continually as newer heights are won. Emerson, indeed, tells us that "a foolish consistency is the hobgoblin of little minds. With consistency, a great soul has simply nothing to do. Speak what you think now in hard words; and to-morrow, speak what to-morrow thinks in hard words again, though it contradict everything you said to-day."

This is strong — perhaps too unqualified; but even inconsistency is better than the dull, donkey-like obstinacy which refuses to move from one position, though the wooing spirit of inquiry beckon it onward, and winged speculation tempt it to scale the clouds.

Still, there should be in writing, as in acting, a fixed and distinct purpose to which everything should tend. If this be to elevate and refine the human race, the purpose will gradually and unconsciously work out its own accomplishment. Not, indeed, through didactic homilies only; every image of beauty or sublimity crystallized in words, every philosophic truth, and every thought that has a tendency to expand the mind or enlarge the range of spiritual vision, will aid in advancing this purpose, will be as oil to the lamp we carry to light the footsteps of others.

As to the subjects that should be written upon, they are many and varied; there is no exhausting them while nature teems with beauty — while men live, and act, and love, and suffer — while the murmurs of the great ocean of the *Infinite* come to us in times when the soul is stillest, like music that is played too far off for us to catch the tune. Broad fields of thought lie before us, traversed, indeed, by many feet, but each season brings fresh fruits to gather and new flowers to crop.

Genius, like light, shines upon all things — upon the muck-heap as upon the gilded cupola.

As to the wrong and wretchedness which the novelist lays bare — it will not be denied that such really exists in this sin-beleaguered world. Wherefore shrink and cover our eyes when these social ulcers are probed? Better earnestly endeavor to eradicate the evil, than seek to conceal or ignore its existence. Be sure this will not prevent it eating deeper and deeper into the heart.

Genius, when true and earnest, will not be circumscribed. No power shall say to it: "Thus far shalt thou go, and no farther." Its province is, in part, to daguerreotype the shifting influences, feelings, and tendencies at work in the age in which it exists — and sin, and grief, and suffering, as well as hope, and love, and joy, and star-eyed aspiration, pass across its pages as phantoms across the charmed mirror of the magician. Genius thrills along "the electric chain wherewith we are darkly bound," from the highest to the lowest link of the social ligature; for true genius is Christ-like; *it scorns nothing;* calls nothing that God made common or unclean, because of its great yearning over mankind, its longing to lift them up from the sordid things of sense in which they grovel to its own higher and purer intellectual or spiritual atmosphere. The noblest woman of us all, Mrs. Elizabeth Browning, whom I hold to have written, in "Aurora Leigh," the greatest book of this century, — the greatest, not from the wealth of its imagery, or the vigor of its thoughts, but because of the moral grandeur of its purpose, — Mrs. Browning, I say, has not shrunk from going down, with her purity encircling her, like the halo around the Saviour's head, to the abodes of shame and degradation for materials to aid in elucidating the serious truths she seeks to impress for sorrowful examples of the evils for which she endeavors to find some remedy. She is led to this through that love which is inseparable from the higher order of genius. That noblest form of genius which generates the truest poetry — the poetry of feeling rather than of imagination — warm with human life, but uncolored by voluptuous passion — is strongly connected with love. Not the sentiment which dances through the world to the music of marriage-bells; but that divine, self-ignoring, universal love of which the inspired apostle wrote so burningly, when, caught up in the fiery chariot of the Holy Ghost, he looked down upon the selfish considerations of common humanity: the love (or charity) "which beareth all things, endureth all things, which suffereth long and is kind," — the love which, looking to heaven, stretches its arms to enfold the whole human brotherhood.

This is the love which, hand in hand with genius, is yet to work out the redemption of society. I have faith to believe it; and sometimes, when the tide of hope and enthusiasm is high, I have thought that woman, with the patience and the long-suffering of her love, the purity of her intellect, her instinctive sympathy and her soul of poetry, might be God's chosen instrument in this work of gradual reformation, this reconciling of the harsh contrasts in society that jar so upon our sense of harmony, this righting of the grievous wrongs and evils over which we weep and pray, this final uniting of men into one common brotherhood by the bonds of sympathy and affection.

It may be but a Utopian dream; but the faith is better than hopelessness; it is elevating and cheering to believe it. It is well to aspire, though the aspiration be unfulfilled. It is better to look up at the stars, though they dazzle, than down at the vermin beneath our feet.

FANNY E. HERRON.

MISS HERRON'S publications have been few, and yet we rank her among the "promising writers of the sunny South." In February, 1867, a poem of four hundred lines appeared in the "Mobile Sunday Times," entitled "The Siege of Murany," which was Miss Herron's first contribution to that journal. "Glenelglen," a romance of other days, and an excellent tale, her first attempt in prose, was written to compete for the prize offered by the "Times;" and, after appearing in that journal, was published in book-form.

Though originally a resident of Virginia, the father of Miss Herron, the late James Herron, civil engineer, was for a number of years in charge of the public works at the Pensacola Navy Yard. Miss Herron is a graduate of the Academy of the Visitation, Mount de Sales, in Baltimore County, Maryland, taking first premiums and gold medal.

The family residence of Miss Herron was burned during the war, and by the fortunes of war she became a sojourner at the Capital of Alabama — although still considering Florida, the land of flowers, as her home.

EXTRACTS FROM

THE SIEGE OF MURANY.

But see, on yonder neighboring plains,
  Where lingers still the day,
Each silvered helm, each burnished shield
  Has caught its latest ray,
And flashes back in mimic light
  The glory Sol had given,
Before the spangled flag of night
  Had draped the dome of heaven.
Whence came yon band in martial gear?
  What daring chieftain led
Yon royal host where Muran's guns
  Rain vengeance on his head?

'Tis he! 'tis he, with eagle glance,
And forehead bold and fair,
With cheek sun-kissed to olive hue,
And waving, midnight hair;
'Tis he, with martial step and mien,
Whose deep-toned voice's sound
Might vie with lyre by Orpheus touched
T' enchant the groves around;
'Tis he, whose mouth of stern resolve
Can melt in smiles so rare,
So soft, so sweet, his men forget
Their months of toil and care,
And rush to death in countless forms
Whene'er he leads the way:
'Tis Wesselengi — he who sits
In tent at close of day.
Though young in years, in deeds of arms
Full many score is he,
As foe hath never yet beheld
Him dastard turn to flee.
Yet when yon dark, stupendous pile
Upon his vision rose,
The evil fortune he deplored
That peopled it with foes.
By nature it was rendered strong,
Impregnable by art;
Yet felt he, never from those walls
With honor he'd depart,
Until time-hallowed Murany
Had owned the kingly power,
Until his monarch's standard waved
Triumphant o'er each tower.
In sullen floods these sombre thoughts
Fast o'er his spirit roll,
Till thus he vented to the night,
The anguish of his soul:

"Oh! must the laurels hardly earned,
Which long have wreathed my brow,
Be tarnished by defeat or flight?
Yield to a woman now?
I've led my hosts o'er mountain snow,
By prestige of my name;
Was't but to watch in darkness set
The day-star of my fame?

No! brighter yet that star shall glow,
And laurels fresh I'll reap;
Again shall fortune greet her son,
Or with my dead I'll sleep."

. . . . . .

O Wesselengi, was it pride,
And loyalty alone,
To keep undimmed thy martial fame,
And stay thy monarch's throne,
That made thee hazard freedom sweet —
Nay, tempt a darker fate —
By venturing unattended thus
Within that massive gate?
Or had the charms of her who dwelt
In yonder turret old
Been whispered in thy midnight dreams,
To make thee rashly bold?

AUGUSTA DE MILLY.

IN Confederate literature, the signature of "Ethel Deen" and the initials "A. D." were pleasant sights; for the article to which they were attached, whether prose or verse, was always readable.

Augusta De Milly is a native of New York city, but having many Southern connections, and the greater portion of her life having been passed in the State of Florida, she claims to be a Southern woman by residence, as she is by feeling.

During the war, Mrs. De Milly contributed to the literary journals of "Dixie," principally the "Southern Field and Fireside," (Augusta,) and "Magnolia Weekly," (Richmond,) under signatures alluded to, and many of her articles, written in a careless and desultory manner, were excellent and much praised. Since the close of the war, her attempts in the writing line have been few: as she expresses it, "a school-teacher has little time to gossip with the Muses." The prose productions of Mrs. De Milly are short sketches, well written and interesting; but, as she says in a note to the writer, "Never having made any sustained effort, I can point to no effort which would at all afford a foundation for a literary reputation."

Her home is in the "land of flowers," where the "fount of perpetual youth" was said to be in ancient days, and indeed where sunshine and beautiful blooms are perennial. "Jacksonville, Florida," is her address.

"IMPLORA PACE."

The most frequent inscription on the tombs in Italy is the above petition.

The spring-time died — so would I gladly die
   And be at rest; for life brings but remorse:
I'd welcome thee, dread Azrael, fearlessly,
   Nor once bewail my yet unfinished course.
Come, dreamless sleep; no phosphorescent spark
Can lure me then to wander in the dark.

Germs wither, buds pale at their birth,
The chilling winds stab blossoms without ruth,
The grain must lie among the tares of earth,
And scudding vapors hide the heaven of truth.
Must I, whose soon maturity was vain,
Take up the burden of my life again?

The summer died — and fain would I too rest
Within thy pitying arms; quick tempests drown
Me with their tears — fierce lightnings scathe my breast,
And the rich treasures of my heart go down.
Oh, be not thou inexorable, Death!
Kiss on my lips thine all-availing breath.

Come thou! the orchid's eyes are calm
That look from the greensward — the shade
Of feathery cedars woos me with its balm,
And the eternal stars smile ever overhead.
How can I hush my heart that moans its pain?
How take the burden of my life again?

See! even the autumn lies beneath his pall
Heraldic. O ye winds that round him sweep,
Could ye, like his, my spirit disenthrall,
Then would I calmly lie — and calmly sleep.
Dews of the mocking vine but parch my lips;
I 'd quaff, O Death! thy cup's nepenthean deeps.

Must I, pale king! so weary of the strife
For fame, for wealth, for fruits that ever cloy,—
I, who had sown the affluence of my life,
And built wide barns for harvestings of joy,—
Must I, who garner blight, not laughing grain,
Take up the burden of such life again?

Between white hills, within his nest of snows
Plucked from the bosom of the brooding cloud,
Dead winter lies — so peaceful his repose,
No royal robes could lure me like his shroud;
My blooms like his are fettered for all time,
Prisoned in bars of ice, and frost, and rime.

Why should I live? My heart is stark and dead
To all sweet influence. Never love-bird's lays

Wake tuneful carols there — such songs have fled
  To where are verdant boughs and blossoming sprays.
Hold out thy sceptre, Death! — if thou dost reign,
Nor bid me bear life's burden yet again.

FLORIDA CAPTA.

Leaning her fair head against the pines,
  Like some faint lily resting on the waves,
In the clear waters — where a white moon shines —
  Idle and dreaming, either hand she laves.

Her listless cheek the green palmetto fans;
  The blue-eyed vine her sighing lips has kissed;
The pitying rivers, from their reedy bands
  Loosening their tresses, fold her in the mist.

And over her the sobbing roses bend,
  Dropping their fragrant tears upon her face;
For her wan temples, with a trembling hand,
  The jasmine breaks her alabaster vase.

In vain, from every sprouting screen around,
  A sweet-voiced bird her plaintive love-song sings;
With the soft moonlight linked and interwound,
  Rippling the air in bright harmonic rings.

A tender memory haunts her where she lies —
  The beauteous Florida! — the queen uncrowned!
And dims the light in her sweet, mournful eyes,
  That see not wave, nor moon, nor aught around.

She feels again upon her bosom bare
  The milky teeth of the young laughing corn;
Her fingers stray among the tangled hair,
  Silken and white, of one yet later born.

No more! no more on any summer night
  They'll draw their nurture from her crescive breast;
No more the breathings of their soft delight
  Shall lull their mother into blissful rest.

Above her, O ye fauns! bend branch and bough;
  Shield her fair form 'gainst the chill, blighting dew;

Pity her dolor, and on her pale brow
  Bind your gray pearls of beaded mistletoe.

For from the dusk in her sweet, mournful eyes,
  That see not moon, nor wave, nor aught around,
Never again shall full-orbed hope arise
  To shine on her — on Florida uncrowned.

BLUE AND GOLD.

Grizzly-bearded, swarthy and keen,
  Sits a jeweller, cunning and cold;
Spectral-eyed, like a Bedouin,
  Counting his gems and gold:

Counting his chaplets of Syrian jet,
  And odorous amber steeped in the sun,
The golden circlets, turquoise set,
  A dowry every one;

Blood-red rubies, pearls like grapes,
  In clusters of purple, black, and white;
Cameo girdles for exquisite shapes;
  Diamond drops of light;

Jewelled masks and filigree fans
  In carved cases of tropical wood;
Aspic bracelets, ouches, and hands,
  Clasps for mantle and hood.

Dreaming a dream of sordid gain,
  The merchant, keen-eyed, cunning, and cold,
Smiles in thought of a yellow rain,
  Ducats and sequins of gold.

Trailing her robes of velvet and lace,
  Through the luminous dimness glows
Viola's form of girlish grace,
  And face like an Alpine rose.

She comes to look at the baubles new,
  To look at the rubies and strings of pearls,
With light in her eyes of turquoise blue,
  And light in her golden curls.

She fans herself with the filigree fans,
  Opal-handled with flame and dusk —
Giving the palms of her slender hands
  The scent of attar and musk.

She tosses the chaplets of Syrian jet
  And amber by with a careless air,
And looks in vain for a jewelled net
  For her beautiful golden hair.

Grizzly-bearded, with spectral gleams
  In the merchant's keen eyes, cunning and bold,
Through the long day he sits and dreams
  Of mingled blue and gold,—

Counting his wealth of baubles and toys,
  Of the hoarded coin which his coffers hold,
A snare for the eyes of blue turquoise,
  A net for the hair of gold.

MRS. M. LOUISE CROSSLEY.

ATHENS, Georgia, was the birthplace of Mrs. Crossley, *née* Miss M. Louise Rogers. On the maternal side, she is descended from an ancient English family, who trace their blood back to a ducal reservoir. Her mother, a famous belle and beauty in her youth, early exchanged her maiden name of Houghton for that of Rogers, and was blessed (according to patriarchal manner of thinking) with a "goodly number of offspring." Perhaps it is to the circumstance of her having been one of a large family of children, that Mrs. Crossley owes, in a measure, her sympathetic, self-sacrificing disposition, and her admirable faculty of self-help. The necessity of sometimes playing the mother's part of comforter or adviser to younger brothers or sisters — the interchange of little confidences and services among each other — nurtured the kindly affections; while the attrition of different characters with her own, quickened and stimulated her mind, without detracting from its individuality.

It is not the purpose of this slight sketch to follow our authoress through all the vicissitudes of her life: enough for us to note the circumstances tending to the development of her intellectual tastes.

In her childhood, she was left much to herself — left to puzzle out her own conclusions from the phenomena of life she saw around her. In the stereotyped "young lady's education" she was not deficient, but her best teachers were nature and experience, and the poets, with whom she communed in sweet, stolen hours. The faculty of her mind which was first to mature was a delicate sensibility to beauty. Every phase and mood of nature was dear to the heart that loved her. The stirring of a dew-shining leaf in the April air; the sailing of a snowy cloud; the voice of a bird; the perfume of a hidden flower; the gurgle of a brook — every beautiful sight or sound of nature awoke a thrill in her heart. But, as yet, she only *felt* the harmonies of nature, she had not essayed to combine and express them in the immortal music of language. Sweet and stolen fancies had visited the soul of the thoughtful girl, but they had been sacred to herself. The first years of her young girlhood had passed, and the future *bas bleu* had given to the public no token of her literary proclivities. The first published production of her pen was written while she was in Southwestern Georgia, an inmate of the beautiful home of Major Edwards. Mrs. Edwards, her aunt on the maternal side, was also the mother of Mrs. Mary E. Bryan, whose star of fame was then rising. The cousins met there for the first time, and it is possible that, in the year of close intercourse which followed, they mutually influenced, in some degree, each other's character.

There are critical times in almost every life, when the slightest circumstance may serve to change the current of destiny; and it was probably owing to this pleasant summer visit that Miss Rogers turned her attention to authorship *so soon;* for, like Miss Edgeworth, her "great respect for the public" would have made her timid about publishing, unless stimulated by the example of one her opposite in this particular. Such a one, she found in her cousin. Although so young, Mrs. Bryan had already sounded nearly the whole gamut of feeling, and now she was reproducing her experiences through the medium of her pen. Passionate, impetuous, and bold, she was rapidly throwing off her daring opinions and sentiments, more from the feverish unrest and turbulent fulness of her mind than from any fixed purpose or reverent devotion to art (such as may have afterward come to be her motive), and publishing with the indifference of one not troubled with any overpowering "respect for the public."

The contagious quality of the *cacoethes scribendi* is proverbial. The daily sight of manuscript, the indifference with which scribbled sheets were dispatched to various editors, had their influence upon the more timid cousin. The long walks through bay-blossoming hummocks, and pine-fragrant hills, under the open skies, was another source of inspiration. The sweet fancies and lovely thoughts that had so long been singing to themselves in the brain of the young poetess, now awoke to audible music. Under the shade of the long-leaved pines, a prose poem, whose theme was "Beauty," was written, read aloud to the admiring cousin, and published. The ice was broken; the eloquent rhapsody, instinct with true poetic enthusiasm, was favorably received by the public, and the fair writer essayed again and again, modestly publishing in newspapers only, and sheltering herself under the *nom de guerre* of "Rena." In 1859, she was engaged as a regular contributor to the "Bainbridge Argus," and her graceful essays, and sprightly sketches of life and character, aided in no slight degree the popularity of that journal. Afterward she wrote some excellent pieces for a short-lived periodical, published in Atlanta; and, later still, under the pseudonym of "Currer Lyle," she contributed some of her most finished articles to the "Literary Companion," a journal of considerable ability, published in Newnan, Georgia. For a short time, during the war, she contributed regularly to the "Southern Illustrated News," under her own name; and in 1866 we find her name among the talented contributors to "Scott's Monthly Magazine." Her nature is very sympathetic, and most tenderly human; and many of her pieces in newspapers, during the war, were replete with a womanly but fervid patriotism, and the tenderest sympathy for the soldier wearing the Confederate gray. We were told by an ex-officer that many were the blessings he had heard breathed upon her name by the Southern soldier, as he read her poems and essays by the light of his camp-fire. We understand that she is now engaged in collecting and composing materials for a volume destined to contain, not only her best productions that have appeared in print, but others, especially two novelettes that have never been published.

I have already too far transgressed the limits allowed me to attempt any analysis of Mrs. Crossley's writings. Her talent is poetical, not philosophical. She mirrors truly and beautifully the more apparent aspects and phenomena of nature and art, of life and character; but the more intricate and less thankful task of portraying the hidden meanings and relations that underlie these she leaves to more analytic minds. She holds that there is, in life and in nature, enough of plainly apparent sunshine and shadow, of joy and sorrow, of good and evil, out of which to weave her mingled web. Her style is elegantly pure and simple; her diction musical, and not unfrequently energetic. In her poetry, she reminds me more of the Ettrick Shepherd than of any other writer whom I can now call to mind.

If I were restricted to a single word with which to describe the personal appearance of Mrs. Crossley, that word should be "noble." It most fully embodies my impression of her gracious presence. It conveys an idea of the sweet dignity, the excellence of mind and heart apparent in her countenance and in her manner. In her presence, one involuntarily acknowledges the power of a pure and serene womanhood.

It is no ordinary face — that which rises before me as I write — the sweet, peculiar smile, one of the chief charms of the changeful countenance; the dark blue, deep eyes, full of vivid expression, and mellowed by long, brown lashes; the white forehead, high and broad, and forever suggesting that noble line:

"The dome of thought, the palace of the soul."

No portrait could do her justice; for it could catch only one of the many phases and flitting expressions of her face. As a friend and admirer remarked: "Her face is an enigma to me—ever so changing in its expression. At times it is pale, passionless, listless; and again it beams with a brilliancy that makes her almost beautiful."

Her social talent I consider of the highest order, because it is not positive; it does not lead her to overpower others by her own individuality—to create discord by antagonism; but rather to diffuse a harmonizing influence through the social elements with which she comes in contact. It has the rare quality which existed in perfection with Madame Récamier, and exists in our own age and country with Madame Le Vert—that sympathetic and assimilating faculty—that magnetism by which one mind may put itself *en rapport* with another, call out its best qualities, win its confidence, and arouse its self-respect; in brief, put it in a genial humor with itself and others. Give me one such harmonious power in society, and I will gladly relinquish to you a De Staël or a Sand, who, however brilliant, are too positively electrical in their natures to be productive of social concord.

I cannot but look forward to a bright future for Mrs. Crossley. She has energy and perseverance, and lately she has attained to a belief in herself—in her own capabilities. She has also that "noble discontent" (intellectually) which prevents her from being satisfied with her attainments, and keeps her ever striving to reach her own high-placed ideal. Examining what she has written, I can see that her range of thought continually widens; her conceptions of life and nature grow constantly more clear; she is perceiving the deep soul of truth which exists in all things, and is bodying it forth with a bolder and more certain hand. She does not allow the flatteries which the well-meaning press of the South showers upon its writers with such a lavish, and, unfortunately, such an indiscriminate hand, to render her self-complacent; but, keeping her own ideal in view, she presses earnestly forward, destined, I believe, to take an enviable rank in the world of letters.

In May, 1866, the subject of our sketch was married to J. T. Crossley, Esq., a gentleman of great worth and respectability — a union, we are told, not only of hands, but also of hearts; and she is now a resident of Columbus, Florida.

MEMORIA IN ETERNA.

Dead in his beauty, young manhood, and pride,
Torn from our hearts and home fireside;
Dead to the honors he could nobly have won,
In the world's great battle he just had begun;
Dead to all friends who loved him so well,
Dead to all foes — if one, none can tell;
Gone from the earth into the unknown,
To solve the great MYSTERY lying beyond
All the tinsel and glare, the pomp and the show,
The care, and the grief and sin that we know;
The soul's grand soarings in this world of ours,
The bliss and the woe, the thorns and the flowers,
That make up this thing we vainly call life,
With all of its death, its sorrow, and strife.

O my brother! my brother, lost, loved one!
Canst thou hear me now call thee, far beyond
In thy unseen home? canst thou see the tears,
That flow from my eyes as the night appears,
And I bow my head low down in the dust,
And wail for thy love, its sweetness and trust?

O pitiless Death!
You 've taken from one, from an old man's heart,
His fondest hope and pride —
A mother's dear and noblest one,
That in his beauty died.
You 've torn from the arms of sisters so dear,
From all their fond caressing,
The darling one of all the loved band —
Their proud, sweet, earthly blessing!
Oh, cruel! most cruel! you took him from me
Without one word of warning:
I thought he still lived, hoped, and loved,
Until that woful morning
They came and told me he was dead,
And left my heart a-breaking,

With the sunlight gayly streaming in,
  To mock my sad awaking.

Dead! O kind Saviour, and not one sweet word
To bless my fond ears, if I only had heard;
No look of dear love to comfort my heart,
No clasp of the hand, so loth here to part;
Without one kiss on the broad, noble brow,
Where death had set his pale signet now,
And darkened the light of the peerless mind,
With its truth, bright honor, and heart ever kind.
Dead! sweet Jesus, and all loved ones away
With but one of the band 'round his death-bed to stay,
And wipe the cold drops from the dear, loved face,
And catch the last words the pale lips traced,
Before the freed spirit took its swift flight
To God's bowers of bliss, eternally bright.

O Death, most dainty old epicure,
On the fairest, the dearest, the lovely and pure
Thou lovest to gorge, and greedily taste
Of flesh as priceless to us as the feast
Of fabled ambrosia the gods supped upon
In their cloud-palace homes; while thou passest on,
And leavest the idiot, the lout, and the clown,
The corrupt, and the bad, with sin bound around,
To live here on earth unscathed, as they stand
'Midst all its bright beauty of sky, sea, and land.

My brother, my darling brother, my pride,
  In this clime near tropical skies
We'll cull the fairest and sweetest of blooms,
  With the softest and purest dyes,
And twine them above thy silent, dark tomb:
  We'll water them with our tears,
And fervently kiss each fragrant, bright flower,
  When twilight softly appears,
And wraps its robe of royal-bright hue
  About thy lowly resting-place,
While humming-birds fairily float on the air,
  Or kiss some flower's pure, sweet face.
    White lilies we'll bring thee,
      For purity's token,
    And roses the loveliest,
      For love unbroken;

Violets blue, and orange blooms too,
Sweet as the home of a dainty fay
Slumbering all the livelong day
In a water-lily, upon some stream
Murmuring ever a happy dream:
Jasmines white, fragrant and pure,
We too will sadly bring,
To mingle with the rose's hue
These dear, sweet flowers of spring;
And the queenly magnolia,
Fair as the flowers
That grow in the gardens of Gul,
'Neath Orient bowers,
Perfume and pearly showers.

Blow, blow, ye sweetest blooms,
Above our darling's grave!
Oh, die not in some upas blast,
But let the dewdrops lave
Your fragrant lips and glowing hearts,
And keep them pure and bright,
While from the skies the stars drop down
Their dreamy, silvery light!
And winds—oh, sigh soft and sweet,
Come with lightest, hallowed feet,
And make low music round that spot,
Sweet as in some fairy grot
Æolian harps were sighing—
Sighing, and dying,
In the completeness
Of their own sweetness.

My brother! my brother! loved and lost,
My heart's own idol—I confess it the most!
Father, forgive!—our idol, dream, and hope,
From youth's bright years all up the sunny slope
To manhood's princely prime.
Thou, the Great Builder
Of the human frame, didst make him in all
The completeness of mortal mould, and gavest
Him to us to love; then, in Thy compassion,
Oh, forgive our worship of the creature
Thou didst make! Father in heaven, I loved
Him so! I know Thou doest all things well,

Then, oh! upbraid me not that I miss his step,
And his presence ever near me, at morning's
Radiant birth, at noontide glow, and evening's
Bridal of the sea and sky — that the world,
Which Thou didst make and fling into wide space,
A globe of glowing, Eden beauty, is now all
A blank to my tearful eyes, as I bow
My weary head beneath the bending blue
Of these star-gemmed skies, and seem still to hear
His dear, loved voice in song, or the melody
Of poesy's written sweetness, which we have
So loved and often read each to the other;
And the rare, sweet music, sparkling or dreamy,
His dear fingers were wont to wake, to still
My spirit, tempest-tossed, in sad, sweet dreams
Of Elysian's fair and ever-happy fields.
My Father! upbraid me not that I mourn
As Rachel mourned in Rama; but let me
Bring my bleeding heart, my shattered dreams,
And lay them on Thy sacrificial altars;
Let me keep the glittering crown, the harp
Of gold, the paradisial fruit in view,
And thus lose sight of my broken idols here —
Not in some loathsome charnel-house, but robed
And crowned before Thy throne, where angels bow —
A glittering, starry throng!

TENNESSEE.

MRS. L. VIRGINIA FRENCH.

MRS. FRENCH'S birth and education are the best the country affords. *Poeta nascitur*, and Mrs. French, aside from being a "born" poet, is a "born" lady. She knows it as well.

Her family, early incidents of her life, and romantic marriage are piquantly spoken of in "Mary Forrest's" elegant work, "Women of the South." Born on the fair shores of Virginia, educated in Pennsylvania, and married in Tennessee, her life has been like herself, varied and cosmopolitan. She is, nevertheless, a true daughter of the Old Dominion; a fair representative of its gay grace, its cordial hospitality, its love of luxury, and its indomitable pride.

The personal appearance of Mrs. French is highly prepossessing, and her manner so gifted with repose as to be unusually tranquillizing in its social influence. Yet there are seasons when the blue eyes flash, and the lips are wreathed in smiles so vivid and genial, that one can scarcely understand how the quiet lady, a moment before sitting so restfully, and listening so patiently, can be the same as she, so suddenly stirred to interest and emotion.

That rarest of all American gifts — wit — has been conferred upon her, in conjunction with poetic genius of no common order; and it is delightful to hear her low, rich laugh rippling out in ready recognition of some point of humor, obtuse to most listeners, and to find her arrow of repartee always on the string, though its point is never envenomed by the poison of bitterness.

Mrs. French possesses a noble nature; full of generous emotions and fine impulses; turning away from all wrong; not so much, perhaps, because of the wickedness of wrong; but because wrong implies something low and mean; and to do wrong, therefore, would be too deep a condescension;—large-hearted and liberal-minded; taking broad views of life and humanity; possessed of a catholic charity which "circles all the human race," and a nature with but one "prejudice," *i. e.*, a healthy and well-developed hatred of all Puritanism — Puritanism, as she understands it, viz., the embodiment of hypocrisy and cant; — radically independent in all things; doing each day "whatever duty lies next to her," leaving the results with God.

"In 1848," says 'Mary Forrest,'* "Virginia Smith and her sister returned from school to their father's house. But a new spirit was rife in the old home; its lares and penates had been displaced, and the two sisters, ever united by the tenderest ties of sympathy, determined to go forth into the world and shape their own destinies. Before the close of the year, they were established in Memphis, Tennessee, as teachers.

"Strangers in a strange city, they put themselves bravely to their self-appointed work, and by their energetic perseverance, no less than their personal and intellectual charms, soon won the confidence of all.

"Having achieved a social and tutorial position, the elder sister began to turn her attention to literary pursuits, contributing occasional articles to the journals and magazines of that region under the name of 'L'Inconnue.'

"In 1852, she became associated with some gentlemen of New Orleans in the publication of the 'Southern Ladies' Book.'

"On the 12th of January, 1853, she was married to Mr. John H. French, of McMinnville, Tennessee."

Mrs. French has published one volume — a collection of her poems, under the title of "Wind Whispers" — in 1856; and a tragedy, in five acts, under the title of "Iztalilxo, the Lady of Tula." She has written enough for half a dozen volumes, or more. She takes all criticism in the proper spirit, having no fear of the "small snarlers," but little reverence for the great ones, and no ambition to become a "serf of the booksellers."

But few ladies whom "we read about" have any deficiencies. Mrs. French is the exception which proves the rule. A serious defect in her organization is want of application. Had she never married, but devoted herself to literature and art, she would assuredly have been eminently successful. But her life is too full of other attractions — home, and home happiness. She entirely repudiates the name of "*littérateur;*" loves books, but cares no more for being put into them than the lark cares for seeing his morning hymn written out on a musical score. A great deficiency this want of ambition; this lack of interest

* "Women of the South," page 440.

in her own reputation. She has no consideration for any work that is *done.* An article completed, the excitement of writing it over, is thought of no more. Literature, which with her should occupy the front rank, does not even take a secondary place in her life and estimation; it is merely a kind of little by-play while the real drama of life goes on. She scatters here and there the effervescence of an affluent intellect, the deeps of which are still clear, calm, and undrawn upon. What the public sees of her writings as yet are merely "gold-blossoms," sparkling quartz, which indicate the precious ore that lies below; the mine itself is unworked, almost untouched. Emphatically a child of the sun, her fancies, bright and beautiful as foam-bells on the deep, never suggest to you the thought of effort or exhaustion, any more than the sigh of an Æolian lyre when "the breeze is spent, intimates that the mighty billows of the air shall surge no more." Her weakness, therefore, so to speak, lies not in any lack of power; but in a lamentable want of exertion. There is no deficiency of nerve to grasp a subject, or of power to discuss, or of keen acumen to analyze it; but there is indifference; and I think it reprehensible to give us merely the spicy fragrance flung off from the cinnamon-tree of genius, while the principle of sweetness in concentrated strength still lies hidden in the heart. Yet if you should undertake to impress upon her the wrong she does herself by trifling away gifts so precious, she would probably laugh archly in your face, and say, with the philosophy of a nature rather Sybaritic in its composition, "It is pleasanter to enjoy than to labor, more especially when both amount to the same thing at last."

As a *littérateur?* If (to borrow the simile of a famous critic) the gifts of others resemble wealth, hers "is an alchemy. If others, so to speak, go out into the mind's Australia, and collect its ores, lying thick as morning dews, she remains at home, transmitting all she touches into gold." Her language, in its elegance and rhythmic flow, is clear and lucid as the pleasant rush of a summer stream; and it has been said that her absolute command of comprehensible words is such that many might, with advantage, employ her to translate their Pedantese into plain English. I have seriously objected to her want of study; yet I must confess that what she writes, most of us can comprehend. We are not compelled to sit down over any poem of hers, gazing with portentous visage and a critic's eye at its obscurity; whispering at last under our breath: "There are sunbeams in this cucumber, if we could but extract them." But she does not put her sunbeams into the cucumber form. No; by all means let us take our cucumbers and our sunshine separately.

"Lady Tranquilla's" chief characteristic in literature is a wonderful versatility, to which scarce any vein of writing comes amiss, as is shown by poems, tales, sketches, letters, etc., written not only at her desk "*en grande tenue*," but scribbled in pencil under some wide-spreading tree, by garden-bound or riverside; in short, anywhere and everywhere, as the spirit moves her. This versatility is acknowledged by our people in the calls they make upon her powers. It fits her also to supply that large and constant drain made upon her time and talents, of which the world knows nothing. You might be in her house for months, and never know she wrote a line, for aught you heard or saw; yet she seems to be a species of perennial fountain, from which hundreds of people who never saw her draw supplies of strength and comfort; never dreaming, doubtless, of the drain they make upon this "sweet water spring," which gives out its supplies freshly and freely; which asks no return, and thinks of no replenishing, save what it draws from heaven. A lady, a thousand miles away, wants a May-day speech for some young favorite; an agricultural editor wants an essay on a given topic; a political friend wants a letter written which shall "bring out all the points;" a stranger widow wants five dollars; a young lady wants a situation as teacher; a novelist wants a book noticed; and so on, almost *ad infinitum;* yet all these applications are answered with a tranquillity equal to the fountain's, and a patience enduring as Job's. I have expected ere this to see her grow rather *blasé;* and she has sufficient knowledge of the world to make her so. I have expected to see her grow weary of its

"Dust and decay,
Weary of throwing her soul-wealth away,
Weary of sowing for others to reap;"

but that time seems as yet to linger by the way. In this connection, it may be well to say that "Lady Tranquilla" is accused of being a great favorite with contemporary *littêrateurs.* She has probably been more be-rhymed and be-sonneted than any other poetess. Her popularity arises from the fact that she claims no especial literary honors, and thus arouses no jealousies. Then, too, she is ever ready to extend favors, but asks none in return. She receives innumerable confidences, but never confides. N. P. Willis says that "to listen to the confidences of others, without ever thinking it worth while to burden them with yours, is a very good basis for a friendship. Nothing bores people more than to return their secrets with your own."

Yes, versatility is the "Lady Tranquilla's" *forte.* It makes her a general favorite. It renders her *par excellence* the journalist. It causes her critics to take each a different view. As for instance, Mrs. C. A. Warfield regards poetry as Mrs. French's strong point, and says of that stinging tribute, "Shermanized:" "Never sprang cooler and keener sarcasm from more tranquil lips. It is the flash of the yataghan from a velvet sheath — the cold, clear gleam of the sword from a silver scabbard."

Mrs. Julia Pleasants Creswell takes the opposite view, and insists that "Mrs. French writes the best prose, with the strongest sense in it, of any Southern writer."

That enchanting poetess, Amelia Welby, for years previous to her death, ceased to write. It is affirmed that she gave as a reason, that she had lost the power, the "faculty divine." It is more than probable that as her mind matured and expanded, she felt that she had not the power to express what she had keen ability to feel, and I have imagined that Mrs. French too has grown away from the past. A revolution has changed us as a people, and she feels that our present needs can scarce be "bodied forth in song." She feels also that she has power to write for a *purpose,* and the fact that those seem to succeed best who write for *no purpose,* keeps her comparatively silent. Her broad views and catholicity of character fit her to grapple strongly with many moral and social evils. This breadth and cosmopolitanism fits her for "shooting her soul" into a score of contradictory characters at once, and a novel from her pen would be unique.

During the late war, by which she in common with all of her Southern sisters was a sufferer and a loser, she wrote many poems and pieces of choice prose on the subjects of common interest — distinguished from most of contemporaneous writing by their tone of graceful and scornful satire, and entire freedom from harshness and vituperation.

Mrs. French has in MS. a valuable addition to Southern literature, in the shape of a novel written during and about the war.

Still in the prime of life, and happy in her domestic relations, as well as comparatively prosperous — for she retains her delightful "Forest Home" and landed possessions, it is sincerely hoped that she may put forth her wing once more, and cleave new heights of unexplored atmosphere.

We confidently believe that Mrs. French is capable, in her maturity of mind, of higher successes than she has yet achieved; and that her imagination, like Burke's, grows and strengthens with her years.

This gradual culmination of powers belongs only to strong natures, which grow like the oak-tree, slowly and surely, and remain vigorous and green when their frailer companions of the forest lie in ruins.

THE ELOQUENCE OF RUINS.

High on a desert, desolated plain
In the far Orient, a stately band
Of giant columns rise. Above the sleep
Of devastated cities, mouldering,
Yet haughtily they stand; grim sentinels,
Calling the watches of a vanished race,
And guarding still from Ruin's felt-shod tread
The mutilated chronicles of Eld.

Heavy with melodies all vast and vague,
Lifts up a solemn voice where Ages lie
Entombed with empires, in the crumbled pride
Of old Byzantium. Dark Egypt's lore
Lies in her catacombs; her histories
In fallen temples; while her Pyramids,
Like ponderous old tomes upon the sands,
Teem with the hidden records of the Past.
Amid their gloomy mysteries, the Sphinx,
A gaunt-eyed oracle, essays to speak,
And the weird whisper of her stony lip
Sounds o'er the tumult of the rushing years.

Greece! how her shattered domes reverberate
The thunders of a thousand gods, that dwelt
On Ida and Olympus! Porticos
That droop above their portals, like to brows
Of meditative marble over eyes
Dim with the haze of revery, still speak
Of ancient sages; and her pillars tell
Of heroes who have sought the Lethean wave,
And shores of Asphodel. Then, rising where

The yellow Tiber flows, some stately shaft,
Like a proud Roman noble in the halls
Of the great Forum, stands — the orator
Of nations gone to dust. The obelisk,
Girt with resistance, gladiator-like,
From his arena challenges a host
Of stealthy-footed centuries!
The lone,
Dark circle of the Druid, with its stones
Rugged and nameless, hath a monotone
Wild as the runes of Sagas at the shrine
Of Thor and Odin. Slow and silently
The pallid moonlight creeps along the walls
In the old abbey shadow. Timidly
It creepeth up, to list the tales they tell
Of beauty and of valor, laid to sleep
In the low, vaulted chancel. Ivy-crowned,
And crumbling to decay, how loftily
Rise the old castle towers! Its corridors
Resound with elfin echoes as the bell,
Wind-rocked upon its turret, sends a knell
From cornice to cavazion. The owl,
A dim-eyed warder, watches in his tower;
And zephyr, like a wandering troubadour,
Sports on the ruined battlement, and sings
To broken bastion, shattered oriel,
And fallen architrave.
The western wild
Spreads out before us, and her voice of might
Shakes the old wilderness. Alone it swells,
Where tropic bloom, and gray corrosion strive
To crush the deep and restless mutterings
Of hoary-headed ages. Dim and strange,
The priest, the vestal, and the dark cazique
Rise on the Teocallis; and below
Flit the swart shadows of the nameless tribes
That peopled Iximaya. Ruins all —
Yet mighty in their magic eloquence!

O "land we love!" O mother, with the dust
And ashes on thy robe and regal brow —
Deeper, and wilder, more melodious far,
The voice of melancholy, wailing o'er
Thy desolated homesteads! *That* awakes

Its echo in the memory; it brings
(Alas! that it should be but memory!)
The carol of the robin — and the hum
Of the returning bee — the winds at eve,
And the low, bell-like tinkle of the brook
That rippled round the garden. Then we see
The great elm-shadow, with the threshold stone
That garnered up the sunshine; and the vine
That crept around the colonnade, and bloomed,
Close-clinging as a love unchangeable.

We dream of gay boy-brothers, sleeping now
'Neath grasses rank on lonely battle-fields —
And seem to feel, perchance, the blessèd light
Of our sweet mother's smile — the holy breath
Of a good father's benison. We think
Of the white marbles where their hearts are laid
Down to a dreamless slumbering; — ah! *then*
Rush the thick, blinding tears — and we can see
No more!

"MAMMY."

A Home Picture of 1860.

Where the broad mulberry branches hang a canopy of leaves,
Like an avalanche of verdure, drooping o'er the kitchen eaves;
And the sunshine and the shadow dainty arabesques have made
On the quaint, old oak settle, standing in the pleasant shade;
Sits good "Mammy," with the child'un," while the summer afternoon
Wears the dewy veil of April o'er the brilliancy of June.

Smooth and snowy is the kerchief, lying folded with an air
Of matron dignity above her silver-sprinkled hair;
Blue and white the beaded necklace, used "of Sundays" to bedeck
(A dearly cherished amulet) her plump and dusky neck;
Dark her neatly-ironed apron, of a broad and ample size,
Spreading o'er the dress of "homespun," with its many-colored dyes.

True, her lips are all untutored; yet how genially they smile,
And how eloquent their fervor, praying, "Jesus bless de chile!"
True, her voice is hoarse and broken; but how tender its replies!
True, her hands are brown and withered; yet how loving are her eyes!

She has thoughts both high and holy, though her brow is dark and low,
And her face is dusk and wrinkled, but her soul as white as snow.

An "aristocrat" is "Mammy," in her dignity sedate;
"Haught as Lucifer" to "white trash," whom she cannot tolerate;
Patronizing, too, to "Master," for she "nussed 'im when a boy;"
Familiar, yet respectful to the "Mistis;" but the joy
Of her bosom is "de child'un," and delightedly she'll boast
Of the "born blood" of her darlings — "good as kings and queens a'most."

There she sits beneath the shadow, crooning o'er some olden hymn,
Watching earnestly and willingly, although her eyes are dim;
Laughing in her heart sincerely, yet with countenance demure,
Holding out before "her babies" every tempting little lure —
Noting all their merry frolics with a quiet, loving gaze,
Telling o'er at night to "Mistis" all their "cunnin' little ways."

Now and then her glance will wander o'er the pastures far away,
Where the tasselled corn-fields waving, to the breezes rock and sway,
To the river's gleaming silver, and the hazy distance where
Giant mountain-peaks are peering through an azure veil of air;
But the thrill of baby voices — baby laughter, low and sweet,
Recall her in a moment to the treasures at her feet.

So "rascally," so rollicking, our bold and sturdy boy,
In all his tricksy waywardness, is still her boast and joy;
She'll chase him through the shrubberies — his mischief mood to cure;
"Hi! whar dat little rascal now? — de b'ars will git 'im shure!"
When caught, she'll stoutly swing him to her shoulder, and in pride
Go marching round the pathways — "jus' to see how gran' he ride."

And the "Birdie" of our bosoms — ah! how soft and tenderly
Bows good "Mammy's" mother-spirit to her baby witchery!
(*All* to her is dear devotion whom the angels bend to bless,
All our thoughts of her are blended with a holy tenderness;)
Coaxing now, and now caressing — saying, with a smile and kiss,
"Jus' for Mammy — dat 's a lady — will it now?" do that or this.

On the sweet, white-tufted clover, worn and weary with their play,
Toying with the creamy blossoms, now my little children lay;
Harnessed up with crimson ribbons, wooden horses, side by side,
"Make believe" to eat their "fodder" — (blossoms to their noses tied.)
Near them stands the willow wagon — in it "Birdie's" mammoth doll,
And our faithful "Brave" beside them, noble guardian over all.

Above them float the butterflies, around them hum the bees,
And birdlings warble, darting in and out among the trees;
The kitten sleeps at "Mammy's" side, and two grown rabbits pass,
Hopping close along the paling, stealing through the waving grass;
Gladsome tears blue eyes are filling, and a watching mother prays,
"God bless 'Mammy' and my children in these happy, halcyon days."

SHERMANIZED!

This poem was written for, and read by Miss Lucy Powell Harris, at a concert given by the pupils of the Houston Street Female High School, in Atlanta, Georgia, May 1st, 1866.

In this city of Atlanta, on a dire and dreadful day,
'Mid the raging of the conflict, 'mid the thunder of the fray—
In the blaze of burning roof-trees—under clouds of smoke and flame—
Sprang a new WORD into being, from a stern and dreaded name:
Gaunt, and grim, and like a spectre rose that WORD before the world,
From a land of bloom and beauty into ruin rudely hurled—
From a people scourged by exile—from a city ostracized—
Pallas-like it sprang to being, and that WORD is—*Shermanized!*

And forevermore hereafter, where the fierce destroyer reigns,
Where destruction pours her lava over cultivated plains—
Where want and woe hold carnival—where bitter blight and blood
Sweep over prosperous nations in a strong, relentless flood;
Where the golden crown of harvest trodden into ashes lies,
And desolation stares abroad with famine-frenzied eyes—
Where the wrong with iron sceptre crushes every right we prized,
Shall the people groan in anguish—"*God! the right is Shermanized!*"

MAN may rule the raids of ruin—lead the legions that despoil—
From the lips of honest labor dash the guerdon of its toil—
"Sow with salt" the smiling valleys, and on every breezy height
Kindle balefires of destruction, lurid in the solemn night;
He may sacrifice the aged, and exult when woman stands
'Mid the sunken, sodden ashes of her home, with palsied hands
Drooping over hungered children—man may thus immortalize
His name with haggard infamy—his watchword, "*Shermanize!*"

Nobler deeds are WOMAN'S province—she must not destroy, but build;
She must bring the urns of plenty with the wine of pleasure filled;
She must be the "sweet restorer" of this sunny Southern land;
Fill our schools, rebuild our churches, take the feeble by the hand,

Aid the press, befriend the teacher, give to want its daily bread;
And never, *never* fail to weave above our "noble dead"
The laurel-garland due to deeds of valor's high emprize,
And won by men whom *failure* could not sink, or — *Shermanize!*

With her wakened love of labor let her labor on in love;
Still, in softness and in stillness, as the starry circles move —
Bearing light and bringing gladness from the leaden clouds unfurled,
As the soft rise of the sunlight bringeth morning to the world;
Grandly urging on endeavor, as the gates of day unclose,
Till the "solitary place again shall blossom as the rose;"
And woman — THE REBUILDER — shall be freely eulogized
By the triumph of her people — then no longer Shermanized.

God bless our noble Georgia! Though her soil was overrun,
And her lands in desolation laid beneath an autumn sun;
With the signal shout "*To action!*" like the boom of signal guns,
She has roused the iron mettle of her strong and stalwart sons.
May her daughters aid that effort to rebuild and to restore,
Working on for *Southern freedom* as they never worked before!
May our Georgia as a laggard never once be stigmatized,
And her PEOPLE, PRESS, or PULPIT never more be Shermanized!

THE AUCTIONEER.

Up with the red flag! wave it wide
  Over the gay and fair;
O'er things of love and things of pride
  It flaunteth everywhere.
Bring the hammer — the auction-block,
  Gather ye hearts of stone —
"*Here's excellent bargains, and premium stock,* —
  Going — going — gone!"

Wrecks of a ruined household band
  Cast on a silent shore;
Heart-breaks scattered along the sand,
  Where the tide comes up no more.
Amid the relics the auctioneer
  Standeth — a wrecker lone;
Bidding them off with a jest and jeer, —
  "*Going — going — gone!*"

Here's a mirror — a faithful friend —
  For, without a shade of guile,
It tells when passions the dark brow bend,
  And it gives you smile for smile.
No more — no more will it counsels lend —
  Ha! hark to that flippant tone —
"How much? — how much for this faithful friend?
  Going — going — gone!"

Here is a purple divan — soft,
  And circled with silken fringe;
Here the lord of the manor slumbered oft,
  And the couch's richest tinge
Was dull and cold to the golden shower
  Which over his visions shone:
"Who bids? — who bids for the dreams of power?
  Going — going — gone!"

A pendule strikes — with a dreamy chime,
  Like that which the spirit hears
In the notes of a curious, quaint old rhyme,
  That telleth of bygone years.
But the owner's passed to another clime,
  His last sad sands are run:
"How much? — how much for the wings of time?
  Going — going — gone!"

Costly lamps: when the golden spire
  Rose o'er the festal board,
How dim it shone to the eyes of fire,
  Where Love's sweet light was stored!
But those eyes grew dark — like stars that roam
  Afar from the "great white throne:"
"Who bids? — who bids for the lights of home?
  Going — going — gone!"

Statues, too: here's an angel band
  Just parting a curtain's fold,
While a cherub places a flowery band
  In the fair young sleeper's hold;
Then a laughing boy, with his two white doves,
  Carved in the Parian stone:
"How much? — how much for the household loves?
  Going — going — gone!"

A dainty volume, clasped with gold,
  Its links still bright and new;
It whispered a love that could ne'er be told,
  And it bound the giver true:
On the first blank leaf it is written now,—
  "Thine—thine alone!"
"*Who bids? who bids for the broken vow?*
  Going—going—gone!"

And here is a picture—pale and fair,
  What a soul looks from its eyes
Through shadowy clouds of golden hair,
  Like a peri from the skies!
So like to *her* in the church-yard laid
  When the autumn rains came on:
"*How much for a beauty that cannot fade?*
  Going—going—gone!"

Here is the carpet, with flowers dense,
  Her fairy feet once trod,
And the little cradle-bed from whence
  Her baby went up to God.
Here is the harp with its broken strings
  Her white hand moved upon:
"*Who bids? who bids for this lot of things?*
  Going—going—gone!"

Thank God, he cannot sell the heart—
  We bury our treasures there;
Warm tears that up to the eyelids start,
  And the baby's lisping prayer;
Songs that we loved in a bygone day—
  Sweet words, many a one;
We bury them deep—where none may say,
  "Going—going—gone!"

THE BROKEN SENTENCE.

A Tribute to the late Lieutenant Herndon.

"A ship went out upon the sea,
  A noble bark, with a gallant crew"—

And in herself a richly-freighted argosy of life and love—the ill-fated "Central America." That dark and terrible picture of her going down amid surging, midnight seas, which has been painted by inexorable fate, and hung upon the walls of time's proud temple, is one upon which our whole country has looked with "bated breath" and tear-dimmed eyes. Then, afar over the ocean waves, "sailed the corsair, death," and, gathered in that dread night-picture, there is the armada of the storm-king — the wrathful sky above, and the black goal of doom "a hundred fathoms down." But, notwithstanding all their terrific grandeur, how small, comparatively, is the meed of attention given to those dread details! Columbia's eagle eye is upon her noble son; the brave commander, the gallant seaman, the humble Christian, the immortal HERNDON. It is as though that great picture contained but one solitary human figure — one single object of interest whereon the soul may centre her intensest gaze. We see him, as, with that heroic devotion to woman, which was one of his first characteristics, he provides for their safety, until every woman and child has left his shattered vessel; we see him don his uniform, the garb in which he so long had served his country, and take his last stand at the wheel-house; we see him uncover to the king of terrors, as the doomed ship fetches her last lurch; with tearful, straining gaze, we see him signal an approaching boat, and order her to keep off and *be saved*, while he himself went down; to the last, mindful of others and forgetful of self — the soul of a warrior, and the heart of a woman!

Beautiful, heroic, and self-sacrificing are such scenes; but there is, in this connection, another still more beautiful and sublime; it is thus related by his kinsman, Lieutenant Maury:

> "As one of the last boats was about to leave the ship, her commander gave his watch to a passenger, with the request that it might be delivered to his wife. He wished to charge him with a message to her also, but his utterance was choked. 'Tell her — ' he said: unable to proceed, he bent down his head, and buried his face in his hands for a moment, as if in prayer, for he was a devout man, and a true Christian. In that moment, brief as it was, he endured the greatest agony. But it was over now. His crowding thoughts no doubt had been of friends and home; its desolation; a beloved wife and lovely daughter, dependent alone for support upon him. God and his country would care for them now. Honor and duty required him to stick to his ship, and he saw that she must go down."

"Tell her — " he began, but the thousand waves of an overflowing heart came rushing over him, like "high, fierce tides trampling in upon low, lee shores," and the last cry of his great soul was drowned amid the tumult. Then and there he had "tasted of the bitterness of death," and it was past. As we look upon him now, we pause in actual awe before the picture imaged in the mind. "Tell her — " said he, but human language had no words to body forth the love, the aspiration, the anguish of that noble soul in this, its hour of terrible trial. And so the strong man bowed his head upon his hands, and bent like a reed before the tempest, feeling only how, in such an hour, heart-throbs scorn the mockery of words. Undaunted by the dread danger — undismayed when all hearts were failing — gazing unblenching in the very face of destruction — ready to take death by the hand and disarm him of his terrors, he bowed down unmanned, and overwhelmed by one simple, loving memory of *her*. And now what remains to be said? What *could* be said, which in pathos and in power would not fall far, far below the single and simple reality of that broken and *forever unfinished* sentence — "*Tell her* — "?

"Tell her" — *what?* Ah! in vain we speculate. In vain we strive through blinding tears to read his heart, and say for him what he could not say for himself. And it is best as it is. Let us leave it so, nor dare to desecrate with our poor surmises the broken column which the master artist was unable to complete. But, do we say *forever unfinished?* Will he *never* tell her?

Far away in some sun-bright "Isle of Balm," more beautiful and more radiant than the Amazonian forests through which he once wandered, will not the language of the *immortal* give him power to utter all that which the *mortal* had essayed in vain? Or in that better land will there be a "fulness of joy" so soul-absorbing, so complete and perfect, that no remembrance of a troubled past, no memory of an unfinished mission, no shadow of our imperfect life shall ever dare intrude? Who of us can tell?

Said his wife, upon the first tidings of the shipwreck: "I know he has perished. He will stand by his ship to the last, and save others by the sacrifice of himself!" A noble trust — and right nobly redeemed! *She* knew he could not be among the rescued, and still be "himself." And what must be her feelings now, as she gazes upon that parting memento, as she thinks of the last time he held it in his hand — the wild, terrific scene around him, and those two solitary syllables which constitute his dying words! To her, now it is as silent as the loved lips of him who sent it from that scene of death; and justly so — for why should it mark time to her whose eternity began with his, who was the life of her life, and soul of her soul?

We leave her with her treasures — a broken sentence and a silent keepsake — the first sounding ever in her heart like the murmur of an ocean-shell cast forth upon a lonely shore, while the slender hands of the last, having ceased to chronicle the flight of time, are ever pointing her away into the opening ages of eternity.

And have we yet no word to say for him? The "heart grows full to weeping" as we linger above his honored memory — but a nation's acclaim is his proudest eulogium, and woman's tears his most fitting epitaph. As Nelson fell, he exclaimed: "Thank God! I have done my duty!" As Webster passed the dread portal which opens into the valley of shadows, he murmured: "I still live!" As Napoleon gathered up life's failing forces to battle with the last enemy, he shouted feebly: "*Tête d'armée!*" But what said the heroic Herndon of *himself?* Nothing. He neither encourages himself with the knowledge of duties well performed — no, he leaves his deeds to speak for him; nor solaces himself with the idea that he will hereafter live in the hearts of his countrymen — no, he leaves that for *them* to say; nor does he proudly assume his province of command, and go forth to meet death as king meets king in battle; nay, he uncovers to the last conqueror, acknowledging him the vicegerent of God, and with a brave heart and firm faith goes down with him silently, and grandly too, into the dark abyss of ocean, and the darker abyss of an unknown eternity.

Silent — silent all! And if we say to the great sea, and the wild winds, and the overlooking skies, "Where is he now?" they are silent also. Perhaps, like drifting sea-weed, cast upon some distant strand, his bones bleach beneath the fiery sun of the tropics; perhaps laid softly down by gently bearing waters, where

> "coral reefs lie bare,
> And the cold sea-maids sit to sun their streaming hair;"

perhaps carried away by the impetuous surge to regions where "night and death" have built their thrones — where giant icebergs go thundering down the deep — where Euroclydon rolls forth its "stern triumphant psalms," and beneath shattered mast and mouldering sail sleep the old Vikings of the Northern Sea. In our cemeteries, "stone spells to stone its weary tale" — we read records of the loved and lost as the long funeral train is passing by, and the dirge is wailing for the dead; but who dares follow *him* to the grave, who went down to death amid the battle of the elements; whose funeral train was long lines of marching billows, and whose burial psalm was the volleying thunder and the sounding storm? We may enter the city's splendid mausoleums, and read engraven on brass and marble the virtues of the dead; we may sit down by some lone grave in the forest, whose only monument is a cluster of snowy lilies, on which the morning dewdrops write their transient epitaph; but who shall venture down, even in thought, to the "dark, unfathomed caves of ocean," where now sleeps the heart which bore up bravely against terror, and danger, and death, but broke in the struggle to utter one little sentence in loving guise, and so left it forever unsaid? The winds and the waves will bring no answer to the questioning voice: "Where is he now?" but we may lay our hands upon our hearts, and answer softly, and truly too: "He is here! he dwells forever in the great heart of his country;" and while we answer thus, we also murmur meekly: "Our God has taken that noble spirit into his eternal rest!"

MRS. ANNIE CHAMBERS KETCHUM.*

IF genuine admiration for Mrs. Ketchum's genius, and the same admiration mingled with warm personal regard for herself as a Christian gentlewoman and ardent friend, could constitute fitness for the labor of love through courtesy assigned me, then this sketch would be among the most interesting of all these narratives of "Southland Writers."

It has never been the present writer's good fortune to meet in person the lady whose name stands at the head of the present article, but several years of familiar correspondence originating in a business way, when Mrs. Ketchum was at the head of the "Lotus," (an entertaining magazine established at Memphis in 1858 or '59,) has afforded more than a passing glimpse of that earnest, fervent nature which appears in everything that emanates from her pen, and constitutes her, according to my ability of criticism, the first poetess of the South — unless we may place Miss Crean in the same rank with her.

Of Mrs. Ketchum's prose-writings, I am not qualified to speak in detail. The "Ladies' Home," edited jointly by Mrs. French and Dr. Powell, gave us, indeed, extracts from "Nelly Bracken," her only published prose volume, unless I mistake, containing specimens of a style simple, terse, vigorous, and devoid of mannerism; the "Lotus" editorials were, oftentimes, tender and touching — imbued with a delicate pathos, whatever the theme; and of her letters — enchanting, artless, soul-breathing — I can only say that they seem to me the perfection of epistolary writing. Poetry, however, seems to be Mrs. Ketchum's natural element, and it is in rhythm that her peculiar bent of mind and feeling seeks its outlet.

My first acquaintance with her name and writings was through a poem which appeared in the "Richmond Enquirer" — copied into that paper from the "New York Churchman," to which it was originally contributed.

The lines struck me as breathing the very soul of poetry and fervent prayer; and, by the way, this religious element pervades almost every-

* Contributed by Miss Mary J. S. Upshur, of *Virginia.*

thing she has written, exerting, as I have cause to believe, a wide influence upon her daily life. The article alluded to is copied entire, thus:

THE MOTHER'S PRAYER.

They sleep. Athwart my white
Moon-marbled casement, with her solemn mien
Silently watching o'er their rest serene,
Gazeth the star-eyed night.

My girl — sedate, or wild,
By turns — as playful as a summer breeze,
Or grave as night on starlit Southern seas,
Serene, strange woman-child.

My boy, my trembling star!
The whitest lamb in April's tenderest fold,
The bluest flower-bell in the shadiest wold,
His fitting emblems are.

They are but two, and all
My lonely heart's arithmetic is done
When these are counted. High and holy One,
Oh, hear my trembling call!

I ask not wealth nor fame
For these my jewels. Diadem and wreath
Soothe not the aching brow that throbs beneath,
Nor cool its fever-flame.

I ask not length of life
Nor earthly honors. Weary are the ways
The gifted tread, unsafe the world's best praise,
And keen its strife.

I ask not that to me
Thou spare them, though they dearer, dearer be
Than rain to deserts, spring-flowers to the bee,
Or sunshine to the sea.

But kneeling at their feet,
While smiles like summer-light on shaded streams
Are gleaming from their glad and sinless dreams,
I would my prayer repeat.

In that alluring land,
The future — where, amid green, stately bowers,
Ornate with proud and crimson-flushing flowers,
Pleasure, with smooth white hand,

Beckons the young away
From glen and hill-side to her banquet fair —
Sin, the grim she-wolf, coucheth in her lair,
Ready to seize her prey.

The bright and purpling bloom
Of nightshade and acanthus cannot hide
The charred and bleaching bones that are denied
Taper, and chrism, and tomb.

Lord, in this midnight hour
I bring my lambs to thee. Oh! by thy truth,
Thy mercy, save them from th' envenomed tooth
And tempting poison-flower!

O Crucified and Crowned,
Keep us! We have no shield, no guide but thee.
Let sorrows come — let Hope's last blossom be
By Grief's dark tempest drowned;

But lead us by thy hand,
O gentlest Shepherd, till we rest beside
The still, clear waters, in the pastures wide
Of thine own sinless land!

The "Home Journal" published Mrs. Ketchum's "Christmas Ballad," of which her beloved "Benny" was the infant hero — Benny, whose pious youth gave such high promise of future usefulness and parental satisfaction in his career through life, whose last Christmas (of 1857) found him keeping the great birthday in his Father's house of "many mansions." While he sang the angel's song there, was there not one on earth whose heart-throbs kept time to the beat of that Christmas carol in its concluding lines?

"He is sleeping — brown and silken
Lie the lashes, long and meek,
Like caressing, clinging shadows,
On his plump and peachy cheek;

And I bend above him, weeping
  Thankful tears, oh, undefiled!
For a woman's crown of glory,
  For the blessing of a child!"

An autograph copy lies before me as I write, bearing far back to the days when it was penned at peaceful "Dunrobin," Mrs. Ketchum's war-ruined home, near Memphis. I am sorely tempted to quote largely from one and another of the valued letters that also came from thence, especially those relating to the war time, and her views of the South and its cause, in which her whole soul was merged; nor can I, indeed, wholly resist inaugurating my transgressions (for which I hope to be pardoned) by an extract from one bearing date in May, '61. Accompanying it came the MS. of a stirring battle-song, copied below, which appeared in the "Norfolk Argus" a short time after. One of the principal inducements to make the extract is to indicate somewhat of the inspiration prompting many kindred productions to that I shall presently copy, which authorship induced the Federal commandant at Memphis to refuse Mrs. Ketchum, later, a pass beyond the lines — she in a state of health vacillating between life and death, and withal in deep affliction — "because of her being a rebel song-writer."

"We had yesterday a frightful storm. Four hours preceding it, there hung a thick, gray mist along the horizon, and the air was so still that the nervous aspen-leaves hung motionless. I looked from my window into the stagnant sky.

"I thought of the stillness in our political atmosphere just now — the sure precursor of coming peril; and when the elements opened their batteries at length, and the tall, stout trees in the wood bowed and broke before their fury, I shuddered to think of the brave and noble that must yield up their lives in the coming conflict. I do not say these things to ——, my pride! I will gird on his sword, God bless him! I will show him I too am worthy of the name we inherit alike from the hero who died in the far-off bygone. But to you, a woman, brave-hearted but tender, I may say that I can sometimes scarcely see for tears.

"He is appointed to the artillery service of the State, our Governor being desirous to have the artillery commanded by West Point gentlemen entirely. His regiment, commanded by Colonel McCown, will march the 1st of June. The City of Memphis seizes every vessel bound North. Yesterday we captured three prizes.

"Yesterday, when —— came home with so much war news — I allude to the seizures, and local and State preparations — I could not resist the temptation to blow my individual bugle just a little, to the extent of the war-song I enclose you."

BATTLE-CALL.

Nec temere nec timide.

Dedicated to her brave countrymen, the Cavaliers of the South.

Gentlemen of the South,
  Gird on your flashing swords!
Darkly along your borders fair
  Gather the ruffian hordes.
Ruthless and fierce they come,
  Even at the cannon's mouth,
To blast the glory of your land,
  Gentlemen of the South!

Ride forth in your stately pride,
  Each bearing on his shield
Ensigns your fathers won of yore
  On many a well-fought field.
Let this be your battle-cry,
  Even to the cannon's mouth,
Cor unum, via una! Onward!
  Gentlemen of the South!

Brave knights of a knightly race,
  Gordon and Chambers and Grey,
Teach the base minions of the North
  How valor dares the fray!
Let them read on each spotless shield,
  Even at the cannon's mouth,
Decori decus addit avito,
  Gentlemen of the South!

Morrison, Douglas, Stuart,
  Erskine and Bradford and West,
Your gauntlets on many a hill and plain
  Have stood the battle's test.
Animo non astutia!
  March to the cannon's mouth,
Heirs of the brave dead centuries,
  Gentlemen of the South!

Call out your stalwart men,
  Workers in brass and steel,
Bid the swart artisans come forth
  At sound of the trumpet's peal.
Give them your war-cry, Erskine!
  Fight! to the cannon's mouth;
Bid the men *Forward*, Douglas! Forward!
  Yeomanry of the South!

Brave hunters! ye have met
  The fierce black bear in the fray,
Ye have trailed the panther night by night,
  Ye have chased the fox by day!
Your prancing chargers pant
  To dash at the gray wolf's mouth;
Your arms are sure of their quarry. Onward!
  Gentlemen of the South!

Fight that the lowly serf
  And the high-born lady still
May bide in their proud dependency,
  Free subjects of your will!
Teach the base North how ill—
  At the belching cannon's mouth—
He fares who touches your household gods,
  Gentlemen of the South!

From mother and wife and child,
  From faithful and happy slave,
Prayers for your sake ascend to Him
  Whose arm is strong to save.
We check the gathering tears,
  Though ye go to the cannon's mouth;
Dominus providebit! Onward!
  Gentlemen of the South!

I think it will be perceived by the specimens already quoted, and others which I shall proceed to quote, that Mrs. Ketchum ignores mere verbiage in expression; that each word has its corresponding idea, and that—to use a homely, but it seems to me expressive phrase—her writings contain no words or phrases thrown in for stuffing. She is exceedingly accurate, saying all she means, and no more—a style impossible of acquisition to a writer less thoroughly imbued with the spirit of his subject. Those who give us sentiment at second-hand always betray themselves, if in no other way, by the employment of some vehicle of speech a little the worse for long use — some pet phrase in demand of poetasters since time, or at least rhyme began. Mrs. Ketchum does not dally to adapt these to her thoughts, seeming to feel that fresh, strong conception is best expressed in the language it originally inspires, and that it confers its own picturesqueness and acceptability on its peculiar spontaneous forms of speech.

In "word-painting," I have thought she rivalled Ruskin at times in his peculiar gift. Who — beyond sympathy with the pathetic beauty of this "Requiem" — but can see therein the chameleon-tinted forests, the "setting" to this central object — the new-made grave? Who but breathes the breath of the autumn flowers, and sees their tantalizing, brilliant beauty — witnesses the white-winged spirit sweep through the "valley's" expanse — and later, the warder-stars come out to guard the battlements she has passed, and passed forever?

Leaves of the autumn time,
Crimson and golden, opalesque and brown,
To this new grave-heap slowly nestling down,
Come with your low, low chime
And sing of her, who, spring and summer past,
In her calm autumn went to heaven at last,
Where there is no more rime.

Flowers of the autumn days,
Bright lingering roses, asters white as snow,
And purple violets on the winds that go
Sighing their sad, sad lays,
Tell with your sweet breath how her spirit fair
Through life's declining kept its fragrance rare,
Fresher amid decays.

Birds of the autumn eves,
Warbling your last song ere ye plume your wing
For milder climes, stay yet awhile and sing
Where the lone willow grieves;
Tell of a nest secure from storm and blast,
Where her white wing — the shadowy valley past —
Rests under heavenly eaves.

Stars of the autumn night —
Crowned warders on the rampart of the skies,
With your bright lances holy mysteries
Upon the gravestone write;

Tell of the *new name* given to the free
In that fair land beyond the silent sea,
Where Christ is Lord and Light.

God of the wind and rain,
Seed-time and harvest, summer-time and sleet!
Stricken and woful, at Thy kingly feet
We bow amid our pain!
Help us to find her where no falling leaf
Nor parting bird doth tell of death and grief,
Where Thou alone dost reign.

I shall copy two others of Mrs. Ketchum's poems into this sketch, prefacing them by extracts from some of her letters: these will lead to a better appreciation of them, especially when I add that her brave husband fell a sacrifice to the dear South's and his own sense of honor and justice, in consequence of wounds received at Shiloh.

"Our conflict is, in the words of your most apt quotation from our holy Bible, between God and Baal. I may lose my ——, my pride and my bulwark, but I shall none the less willingly buckle on his armor and bid God speed him on. . . . Sunshine and fragrance, and sweetest wild-bird music are all around my Dunrobin home. I listen, then look out, and up at the golden, crystal sky, and my tears will not be repressed as I think how degenerate, self-sufficient man refuses the daily lessons taught by everything in nature. Yet I weep not from timorous fear, if I know myself at all. I believe Southern women all are ready to say with Archedamia:

"'We are brave men's mothers and brave men's wives;
We are ready to do and dare,
We are ready to man your walls with our lives,
And string your bows with our hair!'

"You have read this matchless battle-song from 'Chambers' Journal.' It has been ringing through my brain the entire winter, and I find myself often, as I go about my duties, stopping suddenly to listen, as it were, to the stirring lines —

"'Shame to the coward heart that springs
To the faint, soft arms of peace!
If the Roman eagle shook his wings
At the very gates of Greece,
Ask not the mothers who gave you birth
To bid you turn and flee!
When Sparta is trampled from the earth,
Her women can die and be free!'"

The italics are hers. Again she says (January, 1862):

"I have been out with my little hoe all this glorious afternoon, among my flowers, and I found hidden away from the frost, under a dainty coverlet of leaves, this precious violet, which I gathered for you. The long, green spears of the Kinnikinnick are peering out from their russet, mail-clad buds; the turkey-berry, its friendly comrade of the woods, now a denizen with it of the Dunrobin grounds, is swelling in every branch with emulative sap; and across the North Riding, as we call the avenue leading to our home, the dog-wood and Judas-tree are making ready for their fair spring favors. There is a threat of winter yet, early in the mornings, but I feel in my veins and my heart that the blessed spring-time is coming, and for the last week I have literally lived out of doors — now feeding the pigs or hunting hens' nests with Nora and Benny, or lying on the porch in the sunshine, our famous yellow cat — *General Braxton Bragg* — at my feet. The children talk to him, and he answers as intelligently as any other soldier, only in not as good English as some others. . . .

"A letter from my brave soldier yesterday, brings tidings of his continued health and safety. . . . He says it is likely his command will be ordered to Bowling Green shortly, as most of the Western forces are congregating there. All I love best are in that onward march to the *Dark and Bloody Ground*, that beautiful Eden, won inch by inch from the savage in the bygone time, that hallowed land where all my dead are sleeping."

Again: "I do not fear for the safety of our city, but the flower of our land are gathering to the rescue at Decatur, and my head swims to think how soon our homes may be desolated of our sunshine. The history of battles proves the truth of Abbé Fénélon's words: '*La cruelle guerre! Elle moisonne les bons, et epargne les mechants!*' and how dare I hope I shall be blessed above others? . . . Yet I would not have the South retreat one step from the position she has taken. I believe her cause is altogether just, and that history will accord her a degree of forbearance unexampled in the annals of nations."

The subjoined poem, written in 1866, tells its own story:

APRIL TWENTY-SIXTH.

Written in Elmwood Cemetery, upon the occasion of the solemn Floral Festival, commemorative of the Confederate Dead.

Dreams of a stately land
  Where rose and lotus open to the sun,
Where green savane and misty mountain stand —
  By lordly valor won.

Dreams of the earnest-browed
  And eagle-eyed, who late with banner bright
Rode forth in knightly errantry to do
  Devoir for God and Right.

Shoulder to shoulder, see
  The crowding columns file through pass and glen!
Hear the shrill bugle! List the turbulent drum
  Mustering the gallant men!

Resolute, year by year,
  They keep at bay the cohorts of the world:
Hemmed in, yet trusting to the Lord of Hosts,
  The Cross is still unfurled.

Patient, heroic, true,
  And counting tens where hundreds stood at first,
Dauntless for Truth they dare the sabre's edge,
  The bombshell's deadly burst.

While we, with hearts made brave
  By their proud manhood, work and watch and pray,
Till, conquering fate, we greet with smiles and tears
  The conquering ranks of gray!

O God of dreams and sleep!
  Dreamless they sleep; 't is we, the sleepless, dream!
Defend us while our vigil dark we keep,
  Which knows no morning beam.

Bloom, gentle springtide flowers,
  Sing, gentle winds, above each holy grave!
While we, the women of a desolate land,
  Weep for the true and brave!

From the "Sunday Appeal" is copied

MEMORIA IN ÆTERNA.

JUSTUS TRANSLATUS MDCCCLXV.

    Unto thy golden sands
Bright tropic country of my love! once more
I come with exiled feet — how travel-sore!
    From cold and distant lands.

Brightly the sun still shines;
Amid their leaves white blow the magnol flowers;
The mocking-bird throughout the circling hours
Sings in the bamboo-vines:

Fair as Damascus gleam
The city's gardens, 'mid their opulence
Of rose and myrtle flooding sight and sense,
And hill and glen and stream

Glint in meridian light,
Or smile beneath the full and silvery moon,
As if no black eclipse could blot the noon,
No tempest blight the night.

O gentlest friend! we sit
Beneath these drooping elms; the wind blows sweet
Among our Pæstum roses; bright and fleet
The finches sing and flit:

Yet wearily we turn
From their soft wooings to this precious ground,
Along whose silent, consecrated mound
The fires of sunset burn.

What shall I say to thee
Of him, the patriot just — how stammering tell
The virtues of that heart, now resting well
Beneath the myrtle-tree?

From blue Atlantic's bound
To the deep Bravo's mango-bordered shore,
His trumpet, 'mid the battle's shifting roar,
Gave no uncertain sound:

But, firm, and true, and clear,
Cautioned the rash, inspirited the weak,
Rebuked the venal, nor forgot to speak
Rare, noble words of cheer

To brave men, fainting, white,
In hospital wards; to children in their tears;
To women strong in faith and strange to fears,
Toiling by day and night.

And when disaster dire
Furled the red cross, whose light had dazed the world,
His voice was first to blunt the arrows hurled
By a flushed conqueror's ire.

Dark day of overthrow!
Vulnus immedicabile! for thee,
If in the future's Gilead there be
A balsam yet to grow,

Its healing shoot will spring
From holy lives laid down for freedom's sake—
From bold emprise, whose clashing truth will make
The echoing ages ring:

Its blessing will distil
From haunts made classic by heroic deeds—
From Shiloh's plain, from Chickamauga's reeds,
From Malvern's bloody hill.

How proud these memories vast!
Giving us each a dignity and strength
Not born of earth. They make us one, at length,
With the dim, fabulous past.

Ay! vanquished though we be,
O heart! beat rhythmic with my sorrow! we
Are of the Heraclidæ! mount and sea
Attest our high degree!

Another golden age
Dawns from Potomac to the Mexique strand—
With Hector and Andromache we stand
On history's blazoned page:

And from the sulphurous rim
Of black defeat, we join the deathless crowds
Whose shapes, like mountain-peaks above the clouds,
Loom through the centuries dim.

Let bloated, vain success
Be worshipped by the millions of to-day;
Righteous defeat, uncrowned, hath silent sway
To-morrow will confess.

Strike deep, though silently,
O Southern oaks, your roots in Southern ground;
And lift, O palm and laurel, victor-crowned,
Your branches to the sky!

The river's heaving floods,
The mountain-tops, the steadfast stars will say
Unto the cycling ages: IN THAT DAY,
LO! THERE WERE DEMI-GODS!

So finish our selections from Mrs. Ketchum's poems, which, one and all, with all the strong faith they shadow forth in the ultimate triumph of right and truth, will exclude her from the rank of successful poets, so far as popularity is the test of success. Beside her being emphatically the poet of a "lost cause," as it is often called, her style is characterized by a degree of refinement, an elevation both of conception and expression intelligible to the cultivated few, but which the people, so named, will never appreciate; and then that air of mournfulness that touches all she writes, whether of poetry or prose, though here and there stirring a heart to sympathy with its requiem-like, chastened beauty, is not the characteristic most in demand of those who read for relief from the too true tragedies that life sets gratuitously before us all.

Mrs. Ketchum was born and her early life passed in that picturesque portion of her State among the crags of the old Elkhorn River. But I must let her tell something of herself:

"We were three, we fatherless sisters — three little ones in the old Kentucky home, watched over by three older grown-up sisters, to whom we were severally awarded by our dear widowed mother, when our father was called home to heaven. Day by day, when dismissed from the study where our elder sisters taught us, we shouted among the hills, we plashed in the flashing streams. Night after night, in the long, snowy winters, we knotted ourselves in the chimney corner, and listened with wide-open eyes to our dear black nurse's marvellous tales, or, covered up in the warm nursery bed, whispered together of Sinbad the Sailor, with half-closed, sleepy eyes, and at last went off from the fairy world of child romance into the fantastic realm of dreams."

The above prefaced a sad narration of domestic affliction, the loss of one of the devoted trio of sisters above spoken of; and in connection with it, I copy one of the "Lotus" editorials, "Under the Leaves," which I think (without any authority whatever) had for its subject the lamented one just mentioned.

"We have a pleasant shade now, children, under the leaves. There are delicate buds peering out from the leaves of the rose, and glistening emerald beads on the jasmine sprays, almost bursting to display their golden cups. See, out on the slopes, and under the budding trees, the fresh young grass lies like a velvet carpet. The weeping-willows that lean over the high, white wall of the cemetery are fringed with tender leaves; and yellow jonquils, growing on the graves, are tolling their golden bells in every breeze that whispers among the cedars. It is spring-time, and you know all the world is gay in the spring; but the Lotus cannot dance with Laeta now, when the March wind blows his merry, boisterous fife, and the hyacinths, awakened from their sleep, nod and swing in the gamesome frolic.

"There is a gentle river far away, where the rock-moss clings to the tall, gray cliffs, where the wild rose climbs like a fearless child, and over whose clear, murmuring waters the sycamore-trees stretch out their long, white arms in silent benediction. Its waters flow into the Kentucky, the Kentucky bears them to the Ohio, and the Ohio leads them at last to join the armied waves of this grand old river marching to the sea, on whose banks our leafy bower is built. The waters of that far-off stream are singing a death-song now: they have murmured it all the way from the far Kentucky hills, past cities and towns and plantations, where light-hearted children were playing, but none of them understood its meaning—its story was not for them. It tells to the trembling Lotus, as she leans to the solemn water, how the tall, red mountain-pinks will lift their heads on those distant crags, watching in vain for the pleasant eyes that sought them every spring; how the sycamore leaves will stop their whisperings to listen for the light footfall that will rustle the dead leaves at their hoary roots no more; and day and night the Lotus will kiss the blessed waves that a little while ago bathed fair and dainty feet that were whiter than her petals, and mirrored a face that is hid beneath the violets now.

"Laeta, joyful Laeta, has an elder sister, with soft, brown eyes and sweet, majestic manners. Her name is Lucia. She is wise and thoughtful. Through deepest darkness of sorrow she opens a path of light, and where there are only thorny thickets, she can show us safe and pleasant passages. She has sung with the night-wind in the ear of the sorrowing Lotus the story of One who taught the whole world patience in the garden of Gethsemane; she has written on the morning clouds the wondrous legend of the King's Daughter, whose raiment is of wrought gold, and on whose forehead shines the morning-star. Laeta is singing with the mocking-birds; we can hear them in the wood. It is her office to rejoice with every joyful thing. She is good and innocent, and always lovely and unselfish; but Lucia is wiser and knows better what to say when the white rabbit strays away, and the rain washes up the newly-planted flower-seeds, and the black crape hangs at the silent door."

I cannot better conclude this imperfect narration than by adding that the fortunes of our late civil contest left this lady bereft of most her worldly goods, if not all; and that, with true courage, and zeal, and faith, she set herself to the practical work of earning her own living. Her fine mind found employment in the duties of a teacher in the large female school or college conducted in Memphis by a brother of General J. E. B. Stuart; and until an almost ruined state of health incapacitated her for the exertion, she remained in the institution, illustrating the worthlessness of the doctrine that literary women are an incubus upon the body social, separate from their pens and ink; and, moreover, substantiating the fact that Southern women are worthy of all that has been ascribed to them in high heroism — true adaptation of themselves to the changed circumstances their mother-land's misfortunes have brought peculiarly home to them.

AMABARE ME.

When the white snow left the mountains,
When the spring unsealed the fountains;
When her eye the violet lifted
Where the autumn leaves had drifted,
'Neath the budding maple-tree,
Amabare Me.

Now the summer flowers are dying;
Now the rippling streams are drying;
Yet I cry, though lone I linger,
Where the autumn's crimson finger
Burns along the maple-tree,
Amabare Me.

As the wild bird, faint and dying,
Follows summer, faithless, flying,
So my heart, doubts blank are beating,
Broken-winged, is still repeating,
While it follows, follows thee,
Amabare Me.

Soon will winter, gaunt and haggard,
Shroud a new grave, sodless, beggar'd!
Still, though not a flower be planted,
Not a requiem be chanted,
Not an eye with tears be laven,
On a gray stone will be graven,
'Neath the leafless maple-tree,
Amabare Me.

MRS. CLARA COLES.

IN 1861, J. B. Lippincott & Co., Philadelphia, published a beautiful volume, entitled "Clara's Poems." "Clara" is Mrs. Coles, at that time and now residing in the city of Nashville.

"These poems are in many respects well worthy the mechanical labor expended upon their proper presentation; for though they cannot claim, and never were meant to claim a place amid the standard poetry of the language, they are worth, well worth perusal and preservation. Classic in structure, thought, or imagery, they are far from being; elaborateness of verbal finish has not been bestowed upon them; they neither paint nor awaken any of those undeveloped passions, or even sentiments, the revelation of which entitles the poet to the proud title of "original;" but they deal simply and chastely, yet often warmly, with those tender sorrows and feminine fancies felt and nursed by most cultured females, especially by those who have passed much of life far from the frivolities of good society, and dreamed, amid crowds, of heart experiences never realized save to those whose solitariness of sentiment is by circumstances wedded to solitariness of life. The conclusion is forced on the reader of these poems, that the writer had a vague consciousness of possessing a fund of poesy, but had never developed it.

"The very simplicity attained, seems to arise from a dread of using powers, thoughts, and imagery of whose real worth and meaning she was timidly dubious. She is a pleasing versifier, possessed of poetic instincts, but lacking poetic power. She might have been a poet and a *good* one: her book reveals this pleasingly and clearly, but it does no more. This is one side of the verdict of strict impartiality, and were we to stop here it were partiality itself, for we should omit the better features of the poems—music, morality, and a prevailing tone of religious effect, unobtruded, yet, unconsciously to the writer herself, pervading the whole book, and fitting it admirably for the parlor-table, or what-not—a book that may ever safely and profitably be placed within easy reach of young lovers of poesy, in the certainty of yielding pleasure, inflicting no pain and teaching no error. Would we could say the same of greater poets!" Thus said a critic in the "Southern Monthly," 1861.

John T. Edgar, D. D., in an "introductory" to "Clara's Poems," says:

"'Clara' is truly retiring, and as delicate in her claims to attention, as she is in the sweet images which are so meekly and touchingly conspicuous in many of the more tenderly pathetic of her pieces. It will be seen that the great charm of her verse is found, not in their classical allusions or romantic imagery, but in the simple appeals which they so winningly make to all that is unartificial, uncorrupted, truthful, and responsive in the more pure and gentle emotions of every unsophisticated heart. She has had no learned resources from which to draw her inspirations. To such fountains, no former familiarity or more recent acquaintance could have enabled her to resort. The school in which many of her most impressive lessons have been taught has been that of disappointment and sorrow; and to such lessons we are indebted for many of the finest and most thrilling stanzas of her often plaintive and pensive muse."

SABBATH MORN.

Bathed in the orient flush of morn,
  How lovely earth appears!
New tints the opening rose adorn,
  Gemm'd with night's dewy tears.
Soft, whispering breezes sigh around,
  And snowy cloudlets lie
Like angel watchers, floating through
  The calm, pure, azure sky.

The mountain-tops reflect the rays
  That usher in the day-god's beams;
The birds trill forth their songs of praise;
  The wave in gold and crimson gleams:
Oh, beautiful! My spirit drinks
  In copious draughts of love divine,
While gazing on this glorious scene,
  And worships at a holier shrine

Than mortal hands could ever rear,
  Or mortal language e'er portray;
For angel voices, murmuring near,
  Seem wafting my glad soul away.

Sweet, tranquil morn! so clear, so calm;
What soft emotions fill my breast!
Bright emblem of that glorious dawn—
A Sabbath of eternal rest!

SONNET TO SLEEP.

Come, O thou white-winged angel, gentle sleep,
Press thy cool fingers on my tear-stained lids,
Each wearied sense in soft oblivion steep,
Oh, give the rest my sorrow still forbids!
Come, with thy crimson poppy juice, and bathe
My throbbing, care-worn brow;
Ope the rose-tinted, pearly gate of dreams,
And let my weary spirit enter now.
Come, fold thy pinions softly round my soul,
And waft it to some bright and happier sphere,
To meet and mingle for a moment with
Its kindred, who are blest and smiling there,
Waiting with song and harp to welcome me
When death shall close my simple history here.

"WHO IS CLARA?"

She's a queer little woman, that dwells in a cot,
So lowly and simple, the world knows her not;
Where the birds sing all day, and the sweet flowers bloom,
Filling the air with song and perfume;
And peace seems to brood on her halcyon wings,
O'er the dear little nest where unnoticed she sings.

She's a sad little woman, though appearing as gay
As the lark, soaring high at the dawning of day
Far up the blue heavens, to gaze on the sun;
Yet, folding her wings ere his bright course is run,
All drooping and weary she sinks to her nest,
To hide the keen arrow still deep in her breast.

Yes, she's lonely and sad, for death has bereft
Her home of its jewels—not one now is left

To wake its lone echoes with music and mirth;
Like sunbeams they 've passed from the beautiful earth,
Shrouding her spirit in darkness and gloom,
That the sunlight of heaven alone can illume.

And she sits in her bower and dreams of the past;
When twilight's pale shadows around her are cast,
And zephyrs kiss softly the whispering leaves,
Sweet visions of beauty and gladness she weaves
In low, thrilling numbers, that flow from a heart,
Where the world and its follies have never a part.

ADELIA C. GRAVES.

THE stone on which it is written that such a one was born, lived so many years, and died, often furnishes the only record of a long and useful life, of patient suffering and unrequited toil; yet even this is frequently more than the great world cares to read.

The life that has in it no thrilling incident, no wonderful event, no startling tragedy, or mirth-exciting comedy, but which is spent in the quiet performance of every-day duties, has little in it to attract attention from those outside the circle of personal friends.

Such a life is that of Mrs. Adelia C. Graves, the devoted wife, the self-sacrificing mother, the accomplished teacher, and the gifted poet. Had she persisted in following the impulses of her early years, and devoted her life entirely to the pursuits of literature, something would doubtless have been accomplished which would have caused the world to feel much interest in her biography.

She was born March 17th, 1821, at Kingsville, Ashtabula County, in the State of Ohio, and spent her early life upon the romantic shores of Lake Erie. Her father, Dr. D. M. Spencer, was a physician of ability and reputation. He was a man of uncommon mental power, and at one time exerted no small influence in the political circles of his State. But his friends having been defeated in their endeavors to secure his nomination to Congress by the wire-working of his anti-slavery opponent, the noted Joshua R. Giddings, he withdrew from further participation in a conflict where success could be gained only by the use of such means as neither he nor his friends were willing to employ. When Mr. Giddings was elected, Dr. Spencer declared that the ultimate result would be the dissolution of the Union, and a fratricidal war between the North and South. About a quarter of a century has elapsed since that prediction, then denounced as the insane ravings of disappointed ambition.

The children of Dr. Spencer, one by one, as they were free to do so, came and united their destinies with the South. Three of them are buried in Southern soil, and the subject of this sketch is the only one left.

Miss Spencer had in her early girlhood resolved to devote her life to literature. 'The Muses had been the companions of her childhood. Stanzas written before she was nine years old are models of correct versification, and exhibit the beautiful simplicity of expression and happy choice of words which characterize the productions of her more mature years. She wrote because she could not restrain the flow of bright and beautiful thoughts that were forever welling up from her young heart, and taking shape in simple, child-like rhymes.

She loved to be *alone* — passing her time on the pebbly beach, or in the grand old forests that had stood a thousand years near where she had been born. There she could commune with the invisible. There, with no mortal ear to heed, and no tongue to criticize or blame, she could warble out the extemporized lays which *would* be ever coming to her tongue. Her love of nature was a passion, the record of which is beautifully given in some of her earliest unpublished poems.

Miss Spencer married a teacher, Z. C. Graves, President at that time of Kingsville Academy, since founder and President of Mary Sharpe College, Winchester, Tenn.

To Mr. Graves, the highest of all employments, save one, the Gospel ministry, was that of training the minds of the young. The goal of his ambition was to become the greatest of living teachers: not greatest in the amount of money he might amass by teaching, nor yet in the reputation he might gain as the manager of a school; but greatest in his capacity to communicate knowledge, and secure the very highest possible development of the moral and intellectual powers of those who should be objects of his care. In this he was at once seconded by his wife with all the energy of her soul. So long as health and strength permitted, she was with him in the school-room, sharing fully with her husband, not only in its labors, but in all its responsibilities.

A few years after her marriage, Mrs. Graves received a sad injury, which has crippled her physical energies ever since. For five years, at first, she could not walk across her room; and oftentimes now, she is unable to walk a short distance.

In 1850, Mr. Graves, as President, laid the foundation of the Mary Sharpe College, at Winchester. It was designed to be an institution in which the daughters of the South could secure, not merely the fashionable accomplishments of an ordinary boarding-school education, but the same mental discipline and extensive knowledge of ancient and modern languages, the higher mathematics, and the natural sciences which our sons could gain at the very best colleges or universities of the land. The wonderful success of this institution depended, for the first few years, very much upon the patient labor, the indefatigable energy, and the judicious counsels of Mrs. Graves.

That characteristic of Mrs. Graves's poetry which most commends it to our taste, is its extreme naturalness and simplicity of expression. They are beautiful word-paintings, in which every line of light and shade is distinct upon the mental canvas; yet there is no labor for effect, no straining after rhymes, no far-fetched similes; but the verse is in simple Anglo-Saxon words, with a predominance of monosyllables, singing its music as it goes. The rhyming words are there simply because no other words would so well express the thought. Yet while it is thus unstudied and simple, thus devoid of all artistic display, it is full of

"Thoughts not thought before,"

full of the beautiful and the grand.

Mrs. Graves's first-born — the child of hope and promise — fills a soldier's grave! The war and its consequences nearly ruined them pecuniarily. Mrs. Graves at the present time occupies the position of Matron and Professor of Rhetoric in the College. She was formerly Professor of Latin and Belles-lettres.

The Baptist Sunday School Union have published eight little volumes for Sunday-school children, mostly selected from the "Children's Book," which Mrs. Graves edited for several years, and for which she wrote a great deal. These books, at the request of the "committee of the Union," she compiled from her sketches therein published. She has contributed to different periodicals, mostly fugitive poems, and two prose tales, one a prize tale; and "Ruined Lives," published in the "Southern Repository," Memphis, constitute, with the drama of "Jephthah's Daughter," her published works. She has a quantity of MSS. on hand, written as a pleasure and a solace; in fact, because she could not help writing. She is engaged now on a work, entitled "Seclusaval; or, The Arts of Romanism," several chapters of which have been published in the "Baptist," at Memphis.

Mrs. Graves's aim is to instruct and to do good with her pen; consequently, she has tried rather to repress a somewhat exuberant youthful fancy. If Mrs. Graves's health will admit, she hopes to publish several volumes, and also to collect her published and unpublished poems. She has a work on "Woman: Her Education, Aims, Sphere, Influence, and Destiny," (which has been delivered as lectures to the pupils of the college;) "A Guide and Assistant to Composition;" and a poem, entitled "Alma Grey"—all of which we hope to see in print.

HUMAN SOVEREIGNTY; OR, EVERY MAN A KING.

To the young men of our beloved Southland, who, repining not at the past, or despondingly brooding over what might have been, have yet the courage to accept their situation as it is, and the energetic exercise of whose wisdom, goodness, and virtue is yet to constitute the true wealth and freedom of a fallen people, the following poem is most respectfully dedicated, with the assurance that gold, bank-stock, lands, cotton-bales, and negroes make no man rich or great; but the real wealth of any country is to be estimated by the amount of the active intelligence and virtue of its sons and daughters. RESURGAMUS.

Victoria sitteth on a throne, with thronging nobles round,
And with a rich and jewelled crown her queenly brow is bound,
While thousand hands, at her behest, perform her slightest will,
And only wait a wish to know, with pleasure to fulfil.

Her kingdom is the sea-girt isles, and far-off India's shore,
And stretches from the northern snows to great Niagara's roar;
While ocean-gems are crouching low her lion arms to greet,
And strong Gibraltar humbly kneels a subject at her feet.

Queen of a mighty realm, she rules o'er lands so widely spread,
And fearful weight of royalty resteth upon her head;
Millions of beings yield to her their life-career to guide,
While Wisdom, with its hoary hairs, must her decrees abide.

But thou, young man, with sun-browned cheek, a tiller of the soil,
Which, with the fruits it yieldeth thee, rewardeth all thy toil—
The labor-gems that gird thy brow have value rich and great
As diadems of jewels rare that burden by their weight.

Thy God hath given to *thee* a realm, and made thee, too, a king;
And willing subjects unto thee their votive offerings bring;
While thou must reign a sovereign lord, with undisputed sway,
Or yield the master-spirit's rule the subject to obey.

"My mind to me a kingdom is," * wrote one who suffered long
Within the Bastile's gloomy walls, 'mid gratings high and strong;

* Madame Guyon, confined on account of her religion.

And, like a bird, she sat and sang to him who placed her there;
Although a bird shut from the fields of sunlight and of air.

Well was that inborn realm subdued, thus faithfully to bring
The fruits of joy and sweet content, and pleasant memories fling
Among the hopes that budded thick within that grated room,
Where yet the sunlight of the heart in gushing floods could come.

Youth, with the generous impulses that crowd thy opening way,
Thou'rt each a king — monarch supreme — an empire owns thy sway:
'T is true thou wear'st no purple robe, no glittering, golden crown,
Nor bear'st a jewelled sceptre's wand t' enforce thy haughty frown:

Thy kingdom is no wide-spread land, girt by the heaving wave;
But of thyself thou'rt ruler all, from childhood to the grave;
And he who hath a high-born soul, a true and kindly heart,
Addeth to "human sovereignty" its most distinguished part.

No princely dome is thine to boast, no costly marble walls
Reared by the sweat of toiling men, who must obey thy calls;
No pictures of proud artists' skill, no tessellated floors
That echo to the courtly tread of those within thy doors.

Thy palace is the wide-spread earth, its dome the arching sky;
And far more bright than gorgeous lamps the light that meets thy eye —
The glorious sun at morning's hour, the flashing stars at eve,
Among whose rays the moonbeams too their silver tissue weave.

The Architect who built for thee hath fashioned for thy view
Full many a scene of beauty rare, bright flowers of Eden hue,
The greenwood shade, the waterfall, the mountain tipped with mist,
Whose sunny heights and dusky grots the amber clouds have kissed.

What though earth trumpet not thy fame across her lakes and seas,
Nor silken banner waft it forth upon the floating breeze?
If in thy peaceful breast there lives the consciousness of right,
Thou'rt happier than a CONQUEROR returning from the fight.

What though no herald's blazonry trace back thy ancient name,
And find unmixed with vulgar blood thy royal lineage came?
Man's acts proclaim nobility, and not the kingly crest;
For he's the noblest who performs life's trying duties best.

And should men scorn thy mean attire, and dare to call thee "*slave*,"
Hold up thy head, *king of thyself*, and be thou truly brave;
For God hath given thee sovereignty of soul, and mind, and heart,
And absolute thy power must be till life itself depart.

Then arm that soul with heaven-born truth, with justice, and with love;
And fill thy mind with knowledge too, foul error to remove;
Stir well the ground of thy young heart, that it produce no weeds,
But precious fruits of charity, and treasures of good deeds.

Ay, let thy bosom wear the robe of high-born honesty,
And truth gird e'en thy secret acts with its pure panoply;
Then, knowledge-crowned, thy brow serene with holy light shall glow,
And rays of living radiance o'er a darkened world shall throw.

And thou 'lt so rule this precious realm bestowed, fair youth, on thee,
That when is asked thy last account thou 'lt give it joyfully;
Nor fear abash thy pallid cheek, nor tremble on thy tongue,
To meet the Universal King and mingle with his throng.

Prince of humanity! self's rightful, heaven-born lord!
Virtue and goodness bring their own exceeding great reward:
Be free from passion's rule, from ignorance and pride,
And *there 's no nobler work than man, the Godhead's self beside.*

MRS. MARY E. POPE.

MRS. POPE'S maiden name was Mary E. Foote. She is a native of Huntsville, Ala. She married, when young, Mr. Leroy Pope, a member of a branch of the distinguished "Walker" family, of Alabama.

As a young lady, Miss Foote possessed a beautiful, dreamy face, and her form of aërial grace personified the ideal of poesy.

Mr. and Mrs. Pope made their home in Memphis, where she has resided since. Her life has been chequered by misfortune and sorrow, which have only seemed to give occasion for the development of the lofty and noble qualities of her nature. Mrs. Pope is the mother of Lieutenant W. S. Pope, killed at Tishemingo Creek, and mentioned in the life of General Bedford Forrest.

Mrs. Pope has grappled with adversity with a bold, unquailing spirit, and ridden triumphant over the storms of life. She has charge of a flourishing school for young ladies in Memphis, which sufficiently attests the indomitable energy dwelling in her slender and fragile figure.

The sweet murmurings of her muse may be frequently heard floating on the breeze, in the Memphis journals.

THE GIFT OF SONG.

If, when bright visions o'er thee throng,
They clothe themselves in words of song,
And strengthen and refresh thy soul;
Though weak and faint the numbers roll,
    Yet fear not thou to sing.
If common life to thee keep tune
Unto thy spirit's chaunting rune,
And all the actual grows bright
'Neath fancy's soft ideal light,
    Thou hast the power to sing.

If in each living, human face,
Thy unsealed eye doth love to trace,
Through sin's dark, loathsome, outward form,
God's image, ever pure and warm,
Thou art a poet; sing.
When sorrow bows thy burdened head,
And lurid clouds thy path o'erspread,
If in thy grief, on radiant wing,
The muse doth woo thee to her spring,
Fear not to sip and sing.
When life blooms like a new-made bride,
With hope and love and grateful pride,
And earth to thy illumined eye
With Aiden seems in sheen to vie;
If joy is tuneful, sing.
When morning blushes o'er the earth
With rosy softness, bloom, and mirth,
And birdlings from each jewelled spray
Woo thee to hail the new-born day;
If music haunt thee, sing.
If, when thy glances seek the sky,
Where sunset hues its pavement dye,
Thy fettered spirit clank its chain,
Struggling to make its utterance plain;
Unbind the links and sing.
It may be that thy lyre's faint tone
No magic master-key may own;
Thy falt'ring steps may fail to reach
In fame's great temple-shrine a niche;
But yet fear not to sing.
As well the twitt'ring wren might fear
With his soft strain the day to cheer
Because the nightingale's rich note
More proudly sweet at eve doth float,
And thus refuse to sing,
As thou, because on stronger wing
Thy brothers scale fame's height and sing—
Their grand, immortal harps will wake
A thousand lesser shells to take
Part in creation's hymn.
The heaven-descended, god-like power
To mortals is a priceless dower.
Some hearts in silent grief may ache;
But some, if mute, e'en joy would break,
And, sad or glad, must sing.

But if to thee no radiant sheen
Light up the roughest human mien;
If life wear not a glorious light,
Beyond what beams on common sight,
    Be still, nor dare to sing.
If human faith and human love
In thee no sacred worship move;
If in bright nature's open eye
No great, eternal beauty lie,
    Be sure thou canst not sing.
If thy calm pulse and even blood
Course not at times a lava flood,
With suffocating rush of thought,
By noble deeds or evil brought,
    Such cool blood cannot sing.
Touch not with hand profane the lyre,
Unbaptized with the sacred fire.
Study may give the tricks of art,
But cannot the bard's power impart
    To other souls to sing.

THE RAIN.

The rain, the longed-for summer rain,
  Is coming down at last;
Over the city, the wood, the plain,
  A misty veil is cast.
The children of men, with dust-dimmed eyes,
  And a prayer in every heart,
Look fearful up to the cloud-draped skies,
  Lest the welcome signs depart.

The rain, the pleasant summer rain,
  Comes pattering from the eaves;
The grateful music rings again
  From the dust-besprinkled leaves.
O children of men, from sleep arise,
  To worship the loving Hand
That sends the life-stream from the skies
  To heal the fainting land.

The rain, the cooling summer rain,
  How it brightens the crisp, brown grass!
How the odors of blossom and ripened grain
  Sweep by as the sweet drops pass!
The cattle, upon a thousand hills
  On freshened pastures fed,
Are drinking content the tide that fills
  The dried-up streamlet's bed.

The rain, the grateful summer rain,
  It falleth alike on all —
On the child of want in his aching pain,
  On the dweller in splendor's hall;
On him whose heart and hands are clean,
  On the wretch with the mark of Cain;
And lordly man and reptile mean
  Bless God for the summer rain.

The blessed rain of heavenly grace
  Is falling on human souls,
And the stain from the mire of earth's wild chase
  Away on the bright drops rolls;
The heart that in sin lay scorched and dead,
  To a higher life has birth,
Whence flowers of love and holiness shed
  Sweet perfume o'er the earth.

MARAH.

"I went out full, and the Lord hath brought me home empty."

Travel-stained, foot-sore, and weary
  Comes the exile home again;
Lifting eyes tear-stained and dreary
  O'er her life's wide, blasted plain;
With the dust of ceaseless sorrow
  Burning ever on her brow,
Seeks on Labor's fields to borrow
  Strength to meet the empty Now.

Ne'er was queen, with crown-gem studded,
  On the world's most lofty throne,
Richer than with heart-love flooded
  Went the exile from her home.

Mother — oh! the wealth, the glory
  Of that diadem of light;
Words can never tell the story
  Of its treasures of delight.

On the won field, rent and gory,
  Whence the routed foe had fled,
Faded out the light and glory
  When the hero son lay dead.
Empty, shorn, and inly bleeding,
  Groping 'neath a rayless sky,
All the joys of earth unheeding,
  Fain the mother-heart would die.

But o'er sorrow's waves come stealing
  Whispered tones of tender love,
To the darkened soul revealing
  Shapes of light the grave above;
And a form of seraph beauty,
  Hero brow, and maiden cheek,
To hear her song, "Life is duty,
  And the brave the conflict seek."

Travel-stained, foot-sore, and weary,
  Is there strength left to obey?
O'er a life so blank and dreary,
  Can the fainting steps make way?
Saviour, on thy path of sorrow,
  Guide the feet so far astray,
Purge the tear-dimmed eyes to follow
  Thee, the mourner's hope and stay.

VIRGINIA.

MRS. MARGARET J. PRESTON.

MARGARET JUNKIN is the second daughter of the Rev. George Junkin, D. D., a Presbyterian divine of some note in the Southern portion of that Church. Dr. Junkin was President of Lafayette College, Easton, Pa., and of Washington College, Lexington, Va. The successor of the Rev. Dr. Junkin in the presidential chair of the latter College is Robert E. Lee. "Stonewall" Jackson was one of its Professors in the term of Dr. Junkin, whose eldest daughter was the wife of the famous Confederate leader.

Miss Junkin was a frequent contributor to the "Southern Literary Messenger" during the editorship of John R. Thompson. The following poem was published in 1850:

DANTE IN EXILE.

"The prior perceived one day a man coming into the monastery whom none of its inmates knew. He asked him what he wanted; but the stranger making no reply, and continuing to gaze on the building, as though contemplating its architecture, the question was put a second time; upon which, looking round on his interrogator, he answered: '*Peace!*'" — TURNBULL'S *Genius of Italy.*

Peace for the exile banished from his home,
His kindred, and his country? — for the man
Whose very birthplace roots him from her soil
In jealous rage, as though he were a weed
Of noxious influence, and flings him forth
To wither, all uncared for — *peace* for *him?*
Yea, even for *him* — if indignation just
Against oppression and foul wrong can yield
A nutriment, though bitter, strong enough
To still the cravings that his nature feels;
But not for thee, O Poet, with thy soul
Of organism tender, delicate,

Stern, yet with woman's gentlest sweetnesses
Tempering its loftiness — its every chord
Thrilling with an unutterable love
To thine unworthy Florence — with thy heart,
Thy high, heroić, melancholy heart,
In its refinement of ecstatic pain,
Quivering beneath its sorrow evermore!

No peace for *thee!* Thy sadden'd gaze could rest
Upon no other sky that wore a hue
Resplendent as thine own Etrurian heavens;
No stream that flashed in sunshine could awake
The joyousness that thy young years had known
By silvery Arno; and no city seem
So queenly in its proud magnificence
As beautiful Florence, lying lovingly
Within the arms of her encircling hills.
Yet *she* could fling thee from her — she could bear
To bind thy sensitive spirit to the rack
Of an ingenious torture, till thy life
Should wear in broken-heartedness away!
And thou couldst tame thy fiery nature down,
And love her still with an unselfish love,
That nought could quench, even in thy deepest wrong,
Throughout thy years of lingering martyrdom!

She could not take thine all: though sore athirst
For the sweet sympathies that once refreshed
Thy Tuscan home — thou hadst a hidden spring,
Pure, cooling, inexhausted, whence thy mind
Drew strength and solace 'midst its harshest woes;
And even in thy severest poverty
Of hope and comfort — thou, with lavish hand,
Didst pour from out that precious fount of song
Delicious waters that should ever yield
Divine refreshment.

But the living stream,
So clear and full and flowing, and so fraught
With rare delight to others — could not cure
Thy long home-sickness — could not satisfy
Thy painful human yearnings. And the peace
Which thou hadst sought through many wanderings —
Through years of weary banishment, in vain —
Thine aching heart found only in the grave!

In 1857, she published a volume, entitled "Silverwood: A Book of Memories."

Colonel J. T. L. Preston, the husband of the subject of this article, is one of the faculty of the Virginia Military Institute, at Lexington.

Mrs. Preston's most ambitious effort is the poem of "Beechenbrook: A Rhyme of the War."

Mrs. Preston has written because she "thought in numbers, and the numbers came," not for popular notice, nor from necessity, as, alas! so many of her countrywomen have been forced to do since the war, by the reverses of fortune. She is so happy as to be lifted above want or accidents of poverty. She has written for pastime and from patriotism, as the amusement in the pleasant idleness of a life devoted not to literature, but to the womanly cares and pleasures which a large establishment, husband, children, and "society" force upon her.

Mrs. Preston was a frequent contributor from its commencement to the "Land we Love;" General Hill, its editor, being a warm personal friend of hers. She also contributes to various other Southern journals. We subjoin some critiques, Northern and Southern, of "Beechenbrook"—the first taken from the "Round Table," the second from the "Field and Fireside:"

"BEECHENBROOK: A RHYME OF THE WAR.—A publisher's printed estimate of the sale of his publications is usually somewhat imaginative; to use a threadbare but serviceable quotation, 'The wish is often father to the thought.' Yet in this case we see no reason to doubt the entire veracity of Messrs. Kelly & Piet in announcing 'fifth thousand' on the title-page of this volume. It is one which, we should judge, would be immensely popular among the people for whom it was written, and to whose sectional pride and prejudices it appeals in more ways than one. In all respects it is essentially Southern, and in most it is praiseworthy. Its press-work especially shows a standard of excellence which we were not prepared to look for below Philadelphia; and the poems themselves, if they do not quite deserve, still do not altogether disgrace their handsome setting. In two points particularly they challenge Southern admiration: in the first place, they are not absolutely trash, which is quite an advance on the majority of Southern verse; and in the second place, their merit is even sufficient to dimly foreshadow a time when the sunny South shall achieve intellectual emancipation in a literature of its own, and be no longer dependent on New England for poetry, as well as piety, politics, and prints. To the author's own people, therefore, unjaded as yet by the worship of many literary idols, her book must be peculiarly grateful: even we of the North, who are not tainted by that sombre fanaticism that sees no good in Nazareth, may find in it much to admire and applaud. The verse is graceful and flowing, and the language and sentiment prove the author to be a lady of refined and cultivated taste. '*Dulce et decus*' is rather an indecorous liberty with Horace, and we should greatly prefer that Miss (or Mrs.?) Preston had not linked 'breast' with 'caress,' nor turned 'hárassing' and 'suppórt' into 'harássing' and 'súpport.' But after all, we are not so much concerned with Miss (or Mrs.?) Preston's Latin and orthoepy, which might be better, as with her poetry, which might be decidedly worse. The story of 'Beechenbrook'—a story mournfully trite to thousands of aching hearts—is simply and gracefully told; and some of the shorter poems interspersed—'Only a Private' and 'Slain in Battle'—are not without pathos. Of course, the war is regarded from the Confederate standpoint, and equally, of course, there is the usual amount of Southern devotion and Southern invincibility—Miss (or Mrs.?) Preston's rebels being easily victorious against anything less than quadruple odds, which is a rather perplexing statement, considering that Northern bards assure us of its exact converse. But to offset these very natural and not unpardonable flights of fancy, we have much less than the usual amount of 'vandal hordes' and 'despot's heels' that generally trample through and make gory the war-poetry of Dixie, just as the strains of the Federal minstrel are enlivened by the dismal howl of the bondman. The most flagrant error in this direction is a rather invidious comparison of the vulture and the eagle in what is one of the best poems in the book, 'Stonewall Jackson's Grave;' but it is suggested only to be deprecated and dismissed. The stanza will bear quoting:

'The largess of their praise is flung
With bounty rare and regal;
Is it because the vulture fears
No longer the dead eagle?
Nay, rather far accept it thus—
An homage true and tender,
As soldier unto soldier worth,
As brave to brave will render.'

"The last stanza is even better:

'Rare fame! rare name! If chanted praise,
With all the world to listen;
If pride that swells a nation's soul,
If foemen's tears that glisten;
If pilgrim's shrining love—if grief,
Which nought may soothe or sever;
If THESE can consecrate—this spot
Is sacred ground forever!'

"The political tone, if we may so call it, of these poems, is much higher and healthier throughout than we could have expected, or than we were warranted in hoping for by any example of moderation that loyal muses have set. Southern women, we are told, still cherish in their hearts that bitterness of hatred and that stubbornness of rebellion that did so much to prolong the late conflict, and which their husbands and brothers, we believe, have more wisely and nobly dismissed; but if we interpret this volume rightly, if it has not been deftly doctored for the Northern market, we take it as a sign, that, even among the women of the South, at least the more cultivated portion, the right feeling, the true patriotism, is gradually re-asserting itself. The concluding poem, entitled 'Acceptation,' expresses best the spirit which should animate the Southern people; a spirit wherein a very intelligible regret for the past is tempered by submission in the present, and abiding hope for the future:

'We do accept thee, heavenly peace!
  Albeit thou comest in a guise
  Unlooked for — undesired; our eyes
Welcome through tears the sweet release
From war, and woe, and want — surcease
For which we bless thee, blessèd peace!'

"These lines have the true ring; and an extension of the feeling which prompted them will do more to hasten reconstruction than the harangues of a dozen Senators, and the Freedmen's Bureau to boot. The women of the South have done much to destroy the Union; they can certainly do as much to rebuild it."

"It is to be sincerely hoped that the war which has so severely scourged the South will bring some good to the country, beside the lessons of political economy it has impressed upon us all. It is cheering to begin to see already some marked signs of fruition of this hope in the matter of the literary stamina, and taste, and ambition of our people. It has always seemed to us that whatever of genius there is in the South, there has always been wanting some great necessity, some great pressure of circumstances, some great awakening cause to arouse and develop it; and it would seem that the war, in its progress and final effect, is the first gleam of the dawning. It certainly has kindled a poetic fire that has never burned before; and now, while the great avalanche of worthless rhymes which it forced out upon the seething surface are being sunk into their proper places in the dark waters of oblivion, a pearl here and an opal there are being fished out, burnished, and set ablazing in tissues of beautiful gold.

"At first, some good things will be lost in the scramble with the bad; some bad things will be saved in the shadow of the good. At last, all the bad will filter through, and most of the good, and the good only, will be saved.

"Messrs. Kelly & Piet, of Baltimore, have executed a commendable piece of workmanship in bringing out, from all this rubbish, the poems of Mrs.

Preston.* We like the book. It contains some elegant touches that should not be lost.

"To begin with the beginning, and end with the ending, as we propose to do, the leading poem covers seventy-five pages, and is styled 'A Rhyme of the War.' An appropriate title, it is true; but we wish it did not have this double name at all—we have had too much of the war. It is written in the anapestic measure, which is so beautifully employed in the splendid ballads of Scott and Macaulay, and is interspersed with several animated odes in the Pindaric style. The hero is a Colonel Dunbar, and the introductory scene portrays the parting of husband from wife and children, and the sorrow which overspreads his hitherto happy home, Beechenbrook Cottage, when war's rude alarms burst over Virginia, in 1861, on 'a day bright with the earliest glory of May,' and when

'The blue of the sky is as tender a blue
As ever the sunshine came shimmering through.'

The wife, after she prepared the few little articles belonging to a soldier's wardrobe, and after he was ready to leave,

'On the fresh, shining knapsack she pillows her head,
And weeps as a mourner might weep for the dead.
. . . .
And the stout-hearted man is as weak as a girl.'

And then the good wife rouses herself, and, in the very midst of her overpowering paroxysm of grief, throws her arms around her husband's neck, and leaning upon his breast,

'She raises her eyes with a softened control,
And through them her husband looks into her soul,'

while she speaks, with a steady and clear voice, the sentiment of a Macedonian mother to her son, when she told him to 'Go: return with your shield, or on it;' but the griefful wife makes this uninterrupted speech, *twenty-six lines long*, hardly stopping to take breath. It is the heaviest part of the poem. If she had said what she did say with more brevity and more vim, it would have been better. It is a good scene, too much drawn out.

"Beechenbrook Cottage is situate within hearing of the booming of the guns in the battle of Manassas. Mother, daughter, and little son seek a green hillock, and pause to listen:

'Again and again the reverberant sound
Is fearfully felt in the tremulous ground;
Again and again on their senses it thrills,
Like thunderous echoes astray in the hills.'

That is certainly very fine.

* Mrs. Preston is a sister-in-law of Stonewall Jackson.

"Again:

> 'On tiptoe — the summer wind lifting his hair,
> With nostrils expanded, and scenting the air,
> Like a mettled young war-horse that tosses his mane,
> And frettingly champs at the bit and the rein,
> Stands eager, exultant —'

"What? who?

> '— *a twelve year old boy,*
> His face all aflame with a rapturous joy.'

It is really to be regretted that the author should have attempted to fill such a magnificent background for a superb picture with '*a twelve year old boy.*'

"Many and many an eye that peruses this paper will recognize a scene portrayed in Mrs. Dunbar's letter to her husband. It is not hard to find the beauty in these lines: whether it is hard or not to find any truth — and how much of truth — in them we leave the reader to determine. Here is what she writes to him:

> 'Our beautiful home — as I write it, I weep —
> Our beautiful home is a smouldering heap!
> And blackened and blasted, and grim and forlorn,
> Its chimneys stand stark in the mists of the morn!
>
> 'I stood, in my womanly helplessness, weak,
> Though I felt a brave color was kindling my cheek,
> And I plead by the sacredest things of their lives —
> By the love that they bore to their children — their wives —
> By the homes left behind them, whose joys they had shared —
> By the God that should judge them — that mine should be spared.
>
> 'As well might I plead with the whirlwind to stay,
> As it crashingly cuts through the forest its way!
> I know that my eye flashed a passionate ire,
> As they scornfully flung me their answer of — fire!'

"The hero of the rhyme is once wounded ere he receives the fatal shot that deprived his cause of his gallant services, and his bereaved widow and orphans of their husband and father. The allusions to the fields which were fought in the Old Dominion are but incidental, and perhaps, on this account, are more interesting and artistic.

"The poem is a very fair reflection of the feelings of our people, both men and women, during the progress of the war, telling how the women urged the men forward to the front, and wrote them kind letters, burning with patriotic zeal — how the men marched through snows and ice without shoes, and fought battle after battle, with never enough to eat—how the mothers, wives, sisters, and sweethearts toiled day in and day out for the soldiers, the sick and the wounded, their hearts writhing the while with a terrible doubting, hoping, fearing.

"The last two stanzas of this poem are full of vigor and earnestness—a fire that will kindle life enough, even where the process of freezing has been quite completed, to make one appreciate the lines on page 42:

'The crash of the onset—the plunge and the roll
Reach down to the depths of each patriot soul;
It quivers—for since it is human, it must,' etc.

"Besides 'Beechenbrook,' this volume contains 'Virginia,' a sonnet; 'Jackson,' a sonnet; 'Dirge for Ashby,' 'Stonewall Jackson's Grave,' 'When the War is over,' and 'Virginia Capta.'

"There have been but few poems produced by the war so exquisite and thrilling as the 'Dirge for Ashby;' perhaps it has not its equal, if we except Harry Flash's 'Zollicoffer.'

"We cannot resist the temptation to quote a stanza or two from 'Virginia Capta;' they have so much of sublime submission—the conquered to the conqueror—in them:

'The arm that wore the shield, strip bare;
The hand that held the martial rein,
And hurled the spear on many a plain—
Stretch—till they clasp the shackles there!

. . . .

'Bend though thou must beneath his will,
Let not one abject moan have place;
But with majestic, silent grace,
Maintain thy regal bearing still.

. . . .

'Weep, if thou wilt, with proud, sad mien,
Thy blasted hopes—thy peace undone—
Yet brave live on, nor seek to shun
Thy fate, like Egypt's conquer'd Queen.

'Though forced a captive's place to fill
In the triumphal train, yet there,
Superbly, like Zenobia, wear
Thy chains—*Virginia Victrix* still!'"

NON DOLET.

A SONNET.

When doubt, defeat, and dangers sore beset
The Roman Arria, yielding to the tide
Of ills that overwhelmed on every side,
With unheroic heart, that could forget
'T was cowardice to die, she dared and met
The easier fate; and luring, sought to hide
(For her beloved's sake — true woman yet!)
The inward anguish, with a wifely pride.
Not so our Southern Arria! In the face
Of deadlier woes, she dared to live, and wring
Hope out of havoc; till the brave control,
Pathetic courage, and most tender grace
Of her "*Non dolet*" nerved her husband's soul,
Won him to life, and dulled even failure's sting!

CHRISTMAS CAROL FOR 1862.

From "Beechenbrook," a Poem of the War.

'T is Christmas, the season of mirth and of cheer,
The happiest holiday known to the year;
The one that we oftenest love to recall —
Most ancient, most sacred, and dearest of all!
Turn the records of memory over and see
What days of your childhood were fullest of glee —
What scenes are remembered as brightest with joy,
For the old and the young — for the maiden and boy —
When home, with its festive and innocent mirth,
Seemed the sweetest and sunniest spot upon earth,
And the chimes of your heart most responsively rung
To the song that the angels at Bethlehem sung:
Be sure that these white-letter days will be drawn —
Now is it not so? — from your Christmases gone.

How saddening the change is! The season 's the same,
And yet it is Christmas in nothing but name:
No merry expression we utter to-day —
How can we, with hearts that refuse to be gay?

We look back a twelvemonth on many a brow
That graced the home hearthstone — and where are they now?
We think of the darling ones clustering there;
But we see through our tears an untenanted chair.
We wait for a footstep — we wait but in vain;
It will never return from the battle again;
The dear face is hidden cold under the clay;
His Christmas is kept with the angels to-day!
Thank God! there is joy in the sorrow for all;
He fell — but it surely was blessèd to fall;
For never shall murmur be heard from the mouth
Of mother or wife through our beautiful South,
Or sister or maiden yield grudging her part,
Though the price that she pays must be coined from her heart!

We drop the close curtains, we stir up the fire,
And pile up the blazing hearth higher and higher;
We wheel up our chair, and with friends and good cheer
We try to shut from us all visions of fear.
But the spectre *will* come — through the warmth and the light,
The camp gleams before us all shrouded in white.

We tread the soft carpet, and lo! there's the sound
Of the half-frozen sentinel pacing his round.
Come hither, my pretty musician, we say,
Come chase us this gloomy oppression away.
Her hand o'er the instrument gently she flings,
And this is the Song of the Snow that she sings:

"Halt! the march is over;
Day is almost done;
Loose the cumbrous knapsack,
Drop the heavy gun.
Chilled, and worn, and weary,
Wander to and fro,
Seeking wood to kindle
Fire amidst the snow.

"Round the camp-blaze gather;
Heed not sleet nor cold;
Ye are Spartan soldiers,
Strong, and brave, and bold.
Never Xerxian army
Yet subdued a foe
Who but asked a blanket
On a bed of snow.

"Shivering 'midst the darkness
 Christian men are found,
There devoutly kneeling
 On the frozen ground;
Pleading for their country
 In its hour of woe —
For its soldiers marching
 Shoeless through the snow.

"Lost in heavy slumbers,
 Free from toil and strife,
Dreaming of their dear ones —
 Home, and child, and wife;
Tentless they are lying,
 While the fires burn low;
Lying in their blankets
 'Midst December's snow!"

UNDERTOW.

A SONNET.

It is a gift for which to render praise,
 Ceaseless and fervent, that our troubled hearts
 Can hide the harrowing grief that chafes and smarts,
And shut themselves from all intrusive gaze.
 Oft when the murmur of the world grows low,
And the felt silence broods serene and still,
 The inward ear is listening to the flow
Of eddying memories, that flood and fill
 The soul with tumult. Then how blest to wear,
In eyes that yield no sympathizing look,
 A face of tidal quiet, that shall bear
No hint of undercurrents! Who could brook
 That even our nearest, dearest, best should know
 The secret springs of many an hour of woe?

STONEWALL JACKSON'S GRAVE.

A simple, sodded mound of earth,
 With not a line above it —
With only daily votive flowers
 To prove that any love it;

The token-flag that, silently,
  Each breeze's visit numbers,
Alone keeps martial ward above
  The hero's dreamless slumbers.

No name? no record? Ask the world —
  The world has heard his story —
If all its annals can unfold
  A prouder tale of glory?
If ever merely human life
  Hath taught diviner moral —
If ever round a worthier brow
  Was twined a purer laurel?

Humanity's responsive heart
  Concedes his wondrous powers,
And pulses with a tenderness
  Almost akin to ours:
Nay, not to ours — for us he poured
  His life — a rich oblation,
And on adoring souls we bear
  His blood of consecration.

A twelvemonth only since his sword
  Went flashing through the battle —
A twelvemonth only since his ear
  Heard war's last deadly rattle;
And yet have countless pilgrim feet
  The pilgrim's guerdon paid him,
And weeping women come to see
  The place where they have laid him.

Contending armies* bring in turn
  Their meed of praise or honor,
And Pallas here has paused to bind
  The cypress-wreath upon her.
It seems a holy sepulchre
  Whose sanctities can waken
Alike the love of friend or foe —
  The Christian or the pagan!

They come to own his high emprise,
  Who fled in frantic masses,

* In the month of June, 1864, this singular spectacle was presented at Lexington, of two hostile armies in turn reverently visiting the grave of Stonewall Jackson.

Before the glittering bayonet
  That triumphed at Manassas:
He witnessed Kernstown's fearful odds,
  As on their ranks he thundered,
Defiant as the storied Greek
  Amid his brave three hundred.

They will recall the tiger-spring,
  The wise retreat — the rally —
The tireless march — the fierce pursuit
  Through many a mount and valley.
Cross Keys unlocks new paths to fame,
  And Port Republic's story
Wrests from his ever-vanquished foes
  Strange tributes to his glory!

Cold Harbor rises to their view;
  The Cedar gloom is o'er them;
And Antietam's rough, wooded heights
  Stretch mockingly before them.
The lurid flames of Fredericksburg
  Right grimly they remember,
That lit the frozen night's retreat
  That wintry, wild December.

The largess of their praise is flung
  With bounty rare and regal:
Is it because the vulture fears
  No longer the dead eagle?
Nay, rather far accept it thus —
  An homage true and tender,
As soldier unto soldier's worth,
  As brave to brave will render.

But who shall weigh the wordless grief
  That leaves in tears its traces,
As round their leader crowd again
  Those bronzed and veteran faces?
The "old brigade" he loved so well —
  The mountain men who bound him
With bays of their own winning, ere
  A tardier fame had crowned him:

The legions who had seen his glance
  Across the carnage flashing,

And thrilled to catch his ringing "Charge!"
  Above the volleys crashing;
Who oft had watched the lifted hand,
  The inward trust betraying,
And felt their courage grow sublime
  While they beheld him praying:

Cool knights, and true as ever drew
  Their swords with knightly Roland,
Or died at Sobieski's side,
  For love of martyred Poland;
Or knelt with Cromwell's "Ironsides,"
  Or sung with brave Gustavus,
Or on the field of Austerlitz
  Breathed out their dying "Aves."

Rare fame! rare name! If chanted praise,
  With all the world to listen —
If pride that swells a nation's soul —
  If foeman's tears that glisten —
If pilgrim's shining love — if grief,
  Which nought can soothe or sever —
If these can consecrate, this spot
  Is sacred ground forever.

ACCEPTATION.

We do accept thee, heavenly Peace!
  Albeit thou comest in a guise
  Unlooked for — undesired; our eyes
Welcome through tears the kind release
From war, and woe, and want — surcease
For which we bless thee, holy Peace!

We lift our foreheads from the dust;
  And as we meet thy brow's clear calm,
  There falls a freshening sense of balm
Upon our spirits. Fear — distrust —
The hopeless present on us thrust —
We'll front them as we can, and *must*.

War has not wholly wrecked us; still
  Strong hands, grand hearts, stern souls are ours —
  Proud consciousness of quenchless powers —
A past whose memory makes us thrill —
Futures uncharactered, to fill
With heroisms, if we will!

Then courage, brothers! Though our breast
  Ache with that rankling thorn, despair,
  That failure plants so sharply there —
No pang, no pain shall be confessed:
We'll work and watch the brightening west,
And leave to God and heaven the rest!

MRS. S. A. WEISS.

SUSAN ARCHER TALLEY is descended, on the paternal side, from a Huguenot refugee, who settled in Hanover County, Virginia. In an old homestead on an estate in this county the subject of this article was born, and passed the years of childhood.

We are indebted to "Mary Forrest's" volume, "Women of the South," for the following:

"Among the traits earliest developed in Miss Talley were extreme fearlessness and love of liberty. . . . .

"It is said that she was never known to betray a sign of fear; and at the age of five years, in her visits to the neighbors, she would unhesitatingly face and subdue by her caresses the fiercest dogs, which even grown persons dared not approach. A singular power of will and magnetism, like that ascribed to the author of 'Wuthering Heights,' seems to have possessed her. She rode with a graceful, fearless abandon, and loved nothing better than to float away by herself in a frail boat. She was the frequent companion of her father and grandfather in their walks, rides, and hunting and fishing excursions; yet with all these influences, she was ever a gentle child, and remarkable for extreme sensibility and refinement. She delighted in all sights and sounds of beauty, and would sit for hours watching the sky in storm and sunshine, or listening to the wind among the trees, the plashing of a waterfall, or the cry of a whip-poor-will. This life familiarized her with all the voices of nature. A sound once heard she never forgot, but could, years after, imitate with surprising exactness.

"When she was eight years of age, her father removed to Richmond, and she then entered school. . . . . When in her eleventh year, she was released from the thraldom of the school-room by an unexpected dispensation. It had been remarked that for some days she had appeared singularly absent and inattentive when spoken to: being at length reproved, she burst into tears, exclaiming, 'I can't hear you.' It was then discovered that her hearing was greatly impaired. She was placed under the care of the most eminent physicians of the country; but their varied efforts resulted, as is too often the case, only in an aggravation of the evil. She lost the power to distinguish conversation, though carried on in a loud key; a power which she has not wholly recovered. . . . .

"Her parents were at first greatly at loss as to the manner of conducting her education. Fortunately, she was advanced far beyond most children of her age; and now, released from the discipline of school, her natural love of study deepened into a passion. It was soon found sufficient to throw suitable books in her way, and thus, unassisted, she completed a thorough scholastic course. She also acquired an extensive acquaintance with the literature of the day, and her correct taste and critical discrimination elicited the warmest encomiums from that prince of critics, Edgar A. Poe.

"It was not until Miss Talley had entered her thirteenth year that her poetic faculty became apparent to her family; she having, through modesty, carefully concealed all proofs of its development. Some specimens of her verse then falling under the eye of her father, he at once recognized in them the flow of true genius, and very wisely, with a few encouraging words, left her to the guidance of her own inspiration. In her sixteenth year, some of her poems appeared in the 'Southern Literary Messenger.'"

In September, 1859, a collection of her poems was issued by Rudd & Carleton, of New York. This volume secured for her a distinction of which she may well be proud. For rhythmic melody, for sustained imagination, for depth of feeling, and purity and elevation of sentiment, these poems are equalled by few, and surpassed by none of the productions of our poets. They are rich also in those qualities of mind and heart, which, apart from any literary prestige, win for Miss Talley the esteem and affection of all who are admitted within the choice circle of her friendship.

The "war experience" of this lady reads like a romance. It was reserved for Susan Archer Talley to suffer many hardships and privations during the war. Circumstances placed her during a great portion of that period within the power of the enemy — at intervals as a guarded prisoner — at intervals under *surveillance.* As the record of these events is closely connected with many interesting phases of the struggle, and, indeed, in many respects is historical, this sketch of the lady under consideration would be incomplete without some testimony to her adherence, in despite of evil conjunctions, to the principles which, in common with every true Southern woman, she steadfastly maintained.

At the time of the secession of South Carolina from the Union, she was in New York, on her way to Europe, with the ultimate purpose of realizing a cherished wish of her heart, viz., a year's residence in Italy. Prior to the rising of the issue between the North and the South, a devoted friend of the Union, the Northern threat to "whip the South back into the Union" with armed men aroused her Southern spirit; and abandoning her purpose of visiting Europe, she determined to return to her home in the South. About this time she refused to sign a petition of leading Southern women, sent her by Mr. Crittenden, of Kentucky, praying the Legislature of that State not to bring about the secession of Kentucky. In the same spirit, although often since applied to, she has scrupulously refrained from any matter touching upon politics, believing this pursuit to be out of woman's legitimate sphere.

At the threshold of her resolution to seek her Southern home, difficulties beset Mrs. Weiss. Martial law had been proclaimed. Her application for a passport having been refused, she determined to set out alone, trusting to fortune to make her way to the Confederate lines. At Barnum's Hotel, in Baltimore, she was called upon by a gentleman, a stranger to her, who professed to be well acquainted with her, but who declared that he must remain unknown. This gentleman gave her several MS. papers, impressing upon her the importance of their being delivered to General R. E. Lee at the earliest possible moment. The risk was great; but she gladly consented to give her aid, in this way, to the furtherance of the Southern cause. Her manner of secreting these important papers was ingenious. When left alone, she carefully tore them so as not to injure the writing, folded them in slips, and enveloping each in a slip of black silk, plaited them in her hair, which was fortunately long and thick. In this manner she conveyed the precious documents in safety, until it was in her power to confide them to a more speedy conveyance. And this was the first service that she was enabled to render to her beloved South.

Acting under advice, Mrs. Weiss determined to reach Virginia by the Harper's Ferry route. But on reaching Frederick, she learned that the railroad thither had been destroyed, and the bridge across the river burned by order of General Johnston, commanding the Confederate troops at Harper's Ferry, in order to prevent the crossing of the Pennsylvania troops into Virginia. In spite of this disheartening circumstance, she still resolved to go on, on foot, if necessary. An acquaintance placed her in charge of a Charleston gentleman, Dr. ——, and so with him, and in company with another gentleman, who introduced himself as an officer of General Johnston's command returning from a secret mission to the North, she set out on her adventurous and somewhat dangerous journey. Nearly ten miles were traversed on foot by the party. Occasional "lifts" in market-wagons varied the monotony and fatigue of the journey. At intervals of an hour or so, a summons to halt would come from some thicket or other hiding-place, where the pickets challenged them in a low voice; and occasionally an anxious face would appear from amid the foliage, inquiring the news "from above" of the military movements, warning the party of the presence of Federal scouts and patrols ahead, and advising how to avoid them. After a cautious progress, detours very frequently being necessary to avoid detection, the party reached Sandy Hook about dusk. Here it was discovered that the Confederate troops had destroyed all the boats, and that it would be impossible to cross the river. For ten dollars in gold, however, a man for an emergency was found, who consented to patch up one, less injured than the rest, hastily; and in this frail bark the travellers ventured upon the perilous passage. Compelled to move slowly and preserve caution, lest, by the slightest overbalancing, the boat should capsize, two hours were consumed in crossing, the moon shining softly meanwhile. As they stood upon the Virginia shore, finally, a woman, breathless and frightened, suddenly ran through the bushes toward them, and told them that they had landed too low down — that there were Federals near them, and that the Confederate pickets had retreated. The officer determined to go forward; Dr. —— and Mrs. Weiss — the latter sorely against her will — returned to the other side in the boat, and eventually were compelled to make their way back to Frederick.

Mrs. Weiss's next attempt to reach the South was by the Bay Line of steamers. She applied in person to Captain N. Falls, the President of the line, who treated her with great kindness, gave her a free passage to Fortress Monroe; and on a refusal of the military authorities to allow her to land at that point, brought her back to Baltimore. On the following day, a Federal officer, to whom Captain Falls had stated the circumstances of her case, called on Mrs. Weiss, and offered to take her through, as he possessed influence with General Butler, then commanding at Fortress Monroe. After some difficulty, she was permitted to land; and after a few days' detention at the Fortress, during which she received much kindness and respectful attention from the United States officers, she was sent by flag of truce to Coney Island, whence, tired and penniless, she departed for Richmond, to find, on her arrival there, that her once beautiful home near that city had been chosen as the site of a Confederate fort, and that her family was scattered far and wide.

Under these untoward circumstances, Mrs. Weiss obtained shelter and a temporary home with a relative living in Hanover County; but the family soon being compelled to fly thence as refugees, she found a boarding-place in the family of Captain ——, an Englishman, residing on the Peninsula. Here she found herself shut in between the two opposing camps of Yorktown and Newport News. Veterans of the Southern Peninsular Army will well recall the interest which at that time centred about "——'s house" in the minds of the soldiers of either army; and many of them, too, will remember the efforts for their safety and comfort which were constantly being made by the subject of this sketch during her residence "on the line." As a member of Captain ——'s household, Mrs. Weiss's situation was full of excitement and of dramatic incidents. Scouting parties from either side daily visited the house. Skirmishes would take place opposite the back window, and naval engagements would occur on the river in front. Spies and deserters passed and repassed, and parties from either side came constantly to search the house for concealed "rebels" or Unionists. Captain —— was neutral; his wife was a New York lady; their children and Mrs. Weiss were Virginians: thus was it that all parties found representatives in this household. Yet, strange to say, Mrs. Weiss was the only one who was thoroughly trusted by either Confederates or Federals. The latter, although knowing her as an open and uncompromising enemy, invariably treated her with more faith and respect than they exhibited toward the other members of the household. They granted her more than one favor for her own people; and more than once, also, did it occur that her pleadings sufficed to save the house from burning by both General Magruder's and General Mansfield's order.

Upon one occasion, when a party of Federal soldiers had come upon Captain ——'s place, and, in ambuscade, had mortally wounded a Georgia officer, the Confederates, suspecting Captain ——'s faith, were about to take him prisoner and burn the house. Knowing his innocence, and moved by the distress of his family, Mrs. Weiss consented, at their solicitation, to beg a respite until she could obtain General Mansfield's promise that the German soldiers should not again molest the Confederates on Captain ——'s premises. For three miles, on her way to General Mansfield's headquarters, she walked along the river-shore, alone and unprotected, encountering the Federal soldiers in the woods and hollows, in parties of from two to twenty, coarse and brutal in appearance, most of them. From these men, despite their unpromising exteriors and character, she received various acts of rough courtesy, such as the pulling down of a fence for her to pass, or placing a log over a wet place, so that she could cross dry-shod. A most remarkable journey this, at the circumstances attending which even the Federal officers expressed surprise. Her petition was granted by General Mansfield, who sent her home in a private carriage, with an escort and a flag of truce.

Frequently, applications would be made to her from both sides for meetings or exchanges, without the formality of a flag of truce; the Federal officers courteously saying that they would accept her presence as an assurance of good faith — a sure appeal to the chivalrous sentiment of the Southern soldier. Among the officers whom Mrs. Weiss met on this occasion were several true gentlemen, who befriended her during the war, and who, since the war, as circumstances would allow, have been equally friendly in their conduct toward her. They knew her for what she professed to be — a firm, yet open and honorable enemy, doing whatever she could for the Southern cause, yet in a strictly honorable way, and never betraying them where they had trusted her. This was all understood by General Mansfield's officers, who seemed to understand the character of a Southern woman more fully than any of those with whom Mrs. Weiss met, and to respect her accordingly.

From her windows, Mrs. Weiss witnessed the famous battle on the 6th of March between the "Merrimac" and the United States fleet, aided by the "Monitor." She also witnessed the passage of McClellan's army past Captain ——'s house, in their "On to Richmond" movement by the way of the Peninsula; also the attack upon our pickets, and their final retreat. The day previous to this, General Magruder sent two of his staff officers with a lady's horse, urging Mrs. Weiss to come into the Confederate lines at once for safety. Feeling confident that she would not be disturbed, however, she remained at the house. The result proved unfortunate. On the 1st of April, a regiment, commanded by Colonel Vinton, (a son of Dr. Vinton, of Trinity Church, New York,) was sent to guard Captain ——'s house. During the evening of the first day of their arrival, Vinton begged the favor of an interview with Mrs. Weiss. Mrs. Weiss considered this rather in the light of an order, and granted the interview. For three hours he kept her in conversation, in which she expressed herself fully and freely on the subject of the war, Vinton observing at the commencement of the interview: "We are, politically, enemies; but I trust that we may be, personally, friends. Do not hesitate to speak freely to me, on *my honor as a gentleman and a United States officer.*" On rising the next morning, Mrs. Weiss discovered that all her journals, papers, etc., had been removed from her desk; and an hour after an officer quietly presented himself at her door, and handed her a note from General Keyes, which contained the information that that officer requested to see her at his headquarters in camp. Convinced that she was a prisoner, and that no course was left her but to obey, she prepared for travel, and accompanied the officer to the general's ambulance, in waiting. Here she was met by General Davidson, who assured her that she was "under the care and protection of gentlemen, and should be treated as a lady." After a rough ride, they reached General Davidson's tent, which he caused to be prepared for her reception—with a tent-cloth on the floor by way of carpet, and a silken table-cover on the rough pine board, replacing the common tumbler with a silver drinking-cup. After remaining here for a few hours, they proceeded to General Keyes's tent. General Keyes was very courteous, insisting upon her taking some refreshment, and treating her with all respect.

From General Keyes's headquarters, Mrs. Weiss was ordered to be sent to Fort McHenry. On her way thither, as indeed had been the case from the first moment of her arrest, there was no indication of her being a prisoner. She was treated everywhere with the utmost courtesy. General Keyes said, however, that he considered her a most dangerous enemy; and that, "much as he disliked troubling her, duty compelled him to remove her beyond the possibility of influencing either Federal or Confederate officers." She was first sent to Newport News, where the officers of General Mansfield's staff expressed great indignation at her arrest. She was informed by them that she had been made a prisoner on complaint of Colonel Vinton and of a renegade Virginian, one Major Sage, of Fairfax, whom she had offended by some remark. Efforts were made by General Mansfield's staff to secure her release of General McClellan; but without success.

On the 4th of April, Mrs. Weiss reached Fort McHenry. There, fortunately, in the commander of the Fort, General William W. Morris, she recognized an old friend, who had known her from her infancy, and who was well acquainted with her family. General Dix's orders upon the subject of her imprisonment were very severe. His instructions were that she was to be locked up, and kept in a solitary prison, and was never to be allowed to see or speak to any one, except General Morris and the officer of the guard. One or two other lady prisoners, recently released, had been subjected to similar treatment. Mrs. Weiss made no complaint, no petition or compromise. She three times declined to take the oath of allegiance, which was offered to her by General Morris, acting under instructions from General Dix. General Morris informed her upon these occasions that her acquiescence would insure her her liberty.

That Mrs. Weiss's existence at Fort McHenry as a prisoner was not entirely devoid of the amenities of life, and that it sometimes occurred that officers of the United States Army were prompted by generous impulses in their treatment of prisoners, is shown in Mrs. Weiss's own account of her personal experiences while at the Fort. Writing of these days, she says:

"To General Morris's fatherly kindness and indulgence while I remained in Fort McHenry, and to the perfect courtesy and respect with which I was treated, I have no words to do justice. He wished, in order to secure me greater comforts, that I should give parole on certain points, which I declined. How he tried to amuse and interest me in my loneliness, passing many a half-hour at my fireside in cheerful conversation, he himself escorting me in long walks around the ramparts, or inviting me to sit with him on his own piazza in the cool of the evening, and exacting for me from every one the most rigid respect. But oh! the long, solitary hours, in which I would pace up and down my bare room, thinking of my country and of my people — thinking of the battle-fields stained with precious Southern blood, and praying, as I had rarely before prayed, for success to our cause! And then the lonely, almost, at times, maddening feeling of my *powerlessness* in being a prisoner! To know that the tide of life was surging onward without those prison-walls, while I remained a helpless drift upon the shore! Only those who have been prisoners, and *solitary* prisoners, can have an idea of the agony and torment of the feeling. I do not wonder that people die, or go mad under it.

"This did not last more than three months. At the end of that time, General Morris gave me the liberty of the Fort. He allowed no guard about me, and forbade even the officer of the guard to go near my room, unless sent for by me to walk, or to make known my wants. This room was in itself pleasant enough — a large, airy room in the building, occupied by General Morris and his aide. Gradually, by the kindness of General and Mrs. Morris, various comforts were added, until it came to be quite a pleasant and cheerful apartment. General Morris permitted me to walk both within and without the Fort, escorted by an officer, at any time and as often as I liked. He allowed me to see secession visitors from Baltimore, who loaded me with offerings of books, flowers, fruits, and canary-birds as prison-pets. He appointed a nice little German girl to wait on me; and my meals, though taken alone, consisted of every delicacy and luxury that could be desired. And finally, he laid out a little garden-plot in front of the house, and there, with two of the soldiers to do rough work, we amused ourselves in the morning. I had plenty of books, writing and drawing materials; and, on the whole, but for my anxiety in regard to the progress of the war, should have been content. It was here that I wrote the 'Battle of the Merrimac,' which I showed to General Morris, having no fear of him. He spent many an hour in endeavoring to convert me to the Union cause; and he remarked, at length, that I was the most obstinate of all the 'rebels' that he had ever had under his charge. I shall never cease to think of him; the kind-hearted, benevolent man, the firm officer and courteous gentleman, as I then knew him; and to regard him, and also his wife, with the deepest gratitude."

During her imprisonment at Fort McHenry, General Dix was repeatedly petitioned for Mrs. Weiss's release by Federal officers, as well as by Southern sympathizers; but he firmly refused acquiescence with the appeals. He declared that Mrs. Weiss should not be released until the end of the war, if it should last ten years, as he dreaded her influence, as a writer and otherwise. In view of her failing health, General Morris again urged her to take the oath of allegiance, which she again refused, sending word to General Dix at the time that she considered such a proposal to a Southern woman an insult. Her demand for a trial was also refused by the same officer.

In June, Generals Dix and Wool were appointed to an exchange of places, the former taking command at Fortress Monroe, and the latter at Fort McHenry. One of General Wool's first acts was to release Mrs. Weiss. About the last of June, she left Fort McHenry for Norfolk, where she anticipated meeting friends. At Fortress Monroe, she encountered General Dix, who expressed indignation at her release, and who gave orders that she should be watched, and not allowed to leave Norfolk, which town was within the limits of his command, and also that her correspondence should be intercepted. Of these facts, Mrs. Weiss received private information from a Federal officer, whose acquaintance she had made at Newport News, and who was then in authority in Norfolk.

In this condition of surveillance, Mrs. Weiss remained for three months. She finally resolved to run the blockade. One dark night, she left Norfolk in a small boat, travelled up the river past Newport News and Captain ——'s house, the scene of her former strange experiences, past the patrolling Federal gunboats, unseen, as far as Smithfield. Thence the journey to Petersburg was made on foot and in market-carts, in disguise. And at last her journey was completed, and her heart's desire accomplished at the same moment, when, from the Capitol at Richmond, she saw the Confederate flag flying, touched with the splendors of our great and recent victories!

During the residence of Mrs. Weiss at Captain ——'s house, on the Peninsula, she had many opportunities of serving the Southern soldiers, and advancing our military interests. She passed important papers to and fro through the lines, obtained newspapers for our generals, and followed any directions given her, these being, of course, of a strictly honorable nature. It was in consequence of her forwarding a message to General Magruder, regarding the small force at Newport News, just after the sending of re-enforcements thence to Burnside, that the Merrimac made her attack at the time she did, and before she was quite completed. She acted as a *medium* merely, having had facilities for so doing, except in one instance, when, after being taken prisoner, and while on her way to Fort McHenry, she learned from various officers of the number of McClellan's army, the different brigades, his plans, etc., and found means to send information to General Magruder of the same, and that McClellan designed attacking Yorktown, believing the force there to be much larger than, as she knew, it in reality was. Lesser services it was also in her power to render, such as signalling the Confederate pickets of the approach of attacking parties, or of ambuscades. On one occasion, an opportune signal of this kind saved the lives of forty Confederate soldiers, who were approaching directly on an ambuscading party of German Federal soldiers, lying in wait behind a fence. And again, she saved as many more lives from an ambuscading party on Captain ——'s place, by descending the precipitous bank to the river beach, wading some half a mile through the tide, and making her way through a thick and tangled wood and morass to one of the Confederate pickets, two miles distant, whom she warned of the danger, just in time to stop the approach of a troop of cavalry, whose arrival the Federal soldiers were expecting. During the winter in which she remained at Captain ——'s, being the only person allowed to approach the Confederate pickets, she used regularly, every morning, to carry the poor, half-starved men a plentiful hot breakfast of meat, bread, and coffee. Frequently, they would have no rations but bread and potatoes, or rice. Frequently, too, they were barefooted, and otherwise unprotected against the severe cold. In Richmond, also, as did most of the Southern women, she gave her attention to the sick and wounded in the hospitals.

It was upon Mrs. Weiss's return to Richmond from her imprisonment in Fort McHenry, that she commenced writing for the "Magnolia Weekly" and the "Southern Illustrated News." Up to that time, she had written exclusively for the "Southern Literary Messenger," which, however, failed to give her any compensation for her writings. Up to the time of her commencing to write for the two first-named papers, she had never been able to write, satisfactorily, a line of prose, with the exception of one inconsiderable article "On Reading." Poetry had been to her as the breath of life, and her poems had occurred to her almost as inspirations, conceived and written out on a moment's impulse, without labor or difficulty whatever; and in several cases, (as, for instance, in the case of "Summer Noonday Dreams,") without a word being altered. Then, about three years before the war, this power seemed suddenly to desert her entirely; and in this interval she wrote nothing. It returned as suddenly upon the inspiration of the war; but again as suddenly departed. Since three years, she has not written a line of poetry; but, strangely enough, prose now flows readily, and almost without the labor of thinking, from her pen. Providence seems thus to have provided for Mrs. Weiss, at the very moment when she needed this capacity as a sole means of support. As, like most Southerners, she has lost everything by the war, happy for her that facility with her pen which, in a measure, supplies the absence of her lost fortunes!

Mrs. Weiss was too patriotic to regret the destruction of her worldly goods; but the loss of friends, and especially of an only brother, cherished by her with a sister's devotedness, who was drowned in the retreat before Sherman, has cast a permanent shadow over her life. Indeed, since the day when Richmond was taken possession of by the Federal army, and she knew that the war was over, she has felt "as one who mourneth for his friends." Mrs. Weiss is not entirely hopeless, however, of a future recompense for the trials and sufferings of the South. "Our lost cause," she has written, "is as dear to me now as ever; and I glory, even while I mourn, that *we* were enabled to give to the world the glorious spectacle of a handful of men, ragged, worn, and starved, battling with strong hearts and firm, unshrinking hands against an overwhelming host of powerful enemies; and I believe that, though I may not live to see it, the day will come when that cause will reassert itself, and that so much precious Southern blood has not been spilt in vain."

There is one other event connected with Mrs. Weiss's prison-life, the recital of which should properly be incorporated in this narrative of her checkered experiences during the earlier years of the war. This event, concerning her closely, and fraught in its course and conclusion with more of unhappiness than happiness, involves the brief story of her acquaintance with her husband, Lieutenant Weiss, of the Federal army, and her final marriage to that gentleman. Mrs. Weiss met her future husband at Fort McHenry, during the time of her imprisonment in that Fort. As officer of the guard, Mr. Weiss frequently accompanied her in her walks about the Fort and upon the shore. Thus thrown together, a feeling of sympathy prepared the way in the officer's breast for the entrance of a stronger impulse. Their frequent long conversations established, in a few weeks, a more intimate acquaintance than could have been effected, under ordinary circumstances, in a year, and Mrs. Weiss gave him her promise to marry him so soon as she should be at liberty. This promise was given, however, on the express condition that he should resign from the Federal service, and in due time, in an open and honorable manner, espouse the cause of the South; Lieutenant Weiss having, under her teachings, professed to have become convinced of the injustice of the war, and a convert to Southern principles.

About this time, Lieutenant Weiss was ordered South with his regiment. As there was also a probability that Mrs. Weiss would be sent farther North, he insisted upon their immediate marriage, in order that at any time, if need were, she should be able to join him. This marriage was necessarily private; and in order to avert suspicion and possible punishment for infringement of prison rules, it was to be kept strictly secret until he could join her at the South, or she him at the North, as events might render necessary.

The marriage took place on the day before that on which they had expected to be separated; but the orders were countermanded, and Lieutenant and Mrs. Weiss remained at Fort McHenry some six weeks longer. It was at the special request of General Morris that Mrs. Weiss was subsequently allowed to go to Norfolk, where she could daily see her husband, who was at that time stationed at Suffolk.

In August, Lieutenant Weiss obtained his discharge, and hastened immediately to Germany, in order to settle his estate, obtain money, and return and claim Mrs. Weiss openly as his wife. It was understood that he was to meet her in Norfolk in two months, Mrs. Weiss in the mean time going to Richmond.

During his absence, Mrs. Weiss received two letters from him. Then for three years she neither heard from nor of him. This interruption to their correspondence was caused, as Mrs. Weiss afterward learned, by General Dix's intercepting their correspondence, in which manner he became aware of their marriage and their plans. As Mr. Weiss anticipated, a watch was set upon his movements, and thus was it that, at first, he was prevented from coming South.

After her return to Richmond, Mrs. Weiss kept her marriage a secret, in pursuance of her understanding with her husband. Finally, despairing of his coming, she caused the announcement of her marriage to be published, and then made various attempts to join him in New York, where she supposed him to be.

For the purpose of her contemplated journey, Mrs. Weiss was compelled to sell everything she possessed, even to necessary clothing, in order to raise means sufficient to reach New York; and with her infant child and her faithful negro maid, she set out on her difficult and perilous venture. After several days of travel, mostly on foot, for there were at that time no travelling conveniences, Mrs. Weiss succeeded in reaching the Federal lines at Williamsburg.

One step more, and Mrs. Weiss would have been placed within reach of her long-separated husband. But upon that step was a condition — she must take the oath of allegiance. At this alternative she did not for a moment hesitate; but, with a sinking, sorrowful heart, she turned to retrace her weary journey back to Richmond. Nightfall found them in the midst of a dense wood, where Mrs. Weiss was robbed of all her little possessions by two Union men who had promised to guide them. Even her baby's scanty little wardrobe was not spared by these ruffians. For five miles farther through the darkness they walked, passing numerous houses which had been burnt by the Federal troops, and finally came to a ruined farm-house, still occupied by the women of the family, whose husband and sons had all been killed in battle. This family gave to the wanderers all they had — a little milk and a small quantity of bread. At this ruined but hospitable home they rested awhile; and then, resuming their journey, they reached the house of Dr. ——, in New Kent County. Here they were received kindly, and were assisted on their way back to Richmond.

On the fall of Richmond — opportunity, until that time, lacking — Mrs. Weiss joined her husband in New York. But it would seem that churlish fate, not content with clouding the earlier years of her married life with the shadows of multiplied disappointments, had reserved for Mrs. Weiss an unhappy sequel to her marriage. That future content and repose which should have sprung from adversity and trial, failed her when most the promise seemed auspicious. A difference of opinion between her husband and herself brought about a separation. Mr. Weiss desired to send their little boy to Germany, to be adopted by a wealthy brother living in that country. The natural impulse of a mother's heart protested against this action; and when, ultimately, the choice lay between her husband and her child, she and Mr. Weiss parted; and, with her child, she returned to her desolated home, where, in the lonely fort, she lived with the child a solitary life and in extreme destitution. None of her relatives offered to relieve her in her necessitous condition. Her marriage with a Federal officer offended them, and she was thus left alone to struggle with fortune. Subsequently, Mrs. Weiss went to New York, where, at least, the opportunities for one of her cultivated and brilliant intellect were greater than in the devastated South. In that city, she entered a suit for divorce from Mr. Weiss, which, in the summer of 1868, was in progress.

In this reference to Mrs. Weiss's marriage, the writer has been actuated by a desire to explain to many, to whom, perhaps, the explanation brings a new knowledge, the circumstances attending her acquaintance with and marriage to Mr. Weiss. In view of the fact that this explanation has reference to events than which none could be more important in a woman's life, and which, in their course, were known only to familiar and intimate friends, this narrative has been deemed necessary, as making known to that general public which has so long admired the intellectual woman, those truths, intimately associated with her life, which cannot but arouse a generous sympathy.

CON ELGIN.

Con Elgin was a horseman bold,
  A chief of high degree,
And he hath gone with twenty men
  A-sailing on the sea;
Now woe the hour and woe the strand
When Elgin with his men shall land,
  Wherever that may be.

Con Elgin sought the stormy isle
  Across the foaming flood,
And he hath marched with all his men
  Into the Druid wood,
Where dark beneath the ancient oaks
  The Christian temple stood.

Con Elgin slew the old Culdee—
  The priest with silver hair;
He slew him at the altar-stone
  In sacerdotal gear;
He slew the half-baptizèd babe,
  And its mother, young and fair.

He seized the sacramental cup
  The blessed wine to drain;
He mixed it with the Christian's blood
  And quaffed it yet again;
Then, while his eyes in fury roll,
His beard he cleanses in the bowl—
But there is on his blackened soul
  An everlasting stain.

Con Elgin lies in troubled sleep
  Beneath a Druid oak:
Was it the whisper of the wind,
  Or a voice to him that spoke?
"Oh, hard of heart and fierce of hand,
  I sign thee with a sign:
Where'er thou goest, on land or flood,
O'er icy plain, through dusky wood,
  Shall loneliness be thine!"

Uprose the bloody horseman then,
  And loudly laughèd he:
"I bear the spell and wear the sign,
  Thou old and weird Culdee!
Now by the shades of Odin's hall,
That such an ill should me befall,
  That such a curse should be!"

And loudly laughed his followers
  As round about they stood:
But a sudden thrill and a whisper ran
  Through the ancient Druid wood;
And trembled all the Valkyrmen
  As round about they stood.

And now they are upon the sea,
  And far and fast they go;
For lo! the storm is on their track—
The waves are white—the clouds are black,
  And the icy breezes blow.
Oh, that the storm would wear away,
  And the winds would cease to blow!

Yet darker grows the fearful night,
  And loud the tempest's shriek;
They cannot see each other's forms,
  Or hear each other speak:
But though the waves the wilder grow,
And though the winds the fiercer blow,
With stately mast and steady prow
  The vessel onward rides:
They know that some unearthly hand
  The broken rudder guides.

A sudden lull—and in the south
  There dawns a misty day;
There is no cloud, there is no breeze,
But far away o'er frozen seas
  The Borealis' play—
A ghastly light, like that which lies
Within the dying's glazing eyes.

There is no life in all the scene,
  There is no breath—no sound;

But slowly o'er the glassy deep
The icy bars in silence creep,
  And clasp the ship around,
Till mast and sail and deck alike
  In icy chains are bound.

Gloom on the vast, unbroken sky,
  And stillness on the air,
And loneliness upon the sea,
  And silence everywhere;
And in Con Elgin's hardened heart
  A stern and cold despair.

He shrank to see the famished crew,
  So gaunt were they and grim;
He gazed where, sea and sky between,
In lurid haze was ever seen
  The sun's unsetting rim;
But evermore those stony eyes
  Glared fixedly on him.

He spake to them — he called to them —
  Then came a silence dread;
For lo, upon the northern skies
Strange gleams of lurid light arise,
  And gather overhead;
They gleam upon the frozen ship,
  And on the frozen dead.

The faces of the dead were they,
  So rigid, wan, and blue;
Oh, 't was a fearful thing to stand
  Amid that lifeless crew!
And thrice Con Elgin drew his blade,
And thrice his iron hand was stayed:
  Ah, well the grasp he knew!

He paces on the icy deck,
  He chants a mystic rune;
He cursed the long and weary day,
  Yet ended all too soon,
As the lurid disk of the blood-red sun
  Sinks suddenly at noon.

The ghastly dead -- the ghastly dead —
  They chill him with their eyes;
The silent ship — the lonely sea —
  The far and boundless skies!
Oh, that some little breeze would stir,
  Some little cloud arise!

And then uprose a little cloud —
  Uprose a little breeze —
And came a low and slumberous sound,
Like moaning waves that break around
  The stormy Hebrides:
The ice is rent — the ship is free,
  And on the open seas!

He saw the land upon his lee —
  He strove the shore to gain;
And wild and fierce his efforts grew,
  But strength and skill were vain;
Still onward ploughed the fated ship
  Unto the outer main.

A sail, a sail! "What ho! what ho!"
  He shouted from the mast;
And back there came a cheering cry
  Upon the rushing blast:
Their very life-blood chilled with dread —
They saw the living and the dead
  As swift they hurried past!

And long upon those Northern seas,
  At silent dead of night,
A cry would echo on the blast,
And a phantom ship go hurrying past —
  A strange and fearful sight!
And well the trembling sailors knew
Con Elgin and his ghastly crew.

MADONNA.

Madonna, in the golden light,
  Down-pouring on thy pictured form
From the stained window's archèd height,
  Mellow, and rich, and warm—

Lighting the halo on thy brow
Into a living glow,
  Till scarce their radiance seems apart—
Like light and clouds at set of sun
Soft melting into one:
  How beautiful thou art!
How beautiful—as if in thee
    All we might deem of good and fair
That woman hath been, and should be,
  In mind and heart, in form and face,
  In outward charm and inward grace,
In nature's sweet simplicity,
    Were brightly imaged there.

Thy wavy hair, a golden shower,
  Upon thy brow disposed apart,
Half bound beneath the white veil's fold,
Half down thy bosom rolled
  In graceful negligence of art,
Seems like the golden-tinted clouds,
  The golden-threaded clouds of eve
Floating upon the liquid sea,
The waveless, shoreless sea,
  The sea of light the yellow sunset leaves.
Dimpling upon thy parted lip
  A breathing sweetness seems to lie
Like fragrance on a dewy rose;
  Pictured alike to soul and sense,
  The spirit gently breathing thence
Far more than simple words disclose—
  The heart's rich eloquence—
    Longing to pour itself in prayer,
Lest, pent within thy woman's heart,
  Like a fountain in its hidden flow,
  The still-increasing waters grow
Too mighty in their deep unrest—
    Too strong for thee to bear.

Thine eyes beneath their drooping fringe
  In shadowy lustre gleam;
As still and dark their heavenly blue
  As skies within a crystal stream,
In liquid lustre gleaming through,
  So still and softly clear

We scarce may pierce their depths profound,
Or deem their beauty hath a bound,
  Yet ever seeming near.
Softly their earnest light is blent—
  Love and sweet humility—
Watching with mingled smiles and tears
Of human hopes and human fears,
  The baby on thy knee;
The blessèd babe whose starry eyes
  Gaze sweetly upward into thine,
Half in love and sweet surprise,
  While mingling with thy locks astray
Loosely within their baby grasp
  The scattered tresses twine.

Gazing upon thy pictured form,
  The woman's earnest soul revealing,
My soul, uprising from its clay,
Bends lowly to a purer sway
  Of more than earthly feeling—
Something trusting, something holy,
On my spirit dawning slowly,
  With a beauty half divine,
Till thy spirit, meek and bright,
Dawning with a living light
  Stealeth slowly into mine;
Hushing the voice of earthly ill,
  Binding me with an unfelt thrall,
And taming down my haughty will
  To a perfect love of all.
For the meekness in thy gentle eyes
  Doth meekness to my spirit bring,
And love unto my yearning heart
  For every living thing.

AIRLEY.

Oh, greenly grow the alder-boughs
  Upon the banks of Airley,
And on the silver river's breast
  The lilies blossom fairly;

With blithesome echoes, far and near,
  The sylvan shades are ringing,
And shrilly in the hazel copse
  The merle and mavis singing.

But Airley towers are very lone,
  And Airley halls are dreary;
And though the sun be bright without,
  The hearts within are weary;
For she that was the light of all,
  The chieftain's lovely daughter,
Hath fled away with Roden's knight
  Across the stormy water.

He met her in the shady wood;
  He wooed her by the river;
He swore by all the shining stars
  To love but her forever.
And first she smiled, and then she wept;
  Her heart was troubled sairly:
She mounted on his snowy steed,
  And fled away from Airley.

Her cheek was like a summer rose,
  Her smile like summer weather;
Her fairy footstep left the dew
  Upon the purple heather.
Oh! where shall we another find
  Whose beauty blooms so rarely?
'T is morning now at Roden's halls,
  And midnight upon Airley.

Yet dwelleth she a happy bride
  Beyond the stormy water,
And singeth in the stranger's halls
  The songs her mother taught her:
Oh! we shall mourn her many a day;
  Oh! we shall miss her sairly;
Yet happy is the Roden chief
  To win the pride of Airley.

THE BATTLE EVE.

I see the broad, red, setting sun
  Sink slowly down the sky;
I see, amid the cloud-built tents,
  His blood-red standard fly;
And mournfully the pallid moon
  Looks from her place on high.

O setting sun, awhile delay;
  Linger on sea and shore;
For thousand eyes now gaze on thee,
  That shall not see thee more;
A thousand hearts beat proudly now,
  Whose race, like thine, is o'er!

O ghastly moon, thy pallid ray
  On paler brows shall lie,
On many a torn and bleeding breast,
  On many a glazing eye;
And breaking hearts shall live to mourn,
  For whom 't were bliss to die.

THE GREAT STRUGGLE.

Let the world be hushed in awe,
  Let the nations stand and gaze,
And the distant lands and the isles afar
  Be wrapt in a still amaze,
While the wondrous drama is acting on
  In these, the wondrous days.

Lo! the waves of the Southern seas
  Are black with a hostile fleet;
And the very earth to its centre shakes
  With the tramp of a myriad feet,
Where army and army are drawing nigh —
  Nation and nation meet.

From the realms of the chilly North,
  From the East to the Western shore,

The countless numbers are pushing down,
  The gathering legions pour;
And they swear that the plains of the sunny South
  Shall be steeped in Southern gore.

Swords for the strong and brave—
  Chains for the proud and free!
Death to the hands that dare to strive
  For a freeman's liberty!
And they cry aloud, in their boastful pride,
  "Let the world stand still and see!"

Forward! ye hireling hordes,
  And redeem your haughty boast;
For lo! the plains of the roused South
  Are dark with a gathering host,
From the boundless wastes of our Western land
  To Virginia's sea-beat coast.

Steadily on they come,
  With their bearing proud and high;
The fiery-souled and dark Creole,
  And the hunter with eagle-eye;
And there, with a freeman's mien of pride,
The toil-worn cottier, side by side
  With Virginia's chivalry!

A noble race, and brave!
  Meet for a nation's need;
Ready to die a martyr's death
  As to dare a hero's deed;
Marching with firm and steady step
  Where their noble chieftains lead.

Gaunt with famine and toil,
  They pant through the summer heat,
And their rags are turned to a coat of mail
  In the icy winter-sleet;
And the snow of the mountain-top is tracked
  By their bare and bleeding feet.

Yet steadily on they come,
  That stern, determined band,
With the trusty rifle firmly grasped
  In each bare and sunburnt hand.

Thank God! thank God for the noble hearts
  That defend our glorious land!

Yea, plumed and pampered hosts,
  Ye may laugh aloud in scorn;
But the day is near when your pride shall fall,
  And your glory shall be shorn;
And likely shall ye curse the day
  That ever your chiefs were born.

Stand still, O earth, and gaze,
  As the wondrous hour draws near;
For lo! they meet with a mighty shock,
  That the very world may hear—
The sons of the canting Puritan
  And the noble Cavalier.

As once upon England's soil
  They met in the deadly fray—
The Roundhead and the Cavalier—
  So again they meet to-day;
With a hate which time may never quell,
  Nor the world may wipe away.

They meet as the ocean waves
  Meet the firm and living rock,
When wave upon angry wave comes on,
  With a mighty roar and shock.
Yea, steadfast stand, ye Southern bands,
  And their impotent fury mock!

Broken, and shattered, and torn,
  They recoil with an angry roar;
And again they gather, again come on
  In a mightier strength than before;
And again, again they are backward hurled,
And the strength of the conflict shakes the world,
  And the earth is steeped in gore.

O dwellers of sunny France,
  And of England's pleasant strand,
Can ye look on a conflict such as this,
  And calmly and coldly stand?
Can ye see us strive, in this trying hour,
'Gainst the bloody host of a tyrant power,
  And lend no helping hand?

We looked to you in vain,
  Yet our souls are not dismayed;
On a higher power than aught of earth
  Are our steadfast spirits stayed;
For the God of battles is on our side,
  The Lord of Hosts shall aid.

Hark! through the mourning land—
  It is woman's earnest call;
From the cottier's hearth it comes,
  And the old ancestral hall:
"Save us, your wives and children dear,
  From the tyrant's hated thrall!

"Be true, O Southern men,
  Even as we are true;
And let the thought in the darkest hour
  Your fainting souls renew,
That still our tireless fingers toil
  And our prayers ascend for you.

"Stand fast, ye Southern men!
  In the strength of the Lord be strong!
The glorious day shall dawn at last,
  Though the night be dark and long;
And God shall protect our nation's rights,
  And avenge our country's wrong!"

MRS. CONSTANCE CARY HARRISON.

THE subject of this short sketch, whose maiden name was Constance Cary, and who is best known to Southern literature under her *nom de plume* of "Refugitta," is the daughter of the late Archibald Cary and of Monimia Fairfax, his wife, both representatives of ancient families of Virginia. Mrs. Harrison is the elder of two children, and was born, we believe, in Mississippi, to which State her father had removed, shortly after his marriage, for the purpose of practising his profession, the law. Mr. Cary was a gentleman of fine literary abilities, and during his residence in Mississippi was associated in the editorship of a newspaper at Port Gibson, the place of his residence. Mr. Cary subsequently removed to Cumberland, Maryland, where he became proprietor and editor of the "Cumberland Civilian," which journal he edited up to the time of his death.

At the breaking out of the war, Miss Cary was residing with her mother at "Vancluse," about three miles from Alexandria, Virginia, for many years the country-seat of the Fairfax family, and the former home of her maternal grandfather, Thomas Fairfax. Like many others, overtaken by the coming of war, Miss Cary became a "refugee," a term understood with a mournful distinctness by thousands of the best and noblest of the South, and sought shelter, accompanied by her mother, in Richmond, in which city she remained until the close of the war.

It was in Richmond that Miss Cary first wrote under the name of "Refugitta." From both father and mother she had inherited a decided literary taste and aptitude; and hence the lively, sparkling sketches which appeared under that name in the literary papers of the Confederate capital, displayed a more than usual vigor, and their vivacity of style earned for their fair author no little reputation and applause. Among the writers of the four years of warfare that befell the South, none was more popular than "Refugitta," especially in Richmond, where were published most of her writings.

In the autumn of 1865, Miss Cary went to Europe with her mother, remaining there about a year. Some time after her return to the United States, she was married to Mr. Burton N. Harrison, who, during the war, was attached to the person of Mr. Jefferson Davis in the capacity of private secretary. Mr. and Mrs. Harrison at present reside in New York.

M. J. HAW.

IN the fall of 1863, the "Southern Illustrated News," published in Richmond, had the following announcement:

"AN ILLUSTRATED ROMANCE!

"PRIZE OF ONE THOUSAND DOLLARS!

"Having engaged the services of a corps of competent engravers, who are confidently expected to arrive in the Confederacy in a few weeks, the proprietors of the 'Illustrated News' will award a prize of one thousand dollars to the author of the best illustrated romance, to be submitted to them between the present date and the 1st of November next.

"September 5th, 1863."

The time was extended to the 1st of December.

March 1st, 1864, the "News" announced that the prize for the best romance had been awarded to Miss M. J. Haw, of Hanover County, Virginia, for her story, entitled "The Rivals: A Tale of the Chickahominy."

The "committee" stated that, "in recommending the superiority of 'The Rivals,' they base their preference upon the fact that to its other excellences is added that of unity. The story itself is written with a pleasing simplicity of style and a freshness of interest."

Miss Haw had been a contributor to the "Magnolia Weekly," of tales, etc., signed with her initials, the only objection to which were the sombre backgrounds. "The Beechwood Tragedy" was the title of the first story we ever read from "M. J. H.'s" pen. The prize romance was her most ambitious and most successful effort.

Miss Haw had the misfortune to reside during the war "in the midst of battle-fields," and suffered from marauders and so-called scouting parties. The close of the war found her "moneyless," and since that time she has written nothing, save a few articles for the "Christian Observer," having to struggle too desperately for bread to have any time for literature.

MRS. MARY WILEY,

(*"Margaret Stilling."*)

REMARKED a distinguished critic, "A *nom de plume*, in my opinion, should express character. Now, the best that I have seen in the South is that one of 'Margaret Stilling.' It attracted my attention at once." "Margaret Stilling" (the *nom de plume* of Miss Mary Evans) is a native and resident of Amelia County, Virginia. Her father, Dr. M. H. Evans, was a physician of some eminence in his profession. Her mother, who contributed poems to the "Southern Literary Messenger," many years ago, and published a volume of poems at Philadelphia in 1851, was of Northern birth—a Miss Stockton, related, I believe, to the celebrated Commodore Stockton.

The subject of this sketch was educated at the North, and is an elegant, accomplished woman, of high intellectual and musical culture, and a brilliant conversationist.

During the war, Miss Evans was a teacher, yet found time to cultivate the muses, to the pleasure of the "blockaded" Southrons, contributing her elegant productions in prose and verse to the "Confederate" literary journals. Since the war, she has become Mrs. William Wiley, and we presume household duties usurp the hours hitherto devoted to the pen.

A BUNCH OF FLOWERS.

Across the leaves bright sunshine fell,
  Touching their green with gold,
And tingeing, as some lustrous shell,
  Each rosebud's crimson fold.

A dewy network's pearly bands
  Set, diamond-like, with light,
Stretched o'er each flower its gleaming strands,
  With moonlight radiance bright.

While many a tiny, trembling spray,
  Some liquid star-drop brushing,
Would flash from thence one silver ray,
  And show a rosebud's blushing.

With mute delight I gazed on all,
  Some charm my spirit thrilling,
Hearing His voice through nature call,
  Each mystic yearning stilling.

Then 'gainst the wall the shadow fell,
  An outline dim and strange,
As if the colors, limned so well,
  Had known some wondrous change.

'T is thus, O heaven, thy glories bright,
  Fairer than star-gemmed skies,
Fall, shadowed with uncertain light,
  Before our sin-stained eyes.

OH! TELL ME, MY LOVE, DO THE SHADOWY SKIES.

Oh! tell me, my love, do the shadowy skies,
  As they tremble and sparkle above,
Wake not the lost Hope, with her beautiful eyes,
  Shedding glances of holiest love?

Hath the starlight no power to break her repose,
  Or the night-wind to kiss her again?
The flowers, as pale as the purest of snows,
  Do they weep for her presence in vain?

Oh! well do I know there are times when thy heart
  Feels again that sweet rapture of love,
When the flowers and sunshine once more seem a part
  Of those vows still recorded above.

Our love was in sadness, and many a tear
  Fell to prove how immortal its birth,
And years have but shown how surpassingly dear
  It exceeds the love cradled in mirth.

For tears that are wrung from a heart that is true
  Seem to blend with a sunlight divine,
And a shadowy rainbow against the deep blue
  Like a signet of promise doth shine.

'T was the brightest of summers, and thus every year
  Hath a season when memory weeps;
The soul feels a sadness too deep for a tear,
  As the vigils of sorrow it keeps.

Then tell me, O love, do the shadowy skies,
  As they tremble and sparkle above,
Wake not in thy heart all the terrible cries
  Of a stifled and passionate love?

I've marked in thy glances, and heard in each word,
  That the thoughts of the past will not sleep;
I know there are times when a voice will be heard
  That doth make thee despairingly weep.

I know that the present can rivet no chain
  So strong as the linkings of this;
I feel that the future will bless us again
  With a purer and holier bliss.

For love that's immortal can never be stilled,
  And the lips that have quivered shall smile;
While heaven above, that its being hath willed,
  With the brightest of joys shall beguile.

THE OCEAN OF DESPAIR.

There is a boundless, surging ocean,
  Beating forever a dreary shore,
Where darksome waves, with a restless motion,
  Over the sands in anger pour,
With a muttering, sullen sound of fear,
As if they felt some horror near.

Nought of life o'er the waters gliding
  Breaketh the gloom of its sunless day;
But fearful wrecks by its shores abiding
  Show from their spars a ghastly ray;

While many a monstrous, hideous thing
Loathsomely to their sides doth cling.

Bleaching bones, on its margin shining,
  Telling of many a tale of woe,
Point where the breakers are dimly hiding
  Darkly under the waters' flow —
Striving to show, in their warrings vain,
Signs of many a bloody stain.

Up from its depths a voice of wailing,
  Full of a shuddering, awful fear,
Over the billows its sad length trailing,
  Echoes mournfully far and near;
Lifting itself in a quivering sigh,
Far in the dark, o'erhanging sky.

Angry clouds on its bosom shadow
  Many a gloomy, hurrying form,
Wildly with dread o'er the surging billow
  Fleeing fast from the bursting storm;
Looking back oft with a face of woe,
Strangely pale in the ghastly glow.

Alas for the barks, with glad hopes freighted,
  Forever lost on this fatal shore;
Going down with a thunder that grated
  Hoarsely above the ocean's roar!
Who can tell what wild agony burst
Over the soul in those waters curst?

Vain the voice of their earnest warning;
  The pleading, sorrowing, wild-toned cry
Cannot reach to the land whose dawning
  Recks not of that darkened sky;
For others shall steer, not heeding the sight,
To sink as they in darkest night.

OH! LOVE, DEAR LOVE, THE QUIET SKIES.

Oh! love, dear love, the quiet skies
  Are eloquent with tender light;
The perfumed night-wind softly sighs;
  The starlight throbs with strange delight.

A thousand blossoms 'neath the moon
  Lie folded with their treasured sweets,
More beautiful than when at noon
  Their sun-god's smile each trembler greets.

My queen of blossoms, shall the night
  Shed all its jewelled splendor down,
And seek in vain that form of light,
  So worthy of its fairy crown?

See where the pearl-wreaths on the grass
  Flash softly 'neath the night-dew's guise,
Watching to see thee gliding past,
  And catch the splendor of thine eyes.

Oh! love, dear love, the quiet skies
  Cast down for thee that tender light;
The perfumed night-wind in its sighs
  Breathes forth thy name with wild delight.

On this fair eve a thought of love
  Pulses through nature's heart for thee;
Then, while the starlight throbs above,
  Come wander forth awhile with me.

I'll read a story in those skies,
  Where sapphire tints of brightest blue
Reflect the splendor of thine eyes,
  Like olden glories blent with new.

And while the music of thy voice
  Murmurs thy sweet and soft replies,
Like some rich tune, whose notes rejoice,
  Ere on the breeze it slowly dies,

The starlight, with its silver showers,
  The misty tints of melting blue,
The scented winds, the folded flowers,
  Shall plead my earnest love for you.

MISS VIRGINIA E. DAVIDSON.

THE subject of this notice has always been an invalid. Says she, in an elegant letter to the writer: "On this account I have had the misfortune to be uneducated, except so far as a fine private library and an extraordinarily intelligent father's conversation and explanations could supply the painful deficiency."

She is the daughter of Colonel James Davidson, who was well known in Petersburg, Virginia, (the home of Miss Davidson,) as a man of remarkably varied information upon all subjects and sciences, and who occasionally wrote verses. On her mother's side she is, by affinity, connected with the Harrisons, of James River; and the Clairbornes, Maurys, and Fontaines, of this State. Her brother, W. F. Davidson, was an officer in the United States Navy, and was considered one of the finest mathematicians in that highly educated branch of the service: he also wrote poetry; and a sister has also evinced the same talent.

To best illustrate a determined spirit, and showing what can be done when one places their might at the wheel, we would mention that, at the age of sixteen, to use her own words, "I was so illiterate, I did not know or even understand the commonest branches of education, until one night a friend, younger than I, came to spend the evening. She contended with my father about a difference of opinion of Hector, and then of Ajax, Theseus, and Marc Antony. I sat fearful, lest they should call upon me as umpire; for I was entirely ignorant of these heroes. Fortunately, the conversation turned upon the beauties of poetry: upon this subject I knew a little, and gladly did I avail myself of my superficial knowledge. Ignorance was abashed, and I at once commenced, without consultation with any one, a three-hours' task of ancient history and mythological reading, until history became a mania and an idol. This was the commencement of my education."

At the close of the war, Miss Davidson was no better off than the majority of her Southern sisters. "Necessity is the mother of invention, and poverty is the fruitful mother of energies," and at once in

Miss Davidson brain and will and determination awoke, and she wove the incidents detailed to her during social hours of pleasant association *during the war* into book-form, under the title of "Bloody Footprints." Some of the incidents of this volume were published in the "Southern Opinion," Richmond, under the name of "Virginia." Miss Davidson has also written a novel, entitled "Philanthropist," and one which she has called "Principle and Policy." The last named is now in the hands of publishers in New York.

MISS SALLIE A. BROCK

IS the author of "Richmond During the War: Four Years of Personal Observation," a work which, had she written nothing else, would deservedly give her a prominent place among the first female writers of the country. Says a reviewer in a Northern journal:

"It is characterized by a purity of style and thought, a delicacy of sentiment, and an earnestness of conviction that are too rarely found in the publications of the day. The hopes and fears, the resolution and self-sacrifice, the sufferings and privations, the heroism and courage displayed by the Southern people, are described with all the warm affection and loving reverence of a true woman's heart — a heart whose every throb beat in sympathy with the cause of the South. The generous and noble impulses by which, in common with tens of thousands of her Southern sisters, the fair authoress was actuated, are manifested in the general style and character of the subjects treated. She brings to her task a mind fully stored with the most minute information on the principles in controversy. She is thoroughly conversant with the causes that led to the conflict, and this knowledge is employed with admirable judgment during the progress of the work for the enlightenment of the reader. The style is peculiarly pleasing, and the literary character of the book is of the highest order. Full of incident, and of stirring, striking, and often thrilling scenes, the interest of the work never flags. All the joyousness of victory and the gloom of defeat, all the glory and all the horrors of war, are depicted with a lifelike vividness; and the leading characters that appear upon the stage are painted with the fidelity of truth itself. The title of the volume would convey the impression that the scope is limited to Richmond; but this is not so, for the fair authoress takes in the whole range of the Confederacy, and describes the influence of this or that event as affecting the general progress of the contest. There are no less than seventy-six chapters in the book, a fact which will serve to convey some idea of its varied interest. The first opens with the secession of Virginia; and the last, entitled "Life in the Old Land Yet," breathes forth words of hope and encouragement, giving a glowing picture of the future of the South, rousing the faint-hearted, and inspiring the despondent with new life and courage. We heartily commend 'Richmond During the War' as one of the most interesting, valuable, and best written volumes that has appeared since the close of the great struggle."

Sallie A. Brock is a native of Madison Court House, Virginia, an obscure little hamlet among the hills of Piedmont, and overhung by jutting spurs of the Blue Ridge. This little village is distinguished for the wild and romantic character of the surrounding scenery, and the fair intelligence and high moral standard of its inhabitants; and Miss Brock's attachment to her birthplace is shown in the pseudonym for her literary efforts, "Virginia Madison." And this very appropriate *nom de plume* calls particular attention to the many inappropriate ones; and it is a cause for conjecture why so many elegant writers show such questionable taste in their pseudonyms.

Miss Brock, on her father's side, is of Welsh descent. In England, the Brocks were staunch Royalists; and one of the name sealed his devotion to his country and his crown by his blood, upon the Heights of Queenstown, in Canada.

Her mother, whose maiden name was Buckner, was a descendant, from her father, of the Beverlys and the Chews; and from her mother, of the Burtons, the Heads, and the Marshalls, all names inseparably connected with the colonial and revolutionary history of Virginia.

Miss Brock's childhood was passed in her native village, under the tutelage of her father exclusively; and later, under tutors and governesses. She is ignorant of what is usually called "boarding-school experience."

In her childhood, she was fond of study, and devoted to æsthetical pursuits, whether growing out of nature or of art, in the circumscribed sphere of her acquaintance, from which, strangely, nothing could attract her but the *roll of the drum* and the clangor of martial music. Her reward for merit was permission to go out of school to watch the drilling of the officers for the regular spring militia muster. Her soul was so thrilled with enthusiasm, and her pride in the *flag* of our country, "the stars and stripes," so intense, that, though a little child when the Mexican war broke out, she wished she was a man, that she might follow the flag! Her enthusiasm has been completely crushed by the events of the late war. How terrible was the revulsion of feeling, when that flag was used as the ensign for expunging the liberties of her own beloved section, only God can know, who witnessed the midnight agony of soul over the downfall of the Confederate cause.

Will God hold us responsible for this terrible revolt of feeling? Has he implanted within us emotions of patriotism only to show to us the narrow compass of human vision, and the nothingness of ambition?

Has he given us conceptions of right and wrong only to vindicate his power, and to make us miserable?

In the fall of 1850, Mr. Brock removed to the University of Virginia, where his daughter spent the following eight years of her life. There her sphere for improvement was sensibly enlarged, and she enjoyed the advantages of society as moral, refined, highly cultivated, and intellectual as can be found in the country. Her fondness for books grew upon her; in the course of time, she devoted herself to studying oil-painting, and then she indulged the dream of *authorship*.

In the winter of 1858, the Brock family removed to Richmond, and were living in that city when the news from Sumter announced the breaking out of hostilities. Miss Brock's course of life from that time was changed. Dreams of distinction were hushed before the stern demands of duty. There was much for her to do, in common with all of her Southern sisters. She sewed and knitted, and nursed and cooked, and watched and prayed, during the four years of the war, in service for the South and her soldiers; while the delicate health of her mother, and the frequent and necessary absences from home of her father and younger brother, threw upon her the cares of the family. They were severe and onerous, and she bore them with fortitude, feeble enough as she watched her mother's decline to the grave. This was her first personal sorrow; and the only drop of consolation she tastes is in the remembrance that she has been rescued from the great national sorrow, which, like the raven, "never flitting, still is sitting, still is sitting," brooding over the wreck of the buried hopes of a nation. A total change in circumstances and family changes have drifted Miss Brock away from home and friends; and she is now residing in the city of New York, which is the "literary emporium" of the country, where authors much do congregate.

"Virginia Madison's" muse is a busy one, and is becoming to be appreciated by the reading world. Writing gives Miss Brock intense pleasure, and her writings give her readers no less delight.

Her second volume, a collection of poems from Southern poets, is entitled "The Southern Amaranth," Wilcox, publisher, New York, published for the benefit of the "Ladies' Memorial Association," (1869.) This volume contains many poems furnished expressly for this work by the authors; also, many beautiful poems from the muse of the gifted editress. Miss Brock's talents are of a versatile order, excelling in fiction, in poetry, and in what a woman seldom does well, political topics, which she discusses and argues knowingly and eloquently. She has established a reputation as a writer, of which she may well be proud, and which must increase with time: thus considered, her first volume may be looked upon as a bud which must be followed by many magnificent blossoms, which we firmly hope may be fadeless.

WHAT IS LIFE?

"What is Life?" I asked of a wanton child,
As he chased a butterfly;
And his laugh gushed out all joyous and wild,
As the insect flitted by.
"What is Life?" I asked; "oh, tell me, I pray!"
His echoes rang merrily, "Life is PLAY!"

"What is Life?" I asked of the maiden fair,
And I watched her glowing cheek
As the blushes deepened and softened there,
And the dimples played "hide and seek."
"What is Life? Can you tell me its fullest measure?"
She smilingly answered, "Life is PLEASURE!"

"What is Life?" I asked of a soldier brave,
As he grasped the hilt of his sword;
He planted his foot on a foeman's grave,
And looked "creation's lord."
"What is Life?" I queried; "oh, tell me its story."
His brow grew bright as he answered, "GLORY!"

"What is Life?" I asked a mother proud,
As she bent o'er her babe asleep,
With a low, hushed tone, lest a thought aloud
Might waken its slumber deep.
Her smile turned grave, though wondrous in beauty,
While she made reply, "Life—life is DUTY!"

I turned to the father, who stood near by
And gazed on his wife with pride;
Then a tear of joy shone bright in his eye
For the treasure that lay at her side.
I listened well for the tale that should come:
"My life!" he cried, "my life is HOME!"

"What is Life?" I asked of the infidel;
His eyes were haggard and bleared;
Fierce, mocking sneers from his thin lips swell,
And his heart with vice was seared.
"What is Life," I asked, "in its ebb and flow?"
With an oath he muttered, "Life is Woe!"

"What is Life?" I asked of the invalid wan,
As he wheeled to the grate his chair,
And frowned as through the casement there ran
A fluttering breath of air.
"What is Life?" I asked — I asked again:
He languidly coughed, and answered, "Pain!"

"What is Life?" I asked of the statesman grand,
The idol of the hour;
The fate of a nation was in his hand —
His word was the breath of power.
He, sickening, turned from the world's caress:
"'Tis a bubble!" he cried — "'tis Emptiness!"

"What is Life?" I asked of the miser grim,
As he clutched his well-filled bag;
His features were gaunt and his figure slim,
His garment a tattered rag.
"What is Life?" I asked, "the story unfold."
"Life," he chuckled, "life is Gold!"

"What is Life?" I asked of the student of books,
Exploring a ponderous tome;
There are curious things in the rare old nooks
Whence the records of science come.
For a moment he turned from his learnèd perch,
And quickly answered, "Life is Research!"

"What is Life?" I asked of a Christian meek,
As she knelt before a shrine;
The impress of Heaven was on her cheek,
In her eyes a light divine.
"What is life?" I questioned, "oh! trace me its path!"
She pointed upward, and whispered, "Faith!"

"What is Life?" I asked of a man of care,
Bending under the load of years:

He ran his fingers through his thin gray hair,
  And his eyelids were humid with tears.
His voice trembled, "I once was brave;
Life is a shadow that points to the GRAVE!"

I turned and asked of my inner heart
  What story it could unfold?
It bounded quick in its pulses' start,
  As the record it unrolled.
I read on the page, "Love, Hope, Joy, Strife!
What the heart would make it, such is LIFE!"

THE SOLDIER'S HOME.

"You will go home now," said a lady of Richmond to a gallant Mississippian, after the surrender of the armies of the Southern Confederacy. "Home!" he echoed sadly, while a manly tear glistened in his calm, blue eye: "Home — alas! mother earth is my only couch, and the canopy of the heavens my covering. What was once a home is now a monumental ruin. I have no home, unless it be in the hearts of kind and generous friends."

Is it where his infant feet have trod
  In the joy of childish glee,
Like the woodland bird with its merry song,
  'Neath the boughs of the parent tree?
Is it where his boyhood's days were passed,
  And youth's bright dreams began,
Where ambition's dawn, with its kindling pride,
  Gave promise of the man?
    Has the soldier there a home?

Where the cane in rank luxuriance grows
  In the warmth of the genial sun,
Where the "Father of Waters" in his mighty course
  And giant strength doth run?
Where the cotton throws out its snowy fleece,
  Or in that bright "Land of Flowers"
Where the orange-tree yields its golden fruits,
  And the wild rose wreathes its bowers —
    Oh! has he there a home?

In the rich savannas of the South,
  Where springs the pearly grain;
Where the live-oak rears its kingly head
  O'er the forest-trees to reign?

Where the sweet magnolia scents the gale
  And the jessamine's perfume;
Where the myrtle wild, with its livery bright,
  Doth lighten the forest's gloom?
      Not there is the soldier's home.

Is it where the tall palmetto grows,
  Or 'neath the mountain's crest
Where limpid streams o'er their rocky beds
  Dance on and never rest?
Where the cloud-cap throws its silvery veil,
  And the sunset's lingering beam
Kisses its top with a crimson glow,
  And the purple evening's gleam —
      Is there the soldier's home?

On the Old Dominion's blood-washed soil,
  Where every hill and dale
Is tuneful of the sacred past
  As Tempe's classic vale;
Where Freedom's mightiest throes were felt,
  Where Freedom bowed her head —
Her mailed hand on her breaking heart,
  In anguish o'er her dead —
      Not there has he a home.

On the fertile prairies of the West,
  Where the kind and generous soil
To the farmer yields a rich reward
  For all his care and toil;
Where the emigrant's rustic cottage stands,
  And the tall grass, wild and free,
Rises and falls as the breeze sweeps o'er
  Like the billows of the sea —
      Not there is the soldier's home!

For over them all the ruthless foe
  Like locusts dark have trod,
The fields laid waste, the roof-trees dear
  Have levelled with the sod:
The chimneys bare, the blackened walls,
  The ruined hearthstones there —
The silent cottages around,
  Like crumbling tombs, show where
      The soldier had a home!

In the tented field, 'mid the cannon's roar
  And the musket's rattling sound,
Where the drum's long roll and the bugle note
  And the clash of arms resound—
Where foe to foe in human strife
  And deadly conflict meet,
With the hissing ball and the bayonet thrust
  And the dead around his feet—
    Till late, that was his home.

But other homes has the soldier brave,
  From the battle's dim array:
In the loving hearts of the good and true,
  The gentle and the gay,
There is a sacred corner kept,
  Where an altar burns, refined
With the vestal flame of Heaven's own love,
  And the soldier is enshrined
    Within this hallowed home.

Where'er a mansion rears its head,
  Where ease and plenty meet,
At the well-filled board of bounteous store
  The soldier has a seat.
In the mountain cot of the humble poor,
  Or near the swelling tide,
The door may be closed 'gainst the wintry wind,
  But the latch-string is outside—
    And there is the soldier's home!

Then, poor and warworn veteran,
  Oh, cease thy sad complaint!
For earth has always cheery spots
  For the weary and the faint;
And a promise bright to you is given,
  When life's last day is done—
When life's sad battles all are fought—
  When the last vict'ry's won—
    In heaven there is a home!

MISS SUE C. HOOPER.

A QUIET home-existence up to the close, or rather beginning of the war — for "quiet" was hardly to be found in Richmond during the time the "City on the James" was capital of the Confederate States — was that of Sue C. Hooper.

Miss Sue C. Hooper's father, on the death of his wife and an infant daughter, which occurred shortly after the second birthday of the subject of this article, discontinued housekeeping, and the subsequent life of father and daughter was spent as boarders in the home of one or another of their kindred. Says the lady:

"My earliest *distinct* recollection is of a character rather different, I opine, from that of most girls. I could not have numbered more than three or four years, at farthest, when our city had the honor of a visit from the Sage of Marshfield. Reared in the Slashes of Hanover, familiar with the scenes of Clay's early life, and bred in the same school of politics, it was always a marvel to me that Harry of the West was not my father's favorite leader. But, no; it was Webster, from the colder latitude and granite hills of New England. Well, my father could not permit so golden an opportunity of his child's seeing his political idol to pass unimproved; so, girl, almost baby as I was, he hurried me down to the honorable gentleman's reception on the portico of the old Powhatan, then a leading hotel, held me in his arms above the heads of the populace, that in after years I might boast of having heard Webster, the immortal. My impressions of that hour were a source of infinite amusement to my father to the day of his death. Mr. Webster was welcomed by James Lyons, Esq., a prominent member of the Richmond Bar, afterward a representative of that district in the Confederate Congress; and I, after an impartial hearing of both speeches, boldly avowed the opinion that Mr. Lyons was the greater orator of the two, in my infantile judgment. It may have been the elegance and grace of our fellow-citizen, or his sonorous, Ciceronian periods, or perhaps both united, as compared with the stout, portly figure and short, pithy sentences of the New-Englander, as my dim, shadowy remembrance now paints him, which captivated my childish fancy; but there was evidently something in his manner, or appearance, or rhetoric, which indelibly stamped itself upon my mind, and made Mr. Lyons, for a long period, my beau ideal of an orator."

The childhood of Miss Hooper was passed with her maternal grandmother, a woman of strong and well-cultivated mind for the ante-revolutionary period. Politics was her forte. She was never quite so near the climax of happiness as when she could engage a Democrat in controversy, and overthrow (as she conceived) some of his pet theories, by a womanly thrust, or an apt quotation from the Sage of Ashland, her paragon of statesmanship. Who can aver that these surroundings had no influence in shaping the habits of thought and manner of writing of Miss Hooper?

Miss Hooper's father made her, his *only one*, a companion from infancy; taught her to read at an early age, years before she was old enough to go to school; interested himself in her childish pleasures and pursuits. Mr. Hooper was a man of sound judgment and superior practical sense, and was always very ambitious for his daughter.

In her childhood, authorship had been Miss Hooper's hobby; but emancipated from the restraints of the school-room, for several years she had no ambition beyond present enjoyment. It is to Reviews, of which department of literature she is particularly fond, that Miss Hooper is indebted for most of her knowledge of authors, never having had access to a library.

Her first article was published in the "Religious Herald," Richmond, under the *nom de plume* of "Adrienne," which she still retains.

Her first story was published in a literary weekly of Richmond, and was much complimented by the editress; since which time she has contributed to Southern and Northern literary journals. During the war, "Adrienne" was one of the most prominent contributors to the "Magnolia Weekly," Richmond. Her novelettes were lacking in vivacity, and the characters were similar. "Ashes of Roses" we consider her cleverest novelette; some of the scenes being not only lifelike, but capitally delineated. Her best productions will shortly be given to the public.

Shortly before the close of the war, Mr. Hooper died; and with the downfall of the Confederacy, *her* property was all swept away; and single-handed, this true Christian woman prepared to contend with the "cold charities of the world in the battle of life."

A Virginian by birth, having ever resided within the borders of the "mother of States," Miss Hooper is proud of the "Old Dominion," and clings to her, "desolated," as she rejoiced in her "pomp and beauty." She converses fluently and elegantly. As a correspondent, Miss

Hooper is to be praised; her letters are natural and interesting, an index of the character of the writer.

In the writings of Miss Hooper, the defects are those that are inherent in her nature and surroundings. Having never travelled or mingled in "society," so called, her novelettes are necessarily plain, unvarnished records of home-life in the middle class of society; in which, perhaps, the *religious* element predominates too strongly for the mass of readers. We think Miss Hooper has erred in too little following Longfellow's suggestion, "to look into her heart and write."

THE OCCUPATION OF RICHMOND.

I do not believe there ever was a more panic-stricken woman than I, the first day, and, indeed, the first week of the occupation of Richmond by the Federal troops; but, upon present reflection, I admit that the causes for alarm existed more in my imagination than in reality.

Sunday was the loveliest of April days, the morning as quiet as any within four years; and worshippers wended their way to church as peacefully as if "wars and rumors of wars" were mere abstractions. In the afternoon, there were whisperings of evacuation; and, toward evening, elongated visages, the constant whistle of locomotives, and fugitive inhabitants, betokened some unusual commotion; but I remembered the gun-boat panic in '62, and persistently refused to credit the evidence of my senses. Such was my confidence in the success of our cause, that it was not until eleven o'clock that night, when it was positively asserted that our pickets were to be withdrawn two hours thereafter, that I began to realize the situation. That slumber visited not my eyes you will readily believe; but it is too much for your credulity to believe that hope was still inspired by my reflections upon the numerous miraculous interpositions of Providence in behalf of God's chosen people in ancient times, particularly the deliverance of Hezekiah from the hosts of Sennacherib; and I fondly dreamed, even then, that the enemy would never be permitted to enter our "beautiful, seven-hilled city." This delusion was dispelled about dawn by an explosion which shook the house to its very foundation, and I sprang up, exclaiming to my room-mate, "Oh, L——, the Yankees are shelling us!" and shortly after, there was another report more terrific still, which fully convinced me that the enemy had opened a bombardment. These reports we soon ascertained to be from the destruction of the "Patrick Henry," at the Rockets, and the powder magazine, almost in our immediate vicinity; and were but the beginning of the explosions, which were continued throughout the morning at the armory and the arsenal. About sunrise, the mob, who had been sacking the stores all night, completed their work by firing the houses they had rifled. The brooding wing of the destroying angel seemed to hover over us in the dense clouds of smoke which obscured the sun, and made almost a twilight darkness at midday. The fire raged furiously all day, and by night at least one-half of the business portion of the city was in ashes.

About eight o'clock in the morning, in the midst of the consternation about the conflagration, there was a general stampede of the pillagers from "down town," fleeing before the enemy. As everything was remarkably quiet, except in the burning district, and I expected they would enter with "a great flourish of trumpets," I pronounced it all a hoax, until one of our neighbors assured me "he had seen the Yankees on the Square." My first view of them was about ten o'clock, when two regiments of fine-looking, soldierly fellows, whom, but for their splendid uniforms, I might have imagined some of our own brave boys, advanced up the street with a firm, steady tread, and a dignified, martial air. I confess, until then, anxiety for my personal safety had absorbed every other feeling; but when I descried through the closed blinds the "stars and stripes" waving in the Confederate capital, I burst into tears.

The first freshet of my grief having subsided, I became tolerably composed; but, in the afternoon, was again precipitated into a panic by the approach of a colored brigade, who rushed pellmell past our residence, singing, shouting, yelling, firing, the white officers not even endeavoring to restrain them. We anticipated such scenes that night as marked the occupation of Columbia, S. C.; and as these black fiends were encamped only two squares beyond us, we apprehended danger to our neighborhood from their proximity. However, everything passed off quietly, and we scarcely heard a footfall on the street after nightfall.

"Our friends, the enemy," (to quote the polite language of the *late* Mr. Daniel, of the "Examiner," who *fortunately* died the week before the evacuation,) have preserved very good order ever since their occupation. There have been some irregularities and depredations in the vicinity of the camps, particularly before the removal of the negro troops; but, as far as possible, they have been promptly punished. Indeed, *ma chère*, I thought I never knew what gratitude was until the first week of the Federal rule here: every hour we were protected from violence seemed a miracle of grace. The authorities and the soldiery, in the main, have pursued a conciliatory course toward our citizens, and have carefully refrained from any exultation over a fallen foe. At church they are exceedingly respectful and devotional; they have been particularly courteous to ladies; don't even glance at us in the street, except to move aside to allow us to pass. . . . .

An amusing incident occurred not long since on Franklin Street, the fashionable promenade of the city. A belle, in meeting a Federal officer, doubled her veil; but just as he passed, a gust of wind drifted it at his feet.

He picked it up and presented it very gallantly, meanwhile concealing his face with his hat—a suitable reproof for her silly affectation.

Another incident, more interesting still, as showing the temper of the people: Last week, several young ladies, at the passport office, while awaiting their passports, entered into a cheerful conversation, but carefully abstaining from any allusion to the Yankees or the state of the country. An officer in the crowd appeared interested in their discourse, and presently made a casual inquiry. He was answered civilly, but coldly; but, not regarding his repulse, he pursued his interrogatories on indifferent topics. Finding he could elicit no reference to politics or the war, he pertly asked: "Well, what do you think of the success of your Confederacy now?" "Sir," replied one of the girls, "with God nothing is impossible; and I believe with his assistance we shall yet achieve our independence; for we are assured that 'whom the Lord loveth He chasteneth.'" Her questioner, crest-fallen and abashed, hung his head, and was soon lost in the crowd.

We are allowed considerable latitude of speech, of which we are not slow to avail ourselves. Treasonable utterances are not tolerated in the pulpit; but some of our ministers, even in conversation with the Federals, "use great plainness of speech," with perfect impunity. . . . .

On the 29th of April, an order was promulgated by General Halleck, to take effect on the 1st of May, that no minister would be allowed to perform a marriage ceremony without having taken the oath, and the parties contracting marriage should also be required to take the oath. Two of our wealthy young ladies of the *beau monde* were engaged to be married to a pair of North Carolina officers the first week in May; but, upon the appearance of this order, the parties "out-heroded Herod," by being united in Hymen's silken tie on Sunday morning, April 30th—Rev. Dr. Burrows, of the First Baptist Church, officiating. It is said there were at least fifty marriages in Richmond that day.

MATILDA S. EDWARDS.

MATILDA CAROLINE SMILEY was the youngest of twelve children: six sons and six daughters made the old homestead a very bright and happy place.

Matilda was left pretty much to her own inclinations in childhood, and spent many hours wandering through the woods around Grape Hill, (Nelson County, Virginia,) gathering flowers, and listening to the birds and the rippling of the bright waters that sparkled in the sunshine. It was a happy childhood, full of bright, sweet memories. She wrote a great deal; and her compositions, although hidden away, as she thought, securely, were often found by her sisters, who made them subjects of amusement, to her great mortification. One day, the presiding elder of the Virginia Conference, Rev. George W. Nalley, was stopping at the "homestead," and her sister found her blank book and showed it to him. The gentleman saw much good in these juvenile productions, and took them with him, reading them to his friends, and some of the poems appeared in the "Richmond Advocate," then edited by Rev. S. M. Lee. Not long afterward, Mr. Nalley and Bishop Dogget selected poems from the MSS. book, and a volume was published.

About that time, Mr. Nalley persuaded Mrs. Smiley to send Matilda to the Rockingham Institute, presided over by that good man and eminent educator, Rev. John C. Blackwell; a portion of the proceeds of the book of poems was used to defray some of the expenses of her schooling. She spent nearly three years at the Institute.

One by one her sisters left home as brides, until the youngest only was left. She kept up her studies and writings, publishing her articles in the "Louisville Journal," "The Home Circle," and various other Southern journals.

Just before the war, she married Rev. A. S. Edwards, son of General S. M. Edwards, of Washington City. Mr. Edwards was in the Treasury Department of the United States Government, with a comfortable home and good salary. When war came, he immediately resigned his position, and came South to share the lot of the people of his own section. He was in the employment of the Confederate government at Richmond for four years.

Life in Richmond was one of few pleasures and many privations to any, unless they had many "blue-backed promises to pay." Mrs. Edwards, used to the free and open-hearted hospitality of the country, with the pure air and green woods, suffered many privations — one month staying in the house of a rich acquaintance, who let rooms cheaper to them on score of friendship; another month in a damp basement room; and another in the third story of one of the Richmond hotels, then used as a hospital — living on pork, beans, and rye coffee, without sugar. And so life went by from year to year, until the Confederacy ended, and the drama closed with the fall and burning of Richmond.

After the fall of the Confederacy, Mrs. Edwards went back to her childhood's home, "Grape Hill," and opened a female school; but the country was so poor that it did not succeed, and the school was closed.

Mrs. Edwards has little time for writing, surrounded by a family of small children; and like all Southern women, she has many small cares upon her hands. She anticipates publishing a poem this fall.

William Archer Cocke, Esq., the author of "Constitutional History of the United States," a work which attracted considerable attention, enriching our literature, and placing the author high upon the list of Southern authors, in "Sketches of Southern Literature," published in 1863, notices the volume of poems of Matilda "as an agreeable volume of minor poems, which has much of womanly tenderness and delicate sweetness."

MARY J. S. UPSHUR.

MISS UPSHUR, well known under her pseudonym of "Fanny Fielding," has written for nearly every literary journal of the South, prose and poetry, from the "Southern Literary Messenger" to the "Richmond Pastime." She is one of the few writers who entertain the strictest ideas of the responsibility of writers for the press, in any capacity whatever; aiming to be useful in her sphere — "to leave no line which, dying, she would wish to blot."

Miss Upshur's birthplace is in Accomac County, Virginia, on the wave-washed Eastern Shore, where, almost literally, the Atlantic billows rocked her cradle, and the ocean waves sung lullaby. She was removed from here in childhood, and now resides in Norfolk. She is a daughter of William Stith Upshur, (at one time a lawyer of the Accomac Bar, a contemporary of the Hons. H. A. Wise and Thomas H. Bayly,) and a niece of Judge Abel P. Upshur, who was Secretary of State during President Tyler's Administration.

Miss Upshur has an inherent fondness for books — could read "handsomely," it has been remarked, at four years old. Though, when a child, devoted to play, she would frequently indulge in seasons of retirement in a dimly-lighted closet, poring over "Pilgrim's Progress," and other books of a serious character. Much of her childhood was spent in lonely, old country-houses, with little company and many books.

She commenced writing for the press at an early age. Her ambition was to be identified with the "literature of the South." Her first story, of any length, was a novelette, entitled "Florine de Genlis," and appeared in a Norfolk paper. Miss Upshur has written generally over the signature of "Fanny Fielding;" but sometimes over other assumed names, and frequently without any *nom de plume*.

Like Miss Evans, the author of "Beulah," etc., Miss Upshur was educated entirely at home; the difference being that the former was educated by her mother, while the latter lost her mother early, had no elder sister, and was the feminine head of the family from her very juvenile years, and was educated principally by her father.

Miss Upshur's most ambitious prose work, that has been published, appeared in the "Home Monthly," Nashville, 1867, entitled "Confederate Notes," the "prefatory" to which was in the following strain:

"Yes, despite whatever odium may attach to the term, thus is baptized this desultory record, which, written out from an irregular journal of the late war time, and immediately antecedent period, seems not thus misnamed.

"Those blue-backed 'promises to pay' are significant of a grander venture and a nobler hope than mines of gold can express; and exalted in such association, we brave the pronunciamento 'below par,' only wishing the new namesake merited, equally with its original, exemption therefrom.

"Critics of a different turn of mind may vote these 'Notes' discordant, and assign them one characteristic in common with those of the dying swan, whose 'last' are traditionally 'best.' Humoring the metaphor, we feel that not a few are left, yet, upon whose ear the sound will fall like a bar of some old, familiar strain in music, and to whom, though the original melody has died out in air, each echo is a memory of the sweetest song that was ever sung in vain."

"Confederate Notes," said a critic noted for his fairness and clearness of thought, "is a work of great power and deep, earnest thought. The style is terse, graphic, and idiomatic. This work will place the writer indisputably among the leading writers of the South."

The "Richmond Whig" said: "Confederate Notes," (it was published anonymously,) "in a strictly literary sense, and apart from any sectional or political significance contained in its title, is destined, we believe, to make its mark upon the comparatively fallow field of what is called Southern authorship."

The following extract from a letter from Miss Upshur is a picture of her every-day life, showing she is no *bas bleu*, in the popular acceptation of the term:

"A just report of my literary career could, I feel, scarcely be made without some allusion to the peculiar circumstances preventing that entire *abandon* to study and contemplation almost necessary to insure high excellence in one who designs making authorship a profession."

Of the poem "Margaret," given hereafter, she writes:

"I perhaps should tell you that it was written, as so many of my efforts were, disjointed—that is, at odd times, when I was busy with other matters, and yet felt 'a call,' as the Quakers says, 'to write.' I kept pencil and paper in my work-basket, and jotted down a verse at intervals while engaged with a pressing job of sewing.

"Well, I fancy I see certain household achievements interrupting," writes she, "gleaming here and there through breaks — very plain to me, in most things I have accomplished; pots of jam perceptible between stanzas of poems; seams of sheets, of carpets, disjointing the general narrative and final catastrophe of some heroic tale. I do not sigh for more poetic surroundings, or that my lot *is as it is*. There is no poetry without beauty, and use is beauty. A woman can have no higher appointment, I hold, than the keeper of a home. Her first duty is here: if she can shine abroad after this, all well; but this God intended as the centre of her warmth and light. So I believe."

The following poem was extensively copied by the newspapers throughout the country. The "Norfolk Herald" thus prefaces it:

"We take much pleasure in transferring the following beautiful stanzas from the pages of the 'Southern Literary Messenger,' for April, (1859.) They are the production, it seems, of one of the most gifted of the young ladies of Virginia, and one who should rank higher than many whose names have become famous. . . . We commend them to the lovers of the beautiful; for they will find, under their simple style, exquisite figures, conceived in the very spirit of poesy's self."

MARGARET.

Oh! Margaret, pretty Margaret!
  I pray ye linger yet
At the stile beyond the hay-field,
  When the summer sun is set;
And I'll tell ye in the twilight
  What ye never shall forget.

Oh! Margaret, sweet Margaret!
  With face so lily fair,
The sunbeams loved to nestle
  In the meshes of her hair,
And gleam and gleam more golden
  From the light they borrowed there.

Oh! Margaret, sweet Margaret!
  With eyes of violet blue;
Or, when she looked most lovingly,
  Of that celestial hue
The heavens show when cloud-gates ope
  To let the good pass through.

Oh! Margaret, merry Margaret!
  Beyond the meadow mill,
My heart will listen, listen
  For your gentle tripping still;
All its pit-pat echoes waking,
  As of old, at your sweet will.

But Margaret, sweet Margaret!
  Ye'll never come again,
Like the spring-time after winter,
  Like the sunshine after rain;
But I could kiss the blessèd dust
  Where your sweet form hath lain.

But Margaret, sainted Margaret!
  The hay-field and the mill,
The meadow-path, its windings,
  And its little running rill,
Will speak more lovingly of you
  Than the grave-yard, all so still.

And Margaret, blessed Margaret!
  In my heart's love-lacking dearth,
I'll look upon the sunshine,
  And the flowers that strew the earth,
And I'll think I see in each of them
  The types of your new birth.

Then Margaret, sweet Margaret!
  Like sunshine after rain,
Like summer after winter,
  Ye will glad my heart again;
For I'll say they are your messengers,
  And they shall not speak in vain.

The following extracts from a letter from Miss Upshur tell their own tale:

"I suppose the multiform character of my occupations is much the same in degree, and somewhat in kind, with that of many other Southern women now who are writers. The thing has its comical side; a kneeling hero, for instance, just about to make a touching declaration to his adored Daphne, or Sarah, as the case may be, is interrupted by an 'aside,' which reminds, may be, that your latest 'Bureau' pet has gone to S'ciety meeting, and you must go and loaf your bread."

Miss Upshur has recently completed, and expects to publish shortly, novel, entitled "Mabbit Thorn;" and "Confederate Notes" will lso probably appear in book-form.

OUR UNION.

Now give our voices to the breeze — our banner to the sky;
Let stars to kindred stars bear up our orisons on high.
God save our sacred Union! the gift our fathers gave,
For which they fought and bled, and fell in many a hero-grave!

No North — no South — no East — no West the war-cry leading on,
When blood flowed red at Mecklenburg, and Trenton's field was won;
No North — no South — no East — no West when Monmouth's deadly plain
Glowed in its tide of British blood and piled its hosts of slain.

No sectionalist claimed to know who dealt the deadly blows
That purchased life for Liberty, and felled her tyrant foes:
Here on the heights of old Yorktown, and there on Bunker Hill,
The patriot heart and sturdy arm and iron nerve and will

Battled before the Lord of Hosts, the God of land and sea,
Whose fiery pillar led them to the promised land — the free:
The British lion bowed his head and crouched him in his lair
When proud Columbia's eagle soared and cleft the echoing air.

And as our banner's starry folds floated toward the sky,
A band of brothers rallied round and sent their shouts on high:
From far New England's granite hills and ocean-girdled main
The glorious shout of LIBERTY! rang out again — again

Rang out, and louder, prouder swelled, where Southern sons and daughters
Sent simultaneously the shout over our hills and waters!
Should not the sons of sires like these, the offspring of such mothers,
Go hand in hand — one heart — one hope — a loving band of brothers?

Our own beloved, sunny South — our glorious Old Dominion —
Shall our proud eagle bow his head or droop one waving pinion?
Say, stalwart brothers of the North, shall party-strife divide us?
Our foes they of our own household — our enemies beside us?

Now shall we cope as foe with foe, or as with brother, brother?
"*Bear and forbear*" the charmed device till we forget all other?
The passing breeze the watchword waft from icy Northern land
To where our groves and flowery plains by tropic breath is fanned!

The sable sons of Afric's soil, in mercy let them rest
Where God has placed their lòwly lot as seemed unto him best;
In mercy more to them than us, fanatic zeal, be mute;
Do ye not mind who proffered once the God-forbidden fruit?

And in *their* garden of content, say, will ye wildly fling
Apples of discord? Stay your hand! it were a wanton thing
To stir within a human breast thought of what must not be,
By all the laws of God to them — by all His laws to thee.

Perhaps in ignorance ye 've erred: the human heart is prone
To cloud the simple laws of God with doctrines of its own;
No North nor South may say, "'T is thine!" the world-wide weakness, where
Each day brings hourly proof how much *all* need the Father's care.

Perhaps in ignorance ye 've erred: yet better thought may come
By minding meek-eyed Charity, whose work "begins at home;"
And sweeping one's own threshold clean, is better than all other
Cunning device to keep intact the door-stone of a brother.*

Your Sewards, Beechers, Phillipses, who rank and rave of freedom,
And, deadly as the curse that fell upon the olden Edom,
Their blasphemous anathemas pour out upon the land
Where men dare differ with themselves and boldly take their stand.

Who made them judges over us? spokesmen for liberty?
A serious farce — the sable-skinned, but not the white man, free!
Oh! subtle casuists, who preach of "fire and point of sword,"
A fearful freedom that which bids defiance to the Lord!

Dark household enemies! Oh! tell what in exchange they proffer
For the blest boon they take away? — what compensation offer
For the rent flag — dissevered ties? The murderous brand of Cain —
The violated memories — brother by brother slain!

* The answer of the ancient Egyptian to the stranger, who asked how it was the cities of his nation were so cleanly kept, is full of significance, even to this day: "Each man sweeps before his own door," said the compatriot of the Pharaohs.

Say, was it not a sound to make Satan himself seem merry —
The fratricidal shout that shook the hills of Harper's Ferry?
Yet thanks to our wise Governor, under an all-wise God,
Sedition, strife were soon laid low with traitors 'neath the sod.

Did not the shades of those whose bones bleach upon Bunker Hill
Utter their fearful whisperings, when all beside grew still,
Upon the ear of traitor Brown, crying, "Unclean! unclean!
Worse than the leprosy of old your deadly stain hath been!"

Ah! there are hearts of South and North will rally with us here,
Resolved above our grievances to shed the mutual tear;
With honorable burial to consign them to the grave,
And hoist above the starry flag, in triumph yet to wave.

MARTHA HAINES BUTT BENNETT,

THE author of "Leisure Moments," published by E. D. Long & Co., New York, several years ago, (1859,) was born in Norfolk, Virginia. A distinguished clergyman said:

"While the literary execution of 'Leisure Moments' is of a high, if not of the very highest order, the purity of thought, the felicity of the imagery, and the constructive talent displayed in the management of the longer pieces, are as remarkable as they are rare. I can hardly deem it possible that these charming sketches are the production of a lady but just stepping on the threshold of womanhood, so intimate an acquaintance does the fair author display with all

'Thoughts, all passions, all desires,
All that can move this mortal frame.'

It is difficult to say which is the writer's happiest vein. She is alike admirable, whether she essays to strike the keynote of joy or grief."

Mrs. Bennett is descended on her father's side, whom she much resembles, from the English; and on her mother's side, from the French. She is an only child.

She was educated at Ellicott's Mills, near Baltimore, and received her diploma there, and was presented with a gold medal and the degree of A. M. by the Harrisburg Female College.

Miss Butt's first appearance in print was at the age of fourteen, although she had written for several years before that time. She loves the "beautiful and true." She is inclined to be rather satirical—very strong in her attachments.

Says a friend of the lady:

"She is possessed of a fine person, indeed exceedingly handsome; her arm and hand were copied as a model by the artist Barber, of Virginia, for the statue of the 'Fisher Girl.' She understands well the art of conversing, speaking with ease upon almost any subject. She is sprightly, poetic, and imaginative, as her writings indicate."

Says a phrenologist in regard to this lady's character, as viewed phrenologically:

"She would be a good observer—large perceptive faculties; a good thinker—a well-developed forehead; and with large mirthfulness, she would be witty. Indeed, there is a touch of the comic in this intellect; and with her large language and excellent conversational powers, she would be most entertaining. This is the oratorical and musical temperament, overflowing with emotion. There is spirit and temper here, modified, of course, by benevolence; but when such a nature takes the defensive, there will be no half-way work. She is as plucky as she is kind and loving; cautious, but not timid or irresolute; self-relying, but not haughty. She loves her liberty, and will not submit to restraint; but can conform and adapt herself to circumstances. She may be led or persuaded, but cannot be driven. There is great hope, but less veneration; large conscientiousness, but less humility. She has a good degree of spirituality, very large sublimity, with ideality well developed. There is sufficient acquisitiveness to appreciate property, and sufficient love for the beautiful to incline her to make a good display. She is both original and imitative.

"Had she been trained for the stage, especially for the opera, she would have filled the place with credit. Next to this, something in the line of literature or authorship would be the most appropriate. But she would love and appreciate art, and could excel in it. She would make a good linguist, a good reader, and could excel in music, drawing, and in painting. There is much character here; and if duly cultivated, she could shine in almost any sphere."

Miss Butt was a contributor to various periodicals and magazines, in the North as well as the South. Her volume of "Leisure Moments" was a collection of her short tales, essays, and sketches. One journal, in a notice of this volume, said:

"Miss Butt's fine intellectual capacities are well developed in the book which now lies before us. It contains a number of well-written sketches, so different in style one from another that it is hardly possible to imagine they were the product of the same pen. This only goes to show, however, the diversity of her talent. Here we find language which not only reminds us of Fanny Fern, but makes us take it for one of her happiest productions. Another chapter is dashed off in a free and easy style, through which brilliant humor lurks in every sentence. Then again we find an intense depth of feeling, which she portrays in language that calls forth a responsive echo from the hearts of her readers."

July 6th, 1865, Miss Butt was married to Mr. N. J. Bennett, of Bridgeport, Connecticut, and they have made their home in the great city of New York.

In 1866, Mrs. Bennett published, through Carleton, New York, a volume of little tales for children, under the title of "Pastimes with my Little Friends."

MISS SARAH J. C. WHITTLESEY.

THE subject of this sketch, familiarly known to the readers of magazines and weekly journals, for which she has contributed both prose and verse, was born in Williamstown, Martin County, North Carolina, came to Virginia in 1848, and now resides at Alexandria.

Miss Whittlesey commenced rhyming at an early age, and published her first article in the "Edenton (North Carolina) Sentinel," in 1846. She published a book of poems, entitled "Heart Drops from Memory's Urn;" and through M. W. Dodd, New York, 1860, a volume of prose novelettes, entitled "The Stranger's Stratagem; or, The Double Deceit; and other Stories." She received a prize from a North Carolina paper for a novelette, entitled "Reginald's Revenge;" also, from the same journal, a prize for a novelette, entitled "The Hidden Heart." She again was the successful competitor for a prize offered by "The American Union," of Boston, "The Maid of Myrtle Vale" being the title of the successful tale.

In 1866, the publishers in New York of a series of Dime Novels appropriated one of Miss Whittlesey's stories, "The Bug Oracle," and published it without her knowledge or consent.

We believe she has recently, or is about to publish, a novel, entitled "Herbert Hamilton; or, The Bas Bleu." Her longest, and we think most successful novel, appeared in the "Field and Fireside," entitled "Bertha, the Beauty."

HELEN G. BEALE,

THE author of "Lansdowne," is a young lady of the "Old Dominion State," a daughter of William C. Beale, a merchant of Fredericksburg, where she was born and has lived always, with the exception of two years spent in the "Old North State," after the bombardment of Fredericksburg during the war. She spent the day of the bombardment in a cellar at her home. Her father died when she was fourteen years of age. Her education was conducted by Rev. G. Wilson McPhail, now President of Davidson College, North Carolina, until she was sixteen, at which time she began the duties of life as a teacher, and has since spent the largest portion of her life in a schoolroom. Her aim during these years has been, and still is, to perfect herself as a teacher. Being thus occupied all day, she wrote "Lansdowne" one winter, in the evenings, after tea, for amusement.

A lady, who has had close association with Miss Beale, so as to afford her the best facilities for observing the springs of thought and action to which *we* are indebted for "Lansdowne," her first literary effort, writes to me:

"While reading 'Lansdowne,' both in MS. and print, I was confirmed in my idea that *worthy* persons, who are impelled to put their thoughts on paper, throw into their creations their own mental and spiritual life, however unconscious they may be of producing any transcript of themselves. This is seen in the analysis of the *two* most prominent characters of the story.

"We all see, daily, persons resembling the other characters: their traits may have been personified from observations of common life; but *these two* are pure creations of the author's brain — the hero, Theodore Lansdowne, loving, sensitive, tender, and beautiful, being the type of the æsthetic portion of the writer's human emotional economy — an acknowledgment of homage to the truth of the saying, 'A thing of beauty is a joy forever;' while Horace Ashton is a portrayal of another side of her character. In him, we find a crucifixion of *self*, in giving up not only worldly ease and secular ambition, but even love itself, held in abeyance to the call of Divine truth. Here is the culmination, that defines more faithfully than wordy sketch of mine could give, the calibre of the author of 'Lansdowne:' so does she 'fulfil her God-given hest.'

"In person, Miss Beale is very slight, of medium stature, fine skin, bright brown hair, and broad, high forehead; but the eye is a mystery I have not yet fathomed, beautiful, clear brown, calm almost to sadness, as the 'mist resembles the rain;' though if she be moved to mirth, sunshine breaks through the mist, and a most quick, nimble spirit peeps out, full of humor, which has the gift of speech. This lady has written a book worthy of herself, and which, like the companionship of the author, makes

'The cares that invest the day,
Fold their tents like the Arabs,
And as silently steal away.'"

"Lansdowne" was published serially in a weekly journal published in Baltimore—"Southern Society;" and as a narrative of Southern society, it was an ornament to the pages of any journal, and particularly suited to the *one* in which it appeared. Like many illy-managed Southern periodicals, "Southern Society" existed for less than a year.

Professor F. A. March, of Easton, Pennsylvania, (a gentleman of reputation for learning, in Europe as well as in this country,) thus alludes to "Lansdowne": "Over and above its merits as a story, it is decidedly worthy of the honor of appearing in book form, on the score of its value as a memorial of the society which it depicts."

MRS. CORNELIA J. M. JORDAN.

THE subject of this notice was born in the ancient and romantic city of Lynchburg, Virginia, on the 11th of January, 1830.

The maiden name of Mrs. Jordan was Cornelia Jane Matthews. She was the eldest of the three daughters of Mr. Edwin Matthews, at one time mayor of the city; a citizen of sincerest worth, intelligence, and character, highly respected by the entire community, and frequently honored and rewarded with positions of public responsibility. The wife of Mr. Matthews was a sister of the Hon. William L. Goggin, of Bedford County, and was a lady of rare accomplishments, of great personal beauty, and of many marked traits of amiability and excellence. She died when her eldest child was but five years old. Her husband, faithful to her memory, never married again; but devoted himself to the care and training of his children, and sustained toward them, as far as was possible, the relation of father and mother united in one. The three daughters, after their mother's death, lived with their maternal grandmother in Bedford County, till the youngest was old enough to attend school, and then they were placed in charge of the Sisters of Visitation, Georgetown, D. C. It was while in Georgetown that the first attempts of Miss Cornelia to compose, in verse, in accordance with the rules of prosody and composition, were made. Heretofore, she had written "as the spirit moved"—a spontaneous and impulsive utterance. She had sung as a bird, but was now to sing as a trained and cultivated musician. Her "wood-notes wild," which had been merely soliloquies, assumed the form of May-day addresses, verses to her schoolmates, album addresses, etc. These efforts were crowned with the grateful guerdon of flattery and praise: their author began to be known as the "poet laureate," and was always in requisition whenever anything metrical was needed. At the commencement of 1846, the highest prize in poetry and prose was conferred upon her, amidst admiring plaudits. Perhaps no other evidence of triumph ever gave her half the pride and pleasure conveyed by the simple and sincere assurance of her teacher's appreciation and her friends' approval and satisfaction.

The death of Emily, the youngest sister, occurred at this period. She was only fourteen years of age; but united to great liveliness a richly endowed mind and noble heart, which won the affection of all her companions, and the almost idolatrous love of her elder sister. The fair unfolding of a flower so sweet and rare was watched with almost maternal solicitude, and the sudden blighting of the beautiful blossom inflicted a deep wound, whose scar will ever remain to witness its cruel severity. This was the first great sorrow of the poetess. It made a profound impression on her nature, and imparted — unconsciously, no doubt — a melancholy character to many of her pieces. It was in memory of her dead darling that she dedicated her first book, many years after, to "The Fireside and the Grave: the Living and Dead of a Broken Home Circle." The consolation of an assured hope and the gracious promises of the Divine faith were not wanting. But even these could not soothe the great sorrow which despoiled so early the tenderest emotions and aspirations.

The two surviving daughters returned, in 1846, to their grief-stricken father. The spring of 1851 found the elder daughter the happy bride of Mr. Francis H. Jordan, of Page County, a distinguished and accomplished member of the Bar, and afterward commonwealth's attorney. A beautiful home in the Valley of Virginia became now the centre of her affections and the object of her care. It was the fit seat of the Muses, presenting a rare and unrivalled combination of mountain and water scenery. Various poems embalmed its beauties, and evidenced the happiness and tranquil joy which awoke in the married heart of the poetess.

The early years of Mrs. Jordan's married life were spent in the Valley of Virginia; but in the first year of the war, she was called upon to mourn a double loss — that of her only surviving parent and her only child, both of whom died in the short space of one year.

Shortly before the commencement of the war, Mrs. Jordan published a collection of her fugitive poems, under the title of "Flowers of Hope and Memory." The book included the poems which, from time to time, she had written, and which had "gone the rounds" of the newspaper world — waifs upon the sea of journalistic literature. The book was brought out by Mr. A. Morris, of Richmond, Virginia, at a time which was sadly unpropitious; for no sooner was it issued than communication between the sections was at an end and all the horrors of war inaugurated.

About this time, Mrs. Jordan's health became seriously impaired, and she was debarred from writing by a disease of the visional nerve, which had previously threatened her with blindness. However, with the assistance of an amanuensis, she managed to maintain a correspondence with several journals. In April, 1863, she visited Corinth, Mississippi, where her husband held a staff appointment under General Beauregard. It was here that she wrote her poem, entitled "Corinth," which, on its publication after the surrender, was suppressed and burned by order of one General Terry, at that time commanding in Richmond. Mrs. Jordan made this vandalism the subject of a sarcastic communication to one of the newspapers of New York, and detailed how her little pamphlet, entitled "Corinth, and other Poems," of which an edition of about five hundred copies only was printed, had been seized by the timorous military commander as dangerous and heretical. Mrs. Jordan had lost all her possessions by the war, and she had hoped, by the sale of her poems, to obtain return at least sufficient to meet her pressing needs, in that moment of general prostration and ruin. How her hopes were frustrated is shown in the facts that have just been recited.

During the existence of the bazaar held in Richmond by the "Hollywood Memorial Association," about two years ago, the Association published a poem of Mrs. Jordan's, entitled "Richmond: Her Glory and her Graves," the last of any length from her pen.

Mrs. Jordan has always been, even from early childhood, a devotee of the poetic impulse. She is of an essentially poetic temperament. She was especially partial to the poetry of Mrs. Hemans; and she still retains in her possession an old volume of Mrs. Hemans's poetry, thumbworn, faded, and much abused, which has been her inseparable companion for years. A little incident connected with the childhood of our poetess, will show how strongly her nature was wedded to the divine gift of poetry, even at a time when the could have but a faint conception of the poet's mission. On one occasion, an old phrenologist — at a time when phrenology was the fashion — came to her grandmother's residence in Bedford County. Casting his eye around for a subject, he selected the little Cornelia. Running his hand over her head in a very knowing manner, he observed, with a smile: "A pretty *hard* head, to be sure; but one that will some of these days make a poet." The child's heart throbbed wildly at the announcement; and often, in the years that have since passed, has the memory of the old man's words come back to her to give her courage and confidence.

Mrs. Jordan resides at present in Lynchburg. Though her fortunes are altered by the war, and by the result of the unfortunate investment of a large estate left by her father, she still finds a mother's consolation in training and caring for her only child, a bright little girl of six years of age.

It is to be hoped that ere long Mrs. Jordan will give to the world a volume containing all her poems, and especially that entitled "Corinth," the published edition of which, at the behest of a backward civilization, was so wantonly destroyed.

FALL SOFTLY, WINTER SNOW, TO-NIGHT.

Fall softly, winter snow, to-night,
  Upon my baby's grave,
Where withered violets faded lie,
  And cypress branches wave.
Ye bright flakes, as ye touch the ground,
Oh! kiss for me that little mound.

Beneath it lies a waxen form
  Of boyish beauty rare —
The dust upon his eyes of blue,
  And on his shining hair.
Above his little heart so low,
Fall gently, gently, winter snow!

We laid him there when summer flowers
  Gave out their fragrant breath,
And pale white roses watched beside
  That narrow bed of death.
One soft curl from his sunny brow
Is all of him that's left me now.

Ethereal snow, fit mantle thou
  For one so pure and fair;
Fit emblem of the spotless robe
  His baby soul doth wear:
As stormy night-winds howl and rave,
Oh! gently wrap his little grave.

FLOWERS FOR A WOUNDED SOLDIER.

Go, gentle flowers!
Go light the soldier's room,
Go banish care and gloom,
Go, with a voice of home
Gladden his hours.
Tell him of woods and fields,
Tell him of hearts and shields,
Tell him that sadness yields
Kindly to you.
Bear in your sunny smile
Hopes that all cares beguile,
Faith in All-Good the while
Fervent and true.
Go in your beauty drest,
Types of the pure and blest;
Bear to the weary rest,
Holy and calm.
Soothe, soothe his bosom's smart,
Gladness and joy impart;
Breathe o'er the fevered heart
Comfort and balm.
Go in your summer bloom,
Light up the soldier's room,
Drive thence all care and gloom,
Brighten his hours.
Cheer him with memory-gleams —
Pictures of woods and streams,
Boy-haunts and childhood-dreams —
Go, gentle flowers!

THE FIRST VIOLET.

Out from a mossy nook in a dim wood,
Where, silently and lone, my steps intrude
To share thy solitude, thou lift'st to mine
Soft glances, little violet — they shine
Brightly amid the gloom, as if to say,
"Spring, whom thou waitest, is not far away:

I mark her coming — that sweet duty done,
Lifting my timid eyes to greet the sun,
My mission ended, my brief joy complete,
I breathe my life away at Beauty's feet."
Thou speak'st well, sweet blossom, thus to know
That, with thy perfumed petals all aglow,
Thou the sweet prophet art of bird and flower;
Of vernal summer-haunt and woodland bower;
Soft winds, gay streams, and all the glorious things,
Vertumnia droppeth from her dewy wings.
I would compare thee to the first fond smile
That lights with hope and joy the heart the while
From eyes it worships, shedding a soft glow
Of trembling rapture on the depths below —
Where erst, a flowerless, wintry strand beside,
Life's swelling stream rolled on, a cheerless tide;
Now calm and bright, reflecting from afar
The warm, sweet radiance of Love's risen star.

THE BLACKBERRY-VINE.

It climbs o'er the fence in the garden;
  No trouble it costs us to train;
For it loves the old worn, faded panels,
  And clasps them again and again.
It grew there just so in my childhood;
  None knew how it came; but they said
God planted the seed with his finger,
  And straightway it sprang from the bed.

Now and then, as the rain fell upon it,
  We pulled up the weeds all around,
And then carefully lifted the tendrils
  That helplessly trailed on the ground.
So it flourished and grew as I find it
  To-day — a bright, beautiful thing,
With green memories clustering around it,
  And thoughts of my life's early spring.

Ay, thoughts of the days glad and happy,
  When, in spite of rebuke, I 'd resign
Work or books for a romp in the garden,
  Where clambered the blackberry-vine.

How temptingly hung the dark clusters—
  Ah! well I remember to-day
How we gathered the berries in summer,
  And served them for "*dessert*" at play.

Then the butterflies gambolled about it,
  And poised their gorgeous wings,
Just wherever the clustering blossoms
  Their redolent odor flings.
And the bee hushed its musical humming
  To kiss the pure, blush-tinted bloom,
Or to steal from its innocent bosom
  A draught of the honeyed perfume.

Ah! when winter, drear winter was over,
  And birds were again on the wing,
We knew where *one* snug little sparrow
  Would build a soft nest in the spring.
Not up in the broad-spreading oak-tree,
  Nor yet in the towering pine;
But where zephyrs and sunbeams dally
  In the heart of the blackberry-vine.

Oh! I hear even now in the stillness
  A wild song of melody low;
Some dear bird, through the shadows of evening,
  Brings a note of the *long ago.*
And I walk once again in the garden,
  Where roses of memory entwine—
As sweet thought plucks the ripe summer berries
  That grew on the blackberry-vine.

THE SNOW.

Softly, softly, beautiful snow,
Soft on the hills and vales below
Let thy feathery flakes now fall,
Carefully, carefully over all;
Wrap in thy bosom the struggling blade,
Peering through furrows the ploughshare made;
Fold in thy white arms the grain below,
Tenderly, tenderly, beautiful snow.

Over the sheltering roof I love,
Spread thy wings like a brooding dove;
One looks out from her casement there,
Pure as thyself, as thyself as fair;
Give her a message of love for me —
Tell her that, had I thy liberty,
Straight would I follow thy white sails o'er
Tempest and tide to her open door.

Soft on the grave-sod's mantling breast
Let thy hovering pinions rest;
Lightly, lightly, beautiful snow,
Light as the halo that crowns thy brow
Let thy gossamer robe descend
Where the willow and cypress bend
Over the spot where heroes lie,
Under the blue sky's canopy.

They are safe from the storm without;
Safe from the victor's threatening shout;
Safe from the clouds and mists that rise,
Shading the light of earth's changeful skies.
Oh! be each martyr's laurelled head
Safe from the shame of a vandal tread.
Over their sleeping dust so low,
Rest thee now tenderly, beautiful snow.

LAURA R. FEWELL.

MISS FEWELL was born in Brentsville, Prince William County, Virginia, and has spent the greater portion of her life there. Her father died when she was sixteen years of age, and immediately after she commenced teaching, and by her exertions in that way she has educated a younger brother and sister.

She commenced writing during her school-days, when she was chief contributor to a school paper published in the institution where she was educated. She has written a great deal, occasionally publishing in various journals — contributing to Godey's "Lady's Book" under the *nom de plume* of "Parke Richards."

During the war she wrote a novel, "Neria," which has not been published. In 1866, she came to Clark County, Georgia, and established a school, and is now a contributor to "Scott's Magazine" and other journals.

Miss Fewell is the best of daughters; truest of friends, and a Christian.

A VIRGINIA VILLAGE.—1861.

Who does not distinctly remember the spring of 1861? Not for the beauty of the season, though that was as lovely as smiling skies, balmy winds, and odorous flower-cups could make it; but for the cloud, at first scarcely larger than a man's hand, that began to loom up in the political horizon, and the distant mutterings of the storm so soon to burst upon the land. . . . . . Then came the call for troops, and soon the earth resounded with the tramp of armed men. . . . . There was a glory and enthusiasm about the whole thing — in the waving banners, the glittering uniforms, and nodding plumes — that led captive the imagination and silenced reason. In every town where troops were quartered the ladies were affected with "button on the brain;" and seemed to think life was only made to be spent in walking, riding, dancing, and flirting with the young officers. Youth and gayety were everywhere uppermost, unappalled by the spectacle of national distraction.

To a little village situated in the lovely valley lying between the Bull Run and Blue Ridge Mountains, only a faint echo of the din of war had penetrated. Not a single company of soldiers had ever passed through or been camped in its vicinity; and more than one of its young belles read with envious feelings the accounts of the brilliant conquests achieved over the hearts of the Carolinians and other Southern troops by their correspondents in more fortunate towns, and sighed over the hard fate which condemned them to "waste their sweetness on the desert air," for in that light they regarded the members of the county companies, most of whom they had known from their childhood.

This little village merits a description: — It figured in more than one official bulletin during the war. It consisted of one long street, through the middle of which ran the turnpike, and on either side of this the houses — some very pretentious-looking structures of stucco and brick, others frame buildings, stained and weather-beaten — stretched for nearly a mile. Some few houses were situated on side streets crossing the main one at right angles, and there was a pleasant tradition among the people that their town had once rejoiced in back streets, but these, by common consent, were now given up to the hogs and nettles. In spite of these drawbacks, it was a quiet, cosey-looking place, especially when the trees that shaded it were in full foliage, and every garden and door-yard was flushed with flowers whose fragrance filled the air.

A stranger would have thought that this little village, lying in the lap of verdant meadows, encircled by the Briarean arms of the mountains, and so remote from all busy thoroughfares of trade, would have escaped the corruptions of larger towns, and its inhabitants, if not retaining the simplicity of country manners, would, at least, be free from the pride and exclusiveness of city life. But a short residence there would have taught him the fallacy of this opinion. Not in Washington, that modern Gomorrha of pride and vanity, did the strife for fashion and pre-eminence rage higher than in the little village of which we write. It might justly be called the town of cliques, for it boasted as many as any fashionable city extant.

First, forming the *élite* of the place, were the families of the military and professional men, and those of the large landed proprietors residing on estates, and a few aspirants after aristocracy, who kept up an uncertain footing upon the outer bounds, but were not allowed to enter the arena of this charmed circle, from which all new-comers, whatever their personal merits, were rigorously excluded, unless they could exhibit a long list of illustrious ancestors. From this apex — this *crême de la crême* — society descended, in graduating circles, to the lowest phase of social life, which, strangely enough, was found in a *castle;* for so the inhabitant, who had aspirations above her station, termed the mud walls which formed her home. Except a few loiterers, mere lookers-on at life, all the inhabitants of the village belonged to some one of these circles, which were entirely separate and distinct, never infringing on each other's privileges, save in the manner of scandal and backbiting — those time-honored adjuncts of village-life — except when some stray cow or pig trespassed on neighboring property, when there was apt to be an outbreak between the plebeians and patricians, sometimes coming to blows.

MRS. LIZZIE PETIT CUTLER.

LIZZIE PETIT was born in the town of Milton, Virginia, a place of some importance formerly, but which has been swallowed up by the increasing power and wealth of its more widely-known neighbor, Charlottesville. Her ancestry, on the paternal side, consisted of respectable farmers; on the mother's side, she boasted of descent from Monsieur Jean Jacques Marie Réné de Motteville Bernard, an early *emigré* to the colonies, driven from France by political disabilities.

Monsieur de Bernard married in Virginia, and lived on his wife's estates on the James River. Miss Petit had the great misfortune to be left motherless in her early childhood. She was brought up by her grandmother and aunt with tender care and affection, upon one of the beautiful farms lying under the shadow of the Blue Ridge Mountains, in that most picturesque portion of the State of Virginia, near Charlottesville. She was a sprightly child, very precocious, sensitive, and of very delicate beauty. She very soon began to scribble rhymes and write little stories for her own and her cousin's amusement. At the age of thirteen she removed to Charlottesville, where the chaperonage of her aunt enabled her to mingle in the gay society of the city. She was very bright, and a belle among the students at an age when most girls are scarcely released from their pinafores. She was soon trammelled in Cupid's fetters. But accident produced estrangement between her lover and herself, and he departed, to die in Alabama; while she, in the shadow of this disappointment, found relief in the absorption of literary labor. She wrote here her first novel, "Light and Darkness." It was brought out by the Messrs. Appleton, and had very considerable success, both in this country and in England, where it ran through several editions. "Household Mysteries" was her second novel, written at the suggestion of Mr. Appleton. This book was written in the vortex of New York society.

After eighteen months' rest, Miss Petit wrote again; but being advised unwisely, forsook her steadfast friends, the Appletons, and proffered her MS. to the Harpers, who rejected her work. After this, the Messrs. Appleton also refused it. This was a great disappointment to the young girl; and her means becoming limited, she was induced to give a series of dramatic readings, which were so successful that she was thinking of going upon the stage, encouraged by the applause of connoisseurs in the histrionic art. While preparing herself for a "star engagement" proffered her, she nearly lost her life by her gown taking fire accidentally. She was saved by the presence of mind of her friend Mr. Oakley. This severe affliction caused her to pass several months of suffering on her couch; but she was gradually restored to health by the affectionate care of her many friends; one among whom so endeared himself by his assiduous and constant attentions, that upon her recovery she became his wife. She lives now at her husband's residence, near New York, where she enjoys a tranquil domestic peace, and employs her leisure hours in the use of her pen. She is engaged in writing a novel, which will embrace the period of the war.

Mrs. Cutler's sympathies, like those of all the true daughters of Virginia, were with her own people in their recent struggle; but powerless to aid, she could only weep over the misfortunes of her country. Her husband has been a prominent member of the Bar in New York.

SPIRIT-MATES.

I always endeavor to preserve, in every character and circumstance portrayed, the strict unities of truth and human nature.

To a casual observer, the love existing between two such opposites as my hero and heroine may seem rather opposed to probability; but I am sure one who looks farther into cause and effect, will agree with me in pronouncing it the most natural thing in the world.

Ida herself, the perfect type of all that was feminine, delicate in organization, and timid, notwithstanding her sometime flashes of spirit, worshipped in Cameron the type of manliness, bravery, health, strength, and energy. Perhaps, in some respects, the intellect of the woman was superior—that is, she had more of those finer gifts of genius to which men, in all ages, have yielded homage; more of that rare union of ideality and passion, which gives to the harp of poesy the chord which vibrates in the hearts of the multitude; and it was better so: for these qualities, in the exquisite fineness of their moral texture, suit better a woman than a man.

The world may drink in the passionate incense which genius burns on the shrine of feeling, until their whole moral nature becomes purified and elevated; but the "spirits finely moulded," which have given birth to thoughts like these, suit not to come in contact with the jagged edges and rude paths of common life.

Within the world of her own home, a woman of fine intellect and feelings may, unless opposed by extraordinary adverse influences, create an atmosphere redolent of all that the most dreamy and ideal worshipper of the holy and beautiful could desire; but a man must tread rough paths; he must come in contact with the coarse and vulgar elements which compose a portion of the world; and alas! it needs not to tell how often the children of poesy have laved their spirit-plumes in the muddy, turbid waters of the world's recklessness and vice.

It needs not to tell; for their fall, like that of the children of light in the olden time, is never forgotten. The remembrance, like a shadowy pall, darkens future ages with its influence.

But to return to the more immediate theory of our present discussion.

Nature created men and women in pairs. There can be no more doubt of this than the laws of affinity in the science of chemistry. There is the essence of truth in the homely saying, "Matches were made in heaven; but they get terribly mixed coming down."

There is for every one a spirit-mate; one who, morally, mentally, and physically, must gratify every necessity of our being; with whom to live would be happiness: such happiness as would at once ennoble and elevate our nature, bringing it nearer to that of the angels.

And in our search for a being like this, we often pass them in our own blind folly, rather than through the influence of that fabled power men call destiny.

Allured by some passing meteor, turned aside by convenience, caprice, passion, we wander from the star whose light, in after years, we remember with the vain prayer:

> "Oh! would it shone to guide us still,
> Although to death or deadliest ill."

What is the ideal cherished, even though vaguely, in the mind of every one, but a dreamy sense, an unconscious divination — if I may so express it — of the existence of a being formed by nature to blend with and become a part of ourselves?

The loves of a lifetime — what are they but the illusions of an hour, when, deceived by some passing resemblance, we cry, Eureka! and think the bourne is found — until the heart, disappointed, recoils upon itself, or circumstance mercifully tears the counterfeit from our clinging grasp.

God forbid that there should be many loves in a lifetime; for 't is a sad thing, nay, 't is a sin, to waste on many feelings which should be the hoarded wealth of one; like the scattering drops of a rare perfume, which sweeten the common atmosphere, but can never return to the source from whence they emanated.

I have sometimes thought there might be an inner fount shut deep in the soul, never to be unsealed save at the magic touch; never to give forth its wealth of thrilling bliss and unalloyed sweetness to aught save *the one.*

'T is a blessed belief! And yet how sad it is to reflect that many live who are destined never to have the seal removed from the lip of the fountain; many, too, who are surrounded by all the nearer ties of life—ties formed in haste by the force of circumstance, convenience, expediency! Far better to live and die alone, than thus to rebel against the good angel of our nature, clasping the cold corpse of happiness, while its soul sleeps in the unsealed fount of our own bosom, or animates the form of the far-off unseen being, between whom and ourselves we have opened an impassable gulf.

NORTH CAROLINA.

MARY BAYARD CLARKE.

BY JUDGE EDWIN G. READE.

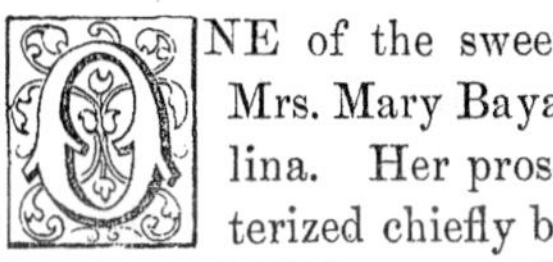

ONE of the sweetest poets and truest women of America is Mrs. Mary Bayard Clarke, a native of Raleigh, North Carolina. Her prose writings, as well as her poems, are characterized chiefly by simplicity, power, and naturalness. Hearing Daniel Webster speak, one was apt to feel, "That is just what ought to be said on the subject; and I could say it just as he has done." The like may truly be said of Mrs. Clarke's poetry: there is no straining after effect — no doubling and twisting to make a rhyme — no climbing after a sentiment, or ranting over a passion — no gaudy dress or want of neat attire. It is just what you would feel; and just what you, or anybody else, would say — as you think. But try it — and it will prove to be just what you *cannot* say. This simplicity and power makes her poetry in the parlor what Daniel Webster's speeches were in the Senate.

Mrs. Clarke is a daughter of Thomas P. Devereux, an eminent lawyer and large Roanoke planter: her grandmother, Mrs. Frances Devereux, a granddaughter of the celebrated logician, Jonathan Edwards, President of Princeton College, was a woman of remarkable intellectual endowments, and well known in the Presbyterian Church, both at the North and the South, for her piety and liberality.

Reared in affluence, thoroughly educated, and highly accomplished, the subject of our notice married, at an early age, William J. Clarke, Esq., of North Carolina, who had entered the United States Army at the beginning of the Mexican war; and after being brevetted as a major for gallant conduct at the battles of the National Bridge, Paso Ovejas, and Cerro Gordo, had retired from the army on a pension granted him for wounds received in the service of his country, and resumed the practice of the law in his native State.

Her position in society was one of ease and elegance; and her contributions to literature were induced by the love of the beautiful and intellectual, and by the ease with which she composed, both in prose and poetry. Her productions were mere pastimes — the pleasures of thought and the scintillations of genius. Her fragile form was soon, however, seen by her husband to be drooping: consumption was hereditary in her mother's family; and, to save her from falling a victim to it, he carried her, first to the West Indies, and finally to the salubrious climate of Western Texas, where she resided, with her little family, at San Antonio de Bexar, until the beginning of the late war, when they returned to North Carolina, and Major Clarke took command of the 24th North Carolina Regiment, and served during the whole war as its colonel. The long and "cruel war" brought adversities in fortune, and then came out all the force of Mrs. Clarke's character, the brilliancy of her genius, and the nobleness of her soul, in educating her children, sustaining her family, and inspiriting her countrymen. Her pen was constantly busy in correspondence, in poetry, and in translations from the French; in which latter she is considered by the best judges — educated Frenchmen — to be particularly happy.

Some of her poems were collected and published in a volume called "Mosses from a Rolling Stone; or, The Idle Moments of a Busy Woman," which was sold for the benefit of the fund for the *Stonewall Cemetery*, in Winchester, Va.; but much the larger, and, her friends say, much the better portion of them have only appeared in the periodicals of the day.

What Mrs. Clarke was some few years ago, is very graphically and truthfully portrayed in a sketch which appeared not long since, from the pen of some unknown admirer who met her in Havana. All her faculties are now matured. Not so beautiful, of course, as when younger, she is yet far more interesting. Her conversational powers are remarkable, and her manners distinguished by their graceful ease and playfulness. Sparkling and impulsive, she is also gentle, amiable, pious, and industrious beyond her strength.

In all she has written, there cannot be found a sentiment that is not as pure as snow, nor an expression unsuited for the ear of the most delicate refinement. Though much of her own history and many of her trials are necessarily shadowed forth in her poetry, there is no appearance in it of an effort to "serve up her own heart with brain-sauce" for the taste of the public.

"The Mother's Dream," in which she says "conflicting duties wore away her strength and life," though doubtless a page from her own experience, speaks directly to the heart of every conscientious mother, and is but a leaf from the life of all who, like her, resolve to climb the hill of maternal duty,

"Unmurmuring at the petty round she daily trod,
But doing what came first, and leaving all to God."

"My Children" were emphatically *her* children. It was published first in the New Orleans "Picayune," anonymously, and as many as a dozen friends, in different parts of the United States, cut it out and sent it to her, because it so exactly suited her and her two little ones. Who, that knows them, can doubt that she expresses her own feelings, when she says,

"Though many other blessings
Around my footsteps fall,
My children and their father
Are brightest of them all"?

How beautiful is her description of "the sweet notes of memory:"

"Like the perfume that lingers where roses are crushed,
The echo of song when the music is hushed!"

And how chaste and poetic the discrimination in "Smiles and Roses," where she says:

"A smile may be given to many—
'T is only of friendship a part;
But I give not a kiss unto any
Who has not the love of my heart!"

These selections are all from her earlier poems: those written later in life have more concentrated force, and more passionate depth of feeling, with equal sweetness and simplicity.

Her lines to General Robert E. Lee are highly poetical and finished; so much is seldom found concentrated and clearly expressed in such a short space:

"You lay your sword with honor down,
And wear defeat as 't were a crown,
Nor sit, like Marius, brooding o'er
A ruin which can rise no more;
But from your Pavia bear away
A glory brightening every day"—

describes General Lee's deportment and conduct since the surrender most accurately; while the closing lines show an appreciation of the feelings hidden under his dignified serenity which must have touched his heart when he read them:

"But who can tell how deep the dart
Is rankling in your noble heart,
Or dare to pull the robe aside
Which Cæsar draws his wounds to hide?"

"Must I Forget?" which was by mistake put among the translations from the French, is not excelled by anything Byron ever wrote for the strong expression of a deep passion; while "It Might Have Been," "Under the Lava," and "Grief," have a depth and force of feeling, with a clearness and terseness of expression seldom found in the writings of a woman. This is but a tame criticism of what will in future be cherished as part of the purest and brightest literature of the age; but space beyond the limits of this article would be needed to do justice to the subject.

The following is a sketch of Mrs. Clarke, taken from a Baltimore paper:

"LA TENELLA.

"Some years ago, during a 'health-trip to the tropics,' it was my good fortune to spend four months in the company of a lady who is now well known in Southern literature, not only as 'Tenella,' the *nom de plume* she first adopted, but also by her real name of Mrs. Mary Bayard Clarke. Sprightly, intellectual, and remarkable, not only for her easy, graceful manners, but also for her delicate, fragile beauty, she was the acknowledged 'queen of society' in the circle in which she moved. The Spanish Creoles are very frank in their admiration of beauty, which they regard as the gift of God, not only to the possessor, but to the admirer of it; and nothing like the *furore* created among them by the blue eyes, fair complexion, masses of soft, sunny curls, and clear-cut, intellectual features of this lady can be conceived of in this country.

"The first time I ever saw her was at the Tacon Theatre. She was leaning on the arm of Mr. Gales Seaton, of the 'National Intelligencer,' and surrounded by three or four British naval and Spanish army officers, in full uniform; and as the party walked into the private box of the Spanish admiral, every eye was turned upon them, and a hum of admiration rose from the spectators, such as could only be heard, in similar circumstances, from a Spanish audience.

"Shortly after this, I met her at a ball given by the British consul-general at the Aldama Palace, and was presented to her by Mr. Seaton, and, from that time, saw her almost daily for the four months during which she reigned the acknowledged queen of the small but select circle of English and Americans residing in the city of Havana; increased, as it is every winter, by visitors from every part of the United States, English, American, and French naval officers, and such other foreigners as speak English. A more brilliant circle than it was that winter it would be hard to find anywhere.

"But while to casual observers Mrs. Clarke was but the *enfant gaté* of society, to those who looked further she was also the highly cultivated, intellectual woman. The Honorable Miss Murray, then on her American tour, was charmed with her, and said she was the only woman she had met in America, who, without being a blue-stocking, was yet thoroughly educated. 'She has not an accomplishment,' said that lady, 'beyond her highly cultivated conversational powers; but they, with her beauty and graceful manners, would render her an ornament to any circle in which she might move.'

"But the lady-in-waiting of Queen Victoria was mistaken, for Mrs. Clarke had two accomplishments rarely found in perfection among ladies: she was a bold, fearless, and remarkably graceful horsewoman, and played an admirable game of chess.

"Speaking one day to Mr. Seaton of her quickness, and the felicitous skill with which she threw off little *jeu d'esprits*, in the shape of *vers de société*, he replied: 'She is capable of better things than she has yet done; and, if she lives long enough, will, I predict, make a name for herself among the poets of our country. I may not live to see the noontide of her success, but I already discern its dawn.' He did not live to see much more than this dawn, but he instigated and suggested much that has brightened that success. Walking one day in the *Quinta del Obispo* with Mrs. Clarke, he said to her, 'I shall expect a poem from you, describing these triumphs of summer as beautifully as you have already described the "Triumphs of Spring."' It was not until years after that 'Gan Eden' appeared in the 'Southern Literary Messenger:' and, although my poor friend had long before died of the disease with which he was threatened when he uttered these words, I saw the effect of them as soon as I read that poem, which is one of the most truthful as well as poetic descriptions of the tropical beauties of the 'Isle of Flowers:'

''T is the Queen of the Antilles
  Seated on her emerald throne,
Crowned with ever-blooming flowers
  And a beauty all her own.
With a grace that 's truly regal,
  Sits she in her lofty seat,
Watching o'er the subject islands
  In the ocean at her feet.

'While its waters, blue as heaven,
Laughing, leap upon her breast,
Where all nature ever seemeth
For a happy bridal drest.
Truly is it called "Gan Eden,"
'T is a garden of delight;
But, alas! the serpent's trailing
O'er the beauty casts a blight.'

"All can realize the beauty of these lines; but none but one who has seen 'a stately ceyba-tree' in 'the poisonous embraces' of a 'deadly *Jagua Chacho*' — a creeping vine of exquisite beauty, which destroys all life in the tree to which it clings — can fully realize the beauty as well as the force of the simile which follows it. Neither can justice be done to the verse,

'Where the cucullos at even —
Insect watchmen of the night —
On the sleeping leaves and flowers
Shed their emerald-tinted light,'

by one who has never seen the long files of watchmen, each with his lantern lighted, start from the Plaza, and scatter over the city of Havana just as the short tropic twilight begins, nor marked the beautiful, pale, green-tinted glow cast by the Cuban fire-flies — cucullos — over the object on which they light.

"Several of the poems in Mrs. Clarke's last book, 'Mosses from a Rolling Stone,' show, to one intimate with him, that Mr. Seaton, who was a man of rare taste and great originality of thought, had at this time much influence in developing the powers which he saw were unknown in their full force to their possessor. Let me not, however, be understood as detracting from Mrs. Clarke's originality by this remark. It is the attribute of art to suggest infinitely more than it expresses, and of genius to catch suggestions, no matter from what source, and reproduce them stamped with its own unmistakable mark; and one of the chief beauties of Mrs. Clarke's poetry lies in her ability to invest with a new and poetic beauty the common things of everyday life. Who can read without emotion those exquisite lines of hers, 'The Rain upon the Hills'? or that beautiful household-poem 'The Mother's Dream'? She is as remarkable for strength as for richness of imagery: there is nothing weak in any of her poems, and some passages of great force and depth of feeling. Take, for instance, 'Aphrodite' and 'It Might Have Been:' when I read them, I felt that Mr. Seaton's prophecy was fulfilled, and she had indeed 'made herself a name among the poets of our land,' and was a literary as well as a social queen.

"I cannot better close this short and imperfect sketch than by giving you an account of the reading of her magnificent poem, 'The Battle of Manassas,' among the prisoners of Fort Warren. Mr. S. Teakle Wallis, of Baltimore, was the first to get the paper in which it was published. It was the hour for exercise, and most of the Confederate prisoners were in the court. Rushing down among them, Mr. Wallis jumped on a barrel and exclaimed, 'Boys, I have something to read to you.' From the animation of his manner, and the sparkle of his eye, they knew it was something they would like, and instantly gathered around him, when he read, with all the emphasis of a poet who feels every word that he utters:

'Now glory to the Lord of Hosts! oh, bless and praise His Name!
For he has battled in our cause, and brought our foes to shame.
And honor to our Beauregard, who conquered in His might,
And for our children's children won Manassas' bloody fight.
Oh! let our thankful prayers ascend, our joyous praise resound,
For God — the God of victory — our untried flag hath crowned.'

"Before he had half finished reading there was not one of those strong men who did not shed tears; and when he had finished, such a shout went up from them that the guards came running out to see if there was not an outbreak among the prisoners.

"I have never seen Mrs. Clarke since we parted on the 'Isle of Flowers,' but I have watched her literary career ever since, and eagerly read all the poems under the signature of 'Tenella.' Latterly, she has turned her attention more to prose than poetry, and is a contributor to 'The Land we Love,' as well as several other periodicals. Her 'Aunt Abby the Irrepressible,' in the first-mentioned magazine, has rendered her name a household word among all its readers. After several years spent in Texas, she returned to her native State, and at present resides in North Carolina. She has won considerable reputation by her translations from the French, and some of her translations of Victor Hugo's poems have been republished in England, where they attracted attention by the beauty of the rhythm into which they are so truthfully rendered.

But her 'Battle of Manassas,' 'Battle of Hampton Roads,' and her 'Rebel Sock,' together with other of her war poems, have given her a home reputation which renders her poems 'household words' by many a Southern hearth."

Mrs. Clarke seldom signs her name to her prose articles. Shortly after her return from Havana, she wrote "Reminiscences of Cuba," for the "Southern Literary Messenger," 1855. She translated from the French for a Confederate publication, "Marguerite; or, Two Loves," and has published considerably under the pseudonym of "Stuart Leigh." "General Sherman in Raleigh," "The South Expects Every Woman to do her Duty," and other sketches, appearing in the "Old

Guard," New York, with "The Divining Rod," in Demorest's "Monthly" in the fall of 1867, and a novelette in "Peterson's Magazine," and "Social Reminiscences of Noted North-Carolinians," appearing in "The Land we Love"—beside contributing as editress to the "Literary Pastime," a weekly journal published in Richmond—show she is an elegant prose writer.

APHRODITE.

'T was in the spring-time of the world,
The sun's red banners were unfurled,
And slanting rays of golden light
Just kissed the billows tipped with white,
And through the waters' limpid blue
Flashed down to where the sea-weed grew,
While rainbow hues of every shade
Across the restless surface played.
Then, as the rays grew stronger still,
They sought the sea-girt caves to fill,
And sparkled on the treasures rare
That all unknown were hidden there.
Roused by their warm, electric kiss,
The ocean thrilled with wak'ning bliss:
Its gasping sob and heaving breast
The power of inborn life confest;
But, though their waves were tossed ashore,
Upon their crests no life they bore.

Deep hidden in its deepest cave,
Unmoved by current, wind, or wave,
A purple shell, of changing shade,
By nature's careful hand was laid:
The clinging sea-weed, green and brown,
With fibrous grasp still held it down
Despite the waters' restless flow;
But when they caught that deep'ning glow,
They flushed with crimson, pink, and gold,
And from the shell unclasped their hold.
Its shadowy bonds thus drawn aside,
It upward floated on the tide;
But still its valves refused to yield,
And still its treasure was concealed.

Close shut upon the waves it lay
Till warmly kissed by one bright ray;
When, lo! its pearly tips unclose,
As ope the petals of the rose,
And pure and fresh as morning dew
Fair Aphrodite rose to view.
First — like a startled child amazed —
On earth and air and sea she gazed;
Then shook the wavy locks of gold
That o'er her neck and bosom rolled,
Loosened the cestus on her breast,
'Gainst which her throbbing heart now prest;
For, ah! its clasp could not restrain
The new-born life that thrilled each vein,
Flushed to her rosy fingers' tips,
And deeply dyed her parted lips,
Spread o'er her cheek its crimson glow,
And tinged her heaving bosom's snow.

Conscious of beauty and its power,
She owns the influence of the hour —
Instinct with life, attempts to rise:
Her quick-drawn breath melts into sighs,
Her half-closed eyes in moisture swim,
And languid droops each rounded limb;
With yielding grace her lovely head
Sinks back upon its pearly bed,
Where changing shades of pink attest
The spot her glowing cheek hath prest.
There all entranced she silent lay,
Borne on 'mid showers of silvery spray,
Which caught the light and backward fell
In sparkling diamonds round her shell.
Thus, wafted by the western breeze,
Cytherea's flowery isle she sees:
Its spicy odors round her float,
And thither glides her purple boat;
And, when its prow had touched the land,
There stepped upon the golden sand,
With life and love and beauty warm,
A perfect woman's matchless form.

The tale is old, yet always new,
To every heart which proves it true:
The limpid waters of the soul
In snow-crowned waves of feeling roll,

Until love's soft, pervading light
Has into color kissed the white,
And in its deep recesses shown
Rich treasures to itself unknown —
Though many restless sob and sigh,
Nor ever learn the reason why;
While others wake with sudden start
To feel the glow pervade their heart,
Flash down beneath its surface swell
And shine on Passion's purple shell,
Change to the rainbow's varying hue
The ties it may not rend in two;
Till doubts and fears, which held it fast,
Beneath love's glow relax their grasp:
Slowly the network fades away,
Like fleecy clouds at opening day,
And Passion, woke by warmth and light,
In deep'ning shades springs into sight.

But man the shell too often holds
Nor sees the beauty it unfolds;
Its close-shut valves refuse to part,
And show the depths of woman's heart.
And tossing on life's billows high,
The purple shell unoped may lie,
Till cast on Death's cold, rocky shore,
Its life and longing both are o'er.
But if Love's warm, entrancing light
Shall kiss the parting lips aright,
And wake to life the beauty rare
Which nature's self hath hidden there,
Beneath his soft, enraptured smile
'T is wafted to the flowery isle,
And Aphrodite steps ashore
A perfect woman — nothing more.

AN EPITHANATON.

General Leonidas Polk, C. S. A., killed on Pine Mountain, June 11, 1864.

"The tear-drops of sorrow may form a rainbow of glory above the grief-stricken head."

Amid the clouds of grief and woe
Again our God hath set his bow,
For o'er the flood of bitter strife
There shines another hero's life —

A hero's life and death, to tell
God loves the cause for which he fell;
For though our tears fall down like rain,
We cannot feel he died in vain.
Baptized by God Himself with flame,
Oh, let his death aloud proclaim
To hearts which sink 'neath grief and fear,
"Look up! look up! for freedom's near!"
Yes, yes, the strife is nearly done,
Or God had left this needful one,
Who on the mountain-top hath died
As Moses did on Nebo's side:
Like him, our promised land he saw
Beyond the rolling clouds of war,
A land of peace and happiness
Which he himself might not possess;
For as the diamond's fragments must,
To polish it, be ground to dust,
Her brightest gems our country yields
To die upon her battle-fields,
And o'er a mourning nation cast
The glory of a life that's past.
And oh! how brilliant is the bow
That from the storm-cloud now doth glow!
For though beside hope's vivid green
The crimson flush of pain is seen,
See joy's bright gold in rich relief
Shine out above our violet grief,
While next to doubt's dark, sombre hue
Comes freedom's pure and dazzling blue.
Thus, woven by a Hand Divine,
Amid the darkest clouds they shine,
While from them gleams the perfect light
Of God's own love in spotless white.
Then chant no dirge, and toll no knell,
But let a glorious anthem swell
In mem'ry of the Church's son,
Who fought the fight, and vict'ry won.

UNDER THE LAVA.

Far down in the depths of my spirit,
  Out of the sight of man,
Lies a buried Herculaneum,
  Whose secrets none may scan.
No warning cloud of sorrow
  Cast its shadow o'er my way,
No drifting shower of ashes
  Made of life a Pompeii;
But a sudden tide of anguish
  Like molten lava rolled,
And hardened, hardened, hardened
  As its burning waves grew cold.
Beneath it youth was buried,
  And love, and hope, and trust,
And life unto me seemed nothing —
  Nothing but ashes and dust.
Oh! it was glorious! glorious!
  That Past, with its passionate glow,
Its beautiful painted frescoes,
  Its statues white as snow,
When I tasted Love's ambrosia,
  As it melted in a kiss;
When I drank the wine of Friendship,
  And believed in earthly bliss;
When I breathed the rose's perfume,
  With lilies wreathed my hair,
And moved to liquid music
  As it floated on the air.
To me it was real — real,
  That passionate, blissful joy
Which Grief may incrust with lava,
  But Death can alone destroy.
'T was a life all bright and golden,
  Bright with the light of love;
A Past still living, though buried
  With another life above —
Another life built o'er it,
  With other love and friends,
Which my spirit often leaveth,
  And into the past descends
Though buried deep in ashes
  Of burnt-out hopes it lies,

Under the hardened lava,
  From which it ne'er can rise,
It is no ruined city —
  No city of the dead —
When in the midnight watches
  Its silent streets I tread.
To me it changeth never,
  Buried in all its prime,
Not fading — fading — fading
  Under the touch of Time.
The beautiful frescoes painted
  By Fancy still are there,
With glowing tints unchanging
  Till brought to upper air;
And many a graceful statue,
  In marble white as snow,
Stands fair and all unbroken
  In that silent "long ago."
It is not dead, but living,
  My glorious buried Past!
With its life of passionate beauty,
  Its joy too bright to last;
But living under the lava —
  For the pictures fade away,
And the statues crumble, crumble
  When brought to the light of day.
And like to Dead-sea apples
  Is love's ambrosia now,
And the lilies wither, wither,
  If I place them on my brow:
And so I keep them ever
  Far down in the depths of my heart,
Under the lava and ashes,
  Things from my life apart.

GRIEF.

"A great calamity is as old as the trilobites an hour after it has happened. It stains backward, through all the leaves we have turned over in the book of life, before its blot of tears, or of blood, is dry on the page we are turning." — *Autocrat of the Breakfast Table.*

'T was such a grief — too deep for tears —
Which aged my heart far more than years;

How old it seemed, e'en when 't was new,
Backward it stained life's pages through,
And, ere another leaf I turned,
On all my past its impress burned.
My happy days a mock'ry seemed—
I had not lived, but only dreamed;
And then, when first I wished it done,
Life seemed to me but just begun:
Begun in bitter unbelief
That Time could dull the edge of grief—
Could give me back my hope and faith,
Or bring me any good but death.
'T was but a moment; yet to me
It seemed a whole eternity!
I felt how gray my heart had grown;
Its plastic way was changed to stone
When Mis'ry there her signet set,
Impressing lines which linger yet.
In each fresh leaf of life I find
The shadow of this grief behind;
For though the page at first appears
Unsullied by the mark of tears,
They'll blister through before 't is read:
A real grief is never dead!
Its iron finger, stern and dark,
Leaves on the face and heart its mark,
As quickly cut—as plainly told
As that the die stamps on the gold;
Though read aright, perchance, alone
By those who kindred grief have known—
Like Masons' signs, which seem but nought,
Although with deepest meaning fraught.
The grief which kills is silent grief;
For words, like tears, will bring relief:
Husband and wife from each conceal
The wounds which are too deep to heal.
But, oh! when Hope and Faith seem dead,
While many a page must yet be read,
And in despair the heart doth sigh
And wish with them it too might die,
Remember that no night's so dark
But we can see some little spark,
And patient wait till dawning day
Shall its red line of light display:

For if we keep our love alive,
Our hope and faith will both revive.
Thus, as life's ladder we ascend,
Our hope shall in fruition end —
Our faith be lost in sight at length —
Our charity increase in strength;
And grief, which stamps the heart and mind,
But coin the gold Love has refined.

LIFE'S FIG-LEAVES.

Life's fig-leaves! Tell me, are not they
The outside beauties of our way,
The pleasant things beneath whose shade
Our inner — spirit-life — is laid?
I own they oft give promise fair
Of fruit which never ripens there;
For though we seek with earnest hope
Some tiny bud that yet may ope,
'T is all in vain — for fruit or flower
The tree has not sufficient power.
And still the earnest spirit grieves,
Which, seeking fruit, finds only leaves.
When such I meet, it calls to mind
The Saviour's warning to mankind:
"The time for fruit was not yet nigh."
Then wherefore must the fig-tree die?
Nature demanded leaves alone;
But yet He said, in solemn tone,
"Let no more fruit upon thee grow,"
That He to us this truth might show:
All life for some good end is given,
And should bear fruit on earth for heaven;
Its leaves and blossoms go for nought,
Unless they are with promise fraught:
No buds for fruit the fig-tree bore,
Hence it was blighted evermore,
And unto man still mutely saith,
A barren life is living death.
And so the parable should teach
That soul which does not upward reach.

MARY MASON.

MRS. MASON is the wife of Rev. Dr. Mason, of Raleigh. She has written several books for children. She is entirely self-taught, and her works are remarkable from that fact, besides possessing considerable literary merit. She cuts cameos and moulds faces; and, for a self-taught artist, her "likenesses" are excellent. Had she made "sculpture" a study from early youth, we warrant that the name of Mary Mason would have been as familiar to the world as is that of "Harriet Hosmer."

A head of General Lee, cut in cameo, is said to be exquisite.

NOTE.—We regret the briefness of our notice of this estimable lady; and have been unable, although striving much, to obtain copies of her publications. Yet we could not forego mention of her, if it was but her name, for she is one of the representative "Southland writers" of the Old North State.

CORNELIA PHILLIPS SPENCER.

MRS. SPENCER is a daughter of Prof. Phillips, of the University, and resides at Chapel Hill, North Carolina. She contributed a series of articles to the "Watchman," a weekly journal published in New York, in 1866, by Rev. Dr. Deems, of North Carolina. These articles were published in a volume, entitled "The Last Ninety Days of the War in North Carolina." This volume is a narrative of events in detail of the war, and personal sketches, showing, says a would-be facetious reviewer, "how the people of the Old North State ate, drank, and were clothed; and telling how the fowls were foully appropriated by vile marauders." The last chapter of the book is devoted to a history of the University of North Carolina.

FANNY MURDAUGH DOWNING.

BY H. W. HUSTED, ESQ.

HIGH blood runs in the veins of this gifted lady, and she came honestly by the talents for which she is so eminently distinguished. She was born in Portsmouth, Virginia, and her literary life commenced in North Carolina, in 1863. The Old North State awards to Virginia the honor of her birth, but cannot waive claim to her literary labors.

She is the daughter of the late Hon. John W. Murdaugh, a distinguished name in the Old Dominion. She was married, in 1851, to Charles W. Downing, Esq., of Florida, and at that time its Secretary of State; and she is blessed in four bright and beautiful children.

Another writer has said of her, and said truly: "Her eyes are black," (they are large and lustrous too,) "her hair of a magnificent, glossy blackness," (and a glorious flood of hair it is!) "her carriage stately, queen-like, and graceful, and in conversational powers she has few equals."

Her health is extremely delicate, but her spirits are always bright, and her heart brave and buoyant.

Many of her works are composed while too weak to leave her bed; and a jolly comedy of three acts, called "Nobody Hurt," was thus dashed off in ten hours. Daniel Webster has been called "a steam-engine in breeches;" but Daniel was a man, almost as strong in body as he was in mind. Mrs. Downing, fragile as she is, has performed an amount of intellectual literary labor which may well entitle her to be saluted as (with reverence be it spoken) a steam-engine in crinoline. When she began to write for the public, which she did with the *nom de plume* of "Viola," she announced her intention in a letter to a friend in these words:

"I shall write first to see if I can write; then for money, and then for fame!"

She has proved to the perfect satisfaction of the court and jury by which her merits were tried that she "can write," and write well. At present, she says, she is in the second stage of her programme; and, in catering to the general public taste, is compelled to bow to its decrees, in instances where her purer Southern taste would suggest a far different and less sentimental style.

One of these days, we trust the land we love will be able to foster, cherish, and *pay for* a literature of its own, and then our authors may write at the same time for money *and* fame. This one of them, in yielding to stern necessity and writing for money, has also achieved ample fame.

Mrs. Downing's first publication was a poem entitled "Folia Autumni," and its success was so great that it was rapidly followed by numerous other poetical effusions, most of which have a religious tinge, and seem the breathings of a subdued and pure spirit. They are all remarkable for musical rhythm, and the easy and graceful flow of feelings which can never be spoken so well as in the language of song.

Among the best of these are her "Egomet Ipse," a terrible heart-searcher; "Faithful unto Death," full of a wild and nameless pathos; and "Desolate," which is not exceeded by any elegiac poem in the language. As a specimen of her minor poems, we select

SUNSET MUSINGS.

Love of mine, the day is done—
All the long, hot summer day;
In the west, the golden sun
Sinks in purple clouds away;
Nature rests in soft repose,
Not a zephyr rocks the rose,
Not a ripple on the tide,
And the little boats, that glide
Lazily along the stream,
Flit like shadows in a dream.
Not one drooping leaf is stirred;
Bee, and butterfly, and bird
Silence keep. Above, around
Hangs a stillness so profound,
That the spirit, awe-struck, shrinks,
As of Eden days it thinks,
Half expectant here to see
The descending Deity!

Love of mine, when life's fierce sun
  To its final setting goes,
Its terrestrial journey run,
  Varied course of joys and woes,

May there come a quiet calm,
Bringing on its wings a balm
To our hearts, which aching feel
"Sorrow here has set its seal!"
May a stillness soft as this
Soothe our souls in purest bliss,
Till the worry and the strife
Of this fever we call life,
With its pain and passion cease,
And we rest in perfect peace.
Love of mine, may we behold
Eden's visitant of old,
When our last breath dies away,
By us at the close of day!

These poems were followed by "Nameless," a novel of merit, filled with sprightly descriptions and delineations of character, but which was, from some unexplained reason, too suddenly crowded to a close, before its plot could be evolved and completed. It is said to have been hastily written in ten days, as a proof whether or not she could write prose. She had already written good poetry which was appreciated and applauded, and her next venture was in prose fiction. "*Tentanda via est*," quoth Mrs. Downing, and spread her trial wings. This trial proved the existence of high power, which has since been wonderfully improved, developed, and matured in her excellent novels, "Perfect through Suffering" and "Florida." Then came a series of poems of a sterner sort, which were deemed by some to be just a trifle rebellious, but which found a responsive feeling deep in the hearts of thousands of true men, who are not willing to wear chains without giving them an occasional shake. Of this style are "Confederate Gray," "Holly and Cypress," "Prometheus Vinctus," "Memorial Flowers," "Our President," "Two Years Ago," "Sic Semper Tyrannis," a majestic lyric, which thrills each Virginian heart to the core, and glorious little "Dixie," which stirs to its fountains every Southern soul, and teaches it

"To live for Dixie! Harder part!
To stay the hand—to still the heart—
To seal the lips, enshroud the past—
To have no future—all o'ercast—
To knit life's broken threads again,
And keep her mem'ry pure from stain—
This is to live for Dixie!"

As Mrs. Downing is a daughter of Virginia, we give her "Sic Semper" in full:

SIC SEMPER TYRANNIS.

They have torn off the crown from her beautiful brow,
Yet she never seemed half so majestic as now,
When she stands in the strength of her sorrow sublime,
As she ever stood, noblest and best of her time!

They have wiped from the roll of their country her name,
Coexistent with glory, coequal with fame;
On the record of Time it will grandly endure
As unchangeably bright as her honor is pure!

They have stolen her crest, which for ages has blazed,
And the motto she loves from its surface erased;
But vain is their malice, and futile their art,
For the seal of Virginia is stamped on the heart!

SIC SEMPER TYRANNIS! We whisper it low,
While the hearts in our bosoms exultingly glow,
As we think of the time, in its sure-coming course,
We will prove it by deeds with a terrible force.

Not the we of this age! WE shall pass from our pain
Ere the bonds of Virginia are sundered in twain;
Yet the day when her children will free her shall dawn
Just as surely as earth in her orbit rolls on!

On her regal white shoulders they press down their yoke,
But her mind is unfettered, her spirit unbroke;
A woman sore weakened, her form they control,
But the points of their arrows turn blunt from her soul!

Like vultures they swoop in a clamorous swarm,
And their talons imprint in her delicate form;
Her treasures they covet, yet blacken and blot
While parting her garments and casting the lot!

As the Jews loved the Romans that horrible night
When the Shechinah took from the Temple its flight,
As the Pole loves the Cossack, and Greeks love the Turk,
We Virginians love those who have compassed this work!

Yes, we love them — as Anthony, righteous in wrath,
Loved Brutus the murderer polluting his path,
When in brazen disgrace he defiantly stood,
His hands redly reeking with Cæsar's warm blood!

Yes, we love them — as Rachel, whose baby lay dead,
Its body apart from its innocent head,
Stung to madness by pain, and infuriate with hate,
In the depth of her anguish, loved Herod the Great!

Though our faces must wear in their presence no frown,
In our souls we despise them and trample them down;
To Virginia in chains, we exultingly cling,
While we spurn them away as a leperous thing!

Not the wrath of a day, nor a season, is ours;
At the white heat of passion it ceaselessly towers;
We will keep it aglow, and its red sparks shall run
Through the veins of Virginians from mother to son!

For Virginia has daughters who stand at her side
And her spoilers in dignified silence deride;
While serene in their strength, every feeling controlled,
Into heroes the men of the future they mould!

'Tis true they are infants now hushed on the breast,
But we teach them a lesson no tyrant shall wrest;
Sic Semper Tyrannis we sow with their prayers —
They will reap with rejoicing the harvest it bears!

To Virginia now prostrate the cross and the sword,
But her future is fair in the hand of the Lord:
When His vengeance sweeps down in a fiery tide,
She shall shine as the gold that is seven times tried!

From God's own chosen people His arm was removed,
While through Palestine Sisera raged unreproved,
Till the work which the Lord had appointed was wrought,
When the stars in their courses for Deborah fought!

Thou mother in Israel, Virginia, shalt wake,
And thy bands of captivity captive shalt take;
At thy feet they shall bow, they shall crouch, they shall crawl:
With Sic Semper Tyrannis thou 'lt trample them all!

They humble Virginia! As well may they try
To sully the stars on heaven's battlements high!
When they crumble to nothing, VIRGINIA shall shine
Eternal, immutable, glorious, divine!

In very playfulness, and as if to show her great diversity of talent and her surprising power of writing by antagonism instead of sympathy, and conceiving what could have only existed with her by the aid of a most lively and exuberant fancy, she has written some of the most musical and genial poems of love and wine since the grapestone choked the old Teian bard.

It may be said of her as of the celebrated French authoress, that she "writes by her imagination, and lives by her judgment." In truth, she seems to rejoice in a sort of "double life" of her own, and to sport *ad lib.* in whichever she pleases. One is the life common to us all; the other, such as poetical fancy alone can build up and people with its own bright and beautiful creations, and which she has described in her poem, "The Realm of Enchantment."

MEMORIAL FLOWERS.

The Lord of light, who rules the hours,
Has scattered through our sunny land
Mementos of His love in flowers
With lavish hand.

This month they bloom in beauty rare,
And more than wonted sweets display,
As conscious of the part they bear
The Tenth of May:

On which the South in plaintive tone,
Of pride and sorrow mixed with bliss,
Speaks: "As a nation, I can own
No day but this!

"I give, on it, my glorious dead
The tribute they have earned so well,
And with each bud and blossom shed
A mystic spell.

"I lay the laurel-wreath above
The cedar with its sacred ties,
And place them with a mother's love
Where JACKSON lies.

"The lily, in its loveliness,
Pure as the stream where it awoke,
And spotless as his bishop's dress,
I give to POLK.

"To Albert Sidney Johnson, moss,
And rosemary, and balm; to these,
Entwisted in a simple cross,
I add heart's-ease.

"The fleur de lis, in song and lay
The emblem of true knighthood's pride,
I place, commixed with jessamine spray,
By Ashby's side.

"Fresh morning-glory buds I twine,
With scarlet woodbine laid beneath,
And mingle with them eglantine
For Pelham's wreath.

"The honeysuckle's rosy drift,
Whence fragrance-dripping dews distil,
I offer as the proper gift
For Ambrose Hill.

"O'er Bender's pure and sacred dust
Let bleeding-hearts and bays be swept;
He well deserved his country's trust,
So nobly kept!

"Let Ramseur's native pines drop down
Their leaves and odorous gums, displayed
To form with ivy-flowers a down,
Where he lies dead:

"While orange-blossoms fall like snow,
To fill the air with fragrance ripe,
And form of MAXCY GREGG, below,
The truest type.

"Where Doles and Bartow rest in death,
Strew hyacinths and mignonette,
And scatter, with its balmy breath,
The violet.

"The fairest of the radiant dyes
Which paint in living gems her sward,
The Land of Flowers well supplies
To honor Ward.

"The grand magnolia's blossoms fall,
Mingling with fern their snowy loads,
And form a freshly fragrant pall
To cover Rhodes.

"Let stars of Bethlehem gleaming lie
As pure as Barksdale's soul, which soars
While he exclaims: 'I GLADLY DIE
IN SUCH A CAUSE!'

"GRANBURY rests in dreamless sleep;
And, heaped upon his grave's green sod,
I let the crimson cactus creep
Round golden-rod.

"Of Zollicoffer, who went first
To plead my cause at heaven's bar,
The am'ranth's buds, to glory burst,
Fit emblems are.

"For Morgan let the wildwood grape
Afford a dewy diadem,
And with its drooping tendrils drape
The buckeye's stem.

"Missouri, from the fertile fields
Washed by her giant river's wave,
The gorgeous rhododendron yields
McCulloch's grave.

"Around the stone with Cleburne's name
Wreathe daisies and the golden-bell,
And trumpet-flowers with hearts of flame,
And asphodel.

"For him who made all hearts his own
  The sweetest rose of love shall bloom,
In buds of blushing beauty strown
  On Stuart's tomb.

"Each nameless nook and scattered spot
  Which hides my children from my view
I mark with the forget-me-not,
  In heaven's own blue.

"Of all the varied vernal race
  I give my cherished dead a part,
Except the cypress: that I place
  Upon MY heart."

MRS. MARY AYER MILLER,

(Luola.)

THE subject of this sketch was born in Fayetteville, North Carolina, but on the death of her father, General Henry Ayer, removed with her mother, when only eight years old, to Lexington, North Carolina, for the purpose of being educated by her uncle, the Rev. Jesse Rankin, a divine of the Presbyterian Church, who had a classical school at that place.

She received the same education given to the boys of her uncle's school, which was preparatory for the University of North Carolina, and began as early as her fourteenth year to show signs of the poetic talent which she has since cultivated with success. She married early a young lawyer, Mr. Willis M. Miller, who gave promise of making a reputation at the Bar, but abandoned his profession about a year after his marriage, and commenced studying for the Presbyterian ministry. This change in the plan of his life, after taking on himself the cares of a family, involved a change in his style of living, which drew his wife almost entirely from literary to domestic pursuits, as his salary, after being licensed to preach, was too small to allow much leisure to the mother of his rapidly increasing family. Consequently, her pen was laid aside for the needle just when her poems, under the signature of "Luola," were beginning to attract attention by the smoothness of their flow and the purity and tenderness of their sentiment. But the spirit of song was latent in her heart, and burst forth, from time to time, in little gushes, which kept her memory alive in the hearts of those who had already begun to appreciate her poetry. In a letter to a friend, she says: "I have never made the slightest effort for popularity, but set my little songs afloat as children do their paper boats: if they had sail and ballast enough, to float; if not, to sink."

Some have sunk; for, like most women who write *con amore*, and not for publication, she does not always give her poems the after critical supervision of the scholar, but is content to throw them off with the easy rapidity of the poet.

But many of them show the fire of genius; and, like the love-boats of the Hindoo girls on the Ganges, cast a light on the waters as they float down the stream of Time, and all are distinguished by some grace which touches the heart, or pleases the fancy for the moment.

As a writer for children, Mrs. Miller has been very successful. The Presbyterian Board of Publication has issued several of her works as Sunday-school books; and her poems in the youth's department of the "North Carolina Presbyterian," and the "Central Presbyterian," published in Richmond, Virginia, have rendered her a favorite among the little ones, who have as keen an appreciation of what is suited to their taste and capacity as older readers have of what pleases them; and such happy conceits as that of "Linda Lee" speak directly, not only to their fancy, but also to their hearts.

Mrs. Miller resides at present in Charlotte, North Carolina, writing occasionally for publication, but as often carrying her poems for days in her memory, until she can steal time from the duties and cares of a wife and mother to commit them to paper.

A few of her poems are preserved in "Wood Notes," a collection of North Carolina poetry made by Mrs. Mary Bayard Clarke, and published in 1854; but most of them have appeared only in the newspapers.

MRS. SUSAN J. HANCOCK.

SUSAN J. HANCOCK was born in Newbern, North Carolina, in the year 1819. Her maiden name was Blaney. Her paternal grandfather belonged to the Irish nobility, and her maternal ancestor was of France, while both grandmothers were Americans. So the eagle of America, with the rose of France entwined with the shamrock of Ireland, would have been a fit emblem for their escutcheon, had they needed one. But the ancestors of the subject of this sketch thought little of the nobility of their ancestry. To be good and virtuous was their aim; content to live respected and die regretted. At the time of the birth of Mrs. Hancock, her father was a prosperous merchant in the town of Newbern, and she seemed born to prosperity; but reverses came, and the family were reduced from affluence. Mr. Blaney was enabled to give all of his children a fair education.

Susan was always of a romantic turn, and from early years exceedingly fond of poetry. Before she ever published a line, she was in her thirty-fifth year. And encouraged by the commendation bestowed upon her verses, she contributed to various Southern periodicals. Nearly all of Mrs. Hancock's poems are impromptu — really but the expression of a full heart; written more to give vent to feelings of joy, adoration, or sorrow, than for any other purpose; and published, not for the sake of fame, but in the faint hope that others, tried and sorrowing as she was, might perchance find consolation, strength, and comfort in their perusal.

At the commencement of the war, Mrs. Hancock resided in Newbern, a Southern town noted for the beauty of its situation, the hospitality and refinement of its inhabitants, and often termed the "Athens of the South." Newbern was one of the first cities on the coast to fall into the possession of Federal troops. And need we draw a picture of this captured town? Mrs. Hancock, after being refused permission to "cross the lines" by General Burnside, was, when General Foster succeeded the former in command of Newbern, sent beyond the lines. Eighty-one persons, including helpless age and weeping infants, were sent out with one week's provision, and placed between the two picket lines. Here they remained until negotiations could be consummated for their removal to "Dixie." She remained here until the close of the war. Her son James fell in battle near Richmond. He was a member of the 2d North Carolina Regiment, commanded by the lamented "Tew," and subsequently by the gallant "Ramseur."

After the "surrender," Mrs. Hancock returned to her old home, where she remained until June, 1868, when she removed to St. Paul, Minnesota. She says: "If anything could make me forget my unhappy past and my beautiful Southern land, beautiful even in her desolation, it would be the warm-hearted kindness with which I have been welcomed in my new Western home."

The following verses are from a volume Mrs. Hancock has prepared for publication:

LITTLE CHILDREN.

Little wild-flowers, gayly springing
  All along the path of life,
How refreshing to the aged
  Are your forms, so full of life!

What is all the labored wisdom
  Musty volumes can impart,
Compared with all the holy lessons
  Found within your guileless heart?

Tell me not of storied grandeur!
  Talk not of Italia's lore!
Nor of vines and gorgeous flowers
  Found on ancient Beulah's shore.

Lovelier far the human blossoms
  Springing round the household hearth;
Sweeter is the ringing music
  Of their heartfelt, guileless mirth.

When the heart is bowed with sadness,
  When the world looks dark and drear,
How reviving falls their laughter
  On the dull and wearied ear!

Wonder not some wither early,
  Fading ere the wintry day;

They are by far too pure and holy
  On this sin-struck earth to stay.

Therefore are they early taken
  To the garden of the blest,
Forever round God's throne to blossom,
  And bloom upon the Saviour's breast.

GOD'S LOVE.

How boundless is the love of God!
  How rich, and yet how free!
It girdles earth and spans the skies,
  And fills immensity.

It buds in every blooming shower,
  And rustles in each breeze,
And falls in every liquid flower,
  And waves among the trees.

It shines in every sunlit ray
  That falls aslant our path,
And glistens in each drop of dew
  On ev'ry blade of grass.

We scent it in the varied sweets
  From woodland flowerets borne,
And view it in the whitening wheat,
  And in the tasselling corn.

It sparkles in the gems and gold
  That deck the kingly hall,
And blushes in the modest rose
  That climbs the cottage wall.

It flashes on us in our walks
  From childhood's laughing eye,
And smiles upon us in the dreams
  Of sleeping infancy.

'Twas love that to the rugged hills
  Their mantling green has given,
And formed the fleecy clouds that float
  Like aërial ships 'mid heaven.

It was this love bespangled heaven
  And lit pale Luna's ray,
And drew the curtain of the night
  To veil the cares of day.

But oh! His love more brightly beams
  From Bethlehem's manger low,
And from the blood-besprinkled cross
  That decks bold Calvary's brow.

His love has made the desert smile,
  And clothed this world in bloom,
And thrown a ray of glory o'er
  The portals of the tomb.

SOUTH CAROLINA.

SUE PETIGRU KING.

MRS. S. P. KING has been complimented by being called the "female Thackeray of America." She is a native of South Carolina — a daughter of the late Hon. James L. Petigru, a prominent lawyer of Charleston. She was early married to Mr. Henry King, a lawyer, and son of Judge Mitchell King, of Charleston. Her husband lost his life in defence of his native city during the late war.

Mrs. King's first book was "Busy Moments of an Idle Woman," this was followed by "Lily." The former was successful, and both were pictures of society. She collected a series of tales she had written for "Russell's Magazine," called "Crimes that the Law does not Reach," to which she added a longer story, "The Heart History of a Heartless Woman," published originally in the "Knickerbocker Magazine," and, under the title of "Sylvia's World," it was published by Derby & Jackson, New York, (1860.) This was the most popular of Mrs. King's books, although her last work, published during the war in the "Southern Field and Fireside," and afterward in pamphlet form, entitled "Gerald Gray's Wife," is her *chef-d'œuvre*. The characters in this novel *are* real people, breathing Charleston air, and were immediately recognized by the *élite* in Charleston society. We know of no book or writer that we can compare Mrs. King to. She is highly original, witty, satirical, and deeply interesting. Her writings are all pictures of society. It is said that her "Heartless Woman of the World" is herself. In society, Mrs. King was always surrounded by a group, who listened with interest to her brilliant flow of conversation. She could talk for hours without tiring her hearers with her sparkling scintillations. Repartee, as may be imagined from her books, is her forte. When William Makepeace Thackeray lectured in this country, and met Mrs. King, he said to her in a brusque manner: "Mrs. King, I am agreeably disappointed in you; I heard you were the fastest woman in America, and I detest fast women." She replied: "And I am agreeably surprised in you, Mr. Thackeray; for I heard you were no gentleman."

Mrs. King is below the medium height, fair; brilliant, variable eyes, black and gray and blue in turn; hair dark, and worn banded across a brow like her father's, high and broad, rarely seen in a woman; lips never at rest, showing superbly white teeth; hands and feet perfect; arms, bust, and shoulders polished ivory, and yet withal not beautiful as a whole; slightly lisping accent; and dress so artistic and ultra-fashionable that nature seemed buried in flowers.

Mrs. King despises foolish sentimentalism, and shows up human vice in all of her books. All of her characters are true to nature. Bertha St. Clair, who is one of the *dramatis personæ* in "Sylvia's World," and also in "Gerald Gray's Wife," is an exquisite portraiture. In the latter the characters are, as we have mentioned, from life—the false Gerald Gray still breathes the air of Charleston. That piece of insipidity, or "skim-milk, *soft* Cissy Clare," is strikingly true to nature, as are pompous Mr. Clare, sturdy old Jacob Desborough, scheming Phillis, and the gallant Josselyn.

The transforming power of love, as displayed in the metamorphosis of plain Ruth Desborough to beautiful Ruth Grey, is very charmingly wrought out.

Mrs. King has published nothing since the close of the war; but shortly after the downfall of the Confederacy, she gave dramatic readings in various parts of the North, and is, we believe, now residing in Washington City.

A LOVERS' QUARREL.

There was not a more beautiful avenue of trees in all the world than that which led to the front entrance of Oaklevel. They were very old—they met overhead, and enlaced themselves with wreaths of moss; the sunlight came flickering through the branches, and fell stealthily and tremblingly upon the clean, smooth ground; little heaps of dead leaves lay here and there, scattered by each breath of the December breeze, and forming their tiny mounds in fresh places as the wind trundled them along.

On a fine, bright morning, some years since, two persons were slowly pacing up and down this grand, majestic walk. They were both young, and both were handsome. She was blonde, and he a dark, grave-looking man.

"Nelly, I don't like flirts."

"Yes, you do—you like me, don't you?"

"I don't like flirting."

"What do you call flirting? If I am to be serious, and answer your questions, and admit your reproofs and heed them, pray begin by answering me a little. Where and when do I flirt?"

"Everywhere, and at all times."

"Be more particular, if you please. Name, sir, name!"

"I am not jesting, Nelly. Yesterday, at that picnic, you talked in a whisper to John Ford, you wore Ned Laurens's flowers stuck in your belt-ribbon, you danced two waltzes with that idiot, Percy Forest, and you sat for a full hour *tête à tête* with Walter James, and then rode home with him. I wish he had broken his neck, —— him!" and a low-muttered curse ended the catalogue.

"If he had broken his neck, very probably he would have cracked mine; so, thank you; and please, Harry, don't swear: it is such an ungentlemanly habit, I wonder that you should have it. And now for the list of my errors and crimes. The mysterious whisper to John Ford was to ask him if he would not invite Miss Ellis to dance; I had noticed that no one had yet done so. You gave me no flowers, although your sister's garden is full of them this week; so I very naturally wore Ned Laurens's *galanterie,* in the shape of half a dozen rosebuds. Percy Forest may be a goose, but he waltzes, certainly, with clever feet; one of those waltzes I had offered early in the day to you, and you said you preferred a polka. Walter James is an old friend of mine, and, for the matter of that, of yours too. We talked very soberly: I think that his most desperate speech was the original discovery that I have pretty blonde ringlets, and when he falls in love, it shall be with a woman who has curls like mine. You best know whether papa allows me to drive with you since our accident: my choice lay between a stuffy, stupid carriage, full of dull people, and a nice, breezy drive in an open wagon, with a good, jolly creature like Walter, whom you and I know to be, despite his compliments to my Eve-like coloring, *eperdument amoureaux* of Mary Turner's dark beauty. Now, Harry, have you not been unreasonable?"

"How can I help being so, Nelly, darling, when I am kept in this state of misery?" answered Harry, whose frowning brow had gradually smoothed itself into a more placable expression. "What man on earth could patiently endure seeing the woman he adores free to be sought by every one — feeling himself bound to her, body and soul, and yet not being able to claim her in the slightest way — made to pass his life in solitary wretchedness because an old lady and gentleman are too selfish —"

"Hush, hush, Harry! You are forgetting. I am very young; papa and mamma think me too young to bind myself by any engagement."

"It is not that. They choose to keep you, as long as they can, mouldering with themselves in this old house."

"Harry!"

"Or else it is I whom they dislike, and refuse to receive as a son. Too young? why, you are nineteen. It is an infamous shame!"

"I will not speak to you, if you go on in this way. You know just as well as I do what their reasons are. My poor sister Emily made a love-match at eighteen, and died, broken-hearted, at twenty-three. Her husband was a violent, jealous man, who gave her neither peace nor valuable affection. He looked upon her as a pretty toy, petted her, and was raging if a gentleman spoke more than ten words by her side, so long as her beauty and novelty lasted. Her health failed, her delicate loveliness departed, and with these went his worthless passion. I was a mere child then — the last living blossom of a long garland of household flowers — when my father laid his beloved Emily in her early grave. I stood by his great chair that sad evening in my little black gown when he returned from the funeral, and he placed his hands upon my head and made a vow that never, with his consent, should his only remaining darling follow in the steps of the lost one. 'No man shall have her who has not proved himself worthy to win her. As Jacob served Laban shall her future husband serve for her, if it please God that she live and that she have suitors.' Day by day, year by year, he has but strengthened himself in this determination; and when, last spring, you applied to him for my hand, he told you frankly that if you had patience to wait, and were convinced of the strength of our mutual attachment, on my twenty-third birthday you might claim a Mrs. Harry Trevor from his fireside."

"But, Nelly, four years to wait! and all because poor Mrs. Vernon had weak lungs — forgive me, dearest Helen, dearest Helen!" But Helen walked on and away from him, with proper indignation.

With impatient strides he passed her, just as they reached the lawn which bordered the avenue and surrounded the house. Extending his arms to bar her passage, "Listen to me, my own dear Nelly," he pleaded. "I was wrong to say that; but you cannot understand, my angel, how furious and intractable I become when I think of those incalculable days between this time and the blessed moment when I shall be sure of you."

"If you are not sure of me now, you do not fancy that you will be any more so then, do you?" asked Helen, gravely; but she permitted him to lead her away from the stone steps that she was about mounting, and back to the quiet alley under the old oaks.

He drew her arm through his, gently stroking her gloved hand as it rested in his own.

"If there is no truth and belief between us to-day, there will be none then," Helen pursued. "I am, in the sight of heaven, by my own free will and wish, your affianced wife. All the priests on earth would not make me more so, in spirit, than I am now. But I respect my father's wishes and feelings; and you must do so too," she added, lifting her eyes with such a lovely look of tenderness that Harry, as he pressed her hand with renewed fervor, murmured a blessing in quite a different tone from the one which he had devoted to the now forgotten Walter James.

He glanced around, and was about to seal his happiness upon the dainty pink lips, smiling so sweetly and confidingly; but Helen, blushing and laughing, said: "Take care: papa is reading yesterday's paper at the left-hand window of the dining-room; and I think, if one eye is deciding upon the political crisis, the other is directed this way."

"We are watched, then!" exclaimed Trevor, passionately, all his short-lived good-humor again flown. "This is worse and worse."

Helen looked at her lover with a calm, searching expression in her blue eyes. "Perhaps papa is right. He has a terror of violent men, and he may like to see if you are always as mild as he sees you in his presence."

Trevor bit his lip and stamped his foot impatiently. Helen hummed a tune, and settled her belt-ribbon with one hand, while she played the notes she was murmuring on the young gentleman's coat sleeve with the other.

He let the mischievous fingers slide through his arm, and "thought it was going to rain, and he had better be thinking of his ride to the city."

Nelly looked up at the blue heavens, where not a speck of a cloud was visible, and gravely congratulated him on a weather-wisdom which was equally rare and incomprehensible.

"But your season, my dear Harry, is always April. Sunshine and storm succeed so rapidly, that you can never take in the unbroken calm of this—December, for instance. Beside, I thought you were to stay all night with us? I know mamma expects you to do so."

"I am very much obliged," said Mr. Trevor, haughtily; "I have business in town."

"Clients? court sitting?" asked Nelly, innocently, and demurely lifting her pretty eyebrows.

"No. There is a party at Lou Wilson's, and I half promised to go. We are to try some new figures of the German."

"Indeed!" Nelly's eyes flashed, and the color stole up deeper to her cheek. "I won't detain you."

She bowed, and turned from him with a cold good-morning. Her heart was beating, and the tears were very near; but she managed to still the one, and send back the others, so as to say indifferently, over her shoulder: "Should you see Walter James, pray tell him that I shall be happy to learn that accompaniment by this evening; and, as there is a moon, (in spite of your storm,) he can ride out after business hours and practise the song. But, however, I won't trouble you; mamma is to send a servant to Mrs. James's some time to-day, and I will write a note."

"I think it will be useless. He is going to Miss Wilson's."

"Not if he can come here, I fancy," said the wilful little beauty, with a significant tone; and then, repeating her cool "Good-by—let us see you soon," she sauntered into the house, elaborately pausing to pick off some dead leaves from the geraniums that were sunning themselves on the broad steps by which she entered.

Thus parted two foolish children, one of whom had a moment before expressed the most overwhelming passion, and the other had avowed herself, "in the sight of heaven, his affianced wife!"

MRS. CAROLINE H. JERVEY.

CAROLINE HOWARD GILMAN, the daughter of Rev. Samuel Gilman, a Unitarian clergyman, and Mrs. Caroline Gilman, the celebrated authoress, was born in Charleston, South Carolina, in 1823.

In 1840, Miss Gilman married Mr. Wilson Glover, a South Carolina planter, and was left a widow in 1846, with three children, one son and two daughters. She returned to her father's house, and immediately began to teach, and for fifteen years carried on a successful school in Charleston.

While engaged in teaching, she wrote papers for magazines, also poems, over the signature of "Caroline Howard;" and finally her novel, "Vernon Grove; or, Hearts as they Are," which appeared serially in the "Southern Literary Messenger," and was afterward published by Rudd & Carleton, New York, passing through several editions, and warmly received by the critics. "Vernon Grove" was copied for the press at night, after being in the school-room all day; and yet Mrs. Glover kept up all her social duties, visiting, entertaining, and seeming always to be as completely the mistress of her own hours as the idlest fine lady.

She is fastidiously neat and particular in all her surroundings, and a wonder for arranging and contriving. While in Greenville, during the war, says a friend, where her apartments and premises were unavoidably small, they were miracles of ingenuity and order.

In ——, 1865, Mrs. Glover married Mr. Louis Jervey, of Charleston, who had been devotedly attached to her for many years. By this marriage she has one daughter. Her son is married; and her eldest daughter has been, like herself, left a youthful widow, with two little children.

In Mrs. Jervey's home circle she is idolized; her temper is perfectly even and self-controlled, her judgment good and ready, and her unfailing cheerfulness and flow of pleasing conversation make her a charming companion. She talks even more cleverly than she writes, and has a vein of humor in speaking which does not appear at all in her novels. Mrs. Jervey is uncommonly youthful in appearance, is above the middle height, with a fine, full figure, and an erect, commanding carriage. Her hair is golden-red and abundant; her complexion is very fair, and with dark eyebrows and lashes she would be lovely: as it is, she is at times indisputably handsome. Her manner is striking, lady-like, perfectly self-possessed—not exactly *studied;* but "her memory is extremely good, and she never forgets to be graceful," never seems to give way to an awkward impulse, and is *always posed* and seen to advantage. A friend says: "I was constantly reminded of Mrs. Jervey by Ristori's attitudes and gestures."

We are sorry to say that this accomplished lady is at present in ill health—prohibited any literary labor, even the most careless letter-writing. Her latest novel, "Helen Courtenay's Promise," (published by George W. Carleton, New York, 1866,) was prepared for the press by dictation of an hour a day to one of her daughters. This novel has been styled the "production of a brilliant, creative fancy."

STANZAS.

Ye strange, mysterious worlds of light sublime,
Far wandering through the trackless maze of time
With measured pace, in one perpetual round—
Unrivalled orbs, with softest radiance crowned,
Can ye with earth, our glorious earth compare?
Ye globes of light, that seem so wondrous fair;
Or can it be that kind, indulgent Heaven,
More lenient still, far lovelier scenes has given?

Do lucid streams in murmuring ripples flow,
And radiant flowers in brightest colors glow?
Do forests dark their branches interweave,
And graceful vines in wild luxuriance wreathe?
Do bright-winged warblers tune their lays of love
In the green alcove of each fragrant grove?
Or have the scenes that on your bosoms rise,
Oh! have their counterpart ne'er met our earthly eyes?

So purely formed, so faultless and so fair,
All earthly dreams but faint resemblance bear;
So far removed from man's degenerate race,
The blest recipients of unbounded grace;

If such there be on yon fair orbs that dwell,
Whose bosoms pure no ruthless passions swell,
For whom no Saviour's precious blood 's been given,
Themselves so guiltless formed, so near approaching heaven —

Known but to Him whose various works divine —
Known but to Him who formed the grand design
Those countless myriads borne from pole to pole,
Whose glittering ranks in regal splendor roll.
Exhaustless theme! to which my soul aspires,
Intensely glow my spirit's tameless fires,
Where all the nobler powers of being reign,
Yet vainly doth it strive your mysteries to explain.

Those star-begemmed and radiant realms divine,
All are thy works, all-glorious Parent, thine!
The more we search, still intricate the more,
How fain would we those azure depths explore,
Whose mystic ways (concealed from all below)
Intensely burns my yearning soul to know,
Yet calmly waits that glorious dawning when
Immortal vision bright beams in the eyes of men.

JULIA SLEEPING.

Hush! let the baby sleep!
Mark her hand so white and slender,
Note her red lip full and tender,
And her breathing, like the motion
Which the waves of calmest ocean
In their peaceful throbbings keep.

Hush! let the baby rest!
Who would wake from blissful sleeping,
To this world so filled with weeping,
Those sweet eyes, like stars o'erclouded,
Those calm eyes with dark fringe shrouded,
Those crossed hands upon her breast?

Hush! let the baby rest!
See each white and taper finger,
Where a rose-tint loves to linger,

As the sun at evening dying
Leaves a flush all warmly lying
  In the bosom of the west!

  See on her lips a smile!
'T is the light of dreamland gleaming
Like to morning's first faint beaming:
Hush! still solemn silence keeping,
Watch her, watch her in her sleeping,
  As she smiles in dreams the while.

  I would paint her as she lies,
With brown ringlets damply clinging
To her forehead, shadows flinging
On its whiteness — or where tracings
Of the blue veins' interlacings
  On its snowy surface rise.

  God hear our fervent prayer!
Through the whole of life's commotion,
As she stems the troubled ocean,
Give her calm and peaceful slumber;
And may sorrow not encumber
  Her unfolding years with care.

  Ah, see, her sleep is o'er!
Flushed her cheek is: she is holding
Mystic converse with the folding
Of the curtains o'er her drooping:
What beholds she in their looping
  Mortals ne'er beheld before?

  Now from her bath of sleep,
Many a deep'ning dimple showing,
She hath risen fresh and glowing,
Like a flower that rain hath brightened,
Or a heart that tears have lightened,
  Tears the weary sometimes weep.

  Herself the silence breaks!
Hear her laugh, so rich and ringing!
Hear her small voice quaintly singing!
She hath won us by caressings:
We exhaust all words in blessings
  When this precious baby wakes.

A SUMMER MEMORY.

Beloved, 't was a night to shrine
  In happy thought *for years*,
A memory of certain joy,
  A spell 'gainst woe and tears.

And why? Was it because the moon,
  More bright than e'er before,
Stooped from her throne to kiss the waves
  That rippled to the shore?

Or was it that the gentle breeze,
  With whispers fond and sweet,
Brought fragrance from some spicy land
  And laid it at our feet?

Ah! never since primeval time
  Was night so fair as this—
So filled with joy, so fraught with peace,
  So marked with perfect bliss.

I seemed to live a fresh, new life,
  A life almost divine,
As on the glittering shore we sat,
  Thy meek eyes raised to mine.

Was it the *night* that brightened all?
  Oft comes the question now—
The *night* that brought such blest content?
  No, dearest, it was *thou*.

CAROLINE A. BALL.

MRS. BALL is the daughter of the late Rev. Edward Rutledge, an Episcopal clergyman of Charleston. Her early life was passed at the North, having been educated at the seminary of the Misses Edwards, in New Haven. Her first poem, or rather the first which caused any sensation, was written when she was sixteen, and was a satirical piece, in answer to an impertinent attack on woman in the "Yale Literary Magazine." It was published anonymously, and was freely discussed, in the presence of the fair author, by the students of her acquaintance, in terms of high compliment, or in condemnation of its severity.

Mrs. Ball is the wife of Mr. Isaac Ball, of Charleston. She never published under her own name until the struggle for "Southern independence" commenced. The poems she wrote were very popular: coming, as they did, from a heart full of love for her fatherland, they spoke to the hearts of the Southern people, inspired by the same mighty love.

Her poems are not studied efforts; but of and from the heart.

In 1866, a number of her poems on the war, originally published in the "Charleston Daily News," were printed in pamphlet form —

IN MEMORIAM

OF

OUR LOVED AND LOST CAUSE,

AND

OUR MARTYRED DEAD:

"Outnumbered — not outbraved."

This book was entitled "The Jacket of Gray, and Other Fugitive Poems."

THE JACKET OF GRAY.

Fold it up carefully, lay it aside,
Tenderly touch it, look on it with pride;
For dear must it be to our hearts evermore,
The jacket of gray our loved soldier-boy wore.

Can we ever forget when he joined the brave band
Who rose in defence of our dear Southern land,
And in his bright youth hurried on to the fray,
How proudly he donned it, the jacket of gray?

His fond mother blessed him, and looked up above,
Commending to Heaven the child of her love:
What anguish was hers mortal tongue cannot say,
When he passed from her sight in the jacket of gray.

But her country had called, and she would not repine,
Though costly the sacrifice placed on its shrine;
Her heart's dearest hopes on its altar she lay
When she sent out her boy in the jacket of gray.

Months passed, and war's thunders rolled over the land;
Unsheathed was the sword and lighted the brand;
We heard in the distance the sounds of the fray,
And prayed for our boy in the jacket of gray.

Ah! vain, all, all vain were our prayers and our tears;
The glad shout of victory rang in our ears;
But our treasured one on the red battle-field lay,
While the life-blood oozed out on the jacket of gray.

His young comrades found him, and tenderly bore
The cold, lifeless form to his home by the shore;
Oh! dark were our hearts on that terrible day,
When we saw our dead boy in the jacket of gray.

Ah! spotted and tattered, and stained now with gore
Was the garment which once he so proudly wore;
We bitterly wept as we took it away,
And replaced with death's white robes the jacket of gray.

We laid him to rest in his cold, narrow bed,
And graved on the marble we placed o'er his head,
As the proudest tribute our sad hearts could pay,
He never disgraced the jacket of gray.

Then fold it up carefully, lay it aside,
Tenderly touch it, look on it with pride;
For dear must it be to our hearts evermore,
The jacket of gray our loved soldier-boy wore.

OUR SOUTHERN WOMEN.

In reply to sundry attacks made upon them by the Northern press.

When war's grim visage o'er us frowned,
And desolation reigned around;
When souls of joy and hope were shorn,
And life-strings rudely rent and torn;
When e'en our bravest were unmanned,
And waves of woe rolled o'er our land,
Our Southern women fearless stood,
And firmly met the raging flood.

When fiercely rang the battle-cry,
Calling our hosts to bleed and die;
When from each home some cherished form
Went out to meet the gathering storm;
When death was showering forth his darts,
And trampling over loving hearts,
Our noble women checked each tear,
And uttered nought but words of cheer.

When, after each terrific fray,
Wounded and faint our brave boys lay,
Afar from friends, afar from home,
Where best-beloved ones might not come;
The gentle women of our land,
With pitying eye and tender hand,
Watched tireless by each sufferer's bed,
And wept above the unknown dead.

When for our cause each hope was lost,
And every soul was tempest-tost;
When homes in ashes round us lay,
And o'er us shone no cheering ray;
When enemies, with taunt and jeer,
Sought to bow *Southern hearts* in fear;
Of all but pride and honor shorn,
Our women paid back scorn for scorn.

Then let the press, by Forney led,
Pour out its wrath on woman's head;
Let those who *dared not* face our men,
And wield no weapon save the pen,
Show to the world how brave they grow
When *woman only* is their foe.
By enemies as vile as they,
Though venom in each word may lay,
Our Southern sisters, true and tried,
Care not how much they are belied;
While loved and honored still they stand
The pride of their own sunny land.

MRS. MARY S. B. SHINDLER.

MARY STANLY BUNCE PALMER is a native of Beaufort, S. C., but removed while very young to the city of Charleston, where her father, the Rev. B. M. Palmer, was the highly honored pastor of the Independent Church on Meeting Street. She was chiefly educated at the seminary of the Misses Ramsay, in that city; but, in consequence of the delicate health which so often accompanies the delicate organism of the gifted children of song, she was sent for a short period to complete her studies in the more bracing climate of the North. She gave early evidence of poetic genius, and many of her school-mates remember with pleasure her impromptu and mirthful efforts in childhood. After her return to Carolina, Miss Palmer became known as a contributor to the "Rosebud" and other similar periodicals. Her graceful manners and sprightly conversation made her at all times a desirable companion; while her ready sympathy and thorough appreciation of the feelings of others rendered her a warmly cherished friend.

In 1835, Miss Palmer was united in marriage to Mr. Charles E. Dana, and accompanied him to the city of New York, where they spent three years, and then removed to the West. They were but a short time located in their new home, when one of those singular epidemics that sometimes sweep over the rich prairies, and enter (none know how) into the new settlements that populate that vast region of country, appeared in the vicinity of their residence, and in two short days Mr. Dana and their only child were numbered among its victims.

Alone, among comparative strangers, Mrs. Dana, rousing into action the latent energy of her character, sought and gained once more her Southern home. As the wearied birdling returns to the parent nest for rest and comfort, so this heart-stricken wanderer came back to the bosom of her family, and, amid the ties of kindred and associations of her girlhood, found consolation for her grief and strength for the duties yet before her.

From early youth she had written, for amusement, occasional contributions for various publications, but now she devoted her fine talents to the task as a regular occupation; and in 1841 published that happy combination of music and poetry known as "The Southern Harp." A similar volume soon followed from her pen, under the title of "The Northern Harp," which met as warm a welcome as her first attempt to adapt her own pure thoughts to the secular music familiar to all. Then came "The Parted Family, and Other Poems," also a success. About the year 1844, Mrs. Dana published a succession of short prose stories, and, soon after, her largest and most remarkable prose work, entitled "Letters to Relatives and Friends," written to defend her changed opinions on the subject of religious faith. Doubts of the creed she had inherited had arisen in her mind, and investigation had strengthened them into a conviction that she had mistaken the denomination to which she should attach herself: therefore she became a Unitarian. The work was well written, and immediately republished in London.

In 1847, Mrs. Dana suffered another most deeply-felt bereavement, in the death of both of her parents, and it required all the support of that religion which she had still continued to investigate, to enable her to bear up under the renewed trial; and, happily for her, light and strength crowned her efforts.

In May, 1848, she married the Rev. Robert D. Shindler, of the Episcopal Church.

"Alas for those who love,
Yet may not join in prayer!"

sings Mrs. Hemans, in her "Forest Sanctuary." But Mrs. Dana-Shindler was spared this bitter experience, for she had once more returned to her belief in the Holy Trinity, and could unite with her husband in all his offerings of praise and prayer, while the Angel of Peace folded its white wings over her chastened, but loving heart.

Mr. and Mrs. Shindler are now residents of Texas.

MISS ESSIE B. CHEESBOROUGH.

ESSIE B. CHEESBOROUGH is a daughter of the late John W. Cheesborough, a prominent shipping merchant of Charleston, South Carolina. Her mother is a native of Liverpool, England. Miss Cheesborough was educated in Philadelphia and in her native city, Charleston, South Carolina.

She commenced her literary career at an early age, writing under the *noms de plume* of "Motte Hall," "Elma South," "Ide Delmar," and the now well-known initials of "E. B. C."

She was a regular contributor to the "Southern Literary Gazette," published in Charleston, and edited by the Rev. William C. Richards; and when Mr. Paul Hayne assumed the editorship, she continued her contributions. She was also a contributor to "Russell's Magazine," one of the best magazines ever published in the "Southland," and to various other Southern literary journals of the past, and to the "Land we Love," of the present era. After the war she was a regular contributor to the "Watchman," a weekly journal, edited and published in New York by the Rev. Dr. Deems, of North Carolina, with which journal she was connected until its discontinuance.

Miss Cheesborough's style is fluent and easy, and she does not pander to the sensational, but is natural, truthful, and earnest, never egotistical, or guilty of "fine writing." She has never published a book, although her writings on various subjects, political, literary, and religious, would fill several volumes.

RENUNCIATION.

I know that thou art beautiful:
  The glory of thy face
Are those dark eyes of witchery,
  That certain nameless grace.
Old Titian would have painted thee
  With joy too deep for telling—

That ivory cheek, the lustrous light
  In golden tresses dwelling.

But, manacled by solemn fate,
  I cannot burst the fetters;
Or write the story of my life
  In precious, golden letters:
Love's star for me can never shine;
  Its trembling light grows dimmer,
As through the dusky veil of grief
  Hope sends a feeble glimmer.

Then go; and in thy happy fate
  Of womanly completeness,
Make strong a husband's loving heart
  With all thy woman's sweetness.
But I must stand without the gate,
  While Eden's glowing splendor
Lights up with its aurora smile
  The glories I surrender.

MANACLED.

Stop, soldier, stop! this cruel act
  Will ring through all the land:
Shame on the heart that planned this deed—
  Shame on the coward hand
That drops the sword of justice bright
  To grasp these iron rings!
On them, not me, dishonor falls;
  To them this dark shame clings.

Manacled! O my God! my God!
  Is this a Christian land?
And did our countries ever meet
  And grasp each other's hand?
O Mexico! on thy red fields
  I battled 'midst the fray;
My riflemen, with steady aim,
  Won Buena Vista's day.

Manacled! Far down the South
  Let this one word speed fast:
My country, thou hast borne great wrongs,
  But this, the last, the last,
Will send a thrill through thy high heart,
  Despair will spurn control;
And these hard irons pressing HERE
  Will enter thy proud soul.

Manacled! Oh, word of shame!
  Ring it through all the world!
My countrymen, on you, on you
  This heavy wrong is hurled.
We flung our banners to the air;
  We fought as brave men fight;
Our battle-cry rang through the land —
  HOME! LIBERTY! AND RIGHT!

Manacled! For this I am here,
  Clanking the prisoner's chain!
We fought — ah! nobly did we fight;
  We fought, but fought in vain.
Down in that billowy sea of blood
  Went all our jewels rare,
And Hope rushed wailing from the scene,
  And took herself to prayer.

Manacled! manacled! words of woe,
  But words of greater shame:
I've that within me which these wrongs
  Can never, never tame;
And standing proud in conscious worth,
  I represent my land,
And that "lost cause" for which she bled,
  Lofty, heroic, grand.

FEASTING THE LIONS.

DEAR MRS. GREEN: — You will be charmed to understand that the Hon. Fitzroy Seymour, formerly St. Maur, is at the Mills House. The Hon. Fitzroy belongs to one of the noble families of England, and also enjoys immense celebrity as a poet. His lady is, no doubt, equally celebrated; indeed, she has written some very sweet things, perfect *bonbons* in the way of poetry. Oblige me by laying down your "Metastasio," and taking up the Seymours.

Before calling, which, with your well-known courtesy to strangers, you will of course do, pardon this gentle hint: make yourself acquainted with the delicious muse of Fitzroy S. It charms an author to find you at home amid his garden of sweets; and the larger the bouquet of his flowers of rhetoric you cull, the closer he clasps you to his heart and approbation.

Accept, dear Mrs. Green, the accompanying volume of poems by this gifted and highly distinguished stranger, and oblige yours, devotedly,

SOLOMON FANTASIO.

January 25.

How delightfully considerate in Solomon Fantasio! It was Mrs. Green's peculiar forte, entertaining distinguished strangers; and Solomon Fantasio, a gentleman of elegant leisure, limited means, and very extended views of hospitality and benevolence, which he carried out at other people's expense, took care that Mrs. Green should never be at a loss for proper objects upon which to exercise her talent.

"I make it a matter of religion," said Mrs. Green to Mr. Green, the day the Fantasio communication arrived, "to entertain strangers, and to use hospitality without grudging."

"That you are deeply religious, Arabella, I am not disposed to doubt, for you gave, last year, at my expense, what you termed a charity ball. This is now a matter of money, and not of religion, and my purse will not stand this everlasting tugging at its strings."

"Tugging at its strings, Mr. Green! your *grassièreté* is remarkable!"

"Well, then, feeding these people, who go away and laugh at us for our pains."

"Go on," said Mrs. Green, majestically. "What else have you to say?" at the same time preventing Mr. Green from complying with her request by continuing the conversation herself. "Do you suppose these people only come here to eat? What an outcry you are raising about nothing!" And Mrs. Green turned away indignantly from her inhospitable lord.

But the Fates, that "lead the willing and drag the unwilling," hauled Mr. Green, kicking and resisting, to his destiny. It was decreed that the Seymours were to be fêted; the lions were to be patted and caressed, and Mrs. Green must introduce them into Charleston society, so that all who desired, could have an opportunity of placing "their hands upon the lions' manes," and "playing familiar with their locks."

Having made herself mistress of the table of contents of the volume of poems by the distinguished stranger — for to drink deep of his Pierian spring was a task Mrs. Green was not equal to — escorted by Solomon Fantasio, she went in quest of the British lions. That night the royal animals roared amid the flower of the aristocracy, in the elegant drawing-room of Merriman Green, Esq. But Southern hospitality is a whole-soul feeling; it must not stop here — it must go and remove the Seymours, bodily, from the hotel, and set them down in the mansion of the Greens. This it did; and here is the grand finalé:

"*Mirum!*" exclaimed Mr. Green, with a waggish smile, on the day after the Seymours had departed.

"What is *mirum*, my dear?" asked Mrs. Green, plaintively.

"That the lions are off, and we are not bitten."

Mrs. Green gazed with deeply rueful visage into the fire, and sighed.

"Who next, my love?" asked Mr. Green.

Mrs. Green replied not; she was even then smarting from the lion's bite, and had no ointment wherewith to mollify it.

"Let me see," said Mr. Green; "we have got through with one Chinese, an out-and-out Celestial; two distinguished Greeks, who were never on those 'classic shores;' three eminently distinguished poets —"

"Oh, forbear your enumeration," implored Mrs. Green, tearfully.

"My dear, why object? *hœc olim meminisse juvabit?*"

"I do not understand Latin, but I do understand English: here, read this, and Mrs. Green thrust a book into the hands of Mr. Green.

"Humph!" he said, reading the title, "Copies of Letters written when in America, to our Friends in England." "Precious legacy!" he continued; "left by mistake, no doubt. Well, we surely have nothing to complain of from these distinguished strangers. We provided their dinners, and they honored us by eating them; they treated us with the most refreshing consideration; they took the back seats in the carriage; drank 'God save the Queen' in my best wine; Fitzroy smoked out my best segars, peace to their ashes; and Mrs. Fitzroy accepted your most sparkling diamonds, which she 'vastly admired.' All of which is charming — but to the letters."

Letter of the Hon. Fitzroy Seymour to the Hon. C. Bedivere Audley.

Dear and Hon. Sir: — My last was from New York; this is from Charleston, a small, dingy town in one of the Southern States of America. Two months ago, I was unfortunate enough to land here, where I have been fêted, feasted, questioned, and bored almost to death. I am really sick of attention, being ready to cry out,

"'Shut, shut the door, good John,' fatigued I said,
'Tie up the knocker, say I'm sick, I'm dead.'"

I have yielded, I hope, with proper resignation to my fate; indeed, rebellion would have been useless. The population flocked around me *en masse*, and one individual, Green by name, greener by nature, [at this racy paragraph "Green by name, greener by nature," kicked the table-leg with unwonted energy, and muttered something not to be mentioned to ears polite,] forced me into leaving my hotel and cohabiting with himself. [" Was there ever a man so slandered by tourist or traveller?" asked Mr. Green, angrily.] I allowed myself to be forced by this Green into his house, imagining that under a private roof I could enjoy more frequent opportunities of studying the much-vexed question of Slavery.

I found that Fame, with noisy trump, had blown my literary celebrity the length and breadth of the land. My volume I found in all hands, and my poetry on all tongues. I was regarded as one whose eyes roll with genuine poetic frenzy. Ah, my friend, what a difference does a trip across the Atlantic make in one's condition! With regard to the literary standing of this place, you will not be surprised to hear that it amounts to nothing. "Russell's Magazine" * is the exponent of the literature of the place: its articles would shame our meanest English periodical; that is, it would be ashamed to publish such unmitigated trash. Its contributors are women!!! boys, and that class of ancients known by the name of "old fogy." I attended a Literary Club, where a prosy gentleman read a prosy essay in a prosy tone, which was responded to by a dozen other prosy gentlemen, and every subject discussed save the one under discussion. Long live Carolina *savans*, say I.

But, my friend, what shall I say of slavery, that foul blot on the people of the South? what new light can I throw upon this dark subject, this ebon theme? Oh, I implore your pity for the down-trodden slave of the white man: extend from the land of Wilberforce sympathy and help. Of all our foreign relations, these our sable brothers demand our greatest attention. I have been an eyewitness to the evils they endure, and the cruel ills their flesh is heir to. They are branded, they are scourged, they are flayed, they are flogged, they are pickled, they are peeled; in short, they are subjected to everything but bleaching. The consequence is, they are a race of invalids, and, notwithstanding I have made diligent search, I cannot find one sable brother or sister who is quite well; in their own peculiar, but expressive language, they are "only so-so." Their enervated condition is a palpable fact. In passing through the streets, how have I thrilled with horror to see as many as half a dozen sable ones, of the masculine gender, leaning at various doors on the tops of their brooms! "What, lazy?" you say. Ah, no, my friend, *they are not* a lazy race, but actually too feeble to sweep continuously for a quarter of an hour; whilst the sable ones of the feminine gender, in a similarly enervated condition, were leaning from the windows, animating by their cheerful converse their companions in affliction, their brothers in bonds. Ah! can we draw from the deep fount of pity too much sympathy to bestow on the poor helot of Carolina? The blackest shades that you have seen of this black picture are not black enough to paint the dark reality. How can the sun shine so goldenly over this sin-stained community? how can the moon spread her silver arch over such a spot? enough of this heart-rending theme. When I reach England—land of the free and the brave—I must, of course, write a book, in which I promise to illustrate my remarks on slavery, by incidents gathered in the house and in the kitchen. The vile institution shall be exposed in all its horrors, and such a picture exhibited that even "the bravest will shrink back, dumb with dismay."

"I have read enough," said Mr. Green, breaking off from the Honorable's letter, abruptly; "now for the lady's."

Oh, dear Lady Barbara! what a place the Fates and Fitzroy have set me down in! Dingy, dirty, disagreeable; utterly without paint; washed only by the rains of heaven. I shall leave it *de tout mon cœur*. I have been bored to death by attention, and deluged with civilities, until, in perfect desperation, I lift up my hands imploringly, and cry: "Hold! enough!" I have attended several parties, at which, "in clouded majesty, dulness shone." The gentlemen congregated in the middle of the room and practised yawn-

* This was published in "Russell's Magazine," September, 1858.

ing, whilst the ladies sat around the edges, stiff, starched, silent. Tacita presided. How I longed for one hour of my dear Lady Barbara's charming "conversation evenings"! One fair dame launched out on the sea of conversation, and in this wise edified her next-door neighbor: "Maum Venus's shortcomings are unbearable; and Maum Flora's long goings, who stays almost forever when sent on an errand; Daddy Neptune is always 'half seas over,' and when wanted to hand the waiter on particular occasions, is in no condition to distribute the edibles." Oh, tender Lady Barbara! how sadly fare the gods and their ladies at the hands of exacting mortals! These wretched slaves, kind Lady Barbara, are most cruelly treated; but I have not the heart to linger on this subject. Fitzroy will, however; his powerful pen, stimulated by his powerful imagination, can do ample justice to the theme. There is a little poem floating in my brain now, which I will pen for your perusal; I will call it "The Slave in Chains." It was suggested to me by seeing a daughter of Afric's land with a gold chain around her neck, said to be stolen from her young mistress's jewel-box. I intend to turn the links into iron — to place manacles on her wrists, instead of the bracelets I saw there, and to pull off her stockings and place her bare feet in stocks. You see, my dear Lady Barbara, there is nothing like giving a complete picture, perfect in all its parts, and in exact keeping with the subject. If I painted a slave in stockings and a gold chain, the English world would say: "Very pretty, but exceedingly unlike." Therefore, to make her in accordance with John Bull's idea, you see the necessity I am under of changing the material of which her chain is made. You are not obtuse, Lady Barbara; you see far down into the clear depths of this idea, do you not?

Now for Charleston ladies! Two words paint the picture — scolds, dowds; the gentlemen overbearing, conceited, always saying, "I and my king," ever elevated on the highest peak of impudence. I am staying with a Mrs. Green; a very good sort of person; quite an obliging creature really, though she will insist upon going to dinner in short sleeves and low neck, and calling it high dress. Mr. Green is ignorant and vulgar; he will call Fitzroy's charming "Ode to the Queen" an "odious." The man is most disagreeably plebeian —

"I'll read no more," said Mr. Green, indignantly; "eat my dinners, drink my wine, smoke my cigars, accept my wife's best diamond, ride in my carriage, and then —"

"Oh, hush, Mr. Green! these letters are charming; go on, pray; we are on the tiptoe of expectation to hear what else the lady says about you. We are laughing merrily at your expense."

Mr. Green looked up pleasantly. "Ah! my friends, *quid rides? Mutato nomine, de te fabula narratur*. Which, being changed into English for your comfort and reflection, reads thus: 'Why do you laugh? Change but the name, and the story is told of yourself.'"

MARY SCRIMZEOUR WHITAKER.

THE author of "Albert Hastings" and various productions, prose and poetical, is a native of Beaufort District, South Carolina. Her father, Rev. Professor Samuel Furman, son of the Rev. Dr. Richard Furman, of Charleston, South Carolina, is a clergyman of the Baptist persuasion, still living at the advanced age of seventy-seven years, and famed for his learning, eloquence, and piety. Her mother, whose maiden name was Scrimzeour, is of Scottish descent, and traces back her lineage to Sir Alexander Scrimzeour, celebrated in Scottish story, whose descendants, in the male line, were hereditary standard-bearers of the kings of Scotland.

Her father having removed from Beaufort to Sumter District, she passed the early part of her life at the High Hills of Santee, probably the most beautiful and romantic portion of South Carolina. There is little doubt that the sublime and picturesque features of the landscape by which she was surrounded sensibly affected her imagination. She gave early indications of possessing a poetic temperament, and pieces composed by her at the age of ten and twelve years were prophetic of the excellence she subsequently attained as a votary of the Muses. She pursued her studies, embracing ancient and modern literature, at home. As she grew up to womanhood, she manifested a fondness for society; and, endowed with personal and intellectual traits which fitted her to adorn any sphere, ere long became one of the attractions of the highly refined circle in which she moved.

She was devoted to history, and her father's library furnished her with the best sources of information. She read rapidly, was in the habit of drawing her own inferences, and of writing comments and criticisms upon the most striking passages she read.

Among the poets, Pope and Campbell were her favorites and models. Pope's translation of the Iliad and Odyssey of Homer were the constant companions of her childhood; and she read them so often, and was so struck with their numerous beauties, that, even to this day, she retains whole scenes in her memory. She is an admirer of Felicia Hemans and L. E. L. She loved them for the deep fountain of feeling which is discoverable in their writings. For the same reason she admired Scott and Burns. She was also attracted by the simplicity and purity of style of these authors, and the high-wrought genius which diffuses such a charm over all their productions.

The critical articles on the poets from the days of Dryden to those of Tennyson, which appeared editorially in the Sunday issue of the "Times" newspaper in New Orleans during the year 1866, and which were greatly admired for their acumen and terseness, were from her pen.

Previous to the late war, she was, for some time, a regular contributor to the Philadelphia magazines, writing under her own name, regarding a *nom de plume* as a foolish species of affectation, and not being ashamed to claim the authorship of anything she wrote herself, nor willing that it should be claimed by others.

In 1837, she, with her parents and two of her brothers, visited Edinburgh, her mother being entitled to a large estate in Scotland, then in litigation, and which she finally recovered. They took lodgings in a fashionable portion of the New Town of Edinburgh, characterized by the elegance and massive character of its private edifices and the beauty of its gardens. Here she passed her time surrounded by friends, among whom were some of the most distinguished literati of that ancient metropolis, such as Campbell, the poet; the Messrs. Chambers, editors of "Chambers's Journal;" Professor Wilson, editor of "Blackwood's Magazine;" Professor Moir, (the "Delta" of that work;) Mr. Tait, editor of "Tait's Magazine;" Burton, the historian; Mary Howitt, and other notables. Campbell was so pleased with her poetry that he encouraged her not to neglect her gift, and complimented her highly, calling her "his spiritual daughter." Some of her fugitive pieces were published, at the time, in the quarterlies of Great Britain.

She often refers to her visit to Scotland, where she spent nearly two years with high satisfaction, styling it the most golden period of her existence.

While in Edinburgh, she formed an acquaintance with a young and distinguished advocate of the Scottish Bar, of high connections, John Miller, Esq., (brother of Hon. William Miller, now member of the British Parliament,) whom she subsequently married. Having received the appointment of Attorney General of the British West Indies, he embarked for Nassau, N. P., with his young wife, but immediately after his arrival there, he was seized with yellow fever and fell a victim to its insidious attacks. Mrs. Miller, assailed by the same fearful disease, recovered from it, and, with a heavy heart, returned in a Government vessel to South Carolina.

The trial which she was called on to endure in the loss of her gifted and distinguished companion was very severe, and tinged with sadness several of the subsequent years of her life. Her vivid descriptions of the scenery of the West Indies, and of the epidemics which annually sweep off so many of its inhabitants, contained in "Albert Hastings," were doubtless suggested by her visit to that beautiful but fatal region.

Gradually she returned to society, of which she became once more the life and ornament. Possessed of conversational powers of a high order, and of a quick wit, that charmed and often startled by its brilliancy, no evening assemblage gathered in her neighborhood was regarded as complete that did not number her among its guests. In short, the youthful Mrs. Miller was very popular — very accomplished. In person, she is rather *petite*, but the elegance and perfect symmetry of her figure, the animation of her expressive countenance, especially when engaged in a literary conversation, the elegance of her diction, the affability of her manners, and the perfect propriety of her dress, (to which no lady should be indifferent, and which, in her case, was always *à la mode*,) made her, whenever she entered a drawing-room filled with cultivated persons of both sexes, "the observed of all observers."

After twelve years passed in widowhood, almost exclusively devoted to literary studies and pursuits, she again married. The individual who was so fortunate as to win her heart and hand, while she was still in the prime of her beauty and womanhood, was Daniel K. Whitaker, Esq., a gentleman not undistinguished in the world of letters, the well-known editor for many years of the "Southern Quarterly Review," a fine scholar, and an elegant and accomplished writer. With him, she has lived happily for twenty years, and has surviving, of six children, two fair daughters, who, in intellect and attractions, bid fair to emulate their distinguished mother.

In 1850, Mrs. Whitaker, at the request of numerous friends with whom, as a poet, she was a great favorite, consented to collect and publish a volume of her poems, which have been highly commended by the best critics, particularly by William Cullen Bryant, himself the first American poet of his age. Her lyrical effusions are characterized by pathos and tenderness. The euphony of her rhythm is unsurpassed by that of Pope himself, of whose musical numbers she was so fond. She confines herself to no one style of versification, but resorts at will to all those forms of "linked sweetness" in which the Muses delight to revel. "The Creole," a tale of some length, descriptive of a West India courtship which ends tragically, is conceived in a very original vein. The beautiful scenery of that fair clime receives its full share of attention from this poet-artist.

There are pieces in the collection characterized by spirit and fire; but the majority of her effusions are deeply tinged with the seriousness that naturally resulted from passages in her early history. The tributes to "Scott," "Byron," "Campbell," "Caravaggio," "Miss Landon," and "Mrs. Hemans," are among the most finished of her compositions. Many of her best pieces, written since this volume was published, (several of them elicited by the scenes of the late war and the gallantry of our generals upon the battle-field,) are scattered in the newspapers and periodicals of the day.

"Albert Hastings" is her first extended effort in the department of novel-writing. The scene of the novel, commencing in the Southern States, ends in England, the birthplace of the ancestors of the hero, where, after struggling manfully with many difficulties which beset him in the outset of his career in this country, he inherits a princely fortune. This work is the precursor of others, which, the writer of this sketch understands, are either finished or in course of preparation.

The following sonnet (a difficult kind of writing, but which has the advantage of embodying *multum in parvo*,) upon Mrs. Hemans, one of the most gifted of England's fair poets, may give the reader an idea of the refinement of her taste and the admirable justness of her discriminations:

MRS. HEMANS.

A SONNET.

O woman poet! wrapped in musings high,
How rich, how soft, how pure thy minstrelsy!
Whose trumpet tones arouse and thrill the heart:
Thy muse-like form and soul-lit face appear,
Like thy own Psyche's, borne on ambient air
To pleasure's fragrant grove and golden isle,
Where blushing fruits and heavenly flowers smile.

Thine was the inborn light which sheds its ray
Around the poet's mind-illumined way:
Forever changing and forever bright,
And swaying all things with its mystic might,
A moral grandeur graced thy melting song,
Which flowed in numbers liquid, sweet, and strong.

THE SUMMER RETREAT OF A SOUTHERN PLANTER.

Noonday sun fell in gorgeous effulgence over a field where long maize-leaves drooped like those of the Indian banana, when salt sea-breezes cease to fan them, and vertical rays glitter on white rocks, burn into the bosom of earth, and blind the eye of the beholder by their intenseness. But this is no tropical scene. On the declivity of a green hill-side rises a rude dwelling, composed of logs, built after the fashion of a pen. A wide passage separates two apartments. This passage, or corridor, is floored with pine boards, which, having been often scoured with sand and the shucks of Indian corn, has assumed an aspect of purity and whiteness truly refreshing. It extends from the front to the back of the house, and whenever there is the least atmospheric agitation, here the wind plays in cooling gusts.

But, as before said, it is noontide now, and stagnation pervades all, both within and without. Great hickory-trees and oaks seem to be sleeping a luxuriant sleep, brooded over by the day-king, as purple wild grapes ripen in luscious clusters on tangling vines, which form untrained arcades down a steep declivity, terminating in a dingle, or branch, cool, and sheltered by tall, magnificent pines, unlike those of the uplands. High wave their green crests, in fine contrasts to rich, blue, cloudless summer heavens, dominating a less stately growth of fragrant gum-trees, cedars, dogwood, and black walnut.

Here the cool spring-house is built over a running stream; and earthen pans, disposed on either side, are crusted over by cream, which will to-morrow be converted into healthy buttermilk and yellow butter, fresh and pure as the stream that wanders beneath, and rich as the golden sky that gleams above them. A large orchard extends on the right side of the dwelling. There the ruddy peach, Tyrian damson plum, large purple fig, and humble melon, lying on the earth, striped with green and white, nestling under grass, and its peculiar serrated leaves, await the hand of the gatherer. Tall sunflowers rise amid these Southern productions, and, ever turning their attention toward their potent lord, stand bravely forth, as though they said, "Perfect love casteth out fear." And so they follow his grand march over the blue empyrean down to his setting, when, their graceful adieu being made, they await to-morrow's sunrise ere, like adoring Persians, they turn them to the east and drink in his morning light.

A large dog lies dozing in the shade of a flower-shaped catalpa. Lazily he slumbers, and from gnats and flies occasionally attempts to relieve himself; flaps his huge ears, whisks his tail, and shows his glittering teeth. A lofty pole, planted firmly in the ground, is hung about with dry calabashes, each presenting an open aperture in front, which has been cut for the admission of swallows and martins, these birds being esteemed as denizens of a farm at the South, for no reason that I could ever ascertain, save that the old African crones, who preside over the plantations in matters of superstitious belief, reverence them.

A farm in South Carolina engages our attention, or rather the summer residence of one of her sometime princely planters. It was the custom of these gentlemen to retire from their plantation, usually situated in the low country, at this season. Their operatives, of African descent, whose lineage and constitution prevented them from incurring the least risk by continued residence in lowland sections during midsummer heats, remained on rice-plantations, on the seaboard and in river-swamps, where cotton was cultivated, while their Anglo-Saxon masters sought refuge amidst pine-barren wastes or on the apex of elevated hills.

The house now introduced on the scene was one in the latter-named region, the dwelling of Mr. Campbell — Scotch, as his name imports, and a true son of that land which not only gives birth to heroes of the sword and autocrats of the great mental republic of the world, but to good citizens, honest, industrious, and enterprising, all the world over. A love of his native land, or at least a memory of it, was traceable in the objects which, on entering either of the apartments separated by the wide passage before alluded to, met the eye. On unplastered walls were Highland scenes, depicted with graphic skill. Falls of the Clyde, Covalinn, Tantallon Castle, and Highland trosacks looked in speaking semblance from rich frames; and disposed on tables, in the midst, were "Blackwood," the "Edinburgh Review," and various periodicals fraught with that sound sense and discriminating intelligence which made Walter Scott the wonder of his age as a novelist, Thomas Campbell the legitimate successor of Dryden and Pope, and a long line of historians, orators, and statesmen the exemplars of their country's glory.

Bating the indications stated, this was a truly American establishment, or rather a sample of Southern summer residences among the wealthy. The house, being plain almost to rudeness, did not lack any accommodation consonant with free ventilation, a warm season, comfort, and use. The stables were as large as the dwelling, and under one extended roof were elegant vehicles, English horses, and attendant grooms, black as ebony, whistling and happy, very cheerfully performing the duties of that fraternity — chopping oats, currying sleek steeds, or putting in order trapping and harness.

Around the low-built but wide house were bare poles supporting a shed covered with green pine boughs, which emitted a healthful odor, and when dried in the sun were removed and replaced by others fresh and verdant.

Coral woodbine and many-flowered convolvulus with passion-flower and yellow jessamine twine around these rude posts and garland with beauty their lofty pilasters. Here humming-birds expand gossamer plumage, hover over India creeper, and insert their long spiral bills into the heart of each fragile and fairy flower. Great black butterflies, with silver-spotted wings, flit from lilac and white althea to scarlet verbena beds, from forest honey-suckle to crimson butterfly-weed, from wild thyme to those unnoted children of our American flora which rejoice in Southern suns and bloom like Eden beneath Southern dews. The grasshopper sings his shrill song, the bluejay whisks amidst sycamore leaves, and the speckled woodpecker rings his horny beak against decaying bark, as, perched midway on some ancient trunk, he plies his ceaseless task. Yet there is silence. All things own the might of heat—all save wild songsters and the busy hostler's whistle.

Down sinks day's grand luminary! Above his evening couch is gathered the glorious drapery of the skies drawn over a cerulean expanse. His lingering beams shoot yellow lustre over the scene. Shadows are being lengthened from skyey tops of towering pines to the lower altitude of man's dwelling. That, with light, is insensibly withdrawn, and soon the chick-will-willow, whip-poor-will, and night-hawk raise their voices, while locusts and katydids chirp in unison, and the harsh-throated swamp-frog sends a hoarse cry from the dingle below.

AUTUMN IN THE SOUTH.

It was autumn now,—the poetic autumn of Southern latitudes. All the trees of the forest were changed in hue, save live-oaks, whose mournful moss swept the earth beneath their wide-spreading branches, and sighed as autumn gales swayed their graceful drapery to and fro, and upright pines, with their strong, tall trunks and plumy crests, which gave out a murmur resembling ocean's distant roll, and laurel-trees, consecrated to victorious wreaths, because we would vainly attempt to perpetuate human renown, and seek its symbol in "the laurel never sere." Bay-leaves were richly spotted, and came flying down at intervals, dying, but greatly beautified by the process of decay. Oaks were shrouded in crimson rich as a monarch's garb. Sassafras and china-trees were golden yellow. The tints softened one into the other, like colors in the rainbow, and everywhere enlivened the forest and adorned the uplands with a mellow grandeur soon to merge into winter's desolation. The great river, wandering in sunlight, seemed to catch the varied hues of overhanging vines, gigantic trees, and many-flowered shrubs, which garnished and glorified its sinuous windings, and drew sustenance from its exhaustless waters. Guided by nature's mysterious instincts, the jetty wild duck floated slowly on Southern waves, rejoicing in the plenty of abundant harvests, and avoiding the bleak gales of a less favored region. Bluebirds were exultant, for, abandoning the task of initiating their young in the mysteries of airy flight, they dismissed the fledglings to their fate, and, sitting free on lofty branches, sang their farewell song to summer, while thrashers and twittering sparrows joined in the lay.

Luscious were the fruits even of uncultivated nature in those Southern lands! Wild-grape arbors wound about the trunks and limbs of her forest-monarchs, and offered purple treasures to the hand of the gatherer. Persimmons, rich as the West-Indian star-apple, were so abundant as to suggest the idea of mere waste in the river swamp. Hickory nuts strewed the ground and covered the overhanging bough; sloes, black as night, hung in clusters about the way of the wanderer, and mellow maypops invited his hand; Chincapins opened their thorny coats, ready for use, and haws, the apples of the wilderness, were ripe as hope in its completion. Fanlike palmettos and aromatic heart-leaves graced earth nearer its surface, where, combined with deer-grass and wild thyme, honey-weed, and wild sunflower, a perfect wilderness of sweets delighted the senses, and carried imagination back to primeval days, when the red warrior pursued his war-path, hunted flying game, launched his light canoe, built his rude cabin, and wooed his dusky bride, himself the most picturesque adjunct of the forest scene. Here arose a green mound, the tomb of his departed ancestors, and occasionally was found an arrow-point of sharpened stone, which once winged its deathful flight through these wilds. Here sage women of Indian tribes, now only known by a name unchronicled in history, collected healing plants of great medicinal virtue, and nutritious fruits, such as the Indian potato and palmetto cabbage, which the paleface, in his agricultural wealth and Æsculapian security, cares not to note. Bell-shaped, sun-colored jasmines wildly flung their fairy-like arches over denuded trunks still standing, and forest trees in all the paraphernalia of half-clad branches, where the squirrel builds his nest and the wild bee hives its honeyed treasures. Here the fat terrapin— another and delicious form of turtle — sprawled in luxurious security on the congenial mudbank where its alderman-like proportions had been matured, and the opossum — choice game of the negro — sleek and well fed, was ready for capture. Partridges, fresh from the pea-fields, everywhere ripened, whistled and settled in whirring groups, while wild turkeys, at times, gave forth their peculiar and unmistakable gobble. Nimble, alert, and fearful, the untamed deer peered through interstices and loop-holes of the redundant undergrowth; but, with the characteristic timidity of its wild race, vanished in an instant. A russet carpet of faded grass and decaying leaves covered earth's surface in the swamp, save where a turbid mud-tinted lagoon or a black quagmire broke the level of the ground; or a fallen trunk, once the puissant supporter of many-leaved boughs, denuded of its honors, lay like bravery conquered, and under its decaying bark the lizard dwelt, and the serpent rolled its scaly length, like cunning, of which it is the type, seeking to disguise itself beneath that which bears no affinity to its own foulness.

MARGARET MAXWELL MARTIN.

THE subject of this sketch was born in Dumfries, Scotland, in 1807, and when eight years of age, accompanied her parents to America. They settled in North Carolina, at Fayetteville; but afterward removed to the beautiful city of Columbia, S. C.

In 1836, she married the Rev. William Martin, of the Methodist Episcopal Church, and shared with him the life of an itinerant missionary.

Mrs. Martin has taught a large female seminary in Columbia for nearly a quarter of a century. Her occupation has not been writing, but teaching, which has occupied her life's prime. Conscientiously she felt that she could not give the Muse her strength — her school had first claims; consequently, her poems have been recreation, and her themes chiefly religious, for she felt she owed God a peculiar debt, that she could only pay by devoting to Him her "one talent," along with all else she possessed.

Says a friend, an author of much reputation and honor to his country — William Gilmore Simms, Esq.:

"Mrs. Martin partakes of the missionary spirit with her husband; and, while he illustrates the Scriptures in sermons which bear glad tidings of salvation to hungering souls, she clothes like lessons in the more melodious garments of poesie, which appeal equally to the affections, the necessities and tastes. . . . .

"In her various wanderings as a missionary's wife, our author has been brought into neighborhoods which should have with us a classical and patriotic distinction. She has sought out and explored their place of mark, and caught up and woven into graceful verse or no less graceful prose the legends and the histories of our colonial and Revolutionary periods. The fields distinguished by the storm of battle, the ruins which mark the decayed or devastated settlement, the noble heroism which makes obscure places famous forever — these she has explored with something of the mood of 'Old Mortality,' and with her pen she has brightened the ancient memories, while newly recording the ancient deeds of heroism or simple virtue. We commend her writings as always possessing a value for the reader who desires truth in its simplicity, character in its purity, and heroism when addressed to patriotic objects."

Among Mrs. Martin's publications are "Day-Spring," "Methodism, or Christianity in Earnest," "The Sabbath-school Offering," a collection of poems and true stories, and two volumes of poetry—"Religious Poems" and "Flowers and Fruits."

That scholarly lady and graceful writer, Mrs. E. F. Ellet, is the author of the following genial notice of "Religious Poems:"

"The author of this book is an accomplished lady of Columbia, the wife of a clergyman of the Methodist Episcopal Church. She has for many years been engaged in teaching, and communion with the Muse has formed the recreation of her useful life. It is a spirit like David's, 'after God's own heart,' that here outpours itself in melody. Rare indeed is the sight of a mind attuned to all things bright and lovely and tender and sweet in nature, consecrating all its powers to the worship and service of God. Such poems, even were they not marked by high literary ability, are fragments of the language of heaven, because they breathe the life and illustrate the grace of Christianity. Faith, childlike and pure; hope, exalted; love, ardent and enduring; patience, humility, and a fair sisterhood of virtues, are reflected in these simple strains. The reader will feel a benign and holy influence stealing into his heart, and will find solace for almost every pang 'entailed on human hearts,' if he reads with a true sympathy. It would be a blessed thing if our poetical literature were more generally imbued with this fervor of religious feeling—this deep love of truth.

"The longest poem in the collection is an epic of the 'Progress of Christianity,' exhibiting God's dealings with His church, from the days of the apostles until now. The second part of this poem illustrates the power which has accompanied the progress of the religion of our Redeemer. Viewing briefly its influence in Scotland, the hallowed Sabbath of the Puritans is considered, and various pictures of human life represented, in which piety has triumphed over trial, sorrow, and death. The following are of them:

'Gaze on that lovely one: consumption's doom
Is hastening her to an untimely tomb:
Hers fortune, friends, and genius; yet all
Must yield her up at Death's relentless call;
Fades day by day the rose-tint from her cheek,
And daily grows she weaker; and, thus weak,
Is she not daunted at the approach of him—
The "King of Terrors," horrible and grim?

Will she not shrink from his unyielding clutch,
Nor seek to evade his blighting, withering touch?
Thus fragile, the last conflict will she dare?
Has she been nerved by mighty faith and prayer?
What words? "I'm ready!" 'T is her own dear voice;
She's more than conqueror—rejoice! rejoice!

. . . .

'See ye yon widowed mother o'er the bier
Of her fair babe, so precious and so dear?
'T was her sole solace since the dreadful day
When death removed her partner and her stay:
This little one, e'en sleeping or awake,
Sweet solace to the poor bereavèd spake.
It lay upon her bosom, and its breath
Was redolent of health—none dreamed of death;
When suddenly 't was from the bosom torn
Of that fond mother, now indeed forlorn;
Yet mark her faith: "The Lord is true and just;
Although he slay me, yet in him I'll trust!"'

The remaining two-thirds of the volume are composed of "Poems by the Lamplight," as the author felicitously calls her paraphrases of Scripture passages. These are applied to the incidents and interests of daily and practical life. "The Beatitudes" form a series, and seldom has sacred truth been more gratefully made familiar to the soul than in the stanzas headed "Blessed are they that Mourn."

MY SAVIOUR, THEE!

When the paths of life's young morning
First I enter'd on, unheeding
Wisdom's well-weighed words of warning;
When my feet were torn and bleeding
With the way, then I was needing
My Saviour, thee!

When the bright sun's daily duty
Lighted life's meridian, beading
That life's slender thread with beauty;
When, by that light, I was reading
Life, then, oh! how I was needing
My Saviour, thee!

When the autumn, mellow, sombre,
  Came, with all earth's hopes receding,
Casting shadows without number;
  When the signs my soul was heeding,
  Of that searing, I was needing
      My Saviour, thee!

When shall come death's midnight awful,
  And my parting soul is deeding
All its sins and sorrows woful
  To the past, dead past, when pleading
  But thy merits, I'll be needing,
      My Saviour, thee!

MRS. CATHARINE LADD.

THE name that heads this article will call a thrill of pleasure to many hearts — for this lady is "one of the most noted and successful of the teachers of the State of South Carolina," and hundreds of her old pupils, many of them now "teaching," scattered throughout the land, remember her kindness and entire unselfishness. "She is the most generous of women; her time, her talents, her worldly goods are at the command of all her friends," says one of her ex-pupils.

Mrs. Ladd is a native of Virginia — was born in October, 1810 — married when eighteen years old to Mr. Ladd, a portrait and miniature painter. Her maiden name was Catharine Stratton.

For several years after her marriage Mrs. Ladd wrote poetry, which was published in the various periodicals of the day. For three years she was a regular correspondent of several newspapers, and published a series of articles on drawing, painting, and education, which attracted considerable attention.

In 1842, Mrs. Ladd permanently settled in the town of Winnsboro', South Carolina, where she established one of the largest institutions of learning in the State, which sustained its well-deserved reputation until closed, in 1861.

Mrs. Ladd has contributed tales, sketches, essays, and poems to various journals under different *noms de plume* — as "Minnie Mayflower," "Arcturus," "Alida," and "Morna."

During the existence of the "Floral Wreath," published in Charleston by Mr. Edwin Heriott, Mrs. Ladd was a regular contributor. Mr. Heriott, in a notice of the literary talent of the South, speaking of Mrs. Ladd's poetical works, said: "They were sweet, smooth, and flowing, particularly so; but, like Scotch music, their gayest notes were sad."

In 1851, she with ardor took up the subject of education, home manufactories, and encouragement of white labor, believing that the ultimate prosperity of South Carolina would depend on it. She reasoned from a conviction that South Carolina could not long compete with the more Southern and Southwestern States in raising cotton, and an extensive system of slave labor would realize no profit.

Mrs. Ladd's plays, written at the solicitation of friends, and performed by them, were very popular. The "Grand Scheme" and "Honeymoon" were celebrated far and wide. The incidents and introduction of characters showed that she had more than ordinary talent for that species of composition. Mrs. Ladd has a wonderful knack of managing young people.

After the commencement of the war, Mrs. Ladd gave up everything to devote herself to the cause of the South. She lived for the soldiers! was elected President of the "Soldiers' Aid Association," which office she retained until the close of the war, and by her untiring exertions kept the society well supplied with clothing. Her pen was unused during the war, the needle and her personal supervision being constantly in demand. In Winnsboro', no church is built, no charity solicited, no ball, concert, tableaux, or fair — *nothing* goes on without her cheerful and ever-ready aid.

Mrs. Ladd is said to be "homely," and dresses to suit herself, never caring about the "latest fashions," ignores "hoops," and always wears her hair short. Her manner is abrupt and decided; but one instinctively feels it to be "kind."

The "Confederate flag" is said to have originated with Mrs. Ladd; the first one, we allude to. The fire of February 21st, 1865, destroyed the literary labor of thirty years. With the assistance of a Federal officer, Mrs. Ladd saved the jewels of the Masonic Lodge in the next house to hers; but the flame and smoke prevented her finding the "charter." By this time the fire had got so much ahead on her own premises, and the confusion was so great, that she lost everything.

It is said that outside of the walls of her school, Mrs. Ladd was the gay, social companion of every young lady under her charge. Following her to the school-room, you instantly felt the change: though not perhaps a word was spoken, every young lady felt it. She has a powerful will and habit of centring every thought and feeling instantly on the occupation of the moment. The confusion of voices or passing objects never seemed to disturb her when writing.

A friend of Mrs. Ladd says: "Her quick motions show the rapidity of thought. Even now, at the age of fifty-eight, were you walking behind her, you might mistake her, from the light buoyancy of step, for a young girl."

CLARA V. DARGAN.

FILLED with aspirations after the true and the beautiful—enthusiastic about music—with *a something* so bright, so star-like about her that we conceive she must be all that is fair and "lovely, and of good report"—few young writers, who have written as much as Miss Dargan, have uniformly written so well, and with so little effort. Says she, "If I did not write *de mon cœur*, I should not be able to write at all." And with study, close application — obeying Horace in placing her manuscript aside for seven years — she must accomplish something that the "world will not willingly let die." A writer who writes only when the spirit moves, hurriedly, often carelessly, scarcely ever revising but once, can hardly be expected to give the world "a masterpiece."

The subject of this sketch was born near Winnsboro', S. C. Her father, Dr. K. S. Dargan, was descended from an old Virginia family, and was noted for his extremely elegant manners and unrivalled conversational powers. Her mother was a native Charlestonian, of French Huguenot blood, a remarkably handsome and graceful lady. Clara inherits her mother's vivacity and love of repartee, fondness for society, her enthusiasm and romance, and her father's manners and conversational powers. For some years the family lived on a plantation in Fairfield, and removed to Columbia in 1852, noted as one of the most beautiful cities in the whole country *then!* Alas that rage for plunder and desire to destroy should have been so deep-seated in the being of General William Tecumseh Sherman!

At the capital of South Carolina, with the exception of a year or so, resided Miss Dargan, until the death of her parents, her father dying in 1865, and the mother two years afterward, scattering the once happy and united family — for with the fall of the Confederacy their wealth vanished.

Miss Dargan was for a time a pupil of Mrs. C. Ladd, who says: "She commenced writing when about ten years of age. I read a story written by her when about eleven; it was worthy of the matured pen of twenty. Nature has endowed her with many rich gifts, which she has not failed to improve; the budding promise of childhood has expanded, scattering many literary gems over her pathway."

Her first publication was a poem, "Forever Thine," in the "Courant," a journal which flourished a brief time under the editorship of the lamented Howard H. Caldwell. It was signed "Claudia," and appeared in 1859. During the following year she wrote several stories for the "Southern Guardian," published in Columbia, under the *nom de plume* of "Esther Chesney," under which name she wrote for the "Southern Field and Fireside" in 1861. In this year she was a successful competitor for the prize offered by the "Field and Fireside" for the best novelette—her story, "Helen Howard," sharing the honors with a novelette entitled "Our Little Annie."

Encouraged by this success, she competed for the prize offered by the "Darlington Southerner," and was successful.

In 1863, she edited the literary department of the "Edgefield Advertiser," then under the control of that elegant scholar and gentleman, Colonel Arthur Simkins: his death dissolved her connection with it. She wrote for the "Field and Fireside" during the war, and after the close of the same was a contributor to the "Crescent Monthly," the ablest periodical ever published in the South, which was edited and published in New Orleans, by William Evelyn, for a short time only. In this magazine appeared "Philip: My Son," considered by many her best story. The late Henry Timrod said "that he considered it equal to any story in 'Blackwood's.'"

Miss Dargan never mixes "ego" with her stories. They are told so naturally that the writer is forgotten entirely in the narrative. As far as a "title" is an index to a story, we append the titles of a few of Miss Dargan's tales: "Nothing Unusual," "Still Faithful," "Coming Home," "Come to Life," "Judith," "Riverlands."

"Charles Anchester," that delightful work of Miss Elizabeth Sara Sheppard, whose short life is one of the saddest of stories, is a great favorite with Miss Dargan. She considers it one of the few books that can be placed next to the "Holy Word." "It is a rare gem, an amethyst of the richest purple, set in the purest gold, chastely carved. It was and is a text-book on more subjects than music to me. So pure and earnest and calm and deep!"

Says she, in speaking of "Mendelssohn's Songs:"

"All he ever wrote, is there such music anywhere, except in heaven? People talk senselessly about Italian operas, and English and Scotch and Irish ballads; these are all very well. I think there is an air or two from 'Lucia,' and one from 'Lucretia Borgia,' and several from 'Ernani,' that are beautiful; but none will compare with those sublime, those soul-full creations."

We have noticed Miss Dargan's musical talents, and music is a highly-developed talent in the family. Clara's two brothers and sisters are not only fine singers, but perform on several instruments; and of course she is a poet. The critic and talented gentleman, author (among other things) of a series of articles on "Southern Littérateurs" — Mr. J. W. Davidson, who was Miss Dargan's literary sponsor — says: "I rank Miss Dargan first in promise among the Southern daughters of song." In person, Miss Dargan is a tall, graceful figure, good eye, and expressive face when conversing.

Said the late Henry Timrod: "If simplicity and pathos be poetry, 'Jean to Jamie' is poetry of the most genuine stamp. The verses flow with the softness of a woman's tears." (1866.)

JEAN TO JAMIE.

What do you think now, Jamie,
    What do you think now?
'T is many a long year since we parted:
Do you still believe Jean honest-hearted —
    Do you think so now?

You did think so once, Jamie,
    In the blithe spring-time:
"There 's never a star in the blue sky
That 's half sae true as my Jamie," quo' I —
    Do you mind the time?

We were happy then, Jamie,
    Too happy, I fear;
Sae we kissed farewell at the cottage door —
I never hae seen you since at that door
    This many a year.

For they told you lies, Jamie:
    You believed them a'!
You, who had promised to trust me true
Before the whole world — what did you do?
    You believed them a'!

When they called you fause, Jamie,
    And argued it sair,
I flashed wi' anger — I kindled wi' scorn,
Less at you than at them; I was sae lorn,
    I couldna do mair.

After a bit while, Jamie, —
    After a while,
I heard a' the cruel words you had said —
The cruel, hard words; sae I bowed my head —
    Na tear — na smile —

And took your letters, Jamie,
    Gathered them a',
And burnt them one by one in the fire,
And watched the bright blaze leaping higher —
    Burnt ringlet and a'!

Then back to the world, Jamie,
    Laughing went I;
There ne'er was a merrier laugh than mine:
What foot could outdance me — what eye outshine?
    "Puir fool!" laughed I.

But I'm weary o' mirth, Jamie —
    'T is hollowness a';
And in these long years sin' we were parted,
I fear I'm growing aye colder-hearted
    Than you thought ava!

I hae many lovers, Jamie,
    But I dinna care;
I canna abide a' the nonsense they speak —
Yet I'd go on my knees o'er Arran's gray peak
    To see *thee* ance mair!

I long for you back, Jamie,
    But that canna be;
I sit all alone by the ingle at e'en,
And think o' those sad words: "It might hae been" —
    Yet never can be!

D'ye think o' the past, Jamie?
    D'ye think o' it now?
'T wad be a bit comfort to know that ye did —
Oh, sair would I greet to know that ye did,
    My dear, dear Jamie!

SLEEPING.

Go down, thou sun, nor rise again;
Sink low behind the purple hills,
And shimmer over western rills,
And gild the dusky moor and plain.

Chant low, ye wildwood birds, chant low;
The cooing ringdove, so forlorn,
Her parted mate as gently mourn,
And thou, sad river, calmly flow.

I sit beside the mossy mound
That gently lies upon my dead;
And violets wave above his head,
And daisies gem the dewy ground.

The willow, like a mourning veil,
Waves quietly above my grief:
The very rustling of the leaf
Against the ruined garden-pale

Murmurs of him who sleepeth here
As sweetly in his narrow bed,
With roses pressed beneath his head,
As if his mother's arms were there.

FLIRTING WITH PHILIP.*

I saw my boy growing rapidly into manhood with the growth of his love. It was the first love of a strong and passionate nature, and a young man's first love so seldom has root in anything deeper than mere physical beauty. Margaret Thorpe was a woman to infatuate enthusiastic natures, especially of boys or very young men. There was a peculiar fascination about her rare loveliness — her manner, half childlike, half dignified — her winning voice, and willowy, graceful figure. At times I believed her utterly unconscious of Philip's sentiments toward her; she seemed to meet his impulsive demonstrations so calmly, and look almost with surprise at any sudden outburst of earnestness: but anon this changed; and when I saw her sitting with downcast eyes and drooping lash under the gaze which he fixed upon her, listening with that peculiar manner she knew so well to assume, and

* From "Philip: My Son," (1866.)

replying in a voice so tenderly cadenced, lifting her violet eyes to his, *then* I knew she felt and believed it. No woman could doubt such evidence.

Philip seemed to grow taller and grander. There was a pride in his bearing; the splendid Antinous-like head, the flashing eagle eye, the quivering finely-cut nostril, the mouth and chin shaped like a woman's in its delicate curves — all were touched with new fire, undying, immortal. As he dismounted from his horse at the gate and walked up the garden-path with his stately step, I heard Margaret, who was watching him from the window, murmur to herself, "*Philip, my king!*" Long years after I heard that same voice, broken by tears, chaunt an exquisite home-lyric, bearing a similar burden of love and pride, as she folded a tiny, white-robed Philip in her arms.

They went out often together, sometimes on horseback, sometimes walking. On these latter excursions, Margaret frequently carried a little basket on her arm, filled with sandwiches and cake, and a bottle of home-made wine; and Philip would take a fishing-rod, while out of the breast-pocket of his coat would peer the azure binding of Tennyson, the inevitable and invariable companion on all occasions, though I heard Philip declare laughingly he could not comprehend one word from preface to finis of the volume, except the poem quoted daily to the praise of his idol, "Margaret." What all this tended to I could not tell. I did not even know if Philip had declared his affection. Like one in a dream, I was content for all things to go on as they had done, and dreaded a change: but it came at last.

Late one evening I was half dozing in my arm-chair by the sitting-room window. The day had been intensely warm, and the entire household appeared overpowered by some influence in the atmosphere. Philip had ridden off before sunset. I saw him dashing down the avenue like one mad, and presently Margaret went up stairs with her light step, humming, in a mocking voice it seemed to me, a foolish little French *chanson*. I had left the two very good friends, in the veranda, after dinner, Philip smoking and playing with Margaret's ball of gold thread, while she sat demurely netting on that wonderful piece of work, half smoking-cap, half turban; but somehow, these latter days, there was a provoking air about Margaret that seemed at times to goad Philip almost to desperation. I knew now she had been teasing him again — my poor boy, who had never been denied the smallest boon in all his short, bright life.

From where I sat, I could see Margaret's white dress gleaming between the rose-vines as she sat on the steps of the piazza, half hid from view by thick clusters of multiflora and drooping sprays of clematis. She had a manuscript book in her hand — while her chin rested in the palm of the other, and her head was bowed in deep revery. There was a step on the gravel, and I heard her say, without raising her head, "Come here, Philip! I have something to read to you;" and she read in a low, steady monotone, peculiarly impressive in its exquisite modulation — flowing on like the sound of water afar off. . . . .

She stopped, and it seemed like the breaking of a dream. Philip sat at her feet: I could not see his face, but I heard his quick breath come and go, as if he panted for relief.

"Margaret," he exclaimed, in a hoarse voice, "don't torture me!"

"Torture you, Philip?"

"Yes, you know you do! Margaret, you have won me with your syren songs, and now you wreck me without a shadow of remorse or feeling."

"It is not my fault that you love me; I never encouraged you."

"Not your fault!" he exclaimed, in that passionate, uncontrollable manner which he so often used of late. "Not your fault? Did you not look up into my face with those beautiful eyes, and say plainly with them, again and again, that you accepted my love? Did you not flatter me with every cadence of your voice, every smile so deadly sweet, to believe that you knew and requited it? And now you call me to fawn at your feet, and listen to verses you knew would craze my very brain, and say it is not your fault that I love you! Oh, Margaret! Margaret!"

"Philip, you wrong me. Listen, for I *will* speak —"

He interrupted her with a gesture eloquent of despair. "Don't, Margaret! I know you are going all over those cruel words again — about my being younger than you, and how I surprise you, and the utter absurdity. All those words mean nothing to me. I don't believe any of it! Just tell me now, once and forever, do you not love me at all — not at all?"

He leaned forward eagerly, and caught her hand. There was a brief silence; and I waited to hear Margaret Thorpe speak. She only said, in a half-suppressed, breathless way, "I am engaged."

I could not endure it. I rose from my seat and went out into the piazza, where the moon, lately risen, shed her clear, pure light over the two figures on the steps; and I saw my boy sitting there as one stunned, looking straight into the false face before him — so fair, and yet so false.

"Margaret Thorpe," I said, "may God deal with you as you have dealt with my son."

FADETTE.

THE author of "Ingemisco" is a niece of the Rev. Dr. Palmer, of the old Circular Church of Charleston; consequently, a cousin of his nephew, the present Dr. Palmer, of New Orleans, to whom her book is dedicated. "Ingemisco" was published by Blelock & Co., New York, 1867. To quote from one of the poet critics of our "Southland:" *

"'Ingemisco' is the tale of a travelling party in Germany. Some of the descriptions are very able, picturesque in scenery-painting, and nervously sketched. The scene of the danger and rescue in the Alpine storm is admirable. The style is good, very fair indeed, with only a touch of feminine affectation, which will wear off as she writes more. There is plenty of that sweet glimmer and soft air-music of romance which we miss so much in most of the fiction of modern days; and much that reminds of the pleasant mirth and genial love that charm us so gladsomely in 'Quits' and the 'Initials.' There is a wild legend, too, told by the Swiss peasant-girl, Luise, of the ancient monastery and the anchorite's cave, which are connected with the fate of Margaret Ross, the heroine of the present tale. It is worthy of the wonderful legendary lore of old Deutschland, and is well told. It is something, in these dull, unbelieving days, to catch into the nostrils of the soul a breath of the witching fragrance of those delicious old superstitions; and I bless the charming craftswoman that she has allowed this quaint embroidery of Sir Walter's magic mantle to linger on her fair shoulder. Thank heaven, there is no pedantry! It is all true woman throughout, with not a bit of the blue-stocking, only traces in plenty of close and artist-like observation in travel and taste in reading. Knowledge is never obtruded. It is a great relief in these days to read clear English, unbroken by huge scientific technicalities or mythological allusions *ad nauseam*, as if the reader were to be put to school again through the medium of a book pretending to be one of amusement.

"The characters are well conceived, and painted with great power. I mean the *two*, the only ones we ever care a button about in a real warm romance of love. Margaret is a proud, high-souled woman, a superb nature, with a world of tenderness in her heart, but with a world of scorn for any baseness, even though born of passionate love for her. The wrong done her by her lover in marrying her against her will, thus forcing her to break her plighted

* C. Woodward Hutson.

word, rouses her strong nature, and shows the true woman better than almost any other trial of trust could show that wonderful mechanism of the affections. Her Ernst, the gallant Polish exile, Count Zalkiewski, despite his one great error, for which he paid so dearly in her heart's estrangement from him, is a noble being, and interests the reader deeply. It is truly a wonderful book for the first. Much as I admire it, it is not half so good as she is. That winter visit I made to the great river region is bright in my memory with many a picture of the pleasant and hospitable homes of transplanted Carolina families. Among those carefully kept visions of a most charming tour, not the least refreshing is that which was lit by the smile of one who is now a princess in Parnassus. As I read her book I could not but rejoice that so true a heart-tale was written by neither Titanide nor Encyclopædе, but by a quiet, *natural* maiden, sweet and modest as the violet she loves."

The "Round Table," New York, in a review of "Ingemisco," concludes by saying:

"As a whole, this book contains so much that gives promise of future excellence, that we hope the authoress will not shrink from that steadfast and patient toil which alone can insure her, in the sequel, that enviable position to which, no doubt, she aspires."

Another Northern reviewer says:

"This book, if we do not greatly mistake, marks the advent of a new and very conspicuous star in the firmament of letters. 'Ingemisco' is an exceedingly clever performance in itself, and involves a promise of richer fruits in the future. The plot is conceived with originality and developed with skill, the characters are drawn with a bold and symmetrical pencil, the descriptions of still life are painted with peculiar gorgeousness of coloring, the dialogue is animated, and some of the situations strikingly dramatic, and the work is illuminated throughout with those subtle glimpses of scholarship which signalize a genuine culture as contradistinguished from the inapposite *sputter* of encyclopædic empiricism. We wish to mark this last statement with the stress of a strong emphasis. In casually turning over the leaves of this book, the eye cannot fail of catching brief and pertinent citations from the most beautiful things in French, Italian, and German literature, and occasionally—as if with a hand deliberately restrained—from the ancient classics. In every instance, these citations are exactly and nicely appropriate to the person, the situation, and the circumstances—are, in short, an unpremeditated outburst of the author's culture, at the point where they spontaneously arise, and not an unnaturally contrived occasion for a palpably meretricious display. To say of a young American author that he brings to his initial effort in the department of fiction a highly-cultivated mind, is to mark an exceptional advantage, whose influence is second only to the possession of genius. But this last great quality is really the dominating feature of this book. It appears in every page, equally attested by colloquy, characterization, or description. In the very first chapter there is a description of an Alpine storm, in which the life of the heroine is almost hopelessly involved, which we do not hesitate to affirm is one of the finest we have ever perused, notwithstanding the subject is equally attractive and familiar, and has exercised all manner of pens, from the 'Great Unknown' to that vast company of little ones who yearly travel the road to oblivion, and contribute to the manufacture of trunks.

"'Ingemisco' will remind every discriminating reader of those beautiful creations which shed, a few years ago, a splendid but fugitive halo around the world of letters—'Initials' and 'Quits.' It is conceived mainly in the same vein as these charming productions. But the pen of 'Fadette' is clearly distinguished from that of the gifted daughter of Lord Erskine, and is, in no respect that we can discover, imitative. On the contrary, its individuality asserts itself constantly, almost to the degree of harshness. We mention the resemblance in question only to indicate what seems to us the great fault of this book. The writer has attempted to condense an interesting story and a book of travels into the same volume. This will not do; it never has done. And, so long as a person engaged in the perusal of a narrative dramatically conceived and evolved must consider it a nuisance to be abruptly interrupted by substituting a book of travels (however well written) for the one in his hands, it never will do. No examples, however distinguished, can justify such a departure from the fundamental laws of art. A novelist is entitled to incorporate into his story just so much of the merely outward conditions of the selected theatre of his fable as is indispensably necessary to the illustration of the supposed facts thereof: if he go beyond this, he is irrelevant—the interest flags—Homer sings of ships—the reader sleeps.

"With this exception, we have only commendation for this admirable book; and we cordially greet—shall we say, the fair authoress, as her *nom de plume* implies?—into the 'magic circle' where fairies dance upon the greensward and imagination weaves into forms palpable and real the colors of the rainbow."

"Randolph Honor" was published by Richardson & Co., New York, (1868,) and was cordially welcomed by the reading world and literary journals. The "Round Table" said:

"In 'Randolph Honor' we have pictures of life which are not wanting in power, and descriptions of scenery drawn with truth and delicacy. The story is not sensational, and its moral tone is unexceptionable; but the plot is meagre, and the great difficulties of character-painting the authoress has not yet mastered. . . . .

"In this work, as in 'Ingemisco,' there appears so fair a promise of future excellence, that we feel justified in saying that the young authoress who produced them is capable, with increased cultivation and mature thought, of achieving something much better than she has yet offered to the public."

And the "poet critic" must have his delightful talk about this delightful second book recorded:

"'Randolph Honor' is a marked improvement on 'Ingemisco.' The characters are ably drawn; and, what is particularly pleasant in this age that gives us spasmodic portraitures for real dramatic delineation, they are ladies and gentlemen. The story is of the war, and is staunchly Southern, true to the ring of those noble tones that died away only when smothered in blood.

"The style *is* faulty. It is injured by a somewhat glaring mannerism, resulting from a tendency to poetic inversion in the mode of expression. But this blemish will wear away as the young writer grows in practice. She is certainly versatile. This last work is totally different from 'Ingemisco.' She is clear, so far, of that vice of the too rapidly productive writers of fiction, whose novels troop out from the publishing-houses in such numbers we cannot keep the run of them—she does not repeat herself. There is, too, great variety in the story, and frequent changes of the locality, perhaps too frequent for the maintenance of the spell upon the reader; for the attachment we form for places in actual life we carry with us into our ideal life, and we like fiction to hallow for us certain spots in association with the persons of the story who have won our liking, and not remove us too capriciously from the scenes thus endeared to us.

"This principle is violated here. We are hurried from the charming Maryland manor-house, Randolph Honor, to Baltimore; from Baltimore to the Steamer 'St. Nicholas,' (the capture of which, by the way, is graphically described); from there and thereabouts to Charleston; from Charleston to Arkansas; and from Arkansas to all sorts of places—the prairies and elsewhere. But the novelty of scenery and of mode of life, I must say, compensate in a great measure for the distracted feeling one experiences in this flitting to and fro. The dramatic action is full of fire and motion. The lady is loved to the heart's content of the reader bent on his heroine's being duly honored. The young men are dashing cavaliers, worthy of the sunny soil they fight for; and 'Miss Charley' is a dashing damsel, much nearer to Joan of Arc and the Maid of Saragossa than Dr. Simms' famous swamp-rider, 'Hurricane Nell.' The life in the West is a fine picture, and shows up well the strong contrasts of culture and roughness in a country of comparatively recent settlement. The darkey wedding is pleasantly described, and the feudal picture it presents of mutual good feeling between beneficent suzerain and attached retainers, readily recognized by us, who have lived under the system, as truth itself, will do well to put alongside the present rancorous hate that glows from the pages of such as Helper of 'No-Joque.'

"Need I say to you who have read the earlier work that the poetic soul of this lady delights in the sweet tenderness and fragrance and the bright bloom of the out-door world, which ought always to lift our hearts to the God who made it so lovely for us. Yes, she loves the good creatures that are so eloquent, though to the material organ they may seem dull. She is of those 'Sunday children' who have the poetic instinct, and to whom nothing that the Divine artist has made is ever mute. Nature, with all its fulness of life and light and freshness, she dearly loves; and the blessed beauty and radiance and vocal melody with which it surges on the soul in a thousand soft wavelets of light and scent and sound, rippling rare undertones of harmony into the dreamy recesses of the heart, draw from her ever and anon tributes of love and praise, and a glad poetic dallying with its wondrous richness in change and varying form."

"Ingemisco" was written with no idea of publication — merely to lighten some heavy hours of the war-time for the author's home circle; and "Randolph Honor," though with imaginary characters, is, regarding war-incidents, drawn from sketches of that which came within the author's own experience or knowledge.

"Fadette's" last publication bears the imprint of Claxton, Remsen & Haffelfinger, and is called "Sea-Drift." Further than that, "Fadette" is a native of South Carolina; her name "we dinna care to tell," but rest assured she cannot long remain masked.

Having told, in the language of others, what her prose is, we will let her poetry tell its own tale.

A PRAYER.

Lord God of Hosts! we lift our heart to Thee!
  Our straining eyes lift vainly toward Thy throne;
  Earth's mists and shadows are so mighty grown,
The gleam of seraph wings we no more see.

Lord God of Hosts! we lift our heart to Thee!
  Our hands are fettered down by galling chains —
  No more the sceptre in our grasp remains —
Beneath the yoke we pass, with Liberty.

Lord God of Hosts! we lift our heart to Thee!
  Our brows are bowed beneath Thy crown of thorn;
  'T is heavy with the blood of those we mourn,
It darkles with the life-blood of the free.

Lord God of Hosts! we lift our heart to Thee!
A ceaseless moan wails on in breeze of morn,
Through all the busy din of day upborne,
And when the gloaming broodeth o'er the sea.

O God of Hosts! turn Thou and hear that moan—
No Southern lips are strangers to its sound,
And, shuddering, in the merry frolic's round
Our prattling children catch its monotone.

Strong men weep now, who never wept before;
Girl-voices sorrow loud and passionate;
Black-stolèd women yearning at Thy gate;
Prayer-worn lips quiver, faded eyes brim o'er.

Thy gate—it is the only open door—
Where standeth Azrael, beckoning one by one,
By which we leave, our pilgrim-goal being won,
This drear God's Acre, crimson-drenched in gore.

Each lowly grave our mountains proudly mark—
Death seared the land throughout with fiery tread:
O Thou who gavest tears to Lazarus dead,
Behold, our mother-country lieth stark.

It is too late for us to raise or save—
We struggled with the blood-hound at her throat,
We saw his savage glare above her gloat:
Teach us to kneel, O God, beside her grave!

Teach us to kneel—to Thee alone, O God!
The tyrant fain would spurn us at his feet—
The gore upon our mother's winding-sheet
Would brand us murderers, trickling through the sod.

Teach us to kneel—teach us to pray, O God!
Not for revenge—for vengeance is Thine own—
But that Thou hear our ceaseless suppliant moan,
And that Thou see we bow beneath Thy rod.

Lord God of Hosts! do Thou lift up our hearts!
Let them not lower 'neath our fetters' weight;
Let not our war-worn heroes cringe to fate,
Nor barter honor in the foe's full marts.

The laurels in God's Acre shelter Thou—
  Let still the people's patriotic tears
  Wash from their shining crests the dust of years,
And dews from heaven vivify each bough.

Oh, garner Thou the lowlier flowers that rest
  Beneath the sod until Thou bid them rise!
  Receive them, meet and deathless sacrifice,
And take them, gracious Father, to Thy breast.

Break Thou, Lord God, our Captive's lengthening chain,
  Wherewith the foe hath him and Freedom bound;
  From deep to deep its clanking doth resound—
Our hearts beat heavy to its dull refrain.

Hear Thou his prayer, to whom alone he prays;
  In loving mercy guard his widowed wife;
  With honor hedge his orphaned children's life;
Untarnished keep Thou aye his hard-won bays.

Lord God! to Thee with him our heart we give:
  O Thou! who heardest Mary's stricken moan,
  Roll from our mother's grave the sealèd stone—
Say to the dead within, "Come forth, and live!"

ANNIE M. BARNWELL.

MISS BARNWELL is one of the youngest of our "Southland Writers," and one who desires to make "literature" her profession.

Annie M. Barnwell is a native of Beaufort, S. C., the eldest daughter of Thomas Osborn Barnwell — until the war, a planter of that place. She was educated entirely in the quiet town of her birth, and, until the war, had seldom quitted it.

From earliest childhood she was passionately fond of reading, and the world of books was a delightful reality to her. Her life has been spent in a narrow circle; and, until the war, it was a very quiet one; but no Southerner can have passed through the last eight years without thinking and feeling deeply and passionately.

Although fond of writing from childhood, noted as the best composition writer in school, she never published anything until 1864, when a poem appeared in a local journal. In the spring of 1866, encouraged by the approval of Rev. George G. Smith, of Georgia, she wrote for publication under the *nom de plume* of "Leroy," a name chosen as a slight tribute of love and respect to the memory of one who holds the first place on her list of friends, the late accomplished Dr. Leroy H. Anderson, of Gainesville, Alabama.

Under this signature she has been a frequent contributor to "Scott's Magazine," (Atlanta,) and the "Land we Love," (Charlotte, N. C.) To the kind and generous conduct of General D. H. Hill, editor of the latter-named magazine, Miss Barnwell owes much, for it encouraged her to persevere in her intention of becoming an author, when the difficulties which lie in the path of every beginner would otherwise, perhaps, have frightened her into turning back.

Miss Barnwell's style is easy and graceful, with the fault of young writers generally, using the "adjectives" profusely. Her most ambitious effort is a tale, entitled "Triumphant," which we hope may be the beginning of many triumphs in the path she has chosen. She resides in Beaufort.

THE BARNWELLS OF SOUTH CAROLINA.

Look forth on yonder field! Lit by the first rays of an October sun, two armies may be seen prepared for battle. On the slope of the hill rests motionless a host, over whom floats a glittering banner, with the device of a warrior worked in gold and enriched with flashing jewels. Upon the opposite eminence the rival army is drawn up in stern array, awaiting the conflict, and eager to bear forward "the three lions of Normandy." A sudden shout of "God help us!" and they dash onward to the fray. From the hillside that shout is answered by the Saxon war-cry, "God's Rood! Holy Rood!" and the battle is begun. Higher and higher the sun rises o'er that fierce and bloody scene. Now, right, perched on the banner of the golden warrior, seemed about to triumph; but anon it is borne back, and the parting beams of the day-god rest on the three lions, floating in solitary pride o'er the hard-fought field of Hastings. The golden warrior trails in the dust, where among his lifeless defenders lies the bloody corpse of Harold, "the last of the Saxon kings." The mighty hand of Norman William grasped the contested prize, and the fair realm of "Merrie England" is the spoil of the conqueror. Among his followers is one who bears the name of Barnevelt or Barnewall, ancestor of the present family of Barnwell.

And now turn from this scene of conflict, and follow to the shores of the Emerald Isle. In the midst of a group of mail-clad warriors and fierce barbarians, stands a fair-haired maiden, daughter and heiress of the savage monarch, Dermot Mac Morrough, king of Leinster. It is her nuptials which are being celebrated in sight of blood and death, and her spouse is yon dark leader of the Norman knights, Richard de Clare, Earl of Strigul; better known as Strongbow. Among the knights who with him made Ireland their home, was Sir Michael de Barnewell, founder of the houses of Kingsland and Trimblestone.

Queen Elizabeth sits alone, with a picture in her hand. It represents several youthful and high-born gentlemen, grouped together, with a motto beneath, asserting that a common object, a common danger is their bond of union. Well knows the queen that this object is her assassination, and the restoration of the Roman Catholic religion, by raising Mary, the captive Queen of Scotland, to the English throne. Closely she studies each form and feature, that they may not approach her unknown and unheeded. Foremost in the group is Anthony Babington, and beside him stands young Barnwell, companion in arms of Strongbow.

Who has not pictured to himself the fatal 30th of January, when the grave, sad face of Charles I. looked forth for the last time upon the realm of which he was the sovereign — then was laid calmly on the block, while he murmured his last word, "Remember!" Who has not thought of his bigot son, pining in a foreign land for the crown his own conduct had lost. Faithful to the house of Stuart, the Barnwells forfeited wealth and power in their defence, as did so many of the Irish nobles.

The daylight is slowly waning in the depths of a mighty forest. With stealthy tread a band of bronzed and stalwart men pass beneath the overhanging branches. Among them are seen tall, erect, sinewy forms, their natural copper hue almost lost in the gaudy paint with which they are covered. Soldiers the band surely are; yet no plume waves in the breeze, save the feathery tops of the dark and mournful pines, and strange bunches of stiff, ungraceful feathers, stuck in the black hair of the wild red-men. The hunter's unerring rifle takes the place of sword and spear, and steel helmet and glittering armor are alike unseen. But the foemen — where are they? Lurking behind the giant trees, crouching low in the thick underbrush, the sudden whistle of the poisoned arrow, as it speeds its unerring flight to the heart of some brave soldier, alone attests their presence. Surely here, in this wild scene, speaking of a new and yet unsettled land, can be found no scion of the proud old Norman stock! Yet, in the veins of yon bold leader of that sturdy band flows the blood of him who fought at Hastings. Colonel John Barnwell had, at an early age, embraced the Protestant faith, and, being discarded by his stern sire, sought a home on the smiling sea-coast of South Carolina. Amid the forests of her fair sister, the Old North State, he did battle with the cruel Tuscarora Indians, and by his prowess won the name of Tuscarora John.

The Revolution came, and found their fiery Norman blood flowing freely in the cause of liberty and right. It is midnight on the broad Atlantic. The English brig "Packhorse," bound to New York, with a band of American prisoners on board, is pursuing her solitary way. Suddenly the deep stillness is broken by shots, cries, and groans. A brief struggle, and the brig is in possession of the prisoners, her course changed for Wilmington, N. C. Well did these brave patriots deserve their liberty. When the British threatened, if the Americans retaliated for the murder of Colonel Hayne, to sacrifice these prisoners, they unanimously signed a paper requesting that no thought of them should prevent the authorities acting as they deemed best for the welfare of their country. Among this band were two grandsons of Tuscarora, John and Edward Barnwell, and his great-grandson, William Elliott, uncle of the gifted and eloquent Bishop of Georgia, and grandfather of the late gallant General Elliott.

Robert Barnwell, another grandson of the Indian hero, at the age of seventeen had received sixteen wounds in the service of his country, and yet lived to take a prominent position in the Legislature of South Carolina and in the halls of Congress. It was his most fervent prayer for his children that they should be remarkable as devoted servants of Christ. And truly has that petition been answered. One of his sons, the polished, courteous gentleman, the eminently wise and Christian statesman, who bears his name, is still spared to his bleeding country. The other, that zealous soldier of the Cross, who labored so faithfully and with such rare success in his Master's vineyard, has entered into his rest. But his mantle fell upon his peculiarly gifted and cultivated son, whose kindly care and heavenly teachings cheered the sick and dying hours of so many of our gallant soldiers. He, too, has passed to his eternal home, but his name lives a household word throughout the South. The brilliant talents of both father and son, and yet more, their ardent, devoted consecration of their all to the service of Christ, shed a radiance around the old Norman name purer and holier than the fame of the proudest conqueror that earth can boast.

The late war found the descendants of the patriots of '76 still at their post, willingly risking fortune, home, and life in the service of the South. Six brave hearts, which beat with love for her, are forever still; and those who live must labor for their daily bread — many deprived of their old and cherished homes. Yet, like all gallant, true-hearted men of the South, they have put their shoulder to the wheel and shrank not from the toil. Methinks they are a fairer representative of the old chivalrous race, though "lands and honors, wealth and power" are no longer theirs, than the titled, sonless old man in London, who, with the snows of seventy winters on his head, still lingers on the confines of the spirit-world, and bears the name of Baron Trimblestone.

Near Dublin, in Ireland, stands the ancient fortress of Drimnagh Castle, once the stronghold of the Barnwells, now in the hands of strangers. The front seems one solid mass of ivy, save where there are openings in the rich, dark green for the windows. The moat, too, is in good repair, and the strong wall still remains, but the old masters live in other homes; yet many of the name, reduced to the humble walks of life, linger around the old castle of their former chiefs. The noble spirit of the days of chivalry still animates them in the midst of poverty and toil; for a late traveller in Ireland mentioned the incident of a child being saved from drowning by a young Barnwell, who in the attempt, alas! lost his own brave life.

And so it is in South Carolina. The old homesteads where the sires and grandsires of the present generation dwelt in refinement, ease, and plenty, where

> "Still they bore without abuse
> The grand old name of gentleman,"

are now the desecrated spoil of the foe. In those old halls which have echoed to the merry Christmas shout, the enemy's foot has trod, and negroes have held their revels.

Picture to yourself a clear, breezy spring morning; the sun shining brightly, the glad notes of hundreds of feathered songsters making the air vocal with their music, and fair nature smiling in her fresh green robes. Pass through this broad avenue of royal oaks, the branches meeting overhead in a majestic canopy of richest green: up the steps, through piazza, hall, and parlor, come with me to a second piazza beyond. And now look forth! Dancing, flashing, sparkling in the sunlight, roll the waters of Broad River on their way to the mighty ocean. Along her banks stretch the green shores, broken here and there by peaceful homes. Yonder glides a snowy sail, sure token of a party seeking the rare sport of drum-fishing. On the right, another avenue of live-oaks winds down to the white, sandy beach; while in front is a small flower-garden. Oh, what new, glad, bounding life seems poured into every vein by that fresh salt-breeze sweeping over the blue river! Heart, mind, and body drink in its inspiriting freshness, and involuntarily you exclaim: "O Lord! our Governor, how excellent is thy name in all the world!"

Such is Laurel Bay, on Port Royal Island, the old homestead of the Barnwells, now in the hands of the United States Government.

The shades of night rest on the scene I have attempted to portray. With stealthy tread, hushed breath, and watchful eye, two forms glide 'neath the deep shadow of the trees, in the direction of the house: they are both young, and both wear the uniform of Confederate gray. The absence of any badge speaks them privates in the service of their country. Yet in their veins flows pure and unsullied the same fiery Norman blood that nerved the arms of the followers of William the Conqueror and Strongbow; that beat in the loyal hearts of those who, with the noble Duke of Ormond, went forth to battle for the royal martyr; that bade old Tuscarora be calm and fearless in the midst of hidden dangers; and that was poured forth freely by the patriots of the Revolution. Suddenly a light flashing through the trees bids them pause, and the loud sounds of uncouth revelry meet their ears. Who can be holding high festival in this desolated home? Another step — and what a spectacle is revealed! Negroes throng the piazza and rooms beyond — lounging on the chairs and sofas — dancing in the old parlor. Shame! shame! The scene is too revolting to dwell on.

Whether this old homestead will ever be the abode of intellectual refinement, hospitality, mirth, and Christian love, as in other days — rising, like the crest of her former masters, a phœnix from the ashes of her desecration — God alone knoweth. But could those brave old ancestors look down from their homes of rest, they would find no stain on their ancient shield; and their descendants still hold firmly to their proud old motto: "*Malo mori quam fœdari.*"

ON SOUTHERN LITERATURE.

Hitherto the South has contributed a comparatively small share to the great mass of American publications. This was, perhaps, owing to the truth of that old opinion that poverty is the soil best calculated to render talent and genius fruitful, not to produce them, for they are rare plants, peculiar to no soil, no climate, and no season ; but merely to stimulate them to a fairer growth, and to ripen their rich and varied fruit. We were a prosperous people; our slaves were carefully housed, fed, and clothed by the masters, who were their protection from those blessings of the free children of poverty, exposure, starvation, and nakedness. We were not obliged to write for our daily bread, and so many who, under other circumstances, would have wielded a successful pen, were content, instead, to satisfy the cravings of their intellect with copious draughts from the cup of knowledge prepared by other hands. Now the case is widely different. Never, perhaps, in the annals of the world, were there so many people of education, culture, and refinement suddenly reduced at the same moment to such a state of absolute and painful poverty. In this condition there is but one alternative — we must work or starve: but where is work to be obtained such as we can perform? Many of us have received the best advantages of education, and with such, food for the mind is a necessity second only to that of food for the body. They cannot get books; and if they could, time is too needful for the task of earning bread, to be spent in anything which does not aid in that object. In this emergency, they seize the pen, and become authors. Eagerly, hungrily they write, striving to feed body and mind at once; now disheartened by the frequent failure of their efforts, now cheered by a feeble gleam of success, but always struggling on for bare existence. Chatterton, poor, lonely, gifted boy, insulted, proud, and shut in by so dark a sky, might well serve as the type of those who will one day be remembered and honored as the founders of a Southern literature.

And it is now, while we are thus at the commencement of our work, that no effort should be spared to lay a sure and strong and pure foundation, that will resist time and change and decay. Is it poetry that is needed to call forth our highest efforts? Surely, we can scarcely have it in a fuller measure than at present. Is it education and refinement? We will never have more than is ours to-day. Is it love of country, and the wish to twine a wreath of immortal bays to crown her brow? Ah! never in her brighter days of pride and hope did we love our sunny land as now, in her hour of woe and desolation — never did we long more eagerly to do her honor. Is it a noble, animating spirit, the sight of gallant deeds and priceless sacrifices, of heroes and of martyrs? Surely, surely the memory of our glorious struggle has not faded yet — we have not yet forgotten the heroes and martyrs, the victories and the sacrifices, the noble deeds and the fearless deaths that marked our brief day of freedom. Or is it examples of faith and trust and self-forgetfulness, of dignity, manliness, and stainless honor that we crave? Look, oh! look around you, and in the lives of thousands of our suffering people you will find examples of all these as fair and as bright as the record of the heroes and martyrs of other days — the Cranmers, Ridleys, and Latimers, the Hoopers, John Bradfords, and Anne Askews, whose names shine like stars amidst the darkness of cruelty, sin, and oppression by which they are surrounded.

MARY CAROLINE GRISWOLD.

IN 1864, the "Southern Field and Fireside" published several novelettes and poems, by "Carrie," which were interesting and naturally written, and consequently popular. "Zaidee: A Tale of the Early Christians," was a very pleasing story; as was "Bannockburn," the longest of these novelettes.

"Carrie," or, rather, Miss Griswold, is rather young, as yet, to have made much progress in the literary line; although, from her published novelettes, etc., we feel warranted in giving her a place among "Southland Writers," as a writer of much promise.

Miss Griswold is a resident of Charleston, S. C.

THE MYSTERIES.

Oh! mystery of mysteries—is Life!
This constant tumult in the human breast,
Where passions wage their never-ending strife,
And hearts still *dream*, but nothing *know*, of rest.
Moments of joy to every heart are known,
But moments only—so shadowy, so brief!
The diamond changes to the worthless stone,
And vanished joys but darken present grief!

Oh! mystery of mysteries—is Love!
To know but *one* in this broad world of ours;
To feel, *one* smile brighten the heaven above
And give new beauty to the fragrant flowers.
To know but one—to live but in one life!
To feel *that* gone, all happiness were fled,
The sunlight darkened, the heart with anguish rife,
And joy and hope lie buried with the dead.

Oh! mystery of mysteries—is Death!
Oh! sad and strange, one moment to behold
The face we love smile back the love we give,
The next, perchance, in death's embrace lie cold:

From the chill touch to shrink in wondering awe —
  Shrink from the casket where once our jewel lay.
Death's mystery is great! An angel spirit sings,
  And we beneath Death's shadow weep for our lost and pray.

THE WHITE CAMELIA.

Circled with glossy leaves, in queenly power
Rested in its purity the marble flower:
No balmy fragrance swept the silent air,
A *dream* of sweetness only lingered there,
Like to a loving heart that stands alone
With o'er each gushing thought a silence thrown:
'Neath the snow-drifts of pride it calmly lies,
Lives in the world awhile, then droops and dies;
Alone with an inward grief that none divine,
It, like the flower, falls without a sign:
Fit emblem thus of pride in all its power,
In dreamy stillness lay — the *marble flower!*

THE BEAUTIFUL SNOW.

The snow-flakes are falling swiftly,
  The children are wild with glee
As they dream of the merry pastime
  The morrow's morn will see;
And faces are bright in their youthful glow,
As they watch the falling, beautiful snow!

Within that pleasant parlor
  The mother alone is still;
She feels not the snow that falls without,
  But her throbbing heart is chill
As she turns away from the fireside glow
To look abroad on the beautiful snow!

God help those eyes despairing
  That gaze at the snow-clad earth;
God pity the mad rebellion
  That in that heart has birth!
The children are gone — and a sound of woe
Breaks through the night, o'er the beautiful snow!

The woman's face all ghastly
  Lies pressed to the window-pane,
But no sound of human anguish
  Escapes her lips again:
'T was the cry of a woman's heart crushed low,
Whose hopes lay dead 'neath the beautiful snow.

The firelight glanced and sparkled,
  Despite of the mourner's gloom;
It gilded the books and pictures,
  And lit up the cheerful room,
While through the casement its crimson glow
Threw a band of light o'er the beautiful snow.

She shrank from the mocking brightness
  That sought to win her there:
Far better to watch the snow-flakes,
  Than gaze at a vacant chair—
A chair, that never again could know
A form *now* still 'neath the beautiful snow.

Many a night-watch had he known,
  And many a vigil kept,
While the snow-flakes fell around him,
  And all his comrades slept;
For his heart was strong in its patriot glow
As he gazed abroad at the beautiful snow.

He, too, had watched the snow-flakes,
  And laughed as they whirled him by,
Had watched as they drifted round him,
  With bright, undaunted eye—
And *now* there rests not a stone to show
The soldier's grave 'neath the beautiful snow.

The mourner's eye roved sadly
  In search of the vacant chair,
To rest in loving wonder
  On a young child slumbering there;
And she caught from the baby-lips the low
Half-murmured words—"The beautiful snow!"

With a sudden, passionate yearning,
  She caught him to her breast,

And smiled in the eyes, that in their calm
  Rebuked her own unrest—
Eyes that had caught their kindling glow
From the father that lay 'neath the beautiful snow.

Again she stood at the casement,
  And smiled at her baby's glee,
As he turned from the feathery snow-flakes
  Her answering smile to see—
Her little child, that never could know
The father that lay 'neath the beautiful snow!

Ah! many a widowed heart doth throb
  In bitterness, alone—
And many an orphan's tears still fall
  Above some honored stone:
For hearts must bleed, and tears must flow
For the loved and lost, 'neath the beautiful snow!

MISS JULIA C. MINTZING.

JULIA CAROLINE MINTZING, the subject of this sketch, comes from one of the most prominent and highly respected families of South Carolina. She is a thorough Southern woman, and she has that intensity of character that distinguishes those women of the South who are truly representatives of their section. By ancestry and nativity a South-Carolinian — her father and mother both having been born in that State — it is not strange that Miss Mintzing should possess that self-consciousness of the Carolinian, which, carried in the persons of statesmen into the political arena of the country, has done so much to mould the public opinion of the South, and, indeed, of Democrats everywhere. In these days of woman-rightism — when the weaker sex tilt against the sterner, mounted upon the hobby of Reform — it would perhaps seem invidious to refer to our sister as one who has always taken a deep and absorbing interest in the politics of the country. But the interest which Miss Mintzing, even from early childhood, has ever manifested in the political questions of the day, has arisen, we may presume, from the necessities of the case. Reared in that fierce school of States Rights which admits of no parleying and no compromise, it would not be singular to find one embodying in herself all the proud traditions of her State, giving to the cause, which in South Carolina partakes almost of the sanctity of a religious creed, her enthusiastic reverence. As the French would say, *ça va sans dire.* This, however, in passing.

In contemplating Miss Mintzing as a writer — our main purpose — we must judge her not so much by what she has done as by her capabilities and her promise of future performance. Her writings, up to within a recent period, have not been voluminous. Circumstances which so many tenderly nurtured of the South have had reason to deplore — the desolations produced by war and rapine — have had much to do with Miss Mintzing's literary efforts. The losses sustained by her family during the war were severe. Happily, the subject of this sketch has found it within her power to call upon her mental armory for weapons wherewith to resist the too pressing encroachments of pecuniary adversity. She has found place for her writings in some of the best magazines and literary papers of the country, and in the pages and columns of these has laid the seeds of a reputation which only needs time to insure its blossoming into fame.

From Miss Mintzing's writings we give two selections, one of poetry, and the other of prose. We commence with the poem:

VICTOR AND VICTIM.

Only a lance in her quivering breast,
Fatally poised in the tourney's jest,
Only a wreck on life's stormiest sea
Wildly adrift for Eternity!
Only a shade on a summer sky,
Only the break of a careless tie,
Only a prayer — O Father — God!
Her passionate cry beneath the rod!
Comfort her, Lord!
Shield with thy sword
From all who oppress,
From all who distress.
Man and his falsity,
Pettiest mockery!
Woman the slanderer,
Friend, foe, and panderer —
Grant her redress!

Why did she pause for the Lorelei's song?
Why did she listen and dream so long?
Why was she blind to the dazzling snare
That lured her on to the end so sair?
Why were the eyes so tender and blue —
And the trysting vows that seemed so true!
Why the soft touch — the passionate thrill,
And the lips that kissed away reason's will!
Back, ye sweet memories!
Off, ye fond reveries!
Hark to the world!
She is but human —
Only a woman!
So crush all feeling,
Weakness revealing,
For we are maskers,
Hypocrite taskers!

Life a poor summer day,
And we the potter's clay
Toys to be hurled!

Was he so brave thus to tilt for her life —
Was he a man in this dalliance-strife?
Flash shield and buckler — blaze helmet and lance
Quick to this tourney — valiant advance!
But the hand that is poising with steadiest aim
Shall quiver with weakness and tremble with pain
When the ghosts of those moments swoop fierce from unrest,
And falsehood's Nemesis holds hell in his breast!
True, 't is but a lance
In the road's advance,
And but a woman
Proves to be human!
Only a heart
Breaks in the jesting;
'T is but a part
Played in life's testing!
Then pity her, God,
As faint, 'neath Thy rod,
Weary in the agony,
She treads her Calvary!

As a writer of prose, Miss Mintzing is just as earnest in her style and in her manner of expressing herself as she shows herself to be in her poetry. Indeed, this earnestness of character is one of her marked attributes. We can well imagine that she would be one to rejoice in the courage of Joan of Arc and in the devoted patriotism of Charlotte Corday — choosing these as memorable examples of the heroism of her sex.

In an article upon Gœthe and Schiller, the illustrious German authors, published in the "Land we Love," Miss Mintzing compares these two masters of the literature of Germany. The following passages from the article in question will afford a fair understanding of Miss Mintzing's characteristics as a writer of prose:

The old city of Frankfort on the Main claims the birth of Johann Wolfgang Von Gœthe, August 28th, 1749. Sprung from the aristocracy, nursed and petted by his beautiful child-mother, his bright, sunny childhood passed.

Impressionable and fiery, we find him, while yet a boy, agonized by the intensity of his first love.

But the heart that through a long life was only to dispense successively, did not break; though the boy-love has, with the boy-faith, so exquisitely idealized the heroine's name in that Faust which thrilled all Germany. Despite the ethics of the poem-drama, which the "rigid righteous" so vehemently decry, the sweet, girlish trust, the faith and pathos of Margaret's love, hold the heart against all judgment.

The pretty poetry of Mignon's episode in Wilhelm Meister pleases, and the refrain of her child-sorrow is still echoing in our hearts, as she pleads for her return to that sunny land where "the gold-orange blooms;" but Margaret, man's spiritualized earth-love, attracts with a sad, sweet witchery which holds us spell-bound as only Gœthe's genius can — lifts us far above the fault, and wrong, and sin, though the hard world thundered its code as the organ rolled the "Dies Iræ," and faint and weary the broken lily fell at the cathedral gates.

But the perfection of Gœthe's womanhood is seen in his conception of Clara — the Clara of "Egmont." Here again the characteristic rather than the morale must appeal! — aye the strength of the passionate devotion of this Amy Robsart of Germany wakens for her an all-absorbing interest. In Margaret, the trust, and clinging, girlish love, are most prominent — the development born of the dangerous guile of the accomplished man of the world; but in Clara it is Egmont's inspiration — the passion called to life by the gallant soldier, brilliant noble, and impetuous lover. Her little songs are exquisite; breathing sometimes a witching coquetry, and always her unselfish devotion. In this drama, less metaphysical than Faust, the scenes are graphic, and the stirring history of the revolt of the Netherlands moves almost as a living spectacle.

Some of Egmont's soliloquies rise into all the grandeur of the truly majestic German, and the famous prison reflection is unsurpassed by anything which even Shakspeare has left to us.

An English writer, comparing the Juliet of Shakspeare with Schiller's Thekla, has remarked that in Juliet is found an "infinity of love," but in Thekla "an eternity;" and in truth the womanly characteristics are wonderfully developed in this rare gallery. Sweet, trustful Margaret pleads her faith-love — for even when dying, her lips fashion the name of her beloved; Clarchen, with more of the strength of passion, exhibits the fathomless depths of her intenser nature; while Thekla, Schiller's pure, self-sacrificing girl-patriot, passes away in the music of her broken heart, as she murmurs her exquisite farewell, in the sweet, sad line,

"Ich habe gelebt, und geliebet!"

And this, his earliest and most spirituelle creation, recalls another of the great lights which brightened the eighteenth century.

John Christopher Frederic Von Schiller was born on the tenth of November, 1759, at Marbach on the Neckar. And what a contrast his infancy and boyhood present, when compared with the cloudless happiness of Gœthe's life. Born in poverty, and educated at a military-monastic school, he was restricted from all intercourse with women; for Charles, Duke of Wurtemberg, thought it most conducive to the intellectual development of his beneficiaries to allow only the visits of mothers and very young sisters. Heart-food and brain-food were alike dusty books; and we find the talent which, in the future, was to give us Don Carlos, Marie Stuart, Thekla, and the thrilling drama of William Tell, diligent in the study of physic and jurisprudence.

But the soul of the thirsting neophyte panted for its native element, and we watch him through the stolen hours of the night, revelling in what was to make his fame throughout the world.

And now the student-life passes away, and we find the independent German spirit boldly and bravely struggling for freedom of thought; and unwilling to submit to the sway and espionage of his old patron, he escaped from the army, and then appeared "The Robbers," the first-born of that wonderful intellect, and a drama of rare talent and marvellous power.

Afterward came Don Carlos, Marie Stuart, Wallenstein, Piccolomini, Revolt of United Netherlands, and, as the last effort and crowning glory, William Tell. The story of Don Carlos, as told by Prescott, in his simple and beautiful English, is familiar to all; but the grace and eloquence of the love-passages in the drama require all the fiery imagination of this grand old master. Marie Stuart, as portrayed by Schiller, has all the womanly dignity with which we love to associate the beautiful Queen of Scotland. The garden scene has become world-renowned since Ristori's perfect rendering and gentle accents have thrilled two continents with their eloquence.

In preparing himself for Wallenstein and the Piccolomini, Schiller collected material for the Revolt of the United Netherlands, a period with which we are now well acquainted through the researches of the terse and elegant Prescott and tireless Motley.

Schiller's life differs entirely from that of his great compeer; for Gœthe, with his rare beauty, seemed born to happiness; while his joyous, expansive heart, ever life-giving, received and gave forth without ceasing, emphatically an absolvent, and, whirled on by destiny, he dispensed what might be called his life-charities: receiving always a more costly recompense, as Gretchen, Frederica, and a hundred others answer to the roll-call of his unresisting and irresistible heart.

But of all the many, the history of Frederica, the timid, shy, yet loving maiden, stands conspicuous in her sweet, forgiving sorrow; a mute, appealing rebuke to the faithless poet. Through long years of neglect and forgetfulness, still she clung to this grand passion of her life: and when wooed, her reply was,

"The heart that has once been Gœthe's, can never be another's."

Schiller, differently situated, had life's hard realities to struggle against; for poverty, with its iron grasp, had seized him, and he had little time for love's dalliance or its joys; in fact, his early isolation from women told plainly in his writings, and his heart-impressions were neither many nor inspiring: therefore we are not surprised at his friendship — love-marriage. Whether the heart of this mighty German could have been otherwise wakened, remains a mystery; but certainly the perfection of womanly passion has never been evidenced in his heroines.

Schiller generally wrote at night, strengthened by very strong coffee: this was the habit of a lifetime, and to and fro, through the cold German midnights, would he pace his room, while the grand conceptions of his magnificent intellect were dreamed into realities.

But the battle, the toil, and the wear of a troubled existence told upon him while yet in the flush of his manhood. An earnest spirit, disdaining the mean and the sensual, his strivings were after the pure, the true, and the good; and as his last-born, his farewell benison to his fatherland, he bequeathed his great drama of William Tell.

Who that has read this does not feel his pulses quicken, as the splendid talent of the author does noble battling for the right? and, as the last flush on the Rütli dies along the Swiss heavens, we feel Schiller's spirit floating upward in its light.

As the one illustrates the German genius, so the other stands colossal as the German talent.

Even the personal appearance of the men seems to speak their especial characteristics. Gœthe was tall and majestic, the handsome man of Germany; with that marvellous beauty which lit every lineament with the reflex of his soul: and Schiller, towering in his rugged outlines, large-featured and irregular, yet always bearing the impress of the great intellect that swayed him with imperial rule.

But they both have passed where, to use Schiller's own language,

"Word is kept with Hope, and to wild Belief a *lovely truth* is given."

And the old German is singing still their echoes — the delicious thrilling minor, and the vibrating, heart-stirring bass — a grandly weird symphony, born in the wild German mountains, and nursed by the blue, rippling Rhine.

Again we listen to the sweet Minnesingers, and again we bow in reverence to the magnificent hymns of the seventeenth century: now the spell of Gœthe's genius lures us, and anon Heine's silvery music wilders, as did his own beautiful Lorelei. The soul-chants of Schiller waken and vibrate to the very depths of the spirit; while Kremer, fiery, impassioned, freedom-loving Kremer, shields us with that last hymn, born while his immortality hovered on the brink of destiny.

And so the mighty host passes onward, onward! marshalled into the far eternity; but their teachings remain forever in our hearts, and as an inspiration from them echoes the sentiment,

> "Whoever with an earnest soul
>   Strives for some end, from this low world afar
> Still upward travels though he miss the goal,
>   And strays — but toward a star!"

Miss Mintzing's personal presence is very attractive. She is of a *distingue* appearance, somewhat above the medium height, graceful in the extreme, and denotes in every gesture the lady of culture and refinement. In conversation, she is earnest; bordering, sometimes, on the enthusiastic — especially upon subjects connected with her State and section — and dispenses a great deal of her own magnetism to those with whom she converses. Her social tastes lead her to pleasure and gayety; and in the drawing-room she is an acknowledged ornament. She is rather of an Italian type, being a brunette of a clear and soft complexion. Her eyes are dark, and her hair is dark-brown and lustrous.

Since the war, Miss Mintzing has resided chiefly in New York. As a writer, her future lies before her. We do not doubt, if she should choose to follow the thorny paths of literature, that she will establish herself among the authors of the South whose reputations will be something more than ephemeral. Hitherto she has never published under her own name.

MARYLAND.

ANNE MONCURE CRANE.

 NEW and Original Novel" was the heading of an article in the "Boston Transcript," written by E. P. Whipple, the essayist, in which he says:

"The most notable characteristic of this book, published by Ticknor & Fields, entitled 'Emily Chester,' is its originality, and it will give novel-readers a really novel impression. All the usual elements of romantic interest are avoided, and new elements, heretofore but slightly hinted in English novels, are made the substance of the work. Since Gœthe's 'Elective Affinities,' we are aware of no story in which the psychology of exceptional sentiment and passion is represented with such keenness and force as in 'Emily Chester.' The play of sympathy and antipathy, in recesses of the mind where will exerts no controlling influence, is exhibited with a patient, penetrating, and intense power, which fastens the reader's somewhat reluctant and resisting attention, and compels him to take interest in what has no natural hold on his healthy sympathies. The character of Emily Chester is not a pleasing one, but it is deeply conceived and vigorously developed. Max Crampton and Frederic Hastings are also types of character strongly individualized, and the contrasted magnetism they exert on the mind and heart of the heroine is vividly represented. The interest and power of the novel are concentrated in these three persons. The other characters are rather commonplace, and seem to be thrown in simply to give relief to the passions of the principal personages. In those parts in which the author is not analyzing and representing the strange mental phenomena which constitute the fascination of the book, she shows immaturity both of thought and observation. . . . . 'Emily Chester' exhibits such palpable mastery of illusive phases of passion difficult to fix and portray, that it cannot fail to make a profound impression on the public."

"Emily Chester" was published without a word of preface to give the least hint of the whereabouts of the author, and was not covered with the pall of "Great Southern Novel!" as is usually the mode novels by Southern writers are announced. It had made a reputation in the North, in Boston, the "Athens of America," before it was announced that the author was a lady of Baltimore.

The Hon. George H. Hilliard thus reviews the book:

. . . . "We have a work of remarkable originality and power, certainly in these qualities entitled to rank side by side with the best productions of American genius in the department of fiction. The interest of the book is entirely derived from psychological sources, that is, from the delineation of character, and not from the incidents of the narrative, which are of a commonplace character, and with hardly the merit of probability. It reminds us of two works of fiction of a past age, Godwin's 'Caleb Williams,' and Gœthe's 'Elective Affinities,' but more of the latter than of the former. Indeed, 'Emily Chester' could hardly have been written had not the 'Elective Affinities' been written before it. We may be sure that the writer of the former is familiar with the latter. Imagine the 'Elective Affinities,' with a distinct moral aim superadded, and written with the intensity and consecration of Godwin, and we get a tolerably fair impression of 'Emily Chester.' . . . . Emily Chester is a young woman of radiant beauty and extraordinary mental powers. One of her lovers is a man of iron will and commanding intellect, from whom she nevertheless recoils with an unconquerable physical or spontaneous repulsion. The temperament of the other is in harmony with her wn; she is happy in his presence, and yet she is ever conscious of his intellectual inferiority, and thus resists the influence of his nature upon hers. Here is the whole web and the woof of the novel. . . . . It is unquestionably a work of genius. It is fair to add that it is a very sad story throughout, and thus not to be recommended to those who have sorrows enough of their own not to make them crave the books that make them grieve. It is a web in which flowers of gold and purple are wrought into a funeral shroud of deepest black. . . . .

"The heroine is an impossible creature. She is a combination of Cleopatra, Harriet Martineau, and Florence Nightingale. She is a being as supernatural or preternatural as a centaur or griffin. She is a blending of irreconcilable elements. She is represented as choosing between one lover who satisfies her intellect, and another who gratifies her temperament, as coolly as she would between a pear and a peach at a dessert. Human beings are not so made. You cannot run a knife between the intellect and the sensuous nature in this way; nor can we think Max Crampton and Frederic Hastings are true to nature. They are to real men what Ben Jonson's characters are to Shakspeare's: they are embodiments of humors, and not living flesh and blood. . . . . And we need hardly add that it is not a healthy book. We lay it down with a feeling in the mind similar to that produced on the body by sitting in a room heated by an air-tight stove. . . . . But, as has been said, there is only one kind of book which cannot be endured, and that is the stupid kind, the book that bores you. 'Emily Chester' will never fall under this condemnation, for it is a book of absorbing interest. From the first chapter the author seizes the attention with the strong grasp of genius, and holds it unbroken to the last. And when the end comes, we lay the book down with a sort of sigh of relief at the relaxation of fibres stretched to a painful degree of tension."

To show plainly the attention this novel attracted among the intellectual portion of the North, I give a criticism from the pen of a female genius of New England, widely known under her pseudonym of "Gail Hamilton":

"The very common fault of this book will have a tendency to conceal from the popular gaze its uncommon excellence. It has all the millinery of a third-rate American novel—the most abounding beauty in its women, perfect manly grace in its men, fabulous wealth surrounding the important personages, with a profusion of elegant appurtenances which, at the present rates of gold, reads like an Arabian Night's entertainment. In style it is sometimes careless, sometimes slightly coarse, and not unfrequently labored. It constantly falls into the vulgar error of making all of its outside women pretty, gossiping, envious, malignant, and hateful, with only here and there a gleam of faint and altogether flickering sunshine, as if womanly splendor were not sufficient of its own shining, but must be set off against a black background. The conversations are sometimes spun out to undue length, and it indulges too largely in philosophy and generalizations. Yet even these drawbacks have their own compensations. The remarks and reflections, if sometimes a little impertinent, are generally sensible and shrewd, indicating an uncommon depth and clearness of insight. The conversations would occasionally be improved by abridgment; but they are earnest and high-toned. . . . .

"I do not know that American novel literature has produced any other work of the kind. Miss Sheppard's 'Counterparts' offers, so far as I can recollect, the only resemblance to be found in the English language. But discarding all resort to hard-featured fathers, mercenary mothers, family feuds, and all manner of *circumstances*, go directly inward, and find in the eternal mystery of the complex human being all the obstacle, the passion and purpose which life requires. This will not, perhaps, add to the popularity of the book; but it makes its power. It may, indeed, be a stone of stumbling and a rock of offence to those conservative novel-readers who love to have a story go on in the good old paths, with which they have become so familiar that they can see the end from the beginning. It is so comfortable to know of a surety that the villain will come to grief, and the knight to joy, however stormy may be the sea of troubles on which he is tossed. All present pain is viewed with a tranquillity inspired by foreknowledge of future happiness. But this book thrusts in upon all these easy-going ways. A beautiful woman, of her own free will, marries a man who is passionately and most unselfishly devoted to her, whom she holds in profound respect and reverence, yet with a feeling little short of loathing. What newfangled notion is this? Alas! it is newfangled only in novels, not in life; and it is only by failing to recognize these subtle yet all-powerful facts, that life has so much confusion. The most careful students, as well as mere casual observers, may fail to comprehend them; but we have learned much when we have learned that there is mystery, that nature has her laws, impalpable but imperative, by obedience to which life is perfected, and by disobedience destroyed; that, deeper down in the heart of man than any words can penetrate, are forces against which it is useless for even the will to contend.

"'Emily Chester' presents this theory in what seems to be an exaggerated form. Perhaps, to state a truth, it is necessary to overstate it. The motto of the title-page avows this: 'It is in her monstrosities that nature discloses to us her secrets.' Max and Emily are scarcely so much man and woman as an impersonation of magnetism. But granting their existence, they act according to rigid natural laws. They are often melo-dramatic; there is a certain overdoing of attitude, gesture, and expression, as if a youthful hand had traced the windings of Emily's inward experience, her changing relations to Max, the effects of his absence and presence, the mingled distrust, repentance, regard, and gratitude. Such things come by special revelation. Emily herself is pure, and pure womanly, an intensified woman drawn with much skill and an infinite pity, sympathy, and tenderness. Her mirth, her coquetry, her gentleness and wilfulness, her great heart-hunger and brain-power, her passionate tastes and distastes, are a mighty relief after the bread-and-butter heroines who mostly trip it through even our good novels. Max is as great an anomaly, in his way, as Emily in hers. From time immemorial the self-immolation has been appointed to woman; but this man, opening his eyes to the evil his indomitable will had wrought upon the woman most dear to him, gave himself a living sacrifice for atonement. With stern, unwearied self-denial, he bore the sharpest pain, if so he may bring to her a gleam of peace. He will have more disciples in his sin than in his suffering; but it is well to know that such a thing is possible, even in conception."

Who is the author of this wonderful book?

A young lady of Baltimore, and her first attempt at writing! It seems strange to me that when the identity of the author of "a new and original novel" became known as being "a daughter of the Southland," and a second volume from her pen appeared, it was almost completely ignored by the "warm admirers" of "Emily Chester."

Miss Anne Moncure Crane is from a talented family. The best translation in English of the celebrated German poem, "Körner's Battle Hymn," I know of, was made by a younger sister—never published. The author of "Emily Chester" was born in the city of Baltimore, and has ever resided in that "city of beauty and talent." "Emily Chester" was her first attempt at writing. She became an authoress by the merest accident. Had any one told her a month before she began *the* book that she would ever write a novel, she would have laughed at the idea. She was twenty years old when her book was written. How true is it "that great events arise from trivial causes!" One evening some one carelessly suggested that a circle of friends should form an original composition class, upon the plan of a reading class—and Miss Crane contribute a novel. The plan was not carried out, but the idea of "writing" had fallen upon fertile soil, and before the next day Miss Crane resolved to seriously attempt to write a book for publication. She began it, and "Emily Chester" was the result—she says, "a greater surprise to me than it could have been to any one else." A very unusual case was that of the publication of this book, and "as an act of justice to the much-maligned race of publishers," we state the case. When "Emily Chester" was completed, it was taken to Messrs. Ticknor & Fields by a lady who was a stranger to them. She was told that they could not even entertain the idea of publishing it, as they were overcrowded with previous engagements; but upon her urging the point, she was politely allowed to leave the book for inspection. Within two weeks from that time they sent a contract for its publication, addressed to the "Author of 'Emily Chester;'" and it was not until Miss Crane returned the paper signed in full that they knew the name of the writer whose novel they had bound themselves to publish. They were aware that it was a first attempt, and that the author was a woman. Miss Crane's literary life has been peculiarly exempt from those trials and discouragements which tradition has led us to believe are almost inseparable from the career of a young, unknown author. Miss Crane is a contributor of brilliant stories and poems to our magazines—among others to the "Galaxy" and "Putnam's Monthly."

Her second book, entitled "Opportunity," was published at the close of 1867, and was welcomed by the many admirers of "Emily Chester," although it did not create such a furore. It is thus noticed in a Southern journal, by Paul H. Hayne, the poet:

"This is no common romance. Depending but slightly upon the nature of its plot and outward incidents, its power is almost wholly concentrated upon a deep, faithful, subtle analysis of character. Indeed, it is rather a series of peculiar psychological studies, than a novel in the ordinary sense of the term. True insight, genuine imagination, a somewhat unique experience of life, are everywhere apparent in its elaborate, careful, and not unfrequently profound portraitures. Even the faults of the work are such as could scarcely have had their origin in a commonplace mind. A morbid, exaggerated force of introspection, laying bare to their very roots the motives of human action, strikes the reader sometimes with a shuddering distaste, the sort of feeling one would experience in beholding too deep and merciless a dissection of any diseased condition, whether of body or heart! Yet how can one fail to admire the strong and subtle gifts by which such results are attained? Moreover, the *general* purpose of the story is noble and exalted. A purity of aim some might call transcendental distinguishes its central *morale*. But its unworldly suggestiveness is charming. Two male characters — brothers — divide the reader's interest. One is a brilliant, susceptible, but frivolous nature, possessing, no doubt, capacities for good, yet too feeble to arrest and to develop them. The other is a strong, passionate, manly, upright soul, who, in the blackest hours of misfortune and doubt, feels (as that gallant Christian gentleman, Frederick Robinson, was wont to observe) that there are instinctive spiritual truths — the 'great landmarks of morality' — which a man (in the midnight of skepticism) must cling to, would he avoid destruction. These brothers, so diverse in temperament, encounter and fall in love with the same woman. She is little more than a girl in years, but her heart and intellect are strangely precocious: and not merely precocious, but wonderful in the exceptional character of their endowments. Her fascination radiates chiefly from *within*. To Grahame Ferguson — the elder and weaker brother — she is led unconsciously to give her affection.

"'Ah!' says the author, referring to this singular heroine — 'Ah! the marvellous fascination of these beautiful-ugly women. To watch the loveliness they seem to keep as too sacred for ordinary eyes, slowly dawn and reach a divine perfection in your sight, what mortal man *can* withstand? If it be only a faint, momentary wild-rose flush upon the usually colorless cheek, a single flash or passing gleam in the lustreless eyes, if you know it to be your very own, that *you* alone have created it, no glory of Greek art can so stir you! This was the miracle Grahame wrought daily; and yet so differently, that he waited each time in expectancy as uncertain as intense. "This is the true, essential beauty!" he was tempted to exclaim. Another truth he awoke to, as he listened to her careless talking, with ever-increasing wonder. Not only was it that *he* recognized her absolute originality, her large structure of mind, but that her thoughts seemed radiant with *that* gleam which "never was on sea or land," her sentences musical with nature's own harmony.'

"Very speedily, however, the shallow, sensuous nature of the man betrays itself by an irrecoverable act of self-committal, and there is a passionate though secret renunciation of him on the part of Harvey Berney, (the heroine's name,) which is depicted with a refined and searching skill, a degree of mind-knowledge and soul-knowledge that are unquestionably remarkable. We cannot follow the various complications of the narrative. It is at a later date that Grahame's brother, Douglas, makes the acquaintance of Miss Berney. These two were evidently fitted for each other; strength to strength, purity to purity, passion to passion. But one of those errors, apparently so trifling, in reality pregnant with fate and death, came between and separated them.

"Douglas was not permitted even to tell his love. Yet how the true, loyal, noble spirit rises gradually from the depression of the blow, and finds comfort in the arms of *duty*, which are finally transformed into the arms of *happiness!*

"Grahame's destiny is of another and sadder kind. It never occurred to him that

'To bear is to conquer our fate.'

Therefore he yields to disappointment and all its insidious temptations, sinks lower and lower in the moral scale, and may finally be regarded as one of those dead souls which, though freed from absolute sensuality, are yet the 'bounden slaves' of *ennui*, sloth, discontent, and that host of effeminate vices which in certain moods are more revolting to us than downright, monstrous, satanic wickedness.

"Underneath the surface of Miss Crane's story and its characterizations, there runs a vein of meaning which only the attentive reader will clearly comprehend. She shows how 'opportunities' may be neglected to the utter misery of the individual; but she rightly and philosophically represents these 'opportunities' as often coming in such 'questionable guise,' that an inspired foresight alone could be expected to take advantage of them. Thus, it is not in the ignorant neglect of 'opportunity' that she pretends to find the seeds of guilt or folly, but in *that illogical and disloyal faithlessness* which sinks weakly under the ban of circumstance, accepts tamely its awards, and never, with the superb audacity of the 'GREAT HEART,' strives to force a way upward, in the very teeth of what we are too apt to call falsely 'providential decrees.' In this way the unlucky Grahame sinks to a level below our contempt. Pursuing an opposite course, his brother not only vanquishes the desperation and despair which beset his reason, but grasps, finally, the serene rewards of an unselfish, manful endurance.

"We close our notice of Miss Crane's production with the remark that no tale has recently appeared, North or South, which is so full of rich evidences of genuine psychological power, a profound study of character in some of its most unique spiritual and mental manifestations, and fervid artistic aspirations, destined to embody themselves gloriously in the future."

Miss Crane looks the "woman of genius," having large features, her nose aquiline and prominent, her mouth large, but rather pleasant, her chin firm, her brow moderate and well arched: her eyes are dark, and have a bright outlook on this world; her hair is dark and very luxuriant—she wears it piled up according to the present "Japanese" style. She is tall, but not ungraceful. She prides herself on making all her own clothes, and being able to do *everything* for herself, which is very commendable. A friend calls her "an universal genius" who is very ambitious, thinking "an intellectual woman ought to do everything." The following characteristic paragraph expresses so much, that we give it place here, against our better judgment perhaps: "In fact, the author of 'Emily Chester' is a steam-engine of a woman, a regular locomotive, and flies desperately along the railroad of life; and one must either subside into the train of cars she leads quietly, or be run over, perhaps crushed to infinitesimal atoms." Miss Crane has formed an "*ideal*" of what an "authoress" ought to be, and she tries to be it! Miss Crane is the *centre* in her galaxy of nebulous stars in the Monumental City.

WORDS TO A "LIED OHNE WORTE."

All earth has that is rare or is treasurable:
  Long I searched for a token, in vain,
Worthy to speak of this love so immeasurable,
  Worthy to be both my gift and her gain.
    Nor palace nor glory,
    Nor name high in story,
These, not these would I bring to my love;
    But what God gave me
    To raise and to save me,
This, 't is this I would bring to my love.

Years go by, and they take what is perishing,
  This world's fashion, which passeth away;
That which I give will need but love's cherishing,
  Ever to live and to bloom as to-day.
    Love's silver lining
    Through life's dark clouds shining,
This, 't is this I would bring to my love;
    All I have shared with none,
    All I have dared with none,
This, all this I would bring to my love.

Pleasure lures, and we follow its beckoning;
  Fame and honor seem life's best ends;
Aught that may stand in our way little reckoning,
  Onward we press, whomsoe'er it offends.
    But when Love's star rises,
    Nought else the soul prizes,
As earth sinks to darkness when heaven shows light,
    Then seem these empty hands
    Richer than golden strands,
With love, and love only, to bring to my love.

WINTER WIND.

Restless wind of drear December,
Listened to by dying ember,
Do you hold the same sad meaning to all other hearts this night?
Sweeping over land and ocean
With your mighty, rhythmic motion,
Has your hasting brought swift wasting to their hope and joy and light?

To them, does your passing darken
Night's black shadow as they hearken;
Filling it with mystic phantoms, such as throng some haunted spot,
With the ghosts of joys and pleasures,
Tortures now that once were treasures?
Does your sighing seem the crying of a soul for what is not?

Does the same weird, weary moaning
Seem to underlie your toning,
Whether risen in your strength, or sunk to wailing, fitful blast?
Do they hear wild, distant dirges
In your falls or in your surges?
Does your swelling seem the knelling for a dead, unburied Past?

"FAITH AND HOPE."

That night, after her mother had fallen asleep, Harvey, scenting tobacco-smoke upon the porch, stole down stairs for a quiet talk with Dr. Dan, or perhaps an hour of silent sitting, as of yore. At first, it proved to be the latter; for, taking her childish place at his feet, and laying her head upon his knee, he put out his hand, and softly stroked her hair with the familiar gesture, but said nothing. Except the necessary aging with years, Dr. Dan was just the Dr. Dan of old. Presently, he began asking questions about her future plans; and then the conversation came back to the present, and even to the past.

"Harvey," he asked at last, "do you ever intend to marry?"

The inquiry had arisen somewhat naturally from others which he had put concerning a strong, true-hearted gentleman, whose apparently hopeless devotion to Harvey seemed but to deepen and strengthen with the deepening and strengthening of his nature.

"That is as God pleases," she answered, rather sadly. "Uncle," she continued presently, and her voice had changed perceptibly, "I was wounded terribly, early in the battle of life, and since then I have been among the halt and maimed."

"Yes, I know it," he replied, and his thoughts went sorrowfully and silently back to those early days.

"Harvey," he said at last, and there was something like despair in his tone, "I want you to answer me one question truthfully. You have worked and won; you have been faithful to what God gave you, and have striven hard to choose the better part: now tell me, has anything in existence yielded you real satisfaction? I frittered away my strength and purpose; I wasted my substance of heart and soul in riotous living, and the punishment of spiritual starvation rests rightfully upon me: you did none of these things; yet tell me what essential, soul-satisfying element has life ever brought you?"

For a moment or two the woman sat motionless, not looking at him, nor at the broad, moonlit heavens above her; but with eyes fixed upon the low, dark horizon, and filled with a hungry, wistful light.

"I shall be satisfied when I awake with His likeness."

This faith and hope were all she had rescued from that failure which she called her life. Ah, me! from the beginning, has any human heart ever truly rescued more?

LYDIA CRANE.

NOT noted in the "literature" of our country, yet we cannot conscientiously omit a place in our volume to the translator of the beautiful "Battle Prayer" that we give. If she so desired, she could occupy a high position among our "Southland Writers," as a translator and as an "original writer."

Miss Lydia Crane is a daughter of the late Mr. William Crane, for many years a merchant in the city of Baltimore; a man of wealth, noted for his extensive contributions to the Baptist Church and charitable institutions. She is a younger sister of the authoress of "Emily Chester" and "Opportunity."

Says a lady who has reverence, admiration, and true, respectful affection for *her*: "Lydia Crane is a noble, suffering woman, a martyr all her life to nervous disease and curvature of the spine, but who rises above pain and wretched health, and studies mathematics when every nerve is quivering with anguish."

KÖRNER'S BATTLE PRAYER.

Gebet in der Schlacht.

Father, I cry to Thee!
Rolling around me the smoke of the battle,
Lightnings surround me and war's thunders rattle,
Leader of armies, I cry to Thee!
Father, lead Thou me!

Father, lead Thou me!
Lead me to victory, lead me to dying;
Lord, by Thy word, be my labor and trying;
Through this world's strife my guide deign to be.
My God, I discern Thee!

My God, I discern Thee!
As in the murmur of leaves that are falling,
So in the thunder of battle appalling,
Fountain of Mercy, I recognize Thee!
Father, bless Thou me!

Father, bless Thou me!
To Thy hands alone my life is commended;
That Thou hast ordained, by Thee must be ended:
In life and in death wilt Thou bless me!
Father, I praise Thee!

Father, I praise Thee!
If war ever good to the earth has afforded,
The holiest cause we have saved and rewarded:
Failing or conquering, I praise Thee!
To Thee all surrendered be!

To Thee all surrendered be!
Though from my heart my life-blood be flowing,
When from my lips my last prayer is going,
To Thee, my God, I surrender me!
Father, I cry to Thee!

GEORGIE A. HULSE McLEOD.

MRS. McLEOD is well known as presiding over the "Southern Literary Institute," of Baltimore, Maryland—a seminary for young ladies which is well known throughout the United States. That Mrs. McLeod is a generous, noble-souled lady, the fact that she gives free tuition to one young lady, the daughter of a deceased Confederate soldier, from each Southern State, amply attests.

Mrs. McLeod was born in Florida, at the Naval Hospital near Pensacola, of which her father, Dr. Isaac Hulse, was then surgeon. She was left an orphan in infancy.

Her first books, "Sunbeams and Shadows" and "Buds and Blossoms," were published in New York, in 1851. Two years after the appearance of her books, she was married to Dr. A. W. McLeod, of Halifax, N. S., where they resided for some time. Her first volume after her marriage was "Ivy Leaves from an Old Homestead," which was followed by "Thine and Mine; or, The Step-mother's Reward," published by Derby & Jackson, in 1857—a book that was received with much favor, and inculcating an excellent moral, showing that a step-mother may supply a mother's place in kindness and care.

Mrs. McLeod, since the close of the war, has published two little volumes, "Sea-Drift" and "Bright Memories." The former is a little story, dealing mainly with school-girls, their ways and thoughts, their joys and trials—a charming book, pure, healthful, and inspiring.

Mrs. McLeod has been a constant contributor to magazines, etc., North and South, under the signature of "Flora Neale," and other *noms de plume.*

Mrs. McLeod is a very industrious writer, conducting a large school successfully, and considering her pen-work as a recreation.

She has recently completed a book for juveniles, entitled "Standing Guard," and a novel, the title of which is very inviting, viz., "The Old, Old Story."

Mrs. McLeod also has in preparation a First-Class Reader, intended for the senior class of the Southern Literary Institute, for which some of the most noted writers have contributed.

MINE!

The fresh green robes spring had given to the earth became gorgeous with the many-colored blossoms springing up everywhere. The June roses clambered over the lattice-work, and sent in on the breath of the south wind a perfumed greeting, to woo into the summer air the happy-hearted.

Never, to Mrs. Rivers, had the summer been so fair, the flowers so lovely. A joy within had shed an influence over outward things—a new, deep joy; for, with the summer blossoms, a bud of beauty, a living floweret, gave an added charm to home. A murmur of praise trembled on her lips, and a happy light was in the soft, dark eyes, as she folded the unconscious little one so lovingly to her heart, murmuring, "*Mine*, all my own!"

A little child! How the memory of Him who was cradled in a manger comes back upon us when we look upon such helplessness! Its very weakness has the power of twining about proud hearts a chain of love and pity, that even man's strong hand may not unbind.

We bless little children, for their presence bringeth purity and joy. Around them cluster affections that are nearer to the love of heaven; and when, from one dwelling and another, the timid doves are won heavenward, their flitting leaves a void which may not easily be filled.

"*Mine!*" What a spell in that simple word—a strangely solemn influence. So to Grace it was. "Mine" is an added charge — an immortal spirit, which must learn through me the way to live — the how to die. Far away into the future her thoughts were fast flitting, weaving, thus early, visions of beauty yet to open upon the baby dreamer. But as shades shut out the sunlight, so darker thoughts were blending with them. What if she were called away ere it should learn to tread life's changing way? Even thus another had been taken from those leaning upon her love—even thus, for the young voices that were echoing around gave to *her* the name lisped *first* to one departed. It was a sad memory, but one which made them seem the dearer, a more precious charge. The new tie that so blessed her should not weaken their claim, but, as a pure and cherished link, bind them more closely together.

THE LOST TREASURE.

The blue fades out from the fair summer sky,
   And my flowers have drooped their bright buds;
The winds of the autumn are scattering the leaves,
   And chanting a dirge o'er their heads.
So the love that made earth always summer to me,
   Has failed me and left me alone;

I sit by the ashes all cold on the hearth,
  And weep for the light that is gone.

I set up, unseen by a stranger's cold eye,
  A stone in my heart's secret shrine:
"In memory of"—and a name is thereon,
  The name of this lost love of mine.
I prayed for him nightly; I blessed him each day,
  The love and the blessing he scorns;
He has crushed from my path the roses I loved,
  And leaves me all pierced by the thorns.

But murmur not, heart—poor, sorrowful heart!
  We will keep loving vigil together;
It may be some day he will seek us again,
  When with him 't is less sunshiny weather.
Let us patiently wait, and pray, and love on;
  Kindly welcome him back, should he come;
But if not, the rich treasures we lose here on earth,
  May be found in a heavenly home.

"STONEWALL."

"Let my men have the name; it belongs more to them than to me."—*Jackson's words.*

Weep for the mighty dead,
  The nation's joy and pride;
Send forth the mournful tidings
  From hill and mountain-side.
Virginia, shroud thy banners;
  Thou had'st no nobler son;
Weep, fettered Maryland, for he
  Thy freedom could have won.

Weep for the hero chieftain
  Who met your greatest need:
Each Southern home is darkened,
  Each Southern heart must bleed.
A thousand would have fallen
  To win him from the grave:
What were a thousand lives to his,
  The good, the true, the brave?

Weep for the good man fallen,
  Ye mothers and ye wives;
Teach your children how his virtues
  May brighten their young lives.
And to his pure example
  Each mother point her son;
So, though dead, he yet shall live,
  As liveth Washington!

Weep for the great and gifted;
  We all have cause for tears,
For him in whom shone brightly
  Each virtue that endears;
And nightly in our praying
  For those who rule our land,
At his dear name we falter,
  Then pray for Stonewall's band.

When the trumpet calls to battle,
  They 'll miss the olden spell,
That ever led to victory,
  O'er mountain, brake, and dell.
They 'll miss his voice in battle,
  And in the hour of prayer,
By council and by camp-fire;
  They 'll miss him everywhere.

Oh, wreathe your brightest banners
  With cypress that shall wave
Above the spot ye hallow
  As Stonewall Jackson's grave!
Then, with reverence and love,
  Years hence shall pilgrims stand,
Sweet memories to garner
  Of Stonewall and his band.

TEXAS.

MRS. FANNIE A. D. DARDEN.

THE subject of this brief article is a native of Texas. She belongs to a thoroughly Southern stock. Her father, General Mosely Baker, a native of the "Old Dominion State," was one of Texas's most distinguished soldiers during her struggle with Mexico for independence, and, after peace was declared, was her bright, particular star of legal acumen and forensic eloquence. Her mother was the only daughter of Colonel Pickett, of North Carolina, and sister of the historian of Alabama, in which State Fannie was educated.

As a lady of birth and culture, as a *littêrateur* of taste and genius, as a native Southerner, and true, unswerving "daughter of the Confederacy," as the wife of a gallant officer — Captain William Darden, of Hood's Texas Brigade — Mrs. Darden's patent of nobility is clear and unmistakable, and therefore, with pride and pleasure, Texas presents her among "Southland Writers" as one of her representative women.

THE OLD BRIGADE.

Hood's gallant old brigade!
Ah! how the heart thrills, and the pulses leap
When once again those well-known words are spoken,
Rending aside the clouds that darkly keep
The present from the past, and bring a token
From that weird, shadowy land, whose silence is unbroken!
Hood's gallant old brigade! what memories throng
With the swift rush as of a torrent leaping;
And far-off strains of high, heroic song
Come like a rolling wave majestic sweeping,
When that mute chord is struck which stirs our souls to weeping!

And was it not a dream, those glorious days
  When hope her banner proudly waved before us;
When, in the genial light of freedom's blaze,
  We lived and breathed with her bright heaven o'er us,
  While every hill and vale rang out her lofty chorus?
When our loved State (whose one bright, glorious star
  Her lonely vigil keeps o'er earth and ocean)
Poured forth her sons at the first cry of war,
  Which thrilled each soul with patriot emotion,
  And claimed from those brave hearts their loftiest devotion.

Nay, 't was no dream, those four long years, when war
With gloating triumph rode her bloody car,
Dragging, enchained, o'er fierce and stormy fields,
Her bleeding victims at her chariot wheels.
Nay, 't was no dream, though vanished are the days
  When glory's splendid pageant moved before us,
Though now no more is seen the lurid blaze
  Which from each gory field lit up the heaven o'er us —
Though fallen is that flag, once proudly floating
  Above the battle's roar where heroes fought
With more than Spartan valor, there devoting
  Those hearts, whose flame from freedom's shrine was caught,
  To that loved cause, the freedom which they sought.

Hood's gallant old brigade! where are they now?
  Those souls of fire, who on the bloody plain
Of proud Manassas swept the usurping foe
  Before them, as the rushing hurricane
Its fatal vengeance wreaks and spreads its mighty woe.
Oh! where are those whose blood baptized the soil
  Of Sharpsburg and the sombre Wilderness,
Who, through long years of strife, and pain, and toil,
  No want could sadden, and no power depress —
Who charged the foe on Malvern's fatal hill,
  And where the mountain's brow frowns darkly down
On Boonsboro', and on the historic field
  Where Richmond looked on deeds whose high renown
Amazed the world, and in the valley deep
Where Chickamauga's heroes gently sleep?

But few remain of those, who, side by side,
Together braved the storm; and far and wide

Hood's Texans sleep a dreamless sleep, nor mark
The times nor changes, nor the heavy cloud
That wraps their once-loved land in pall so dark.
The past has fled, but thickly memories crowd
Upon us, and the phantom years return
With distant echoes from its shadowy shore.
Our bosoms throb, our hearts within us burn;
We hear again the deep artillery's roar,
And see our banner in the light of day
Borne high aloft upon the buoyant air;
And columns deep of those who wore the gray
Are marshalled as of yore — the foe to dare.
The past comes once again, and memories throng
With the swift rush as of a torrent leaping;
And far-off strains of high, heroic song
Come like a rolling wave majestic sweeping,
When that mute chord is struck which stirs our souls to weeping.
The past comes once again, but stays not long;
Its forms dissolve, its glorious splendors fade,
But still is heard the burden of its song:
And distant ages shall the strain prolong,
Which tells thy immortal deeds, Hood's gallant old brigade!

MRS. MAUD J. YOUNG.

MRS. M. J. YOUNG, daughter of Col. N. Fuller, Houston, Texas, is a native of North Carolina. Through her father she is a lineal descendant of John Rolf and his wife, Pocahontas, and blood kindred of the Randolphs of "Turkey Island" and "Roanoke," and of the Bollings, of Virginia. Her great-grandfather, Michael Pacquenett, a Huguenot from Bordeaux, France, came to this country after the revocation of the Edict of Nantes, and is mentioned in Hawkes's History of North Carolina as a freeholder in that State in 1723.

On her mother's side she is descended from the Dunbars, Braggs, and Braxtons, of Maryland and Virginia; and the Marshalls, of Marsh Place, Essex, England. Her grandfather, Dr. John Marshall, a man of vast erudition and finished accomplishments of mind and manner, was educated at Eton and Oxford; Trinity College, Oxford, conferring upon him two degrees. After completing his education, during a travelling tour in this country, he met Miss Mary Bragg, (aunt of General Bragg, of the Confederate Army,) and became so enamored of the fair American that he did not return to England until he had wooed and won her for his wife. Their youngest daughter is the mother of the subject of this sketch.

Miss Fuller was married in her twentieth year to Dr. S. O. Young, of South Carolina, a man of superior mind, thorough cultivation, and elegant address. His family are connected by ties of blood and frequent intermarriage with the Bonners, Lees, Pressleys, Calhouns, and Bonhams, families whose names are interwoven with the literary, political, judicial, religious, and military history of South Carolina since the first Revolution. He died the first year of their marriage, leaving an only son, to whose education and training Mrs. Young's life has been devoted. This son is now, after having completed his college studies under General Lee at Lexington, pursuing the study of his profession at the Medical School in New Orleans, and bids fair to be a worthy representative of his family name and honors.

After showing Mrs. Young to be so truly a daughter of the South, it need scarcely be added that she was true to the traditions of her race in the late struggle. During the war, her pen, guided by the thrilling impulses of her soul, dropped words of comfort and songs of fire that soothed the souls and inspired the hearts of her countrymen from the Potomac to the Rio Grande. The 5th Regiment of Hood's Texas Brigade sent their worn and bloody flag home to her, after it had been covered with glory on a hundred battle-fields. She was enshrined in thousands of stern, true hearts, under the title of "The Confederate Lady" and "The Soldier's Friend." The commanding general of the Trans-Mississippi Department caused her appeals to be published by thousands and distributed through the army during the dark days after Lee's surrender, when it was still hoped that Texas would constitute herself the refuge and bulwark of that cause which none could deem then "lost." General Kirby Smith, General Magruder, General Joseph Shelby, and "The Confederate Lady" came out in a paper addressed to the "Soldiers and Citizens of Texas, New Mexico, and Arizona." This sheet, whose thrilling and soul-stirring appeals were enough to have created heroic resolutions under the very ribs of death, was printed by military command, and posted in the towns and served broadcast over camps and country.

Since the war, Mrs. Young has in all her writings made more or less practical application of her subjects to the times; comforting, consoling, and encouraging her people—yet never bating one jot or tittle of her convictions concerning the past. To fail is not to be wrong, we can acknowledge defeat without believing ourselves in error, is her maxim. A distinguished officer of General "Stonewall" Jackson's regiment, after a visit to Texas, writes of her as "the vestal matron, guarding with religious and patriotic devotion the home-altars of her beloved State."

In an essay entitled "Weimar," she exclaims:

"Shall any young Southron fall into despair, or feel that he can never achieve greatness or distinction, now that his patrimonial acres and slaves are gone, when he reads the great Schiller congratulating himself upon the possession of an income of one hundred and twenty dollars? Go to your libraries, my young countrymen, and read the splendid thoughts that God sent Schiller in his poverty, and see how, in his humble cottage, in the capital of a duchy whose entire territory is scarcely larger than your plantation, he made a glorious fame, and crowned the brow of his native land with wreaths as immortal as her mountains, and beautiful and bright as the sparkling waves of her broad, blue Rhine!"

Again she writes:

"To contemplate Weimar, her insignificant territory, her poverty, her weakness, her dependence, and to see her become the nursing mother of the whole German Empire, and that too, not by wealth, or arms, or diplomacy, but simply through the mental powers of her children, we are constrained to admit that the grandest possibilities of humanity lie within the grasp of every condition; and that the watchword of youth should be that terse but comprehensive command of the Bible, 'Despise not the day of small things.' The best things of this world have owed nothing to extraneous circumstances —the power has been from within—fashioning, elevating, and purifying the individual, then the masses. No thought of failure should weaken your energies. 'Heart within, and God overhead.' You have not only a right to the brightest hopes, but a solemn duty to make those hopes verities."

Mrs. Young has written under several *noms de plume.* Her two works of greatest length are "Cordova," a religious novel, and a work on botany, soon to be issued, illustrative principally of the flora of Texas. Essays, short poems, and stories for magazines and newspaper publications, make up the bulk of her writings.

Simms, in his volume of Southern poems, has her "Song of the Texas Ranger." It was published originally without her name, as the most of her war poems were.

She has embodied in stories several of the legends of her State—among them, one of the famous watering-place, Sour Lake. Under the garb of a fairy story, she relates the story of secession, and the downfall of the Confederacy, pointing, in conclusion, to the only hope of happiness left us—*labor, and an unselfish devotion to the welfare of each other.*

A leading paper, in speaking of this, says:

"'The Legend of Sour Lake,' by M. J. Y., is really one of the finest prose poems we have read for many a day. Though not in verse, it is genuine poetry from beginning to end. Would that all the wild and beautiful legends of our wide field of poetic treasures—Texas—could be put in enduring form by the literary artist. This romantic Indian tradition, so beautifully rendered, and whose glorious symbolisms are so happily applied to the instruction of the Southern people, will not die."

Rev. Mr. Carnes, himself one of the purest and most talented of writers, says that the "'Legend of Sour Lake' is a tale worthy the author of Undine itself," etc. The proprietors of the Lake presented the writer with the freedom of the springs.

One of Mrs. Young's best productions is an essay upon the relative character of the mind of man and woman. She takes ground against the "New School lights," denying woman's mental equality in kind, though she claims it for her in degree. She has chosen Milton and his "Paradise Lost," and Mrs. Browning and her "Drama of the Exile," as illustrations of her theory. The essay is too long to give entire, and to make quotations would only be an unsatisfactory marring of the whole. The "Telegraph" has been the most frequent medium of her communications, Mr. Cushing, its editor, being the Nestor of the press in her State, and the kindly guardian of every genius in its boundaries.

The writer of this sketch is reluctant to leave her pleasant task without making some mention of the sweet atmosphere of sympathy and feeling which emanates from and surrounds Mrs. Young in her social and private life, and of the brilliant light which her genius sheds upon those who come in immediate contact with her. Not only are her conversational powers incomparable and her manners perfect, but she has that silent tact and ready understanding which brings forward the *best* that is in those about her, and makes them feel, after leaving her, that they have themselves shone in truer and sweeter colors than their every-day garb. She is enveloped in incense from grateful hearts day by day; she is the "comforter," the "Christian," to those who come within her orbit. In her town, and in the country surrounding, no bride is pleased with the adjustment of her orange-blossoms unless Mrs. Young's fingers have helped to arrange them; no schoolboy is satisfied with his prize until she has smiled upon it. Grief comes to be folded to her heart, and happiness begs for her smile. She has drunk herself most deeply of the cup of sorrow — she has been scorched by the flames of affliction; but she has risen refreshed and strong from the bitter draught; she has come out brightened and purified, "even as refined gold" from the heat of the furnace.

In person, Mrs. Young is tall, with a commanding grace. She has beautiful dark eyes, an expressive mouth, and a soft, clear voice. Clad always in soft, black, flowing robes, and moving, as she does, like a dream, her memory haunts all who have once seen her, and her wonderful presence leaves a sense of itself wherever she has been.

HOUSTON, *November*, 1864.

SOLDIERS AND OFFICERS OF THE FIFTH REGIMENT
OF HOOD'S OLD BRIGADE:

My Dear Brothers: I received from your committee — D. C. Farmer, Capt. Company A; W. T. Hill, Capt. Company D; and A. C. Woodall, 1st Lieut. Company D — the letter, and the worn and battle-torn flag you did me the honor to send. Words are totally inadequate to express my feelings. The 8th of October will ever be remembered by me as the proudest of my life, yet mingled with the deepest sadness; for, more eloquent than speech, more powerful than Cæsar's gaping wounds, was the story told by its blood-stained, weather-beaten, bullet-scarred folds.

The weary march, the aching feet and throbbing brow, the cold bivouac, the lonely picket, the perilous scout, the gloomy hospital, the pride and pomp of battle array, the shock of arms, the victory, and oh! those silent, nameless, grass-grown mounds, strewn from Richmond to Gettysburg, from Chickamauga and Knoxville to the Wilderness and Petersburg — mounds whose shadows rest cold and dark upon a thousand hearts and homes in our once bright and happy Texas — all these came rushing thick and trooping over heart and brain; and, clasping the bloody banner to my heart, with a burst of tearful anguish, I could but exclaim: "Oh that my eyes were a fountain of tears, that I might weep over the slain of my people!"

Maximilian's august dame felt not half the pride and delight when upon her brow was placed the glittering crown of Mexico, that I do in being made the custodian of your flag. It shall be preserved as long as one of my name or blood exists. And when my son and younger brother gird them for the strife, I shall place the Bible and that flag before them, and on those swear them to fidelity to God and the Confederacy, to Liberty and Truth; and, invoking the benediction and guardianship of Heaven and the countless army of martyrs — swelled to a countless number by the slain of our Southland — deem them fully panoplied and armed for the

"Battle-field of armies,
Or the battle-field of life."

You bid me "hang the flag upon the outer walls," to strike terror to the hearts of the cowards skulking at home. Ah! my noble brothers of the Fifth! if the sable-clad forms of the mourning women and children — if the numberless maimed soldiers who greet us at every turn — if the cold contempt of proud beauty's eye — if the averted faces of our gray-haired sires — if the form of the Confederacy, beleaguered with foes and bleeding at every vein, strike no remorse, and inspire no patriotic deeds, think you this flag will? They are joined to their idols — money-making and selfish ease; so we will let them alone, hoping for the day soon to come when you shall return and scourge them from the land. If honor or peace or safety were depending upon them, we would long ago have worn the Yankee yoke and ate the bread of slaves. But, thank God! our liberties have not been in their keeping, but in theirs who sprang to arms as the first gun from Sumter awoke the echoes of the South; and well have you proved yourselves worthy of the task. You have saved us (under God) from destruction, and made our name the most glorious on earth. Already we see the daystar of peace; and no men have so contributed to its rising as "the soldiers under Lee." With a worshipful love and enthusiasm, our State contemplates the deeds of Hood's Brigade. From the first hour that you drew your battle-blades, glory adopted you as her own; and fame, plucking the brightest star from her crown, placed it on your banner, and the world has watched it since, growing in magnificence and brilliancy, ever in the forefront of conflict, gleaming like a Pharos of hope and success over the black and surging billows of a hundred battles. Methinks, in ages to come, should our beloved land be called to pass through another long and bloody struggle like this, that the old worn and tattered banner of the Fifth will be taken like the "heart of Bruce" along to the field, and when numbers overwhelm and all seems lost, they will fling it to the breeze, knowing that power almost to waken the dead lives in its heart-stirring folds, and that its faded cross and blood-stained stars will call to them like a clarion to rise and strike — to be worthy of being the countrymen and descendants of "The Old Texas Brigade."

You ask that I shall, with it, wave you a welcome when you return. Ah! the very thought of that return thrills me with emotion. I weep for joy. That day, so looked for, so long delayed, so sought for at God's throne, day and night, by a thousand grief-worn, anxious hearts — in that day how doubly sacred shall this flag seem, when, with tearful eyes, we shall speak of the noble dead who fell bearing it onward! We will remember that

"Never yet was royal banner
Steeped in such a costly dye;
It hath lain on many bosoms
Where no other shroud shall lie."

And thus revering them, doubly dear shall be the blessed fruits that their toils and yours have won for us. God in his mercy grant that no more of your numbers shall fall, and that, ere many months shall have rolled away, you may crown your muskets with roses, and, with your bands playing "Home, Sweet Home," turn your feet away from the bloody grounds of the old Mother State to the quiet hearths and loving hearts in your proud prairie homes!

Then will our State rise up to meet you; streets and thoroughfares will be crowded; old men, leaning upon their staves, with trembling hands will shade their eyes to better behold the warriors who have won such imperishable renown, such good things for the country as to enable them, when the summons comes, to lay their gray heads calmly down in the grave, feeling that all is well in the land that you defended. In the name of the God of Israel they will bless you. Matrons, feeling nobler than the grandest old Roman mothers, will hail you as sons. Young men will say, "They are my countrymen," and will grow braver and purer and nobler with the thought; young maidens, blushing at the very excess of their enthusiasm and admiration, will wave you a loving welcome of smiles and tears. Your mothers, wives, sisters — ah! I cannot proceed, my feelings overwhelm me. God hasten the day — hasten the day!

With deep gratitude and affection, honored Fifth Regiment, I remain ever your friend and proud countrywoman,

M. J. Young.

MISS MOLLIE E. MOORE.

FURNISHED BY A GENTLEMAN OF TEXAS.

NATURE has wrought such profusion of beauty over the prairies of Western Texas, that the lover of the romantic and picturesque is often too much bewildered, as he travels the rolling hills and mimic mountains about the upper tributaries of the Colorado and the Guadalupe, to decide where she has been most lavish of her exquisite touches.

But would you find yourself lost in a Western Eden, and believe that you had passed, unwitting, into the spirit-land? Then pause in your travels amid the hills of the "Rio San Marcos."

Ask you how, away in this solitude, the mocking-bird learns to sing the thousand songs she never heard of bird, or instrument, or human voice?

Answer your own question, by finding the forest, prairie, flower and foliage, the winds and waters burdened with the very spirit of song: the vocal organs of the happy bird are only the instrument through which the music gushes.

And here it was, before she was nine years old, our Texas poetess, Mollie E. Moore, first sang her tuneful songs — and, without a master other than nature's voice, learned, like her feathered friend, to sing the songs she never heard; and, like that mistress of the winged minstrels, she sang "because she could not help it." Poetry gushed from her *pen* as the mere instrument of utterance. *She* is our "Texas Mocking-bird."

Dr. Moore emigrated from the banks of the Coosa, in the State of Alabama, where "Mollie" was born, when she was a mere child, and found a home in Texas such as we have described. Here he resided till his child, the only daughter of a large family, had imbibed the elements of poesy. He could command but few advantages of education for his children beyond their home circle; but he had some books, and a taste for natural beauty and natural science. His wife, too, had a gift for song and versification, readily caught by their little darling. No bird sang, or wind sighed, or grasshopper chirruped, or prairie-plume nodded, that Mollie's heart did not respond; and the passion for natural beauty, in all its thousand phases, that she sketches now with the hand of magic, was so deeply inwoven with her very being, that she lived a kind of fairy-life during her few years on the banks of the "Rio San Marcos." But read her own sweet song of her childhood's home:

"THE RIVER SAN MARCOS."

Far o'er the hills and toward the dying day,
Set like a heart — a living heart — deep, deep
Within the bosom of its wide prairies,
Lies the valley of San Marcos. And there,
A princess, roused from slumber by the kiss
Of balmy southern skies, the river springs
From out her rocky bed, and hastens on,
Far down the vale, to give her royal hand
In marriage to the waiting Guadalupe.

Like some grim giant keeping silent watch,
While from his feet some recreant daughter flies,
Above, the hoary mountain stands, his head
Encircled by an emerald-pointed crown
Of cedars, strong as those of Lebanon,
That bow their sombre crests, and woo the wind,
Drunken with fragrance, from the vale below.
About his brow, set like a dusky chain,
The mystic race-paths run — his amulet —
And nestled squarely 'gainst his rugged breast.
Perched quaintly 'mong the great, scarred rocks that hang
Like tombstones on the mountain-side, the nest
The falcon built still lingers, though the wing
That swept the gathering dust from off our shield
Hath long since drooped to dust!

. . . .

And here, down sloping to the water's marge,
The fields, all golden with the harvest, come:
And here, the horseman, reining in his steed
At eve, will pause, and mark the village spires
Gleam golden in the setting sun, and far
Across a deeply-furrowed field will glance
With idle eye upon a stately hill,
That, girt with cedars, rises like a king
To mark the farther limit of the field.
'T was here, between the hill and river, stood

A shaded cottage; and its roof was low
And dark, and vines that twined the porch but served
To hide the blackness of its wall. But then
'T was home, and "heaven is near us in our childhood."
And I was but a child; and summer days,
That since have oftentimes seemed long and sad,
Were fleeter then than even the morning winds
That sent my brother's fairy bark, well balanced,
In safety down the river's tide. Alas!
Is there, can there be aught in all the world
To soothe the sick soul to such perfect rest
As filled its early dreams? Is there no fount,
Like that of old, so madly sought by Leon,
Where the worn soul may bathe and rise renewed?
. . . .
Well I remember,
Down where the river makes a sudden bend,
Below the ford, and near the dusky road,
Upon her bosom sleeps a fairy isle,
Enwreathed about with snowy alder-boughs,
And tapestried with vines that bore a flower
Whose petals looked like drops of blood —
We called it "Lady of the Bleeding Heart" —
And through it wandered little careless paths.
. . . .
And o'er this living gem
The very skies seemed bluer, and the waves
That rippled round it threw up brighter spray.
Upon the banks for hours I 've stood, and longed
To bask amid its shades; and when at last
My brother dragged, with wondrous care, his boat —
Rude-fashioned, small, and furnished with one oar —
Across the long slope from the stately hill
Where it was built, ne'er did Columbus' heart
Beat with a throb so wild upon that shore
Unknown to any save to him, as ours
When, with o'erwearied hands and labored breath,
We steered in safety o'er the dangerous way,
And stood, the monarchs of that fairy realm!
My brother! how I wish our wayward feet
Once more could feel that lordly pride — our hearts
Once more know all their cravings satisfied!

Sweet valley of San Marcos! few are the years
That since have linked their golden hands and fled

Like spirits down the valley of the past;
And yet it seems a weary time to me!
Sweet river of San Marcos! the openings seen
Between thy moss-hung trees, like golden paths
That lead through Eden to heaven's fairer fields,
Show glimpses of the broad, free, boundless plains
That circle thee around. Thine own prairies!
How my sad spirit would exult to bathe
Its wings, all heavy with the dust of care,
Deep in their glowing beauty! How my heart,
O'ershadowed with the cloud of gloom, would wake
To life anew beneath those summer skies!

. . . .

Oh, river of my childhood! fair valley-queen!
Within thy bosom yet at morn the sun
Dips deep his golden beams, and on thy tide,
At night, the stars — the silver stars — are mirrored;
Through emerald marshes yet thine eddies curl,
And yet that fairy isle in beauty sleeps,
(Like her of old who waits the wakening kiss
Of some true knight to break her magic sleep;)
And yet, heavy with purple cups, the flags
Droop down toward the mill; but I — oh! I
No more will wander by thy shores, nor float
At twilight down thy glassy tide! — no more.
And yet, San Marcos, when some river-flower,
All swooning with its nectar-drops, is laid
Before my eyes, its beauty scarce is seen
For tears which stain my eyelids, and for dreams
Which glide before me of thy fairy charms,
And swell my heart with longing,
Sweet river of San Marcos!

Dr. Moore afterward removed to near Tyler, in Smith County, Texas, where a more cultured association soon developed another phase of his daughter's life; and the many modest verses that never expected to see the light, but which the poet always retains with affection, as bearing with them the history of the spirit's joys in its buddings, found their way, through admiring friends, to the light they would scarcely bear without the photograph of the girlish writer to vindicate their unpretending juvenility.

It was not long (in her fifteenth year) till some of her verses found their way into the "Houston Telegraph," then under the editorship of the acute and scholarly E. H. Cushing, Esq. With the ready appreciation of a man of wit and letters, Mr. Cushing encouraged and invited the contributions of the young and gifted writer, without knowing how young and uninstructed she was. Further information induced Mr. Cushing to invite, and procured a visit to his family of his youthful contributor. Like the true patron of genius, he sought, by every proper aid, to afford it the means of development. He and his noble-hearted wife prevailed upon her parents to allow their daughter to become a member of their family whenever they could part with her society at home, and, in the absence of good schools, (all broken up by the events of the war,) avail herself of the use of his personal instruction, and his extensive and well-selected library.

Thus for three years, until after the close of the war, our young writer spent a large portion of her time in the city of Houston, in association with ladies and gentlemen of cultured intellect, and in the reading and study that have developed her taste, and made her the true poetess and the elegant and charming woman — a favorite in every circle in which she moves. Somewhat subsequent to this period, we believe it was, she received the aid in her selections of reading and study of the somewhat mystic and profound critic and theologian, Rev. J. E. Carnes.

Miss Moore's pen has never been long idle; and although but few of her productions have seen the light, her literary correspondence has widened, and her prose as well as poetic writings have grown voluminous for one still so young.

In 1866, her father removed, with his family, to Galveston, thus bringing his daughter's two homes within a few hours of each other, and giving her additional advantages of society and the seaside promptings to her muse.

A season of travel through the East and North with Mr. Cushing's family and some other friends, the meeting with many writers of note, and, above all, that monster to all young authors, the publisher, and seeing a volume of her own thoughts collected and published by her friend and patron, were the prominent events of the next season. Then came that terrible shock — her first great grief — the death of her loving and excellent mother, each event, in its turn, giving a new tinge to her productions, or hushing her muse to silence in the presence of unutterable thoughts and emotions.

Thus a large family of brothers, the younger ones scarcely beyond infancy, together with her widowed and stricken father, were thrown entirely upon the care and affection of this slender and frail girl of books and poetic vocation. Yet, as if with one of her own intuitions, she adapted herself to the necessities around her with a maturity and earnestness beyond praise. Yet never has her life appeared more beautiful, nor her pen gushed with a more full and genuine inspiration, than when discharging, with such tender devotion, all these onerous cares thus devolving upon her.

It must not be inferred, because Miss Moore's very versatile muse oft grapples with the grave and the lofty, or weeps in sadness, draped in gloom, that her life and manners are usually austere, or her pen always clothed in mourning. On the contrary, she illustrates a trait not uncommon with poets and persons of exalted fancy. In conversation with friends, in society, and in the hospitalities of her own house, she wears a cheerfulness and humor that would leave an impression of the happy girl taking life and its cares rather lightly. Many of her fugitive pieces illustrate this joyous temper, and prove her humor to be genuine. The poem which follows contains the scintillations of a merry heart:

STEALING ROSES THROUGH THE GATE.

Long ago, do you remember,
  When we sauntered home from school,
As the silent gloaming settled,
  With its breezes light and cool?
When we passed a stately mansion,
  And we stopped, remember, Kate,
How we spent a trembling moment
  Stealing roses through the gate?

But they hung so very tempting,
  And our eager hands were small,
And the bars were wide — oh! Kate,
  We trembled; but we took them all!
And we turned with fearful footsteps,
  For you know 'twas growing late;
But the flowers, we hugged them closely,
  Roses stolen through the gate!

Well, the years have hasted onward,
  And those happy days are flown;

Golden prime of early childhood,
  Laughing moments spent and gone!
But yester e'en I passed your cottage,
  And I saw, oh! careless Kate,
Handsome Percy bending downward—
  Stealing roses through the gate!

Stealing roses where the willow
  O'er the street its long bough dips!
Stealing roses—yes, I'd swear it—
  Stealing roses from your lips!
And I heard a dainty murmur,
  Cooing round some blessed fate:
Don't deny it! was n't Percy
  Stealing roses through the gate?

We do not propose writing a critique upon her productions, but must make note of a few pieces that show her versatility. We open the volume of poems, that casket of jewels, ("Minding the Gap, and Other Poems,") presented to the public by Cushing & Cave, Houston, 1867, the first literary production (we believe) ever published in Texas; and the very dedication to her friend and patron will indicate the originality, the tenderness, and poetic beauty of Miss Moore's mental constitution. First in the compilation is "Minding the Gap," which is suggested by a custom prevalent in the rural districts of Texas, which may not be understood elsewhere. At harvest-time, a length of the fence is let down to allow the wagons to pass to and fro. To keep cattle out, the children are set "minding the gap." It evinces one of her strong peculiarities. Its description is exceedingly graphic and beautiful, while the style of transition, from the simple idea of "minding the gap" in the field-fence, to the heartful reflections upon those "open places of the heart," where, in maturer life, the spirit's foes are ever seeking such wily entrance, is not only tender to tears, but may be said to be one of Miss Moore's decided individualities.

MINDING THE GAP.

There is a radiant beauty on the hills—
  The year before us walks with added bloom;
But, ah! 't is but the hectic flush that lights
  The pale consumptive to an early tomb—

The dying glory that plays round the day,
Where that which made it bright hath passed away.

A mistiness broods in the air — the swell
  Of east winds, slowly wearing autumn's pale
With dirge-like sadness, wanders up the dell;
  And red leaves from the maple branches fall
With scarce a sound. This strange, mysterious rest!
Hath nature bound the Lotus to her breast?

But hark! a long and mellow cadence wakes
  The echoes from their rocks! How clear and high,
Among the rounded hills, its gladness breaks,
  And floats like incense toward the vaulted sky!

It is the harvest-hymn! a triumph tone;
  It rises like those swelling notes of old
That welcomed Ceres to her golden throne,
  When through the crowded streets her chariot rolled.
It is the laborer's chorus! for the reign
Of plenty hath begun — of golden grain.

How cheeks are flushed with triumph, as the fields
  Bow to our feet with riches! How the eyes
Grow full with gladness, as they yield
  Their ready treasures! How hearts arise
To join with gladness in the mellow chime —
"The harvest-time! the glorious harvest-time!"

It is the harvest, and the gathered corn
  Is piled in yellow heaps about the field;
And homely wagons, from the break of morn
  Until the sun glows like a crimson shield
In the far west, go staggering homeward-bound,
And with the dry husks strew the trampled ground.

It is the harvest; and an hour ago
  I sat with half-closed eyes beside the "spring,"
And listened idly to its dreamy flow;
  And heard afar the gay and ceaseless ring
Of song and labor from the harvesters —
Heard faint and careless, as a sleeper hears.

My little brother came with bounding step,
  And bent him low beside the shaded stream,

And from the fountain drank with eager lip;
  While I, half rousing from my dream,
Asked where he'd spent this still September day—
"Chasing the birds, or on the hills at play?"

Backward he tossed his golden head, and threw
  A glance disdainful on my idle hands;
And, with a proud light in his eye of blue,
  Answered, as deep his bare feet in the sands
He thrust, and waved his baby hand in scorn:
"Ah! no: down in the cornfield, since the morn,
            I've been mindin' the gap!"

"Minding the gap!" My former dream was gone!
  Another in its place: I saw a scene
As fair as e'er an autumn sun shone on—
  Down by a meadow, large and smooth and green,
Two little barefoot boys, sturdy and strong
And fair, here in the corn, the whole day long,
            Lay on the curling grass
              Minding the gap!

Minding the gap! And as the years swept by
  Like moments, I beheld those boys again;
And patriot hearts within their breasts beat high,
  And on their brows was set the seal of men;
And guns were on their shoulders, and they trod
Back and forth, with measured tread, upon the sod,
            Near where our army slept,
              Minding the gaps!

Minding the gaps! My brothers, while you guard
  The open places where a foe might creep—
A mortal foe—oh! mind those *other gaps*—
  The open places of the heart! My brothers, keep
              Watch over them!

The open places of the heart—the gaps
  Made by the restless hands of doubt and care—
Could we but keep, like holy sentinels,
  Innocence and faith forever guarding there,
Ah! how much of shame and woe would flee,
Affrighted, back from their blest purity!

No gloom or sadness from the outer world
  With feet unholy then would enter in,
To grasp the golden treasures of the soul,
  And bear them forth to sorrow and to sin!
The heart's proud fields — its harvests full and fair!
Innocence and love, could we but keep them there,
          Minding the gaps!

One turns the leaves of the volume, and finds they would select almost each piece they read as sample of Miss Moore's poetic gifts.

"The Departing Soul," in its dialogue with the body, has a depth of thought that would do credit to the maturer minds of the great poets. It depends not at all upon its special rhythm, for you read its blank verse as if following the thoughts of Bryant or Cowper, without seeing the words, only living and wrestling with the searching and thrilling conceptions.

"Reaping the Whirlwind" is powerfully presented. The religious lesson is developed in an allegory as original as it is truthful and poetic. This spiritual trait, that is usually deemed a great beautifier of the female character, runs like a modest silver thread through the whole web of her poetic constructions. But the intellectual trait, that will at least rank second in the estimation of cultured minds, is the *reflective.* And in this class you might rank nearly every piece she writes. The original and independent manner in which our poetess weaves the reflective into her verses, even on the tritest themes, is fast asserting her claim to fame. She has no mentor, no model, no guide but her own perception of the lofty, the true, and the beautiful. She wrote before she knew there were models; and still she writes, with an untrammelled independence, the thoughts, the reflections, the fancies, just as they flow through the mind of this "our Texas Mocking-bird," our own "Mollie Moore."

The patriotic is a large element in her earlier writings. It found ample promptings just as her mind was developing into the open world. It glows in many of her longer poems, and often creeps in by stealth as she writes upon other themes. The deep impressions made by the sufferings of her people, her friends and family, up to the close of the war, have tinged her mental character for life.

Taking Miss Moore's poems all in all, they indicate a wide range of excellence, a lofty sweep of thought, a subtle gift in allegory and personification, and richness in exquisite fancies.

REAPING THE WHIRLWIND.

My friends and I went forth to reap
  Our fields at full of day;
We laughed and sang along the paths
  As birds in early May.

Peace sat with hands upon her lap,
  (Lilies were in her hair;)
I said, "My harvest-time has come;"
  I said, "Come, help me bear

"My sheaves — come, help me reap my fields."
  But Peace said, sadly, "No,
I cannot help you reap your fields;
  I did not help you sow!"

I called to Faith along the ways:
  "My harvest-time has come;
Come, help me reap my golden fields,
  And bear my harvest home."

But Faith kept firmly up his way,
  And answered from the steep,
"Where was I when your fields were sowed
  That I should help you reap?"

I looked in Love's supernal eyes;
  "Ah! come," I said; "to-day,
My grain is ripe for gathering; come,
  And bear my sheaves away."

Love wept, alas! and from her eyes
  Most tender tears did flow:
"I may not help to reap those fields
  I did not help to sow!"

All on a sudden fell the storm,
  And winds were rudely blown;
I wist not why the sun kept hid,
  But reaped my fields alone.

I brought no sheaves unto my Lord
  Within my aching arm;
My friends *they* brought home Peace and Love,
  But *I* brought home the storm!

GOING OUT AND COMING IN.

Going out to fame and triumph,
  Going out to love and light;
Coming in to pain and sorrow,
  Coming in to gloom and night:
Going out with joy and gladness,
  Coming in with woe and sin;
Ceaseless stream of restless pilgrims
  Going out and coming in!

Through the portals of the homestead,
  From beneath the blooming vine;
To the trumpet-tones of glory,
  Where the bays and laurels twine;
From the loving home-caresses,
  To the chill voice of the world—
Going out with gallant canvas
  To the summer breeze unfurled.

Through the gateway, down the footpath,
  Through the lilacs by the way;
Through the clover by the meadow,
  Where the gentle home-lights stray;
To the wide world of ambition,
  Up the toilsome hill of fame,
Winning oft a mighty triumph,
  Winning oft a noble name.

Coming back all worn and weary—
  Weary with the world's cold breath;
Coming to the dear old homestead,
  Coming in to age and death:
Weary of its empty flattery,
  Weary of its ceaseless din,
Weary of its heartless sneering,
  Coming from the bleak world in.

Going out with hopes of glory,
  Coming in with sorrows dark;
Going out with sails all flying,
  Coming in with mastless bark:
Restless streams of pilgrims, striving
  Wreaths of fame and love to win,
From the doorways of the homestead
  Going out and coming in.

CLOUDS.

Misery springs from much besides crime,
  And grief from other than sin;
Alas! it drives me wild to know
  The things that might have been.

He questioned her, one shining night:
  "My love, dost thou love me?"
"*Why, nay,*" she answering said, but smiled—
  A smile he did not see:

A smile he did not see—oh, blind!
  The smile belied her *nay:*
Oh, fool! and in that moment Fate
  Passed on! (Fate makes no stay.)

They parted thus: he won his way
  Along the years; he gained
The things men sigh for; but with each
  Fair boon from fame attained,

He heard that gentle, mocking voice:
  His heart cried, lonesomely,
Its great, dumb cry for want of that
  One smile he did not see!

She from her wreathed lattice leaned—
  Leaned sighing, blind with tears:
"Oh! give me back one moment, Fate—
  One word!"— So go the years.

It almost drives me wild to see
  The things that are daily seen;
Grief breaking the hearts that do no crime,
  Yea, those that do no sin!

FIRELIGHT.

The feet of them that bear out the dead seem to be again at the door,
And the coffined faces smile their dim, sweet, patient smiles once more!

Oh, my dead! In the summer-prime of roses and fairy-rings,
I could put you aside with the hopes that were, and the half-remembered things;

But the first faint glow of the firelight that reddens upon the wall
Goes into the shadows where you lie, and finds and unveils you all!

Slowly into the embers sink the woods and flowers, and the clear,
Shrill songs of the summer-birds, and the sweet, warm haze of the air;

And rises slowly the cloud of prayers that darkened the way to heaven,
When the light went out of the beautiful eyes, and the loving hearts were riven!

The pain of the old unhealed wrongs, the hurt of the olden stings:
The first fire lighted at even-fall, yea, this is what it brings!

THE SAND-HILLS.

Between the sobs of the sea, oh, hear!
Between the cries of the sea,
Out of the sand-hills, sweet and clear,
The music and minstrelsy!
Each gnome-band singing before the king
And the lords of grand degree;
And the queens and their trains sit listening,
In the sand-hills by the sea.

Oh, sweet beyond song in mortal hall,
Oh, clear beyond mortal tone,
The unseen song, with its tender fall,
The horns and the trumpets blown!
Not all may listen who pass this way;
He only the sounds hath known
Who is true in his heart, let come what may,
And faithful to one alone!

The brawny fisherman dragging his net,
  He heareth the sweet gnome-bands,
And straightway blesseth his fair Janet,
  His flower of foreign lands!
A dreamer here and there heareth too,
  And presseth his true-love's hands;
But what know the most (for the most are untrue)
  Of the music beneath the sands?

Ah! love, ah! sweet, as you pass this way,
  Oh, listen for love of me!
One more proof for my heart, I pray,
  Of music and melody!
So shall my soul be full of the spring,
  And love shall wait at my knee,
While the gnome-bands play for their queen and king,
  In the sand hills by the sea!

An engraving of Miss Moore is the frontispiece to her volume of poems. It is an excellent likeness, having the fault of looking too stern, and much too old. "Looking at this engraving, we see a girl hardly out of her teens, with a face which evinces refinement and culture of the highest order: it is not beautiful, nor would we consider it pretty; but it is a face altogether remarkable — of the kind you love to look at, return to again and again; and having seen it, it is not easily forgotten."

No great poem has yet been given to the public by Miss Moore; but we shall hope, from the promise given in many fugitive and a few more lengthy poems, that as years flow on, and her mental character ripens in its development, her spirit-fancies may find utterance in elaborate works of genius.

www.ingramcontent.com/pod-product-compliance
Lightning Source LLC
LaVergne TN
LVHW021122110826
845150LV00005B/914

* 9 7 8 1 4 2 5 5 5 1 3 6 0 *